The Philippines:

Land of Broken Promises

James B. Goodno

Zed Books Ltd.
London and New Jersey

The Philippines: Land of Broken Promises was first published by Zed Books Ltd, 57 Caledonian Road, London N1 9BU, UK, and 171 First Avenue, Atlantic Highlands, New Jersey 07716, USA in 1991

Cover design by Andrew Corbett
Laserset by Selro Publishing Services
Printed and bound in the United Kingdom by
Billings and Sons Ltd, Worcester

British Library Cataloguing in Publication Data

Goodno, James B.
The Philippines: land of broken promises
1. Philippines. Social change
I. Title
959.9047

ISBN 0—86232—862-4
ISBN 0—86232—863—2 pbk

Contents

About the Author

James B. Goodno was an accredited foreign correspondent in the Philippines during the crucial years of the transition from the Marcos dictatorship to the new Cory Aquino administration. During this time he contributed on a regular basis to *In These Times, Pacifica Radio, Religious News Service,* and *US Radio.* In addition, his articles have appeared in many other outlets including *Miami Herald,* the *Utne Reader, Z Magazine* in the United States and *South* in London. Since returning to the US, he has been an editor with *Dollars & Sense* magazine.

Acknowledgements

I arrived in the Philippines knowing nobody. During the years that followed, far more people than I can possibly thank have assisted me in getting to know the country, its people and its politics. Behn Cervantes, José Castro, Marites Vitug, Boy Tripon, Cooper Resebal, Tom Fawthrop, James Clad, Bobbie Malay, 'George', Leto Villar, Capt. Rex Robles, Dan Vizmanos, Dan Swanson, Sen. Wigberto Tanada, Sen. Butz Aquino, Mar Canonigo, Rep. Bonifacio Gillego, Alex Magno, Ricardo Ferrer, Orville Solon, Brenda Gonzales, Joe Collins, Vic Ladlad, Fides Lim, Leoncio Co, Fanny Leyva and countless others made my stay and this book possible.

Tragically, some people will not be able to receive my thanks. Lean Alejandro, Al Cortez, Manny Sanchez, 'Francisco' and Brig. Gen. Oscar Florendo offered their time and in many cases friendship before being killed in the political violence sweeping the nation. They and their families receive my eternal gratitude.

My wife's family, the Leyva's of Antipolo, Rizal, made me feel at home and showed me sides of Philippine life I otherwise would not have experienced. My own family — especially my parents, Ada and Bill Goodno — offered continuing support and without them my endeavours would have been impossible.

Outside the Philippines I would like to thank Barbara Goldoftas, Sheryl Larson and her colleagues at *In These Times*, Dan Conalson, Walden Bello, Patricia Horn, Thea Lee and Tim Wise, and especially Robert Molteno of Zed Books for offering support and encouragement during the production of this book.

My wife, Daisy Leyva, looked on this project as her own. She offered invaluable criticism, encouragement, information and intellectual stimulation. Without her this book might never have happened.

It is dedicated to my father — William C. Goodno, Sr. (1926—1989) — and my daughter — Nikita Dellia Goodno (b.1989) — whose birth provided me with the inspiration I needed to carry on.

Chronology

BC   Migrants cross land bridge from Asian mainland and settle archipelago.

900   Chinese establish coastal trading posts over the next 300 years.

1400   Muslim clergy start to bring Islam to the Philippines from Malaya.

1521   Magellan lands on Cebu, claims region for Spain. Lapu Lapu slays Magellan, drives expedition from islands.

1543   Ruy de Villalobos sails from Mexico to Mindanao. Names archipelago after Crown Prince Felipe II.

1565   King Felipe II commissions Miguel Lopez de Legazpi to colonize Philippines. Augustine missionaries arrive with colonizers.

1762   British occupy Manila for two years.

1796   US trading vessel calls at Manila.

1815   Galleon trade with Spain's Mexican colony ends.

1834   Spain opens Manila to foreign investment and trade.

1872   Cavite mutiny breaks out, is suppressed. Spain executes Filipino priests José Burgos, Mariano Gomez and Jacinto Zamora.

1887   José Rizal's political novel *Noli Me Tangere* reaches Manila, generates furore.

1892   Rizal returns from Europe but is confined to Mindanao. Andrés Bonifacio founds the *Katipunan*.

1896   Colonists imprison and kill hundreds of Filipinos in Manila. Bonifacio and the *Katipunan* launch the Philippine revolution. Emilio Aguinaldo and rebel forces capture Cavite. Colonial authorities execute Rizal.

1897   Spain recaptures Cavite. Aguinaldo establishes government, executes Bonifacio, signs accord with Spain and leaves for Hong Kong.

1898   Battleship *Maine* blown up in Havana harbour. US goes to war with Spain. Cmdr George Dewey destroys Spanish armada in Manila Bay. Aguinaldo returns on US ship, declares Philippine independence. Treaty between US and Spain grants US authority over archipelago.

1899   23 January Aguinaldo sworn in as president of Philippine republic. 4 February war breaks out between US and Philippines. US Senate votes to annex the Philippines.

1901   Aguinaldo captured after guerrilla war of resistance and swears allegiance to US. Civilian administration takes over. Scattered resistance continues throughout decade.

1907   Manuel Quezon, Sergio Osmena, etc. establish *Nationalista* Party. First Philippine assembly elected. Osmena elected speaker.

1916   US Congress authorizes eventual independence.

1922   Quezon defeats Osmena in race for presidency of new Philippine Senate.

1924   Crisanto Evangelista and other labour leaders establish *Partido Obrero de Filipinas* (Philippine Workers' Party), forerunner to PKP (*Partido Komunista ng Pilipinas*).

1930   PKP established.

1932   Evangelista arrested, PKP outlawed.

1934   Tydings-McDuffie Act provides 10-year transition to independence and interim commonwealth government.

1935   *Sakdalist* rebellion. Quezon elected president, Osmena vice-president. Gen. Douglas MacArthur takes charge of Philippine defence.

1937   PKP regains legal status.

1938   US High Commissioner Paul McNutt proposes to postpone independence. PKP merges with Pedro Abad Santos's Socialist Party.

1941   7 December Japanese attack Pearl Harbor and Clark Field. 22 December Japanese land on Luzon.

1942   Japan takes Manila. Quezon proposes and Roosevelt rejects Philippine neutrality. MacArthur retreats to Australia. In March *Hukbalahap* (*Huk*) established with PKP member Luis Taruc in command. Quezon and Osmena flee to US where they establish a government in exile.

1943   Japanese establish puppet republic with José Laurel as president.

1944   Quezon dies. MacArthur and Osmena land in Leyte.

1945   US captures Manila, much of the city destroyed.

1946   Roxas defeats Osmena for presidency. Left opposition evicted from Congress, which approves Bell Trade Act. 4 July independence granted. Congress passes 'parity' amendment granting special rights to US investors.

1947   Military Bases and Military Assistance Agreements signed with US.

1948   Roxas outlaws *Huk*, dies of heart attack. Elpidio Quirino assumes presidency. Negotiations with *Huk* fail, fighting between *Huk* and government escalates.

1951   US-Philippine mutual defence treaty signed. Col. Edward Lansdale arrives in Manila as adviser to new defence secretary, Ramon Magsaysay.

1953   Magsaysay defeats Quirino in race for presidency.

1954   Newsman Benigno Aquino negotiates Huk leader Taruc's surrender. Government jails Taruc.

1957   Magsaysay killed in air crash. Carlos García sworn in as president, elected to new term.

1961   Vice-President Diosado Macapagal defeats García in race for presidency. Macapagal promises to serve the 'common man.'

1962   Macapagal negotiates agreement with IMF, removes import controls.

1965   Ferdinand Marcos defeats Macapagal in bid for re-election. Marcos backs dispatch of military civic action unit to Vietnam.

1966   US President Lyndon Johnson agrees to 1991 as new expiration date for Military Bases Agreement.

1967   Philippines joins Association of South-East Asian Nations. José Maria Sison breaks with remnants of PKP.

1968   Student demonstrators call for social reforms and end to Vietnam War.

1969   Founding congress held to re-establish CPP (Communist Party of the Philippines), Sison becomes chairman, NPA established by merger with surviving *Huk* band led by Bernabe Buscayno. Marcos becomes first Philippine president to be re-elected.

1970   First Quarter Storm starts with clash between police and demonstrators following Marcos's state of the nation address in January. Peso devaluation fuels price increases, food shortages, unemployment and unrest. Radical students and others stage series of anti-Marcos, anti-US, pro-poor demonstrations. US senators accuse Philippines of misusing funds supplied for Philippine forces in Vietnam. Marcos threatens to impose martial law.

1971   Students seize University of the Philippines, establish Diliman Commune. Opposition rally at Plaza Miranda bombed. Marcos blames communists and Benigno Aquino, suspends writ of *habeas corpus*, threatens martial law again. Opposition wins Senate election.

1972   8 September Defence Secretary Juan Ponce Enrile warns of impending Communist rebellion, bombings in Manila follow. 22 September Enrile stages ambush of his own car. On same day Marcos imposes martial law, shuts down newspapers, bans rallies and begins arresting his foes, including Benigno Aquino.

1973   Referendum approves Marcos's request to stay in office beyond the end of the year. CPP establishes Preparatory Commission of National Democratic Front (NDF).

1974   Catholic bishops call for end to martial law, but Supreme Court upholds it. Parity agreement expires.

1975   Anti-martial law demonstrations and labour strikes.

1976   Opposition boycotts referendum on martial law, 91 per cent vote to continue dictatorial rule.

1977   Aquino sentenced to death, international protest follows, Marcos orders trial reopened.

1978   Parliamentary elections pit Marcos's New Society Movement (KBL) against Aquino's People Power coalition. KBL sweeps in but vote marred by fraud. Widespread protest. Marcos becomes prime minister and president, Imelda joins cabinet.

1979   Military Bases Agreement amended to allow Philippine flag to fly over bases, but US retains unhampered military use. Light-a-Fire Movement conducts bombing campaign in Metro Manila.

1980   KBL wins local elections, Salvador Laurel breaks with Marcos, Aquino released and flies to US for medical treatment. New opposition alliance formed.

1981   Martial law lifted, but Marcos keeps power to rule by decree. Papal visit. Marcos re-elected in contest boycotted by opposition. US Vice-President George Bush attends inauguration, praises Marcos's commitment to democracy.

1983   Aquino returns to Manila, shot at airport. Two million join funeral procession. Demonstrations, periodic violence. Investigation into murder begins.

1984   Legislative elections held. Opposition divided into 'boycott' and 'participation' camps. KBL wins 89 of 143 seats in fraud-marred election. Parliament of the Street holds frequent anti-Marcos demonstrations. Spiralling economic crisis. CPP and NPA (New People's Army) grow rapidly. Panel investigating murder concludes military killed Aquino.

1985   Gen. Fabian C. Ver and 25 others charged with slaying Aquino. Ver goes on leave, Fidel Ramos becomes acting chief of staff of AFP (Armed Forces of the Philippines). RAM (Reform the Armed Forces Movement) surfaces. *Bayan* formed, splits. *Bandila* formed. 16 October CIA chief William Casey, representing Reagan, meets Marcos, then Sen. Paul Laxalt. Marcos announces snap election. Ver and others acquitted. 1.2 million Filipinos petition Cory Aquino to run against Marcos. Cory agrees.

1986   Violence escalates, at least 30 killed on election day, 7 February. Marcos and Cory both claim victory, Cory charges fraud. 22 February Enrile and Ramos defect. Millions join uprising against Marcos regime. Washington offers refuge, urges Marcos to step down. 26 February Marcoses flee. Aquino orders release of political prisoners, seeks negotiations with NDF. First two anti-Aquino coup attempts foiled. New constitution drafted. Labour leader Rolando Olalia murdered. Ceasefire with NPA.

1987   Ceasefire breaks down, military kill 13 peasant demonstrators near presidential palace. Public ratifies constitution after third military mutiny put down. Army kills 17 peasants in rural town. Concern grows about renewed human rights abuses. Pro-Aquino forces win majorities in House and Senate elections. Bloody coup attempt by RAM members fails. Activist Lean Alejandro murdered. Three Americans and one Filipino killed by NPA near Clark Air Base.

1988   Provincial elections. US agrees to pay $481 million a year for use of military bases. Marcoses indicted by US grand jury for fraud and embezzlement.

1989   28 September Ferdinand Marcos dies, 1 December RAM tries again. Coup attempt splits military, government calls on US for air support.

1990   Cabinet revamped. Negotiations start on status of military bases.

Acronyms and Organizations

Acronyms

ABB	Alex Boncayao Brigade
ADB	Asian Development Bank
AFL-CIO	American Federation of Labour-Congress of Industrial Organizations
AFP	Armed Forces of the Philippines
ANP	Alliance for New Politics
ASEAN	Association of South-East Asian Nations
ATOM	August 21 Movement
Bandila	*Bansang Nagkaisa sa Diwa at Layunin* (A Nation United in Thought & Purpose) — social-democratic-led alliance
Bayan	*Bagong Alyansang Makabayan* (New Patriotic Alliance) — legal national-democratic coalition
BCC	Basic Christian Community
BCC-CO	BCC-Community Organization
Bisig	*Bukluran sa Ikauunlad ng Sosyalistang Isip at Gawa* (Movement for the Advancement of Socialist Ideas & Action)
BPMM	Buy Philippine Made Movement
BRC	*Barrio* Revolutionary Committee
Cafgu	Civilian Armed Forces Geographic Unit
CAO	Civil Affairs Office — secretive military agency
Causa	International anti-communist organization backed by Revd Sun Yung Moon's Unification Church
CBCP	Catholic Bishops Conference of the Philippines
CCAP	Coordinating Council on the Philippine Aid Programme
CCP	Cultural Centre of the Philippines
CHDF	Civilian Home Defence Forces
CNL	Christians for National Liberation
Comelec	Commission on Elections
Con Com	Constitutional Commission — draft constitution, ratified 1987
Con Con	Constitutional Convention — draft constitution, ratified 1973
CORD	Coalition of Organizations for the Restoration of Democracy — coordinated anti-Marcos campaign in 1984. Also called Coalition of Organizations for the Realization of Democracy
CPAR	Congress for a People's Agrarian Reform
CPDF	Cordillera People's Democratic Front
CPLA	Cordillera People's Liberation Army
CPP	Communist Party of the Philippines — new party established at end of 1960s
CRC	Cellophil Resources Corporation
DA	Democratic Alliance — post-war legal left alliance
DENR	Department of Environment & Natural Resources
EC	European Community
EDSA	E. de los Santos Avenue

EFF	extended fund facility
ESF	Economic Support Fund
FFW	Federation of Free Workers
FITL	Federation of Igorot Tribes for Liberation
GAD	Grand Alliance for Democracy
HMB	*Hukbong Mapagpalaya ng Bayan* (Peoples' Liberation Army)
Huk	*Hukbo ng Bayan Laban sa Hapon* (Peoples' Army to Fight the Japanese) — left-led peasant resistance during Second World War. Later reconstituted as HMB
ILA	Igorot Liberation Army
IMET	International Military Education & Training Program
IMF	International Monetary Fund
INP	Integrated National Police
JAJA	Justice for Aquino, Justice for All — alliance of anti-Marcos groups established after Aquino assassination
JUSMAG	Joint US Military Advisory Group
Kaakbay	*Kilusan sa Kapangyarihan at Karapatan ng Bayan* (Movement for the Power & Rights of the Nation) — nationalist anti-Marcos organization led by José Diokno
Kaiba	women's political party
Kasapi	*Kapulungan ng Mga Sandigan ng Pilipinas* (Organization of Philippine Defenders) — democratic-socialist organization established in 1970s
Katipunan	*Kataastaasang Kagalang-galangang Katipunan ng mga Anak ng Bayan* (Supreme Exalted Society of the Children of the Nation) — 19th century revolutionary organization established and led by Andrés Bonifacio
KBL	*Kilusang Bagong Lipunan* (New Society Movement) — Marcos's party
KM	*Kabataang Makabayan* (Patriotic Youth) — radical youth movement established in 1960s. Forerunner of new CPP
KMP	*Kilusang Magbubukid ng Pilipinas* (Peasant Movement of the Philippines)
KMU	*Kilusang Mayo Uno* (May First Movement) — alliance of left-wing labour unions
Kompil	*Kongreso ng Mamamayang Pilipino* (Congress of the Philippine People)
KRB	*Komite Rebolusaryong Baryo* (*Barrio* Revolutionary Committee)
Laban	*Lakas ng Bayan* (Power of the People) — anti-Marcos coalition first established for 1978 parliamentary election
LACC	Labour Advisory & Consultative Council
LDP	*Lakas ng Demokratikong Pilipinas* (Strength of Philippine Democracy) — 'super-party' formed by supporters of Aquino government
LMLC	*Lapiang Mangagawa* (Workers' Party) Labour Centre
LOI	Letter of Intent
LTK	*Lingkod Tao Kalikasan* (In the Service of Man & Nature) — environmental group
MAI	Multilateral Aid Initiative — also known as Philippine Aid Programme or Mini-Marshall Plan
Masaka	(Free Association of Peasants) — peasant organization of old PKP
MDP	Movement for a Democratic Philippines — early 1970s united front
MILF	Moro Islamic Liberation Front
MISSSA	Mindanao Sulu Secretariat for Social Action

MIT	Massachusetts Institute of Technology
MNC	multinational corporation
MNLF	Moro National Liberation Front
MP	Military Police
Namfrel	National Movement for Free Elections
NASSA	National Secretariat for Social Action
NCCP	National Council of Churches of the Philippines
NDF	National Democratic Front
NFSW	National Federation of Sugar Workers
NIC	newly industrialized country
NPA	New People's Army (also known as *Bagong Hukbong Bayan*) — armed wing of new CPP
NSSD	National Security Study Directive
NUC	National Unification Committee
NUCD	National Union of Christian Democrats
NUSP	National Union of Students of the Philippines
PARC	People's Agrarian Reform Council
PC	Philippine Constabulary
PCCA	Presidential Commission on Culture and the Arts
PDP	*Partido Demokratiko Pilipinas* (Philippine Democratic Party) — largest social-democratic party. Merged with *Laban* to establish PDP—*Laban* during final years of Marcos regime
PDSP	*Partido Demokratiko-Sosyalista ng Pilipinas* (Philippine Democratic Socialist Party)
PETA	Philippine Experimental Theatre Assembly
Philex	Philippine Exchange Company
PKM	*Pambansang Kaisahan ng mga Mabubukid* (National Peasants' Union)
PKP	*Partido Komunista ng Pilipinas* (Communist Party of the Philippines) — old Communist Party
PNB	*Partido ng Bayan* (Party of the People) — legal left-wing political party formed by ex-CPP leaders and mass activists in 1986
PRG	Provisional Revolutionary Government
PRRM	Philippine Rural Reconstruction Movement
RAM	Reform the Armed Forces Movement
Sakdal	agrarian populist movement of the 1930s. Leaders aligned with Japan
SMA	subversive mass activist
SOT	Special Operations Teams
SP	Socialist Party — merged with PKP in 1930s
Tambuli	democratic socialist organization
TUCP	Trade Union Congress of the Philippines — conservative wing of Philippine labour movement
Unido	United Nationalist Democratic Organization — right-wing party led by Salvador Laurel
UP	University of the Philippines
USAFFE	US Armed Forces in the Far East — US-Philippine forces during Second World War
USAID	US Agency for International Development
VOA	Voice of America
VPD	Volunteers for Popular Democracy
WACL	World Anti-Communist League
WFTU	World Federation of Trade Unions

Organizations

April Six Liberation Movement — anti-Marcos urban guerrilla organization

Bantay Bayan (People's Watch) — unarmed anti-communist vigilante organization

Batasang Pambansa (National Assembly)

Convenor Group — anti-Marcos group for selecting presidential candidate

Core Group — RAM leadership

Haribon Foundation — environmental group

Iglesia ni Kristo (Church of Christ)

Independent Caucus — Marxist group originally in Bayan. Forerunner of *Bisig*

Kabataang Barangay (Village Youth) — pro-Marcos youth group

La Liga Filipina (The Philippine League) — 19th-century reform organization set up by José Rizal

Liberal Party — traditional political party established in 1946

Light-a-Fire Movement — anti-Marcos urban guerrillas

Nationalista (or Nationalist) Party — traditional political party set up in early 20th century

Partido Obrero de Filipinas (Philippine Workers' Party) — forerunner of old PKP

Task Force Detainees — left-wing human rights organization

Foreword

During the four and a half years I spent in the Philippines I witnessed the rise of a broad movement for democracy, the fall of a dictatorship and the advent of what many hoped would be a new era. I shared in the euphoria of that unforgettable sultry Manila night of 26 February 1986 when, in the grounds of the presidential palace during the first hours after Ferdinand and Imelda Marcos had fled on a US helicopter, tens of thousands of people ended their long march to freedom. I shared the hopes of so many people at that moment. Not, I believe, because I had faith in Cory Aquino's ability to get to the root of the nation's problems, nor because I thought that Juan Ponce Enrile and the dashing young men of the RAM (Reform the Armed Forces Movement) had truly undergone a conversion to democracy, but because I believed that the revolution belonged to the people.

In the first two years I saw a nation awaken and a ruthless regime crumble. I met scores of people — on the streets of Manila, in the slums of Davao, the mountains of the Cordillera and the halls of parliament — fighting for their new day. I saw their courage as they — unarmed — faced the armed might of a violent state on picket lines and during demonstrations. I marvelled at their dedication as we spent a long night separated from the military by steel and barbed-wire barricades near Malacanang Palace, waiting for the inevitable fury of the assembled troops. Strikes, demonstrations, election campaigns, guerrilla war, the constant threat of violence. I witnessed it all. And I grew ever more impressed with the people involved.

Cory Aquino's campaign for the presidency was the culmination of this uprising, which began — if a starting point must be pinned down — with the assassination of her husband, opposition leader Benigno S. Aquino, Jr., on 21 August 1983. Her campaign differed from all that had gone before. Part religious crusade, part popular uprising, it promised deliverance, it promised liberation.

Sadly, liberation — especially for the millions of poor people who make up the majority of the Philippine population — has not arrived. This is not entirely surprising. Even at the moment of greatest hope, immediately after the departure of the much hated Marcoses, the odds were stacked against those who advocated rapid, radical change — the radical democrats, socialists and Marxists who make up the Philippine left. A misguided, ideologically prompted boycott left the most powerful force for radical change — the Communist-led NDF (National Democratic Front) and its NPA (New People's Army) — outside the coalition that came to power. Weak organization and political illusions dogged other advocates of thorough-going change. On the other side, business executives, military officers, provincial bosses, foreign powers (most notably the US) and wealthy planters shared access to power and a broadly conservative agenda. While they might fight amongst themselves — often violently — over details of programmes, control of the government machinery and particular political disagreements, they shared a basic opposition to radical change and a commitment to countering insurgency by military means.

Very quickly the promise offered by the Aquino government vanished. Once again — as had happened throughout their history — Filipinos watched their more affluent compatriots and leaders break the promises they had made during their drive to power. But this time there was something qualitatively different. The shared experience of struggle against a dictatorship and for a just peace remained part of the national consciousness. In that, there was hope.

Scores of dedicated Filipinos keep this hope alive. Despite its problems, which will be discussed, the revolutionary left continues to present an alternative vision that finds support amongst a significant portion of the poorest Filipinos. The Communist Party of the Philippines has not been untouched by the dramatic events affecting the international left, especially in Eastern Europe and the Soviet Union, but it still leads one of the strongest left-wing insurgencies in the world and, though far from victory, is a factor in Philippine political life. This alone makes it an important and fascinating subject for study.

Coup attempts, guerrillas, vigilantes, an exotic locale, an attractive heroine, vile and vicious villains, a complex and often contradictory culture, foreign intrigue, religious passion. What can make a place or a story more attractive? These attributes and the wonderful friends I made rapidly drew me into the Philippine scene. As a freelance journalist, I was perfectly placed to witness a historic occasion in the making. My interest — intellectual, political, romantic — grew with each passing day. So too did my sorrow as the failures of the Aquino government and, more important, the movement that brought it to power, became clear.

In the pages that follow I have attempted to paint a picture of life in the Philippines. My goal has been not to take sides, but to help people outside the Philippines understand better the plight of the Filipino people and the complexity of their society, appreciate the depths of the problems confronting them, and become aware of the dedication of people in the movements for social justice. How you, my readers, make use of this information and my experiences is left to you — but I hope it is used in a positive manner, for we outside the Philippines have now, and have long had, an impact on life in the archipelago.

I close my account with the coup attempt in December 1989. Following that coup, Cory Aquino once again revamped her cabinet. However, while the faces changed, the political and economic make-up of the government remained essentially the same. (Aquino tried to add one progressive to her cabinet, as secretary of agrarian reform; Congress refused to approve his appointment.)

Despite changes in their rhetoric, neither Aquino nor her government, nor the largest and most prominent opposition groups (including those in the military) have brought forward new approaches to the nation's many and multiplying problems. That Marcos's leading crony — Eduardo Cojuangco — is now viewed by some serious analysts as presidential timber demonstrates the bankruptcy of political life within dominant circles.

Steadily increasing prices, an energy crisis brought about by drought and overcrowding, ever worsening pollution and persistent poverty make for a rather bleak future. The threat of further coup attempts seems unabated. Emigration is viewed as an ever more attractive alternative. Yet many Filipinos have not given up dreaming of a better day in their own country. That they continue to work and struggle in these dark times gives cause for us all to have hope in our own future.

James B. Goodno
Boston, Mass., 1990

1

The Unfinished Revolution: Sketches of Philippine Life

On the island of Negros sugar workers idle away as many as six months a year. Hungry children latch onto their mothers' breasts in a desperate bid to suck the last drops of milk before dying, or entering the local hospital's malnutrition ward where death strikes with painful frequency. Older brothers and sisters chew sugar cane to ease their stomach pains. Men and women cannot find work during the off season when sugar is neither planted and cultivated nor harvested and milled. No work means no pay and no benefits for most of the island's 250,000 sugar workers.

In Metro Manila tens of thousands of people live in hovels in overcrowded shanty towns. Many spend their days scavenging in stinking rubbish dumps for items of some small value. Blind people, migrants from the countryside and small children clothed in rags press their hungry faces against air-conditioned car windows and beg. Criminal syndicates confiscate part of their take. Others peddle newspapers, sweets, flowers and individual cigarettes to motorists and passengers on hot, jam-packed city buses. Together they breathe the poisonous fumes of the grey diesel-scented air.

In Olongapo City young women and sometimes men rent their bodies to pleasure-seeking American servicemen. Manila's bars and brothels draw clients from around the world and working girls from most — probably all — of the Philippines' 73 provinces. Even in small seaside resorts, boys and girls, some still years short of puberty, join the flesh trade. UNICEF estimates that more than 20,000 Filipino children work as prostitutes.

The scene varies from place to place, but has two common denominators — poverty and oppression. Senate President Jovito Salonga claims that 81 families control the economy, but not on their own. Foreign corporate investors and creditors — the Philippines' international debt exceeds US $30,000 million — also hold extensive economic power. But most of the 63 million Filipinos live below the

1

poverty line; they were the main supporters (though not the leaders) of the movement against Ferdinand Marcos's dictatorship and for Cory Aquino's promised democracy.

Corazon Cojuangco Aquino had never known poverty. She had been born into a prominent rural family and had grown up in the midst of wealth, prestige and political power. She had studied in Catholic schools in Manila and the US and had made her début at the glamorous Manila Hotel. After completing only one year of law school the future president had married into another prominent provincial family (the Aquinos) and settled into a relatively quiet life as the wealthy spouse of a fast-rising political star.

Cory's father, José Cojuangco, had left his children enough property and wealth to lead lives of leisure. At the top of the list of properties she and her brothers and sisters had inherited was a 6,000-hectare sugar plantation in Tarlac province, about 160 km. north of Manila. The Cojuangco family plantation, *Hacienda Luisita*, is untypical of the Philippine countryside. It is big, profitable and planted in sugar — a major export crop, but one that uses less than 3.3 per cent of the nation's farm land. Many of *Hacienda Luisita*'s 20,000 residents and all the migrant workers employed on it annually live an unfortunately typical life. They survive amidst poverty, malnutrition and what a dissident manager called 'subhuman conditions'.

To enter *Hacienda Luisita*, one has to pass several checkpoints manned by a private security force. Without clearance, a stranger cannot enter, even to visit a family in one of the 11 *barangays* (villages) built on hacienda land. The road from the guardhouse leads past sugar-cane fields, villages for the employees (some hidden behind tall bamboo fences), corporate headquarters and the sugar mill. A side road leads past another checkpoint to the stately homes of the Cojuangco family, the country club, the golf course, the stables and the slightly less stately homes of top-level managers.

Tucked away behind the mill stands a compound housing some of the 2,000 cane cutters brought in each year to work the fields of the sprawling plantation. The *sacadas* (migrant workers), who cut cane for two to three months a year, live in exceedingly cramped quarters. Fights, gambling and drinking help pass the time in these human stables where, by mid-afternoon, only flies and less visible vermin outnumber the sweltering men, women and children. 'We will not show you the other living quarters,' said the manager who steered us off the guided tour. 'We do not want you to see the darker side of *Luisita*. This is the most livable of the hacienda's housing areas for *sacadas*. At least the floors are concrete.'

Seasonal employment on sugar plantations in Central Luzon (such as *Hacienda Luisita*) allows the *sacadas* to escape from the appalling poverty of Negros and other Visayan islands. The collapse of the local sugar-based economy — sparked in part by shrinking world markets, corruption and bad policies — brought malnutrition, disease, despair and revolt to the Visayas (the central island group) during Marcos's waning years. And these problems have remained under Aquino. As the disenchanted manager noted, 'if these migrant workers can endure working here under these conditions, you can imagine what kind of life they lead where they come from.'

A lucky and thrifty *sacada* may return to his impoverished and perhaps war-torn province with a few hundred or even a thousand pesos.* Others, like a young man from Escalante, Negros Occidental — a town that gained notoriety in 1985 when soldiers gunned down 29 demonstrating sugar workers, peasants, students and activists — go home broke. But even those who leave Tarlac with empty pockets after a season of hard work would return to *Hacienda Luisita* if offered the chance.

For the majority of the hacienda's resident employees, living conditions are not quite as dismal as they are for the *sacadas*. Still, problems caused by underemployment, poverty, indebtedness and insecurity plague regular workers and local seasonal employees alike, and even some managers. 'See that nice fence over there?' asked our guide, pointing to a bamboo wall along the main road. 'It was built to hide the deplorable conditions behind it.' On the other side of the fence is a village housing hacienda employees and their families.

This particular *barangay* resembles countless other villages in the Philippine countryside. Some of the small houses are tidy and sturdy, others ramshackle or temporary. Tiny *sari-sari* stores dispense soft drinks, San Miguel beer, sweets, snacks and canned foods. The worker-owners earn a little extra income from these stores. Scores of children play on the dusty, unpaved roads. As in many rural communities, after warmly welcoming their visitors *Hacienda Luisita*'s workers and residents complain about their living conditions. 'The water pump broke down because of the molasses from the mill,' said Chito Ocampo. 'We now have to pay a minimum of 25 pesos a month for water. We cannot afford it. It should be free. They also make us pay for electricity. A cigarette gives better light than the electricity they provide us with. As it is, we can barely make both ends meet.'

---

* According to the *Far Eastern Economic Review*, the official exchange rate stood at 22.20 pesos to the US dollar in December 1989.

Managers, skilled employees and mill workers are the most fortunate of *Hacienda Luisita*'s residents. They work the whole year, receive more benefits than the more numerous field workers and live in company houses, complete with free electricity. But year-round employment exists for only a handful of the hacienda's regular employees. Most work full time for six to seven months a year and complain about the lack of employment and income during the off season. 'It is nearly impossible to survive during the off season,' Jojo Espino, a young farm-hand, told us. 'I have no work for almost six months.' Espino had grown up on *Hacienda Luisita* where his father had worked before him. He had dropped out of school after the sixth grade and the best work he had been able to find had been on the hacienda. He wanted to become a construction worker but could not find that kind of job. 'My only skill is weeding,' he said sadly.

To survive during the off season, Espino, Ocampo and their neighbours and co-workers have to borrow from the Cojuangco family, the plantation store or (if they·are lucky) their better-off friends or relatives. The company deducts these loans from the workers' pay packets when they return to the fields. 'I wish I could show you my pay packet,' said Ocampo. 'Sometimes we get no more than a few pesos a month because of our debts.' Travellers in the rural Philippines hear similar complaints from the sugar workers of Negros, from tenant farmers and peasants in the rice and corn-growing areas and from labourers in the coconut groves of the hilly regions. Indebtedness to the *haciendero*, the landlord or the local usurer is a common complaint and a source of agrarian discontent.

To much fanfare, on 11 May 1989 the Cojuangco family announced its intention to participate in the nation's agrarian-reform programme. Their plans, however, promised little change for the majority of the hacienda's employees. The somewhat questionable benefits were limited to 7,000 permanent farm workers, who became minority owners of the corporation that owned the plantation. Collectively they now own 33 per cent of the corporation, with the Cojuangco family owning the other 67 per cent. They gained no influence over corporate practices and their monetary gain may also be minimal. The Cojuangco family retained control over the more profitable sugar mill and most analysts expect the beneficiaries to receive no more than 70 pesos a month in corporate dividends — hardly enough to feed an average family for one day.

Middle managers and professionals on *Hacienda Luisita* also have complaints. They too suffer from indebtedness. They borrow from the company to send their children to good schools or to improve their standard of living. These debts — incurred through monetary need, contractual agreement or the deeply-rooted *utang na loob* (debt of gratitude) — can tie a family to the hacienda, but not always for life. A manager who complained about his debt said that he would leave when his children finished college and were 'free of the hacienda'.

Employees on *Hacienda Luisita* and in the mill have the advantage of being unionized. Separate unions represent farm and mill workers. Both have contracts, but the mill workers have more benefits. Aside from year-round employment, higher pay and company housing, they get free hospitalization and medicine throughout the year. The farm workers are less fortunate. Their pay is only slightly higher than that of non-unionized workers on smaller farms in the area. Though their contracts provide some job security, their annual incomes and benefits offer little opportunity for a better life.

We met Dr Restituto Balmaceda who runs the hacienda's 35-bed hospital. It has an operating theatre, delivery room and nursery and employs four doctors and eight nurses. Mill workers are entitled to full medical benefits, including pharmaceutical and outpatient services, but farm workers must work 45 days a year to be included on the 'master list', which entitles employees to free hospitalization, but not to medicine or outpatient treatment. Low-paid farm workers complain about this.

Malnutrition among children on *Hacienda Luisita* occurs with troubling frequency. Though the children of *sacadas* and casual labourers are the most likely to suffer from malnutrition, dietary deficiencies also affect regular farm workers' children. 'Low wages are the main factor,' Dr Balmaceda said. 'The thing to do is increase the workers' pay. That will solve the problem.' In 1986 over 80 per cent of rural families earned less than 30,000 pesos. The remaining 20 per cent make up the small rural middle and upper classes. Professionals, managers, traders and especially landowners control the bulk of the wealth and power in the countryside.

The villages on *Hacienda Luisita* are divided by class. Supervisors, middle-level managers and professionals live in comfortable but simple houses near the mill, offices and hospital. The Cojuangco family and upper-level managers, however, are housed in a luxurious village near the country club and need not be exposed to their employees' poverty. But when disenchantment strikes, it is not only because of the inequalities of life on the hacienda or in the countryside. *Hacienda Luisita*'s residents are on the whole willing to concede the management a good life so long as they are treated with dignity. But this is not always the case. Some say that the management cares more for the animals than for the people on the hacienda. They resent the way in which the president's brother, Congressman José 'Peping' Cojuangco, pampers his race horses and roosters. His horses live in cool, comfortable stables and the fighting cocks occupy individual shelters. Extra care protects them from disease.

The breakdown of paternalism and of the close relationship between *haciendero* and worker has brought further disenchantment. Older workers fondly recall how the current owners' father used to host fiestas for hacienda employees and their families. Young and old would gather for feasts and entertainment and stare longingly at film stars, singers and other popular idols performing on temporary stages. These breaks in the hard and mundane routine rarely occur today. Now the Cojuangco family and the residents of the hacienda only seem to mix at election time. And it is not only in sugar-growing areas like Negros that the breakdown of traditional relationships has helped create an atmosphere ripe for unrest. Benedict Kerkvliet noted it in the rice-growing areas of Central Luzon during the 1930s.[1]

The breakdown of paternalism and the slow transformation from Philippine-style feudalism to agrarian capitalism is still continuing and is affecting the lives of farmers and farm workers throughout the country. Despite this, however, the landowner's power remains a potent force in electoral politics. The majority of poor residents in Tarlac and on *Hacienda Luisita*, for example, voted for Peping Cojuangco in the 1987 congressional election. Though the immediate causes of rural discontent vary, poverty, exploitation and oppression are common factors. Impoverished farm workers and peasants regard land (the symbol and source of wealth in the country) as the solution to their problems. Advocates of change, whether reformers or revolutionaries, agree that agrarian reform — with the redistribution of land as its centrepiece — is not a panacea, but a necessary first step towards addressing inequality and other social and economic problems.

On becoming president Cory Aquino was aware of the land problem and of its relationship to the people's living standards. 'As I look at the nation today,' she told an excited audience in Davao City, 'I see [that]... land is the anchor of hope; land is your home.' As her words reverberated throughout the Philippines, large numbers of workers and farmers, whom she had earlier referred to as the 'co-creators of our nation's wealth,' rallied to her side. And this despite both the Marcos government's and the revolutionary left's hostility. She told the crowd:

> The two essential goals of land reform are greater productivity and equitable sharing of the benefits and ownership of the land. These two goals can conflict with each other. But together we will seek viable systems of land reform suited to the particular exigencies dictated not only by the quality of the soil, the nature of the produce, and the agricultural inputs demanded, but

above all by the needs of the small farmers, landless workers, and communities of tribal Filipinos whose lives and personal dignity depend on their just share in the abundance of the land.

She also promised to use *Hacienda Luisita* as a model for the nation to emulate. As she put it, 'I shall sit down with my family to explore how the twin goals of maximum productivity and dispersal of ownership can be exemplified for the rest of the nation on *Hacienda Luisita*.'

Presidential candidates had long been promising land reform. Ramon Magsaysay had made agrarian reform the lynchpin of his reform-oriented, anti-communist agenda in 1953. Diosado Macapagal had emphasized the need for land reform during his presidency in the early 1960s — both had instituted limited changes. And shortly after declaring martial law in 1972, Ferdinand Marcos had included land reform as an essential element in his 'revolution from the centre', but nothing much had come of that. Many Filipinos had expected more from Aquino. This was not only because agrarian problems were more severe than at any other time in the nation's history, but because they viewed her as more than just a presidential candidate. She did not simply campaign for office, she led a national crusade for liberation. She symbolized hope and a desire for change.

But four years into Aquino's presidency very little had changed in the Philippine countryside. An executive order on agrarian reform issued in July 1987, less than a week before Aquino surrendered legislative power to a newly-convened Congress, had offered too little too late. She had left key elements of a 'comprehensive agrarian-reform programme' to Congress. *Hacienda Luisita* and other plantations continued to be run in essentially the same way as they had been in the past. Landowners, planters, and their relatives and allies had kept their hold on state power. As peasant groups had feared they would, the landed classes still dominated the new House of Representatives.

Having no power in Congress or in any other branches of government, peasant and farm-worker organizations have had to rely on extra-parliamentary politics — marches and demonstrations, alliance building, information sharing and land occupations. Militant groups, such as the KMP (*Kilusang Magbubukid ng Pilipinas*, or Peasant Movement of the Philippines), have led the bulk of these mass actions and have borne the brunt of state and private repression. The most noteworthy instance of a public attack on the peasant movement came in January 1987 when government troops gunned down 13 KMP supporters during a march near the presidential palace in Manila. KMP organizers in the countryside still face opposition and harassment from the military (which considers it a communist front), from state-supported anti-communist vigilantes and from landowners' private armies.

The 'open mass movement,' to which the KMP belongs, is but one part of a potent movement for radical change. Its backbone is the underground left consisting of the NDF (National Democratic Front) and its 14 constituent groups, including the CPP (Communist Party of the Philippines), the NPA (New People's Army) and CNL (Christians for National Liberation). The CPP plays the central role in the movement as the leader of the NPA, as an organizer of and prime mover in the NDF, and as an actor — sometimes with a lead role, sometimes a supporting part — in an array of legal organizations. The underground left finds its greatest strength in the countryside where, as we shall see, on 26 December 1968 a small band of young intellectuals gave birth to the party and where the government presence is often either minimal or distrusted.

Guerrilla fronts exist in at least two-thirds of the country's provinces. About 10,000 Filipinos belong to the NPA as full-time armed guerrilla fighters. Thousands more serve as local militia members or part-time guerrillas. In many of the places it operates, the revolutionary movement originally gained its foothold by appealing to local aspirations. These included putting an end to land grabbing in parts of Mindanao, defending tribal autonomy in the mountains of the Cordillera, or fighting poverty in the Visayas. In some places it went further by adapting to and utilizing local cultural forms to further organizational work and acceptance.

A glance at life in Albay province in the Bicol region provides an example. In early 1987 government troops controlled the town centres, national highways and some of the roadside, but many of the small farming villages in the rugged interior belonged to the revolutionaries. Red fighters and revolutionary organizers were ready to beat a hasty retreat if they had to, but they put their energies into building stable organizations and basic units of revolutionary authority and participation, expanding areas of influence, recruiting members and fighters, and implementing or experimenting with socio-economic change and development.

CPP cells and organizations of peasants, women and youths exercised rudimentary political power in the more 'advanced' villages, while *barangay* militias and local guerrilla units policed the area. Regular guerrilla units or mobile fighting forces passed through the consolidated villages on their way to and from 'expansion areas' and ambush sites. Guerrillas on leave relaxed with families and helped with chores. Armed rebels hopped on board mini-buses and public jeepneys to move from small roadside villages to paths leading to the interior, but only after making sure there were no soldiers around (local residents formed a simple but effective intelligence network).

Effective organizing and a positive response to questions about ownership and use of land and control of wealth had much to do with the success of the revolutionary movement in the part of Albay we visited. 'Before the comrades arrived,' Generoso, a peasant member of a local CPP cell, told us, 'I was innocent enough to believe the owner of the land had the right to do with it as he pleases.' A neighbour disagreed. 'We realized we had a right to the land,' he said, 'but we had no force to support our claim.' A CPP cadre originally from a nearby village chimed in: 'The people's attitude was that the landlord was so rich there was nothing they could do, they were powerless, besides, the government favours the rich.'

The farmers sat in a shady area just outside a small *nipa* hut discussing their problems and ideas. Fields of corn and upland rice covered most of the hillsides. *Carabao* and under-nourished cows grazed alongside the paths to a coconut grove. Most residents lived in small huts near the concrete school or small chapel, or scattered amongst the fields. Batteries provided the only electricity for flashlights and a radio. The community was poor but proud. Older men spoke most often. All the men supported the revolutionary movement. Farmers said they owed the improvements in their lives to the NPA and CPP cadres. They offered guerrillas and cadres food, places to sleep and a portion of their meagre income.

About ten years before the *kasamas* (comrades) arrived, villagers said that a new landlord had fenced off the rice and corn land they had rented from him and converted it into a pasture for his cattle. The peasants left without fighting. At first they said their troubles were not great, but problems mounted. Some former tenants planted crops outside the fence on tiny unused plots owned by smallholders. Others ran small stores, moved to nearby villages or sold their labour. 'It was a serious hardship for me,' said Marcial, who went from tenant to labourer. 'As a hired hand, life is harder because you have to work all day long; as a tenant you can find time to rest.'

In 1978 things slowly began to change. The PC (Philippine Constabulary) established a base in the town, but did not do much. Residents said the soldiers failed to detect the rebel Armed Propaganda Teams that began operating in the community around the same time. The farmers at first feared the rebels. They did not know this new armed group or what it stood for, but, by 1981, when the PC pulled out, the 'comrades had won the trust of the population.' They did so by treating the people respectfully, protecting tenants from eviction and developing contacts with key people in the community.

In 1980/1, after unsuccessful attempts to petition the landlord to open up the land, the peasants turned to the rebels for help. A *kasama* responded to their request by saying that 'the land should be open because cattle continue to live while the farmers are dying.' The watershed occurred at the end of 1982 when the CPP established a village organizing committee. The rebels began to confiscate cattle and seized 48 animals before the owner stopped using the land. For much of the next year the land lay fallow while the peasants tried to negotiate with the landowner. When nothing came of it the peasants, with support from the CPP and NPA, began to plant the land. One of my companions kept notes on the CPP's role in the struggle:

> The role of the Party in the land invasion was quite clear. The comrades had been instrumental in forming the peasants' organization. The NPA were the ones that took the cattle, at first, a few at a time. Then, the big bunch was taken in December of 1982. During this phase it was reported that one squad of armed NPAs (around 12 people) were supporting the civilians. It was the comrades who told the farmers they should act now — forcibly enter the land and plant, this was in 1983. It was also a Party comrade who divided up the land when the farmers did enter the pasture land. The farmers said that if the comrades had not visited them, they would never have taken the cows. They were afraid to be sued or that they would be punished by the military. During all this time, they felt they had a right to the land, but they were just too afraid to move on their own.

In organizing the land seizure, the CPP responded to the wishes of the local population and followed its own *Revolutionary Guide on Land Reform*. This document advocates reducing rents on farm land, eliminating usury and, eventually, replacing landlordism with control of the land by those who till it. It says:

> This programme for land reform has a minimum goal of lowering to the maximum limit land rent and eliminating usury. This programme has a maximum goal of free land distribution to landless tillers or those who do not have enough land. In addition, this programme aims to improve the conditions of farm workers on the haciendas based on capitalism.[2]

The programme encourages farmer organizations to establish cooperatives and sets out a system for taxing residents and businesses in areas influenced by revolutionary authorities. In practice, however, establishing cooperatives has not been easy and there are reports that the CPP is re-examining its ideas about collective agriculture.

Peasants farm most of the former Bicol pasture individually or with their families. The CPP made several attempts to organize cooperative labour on part of the land, but its efforts failed. Organizers traced the resistance to cooperatives to traditions and close family ties, but planned to continue pursuing cooperative development and organizational efforts. Results from a neighbouring coconut-producing village, where attempts to organize simple cooperative work teams had succeeded, cheered them.

CPP organizers worked with peasants and farm workers in other ways to improve their standard of living. They implemented animal distribution projects, developed a *carabao*-powered sugar mill, and planned fish ponds. Al Cortez, a member of the CPP's Bicol staff, mentioned the importance of such projects during our final day in the guerrilla zone. 'We recognize the fact,' he said, 'that as our formations grow larger, and we rely more on the support of the masses, there will come a time when, if we do not really pay attention to increasing their income, their support could wane.' This part of their plan seemed to be working well. 'The benefits of the revolution are material,' said one tenant. 'The sharing relations are much better.' One farmer called Bentot added, 'I can now send four of my nine children to school. Before, when I had only four kids, I could not send any.'

The tenants supported the movement by giving it a share of the harvest. 'We felt a debt of gratitude for the *kasamas* who helped us in the struggle and, thus, we were willing to give up some trees for them,' said one coconut farmer. These farmers believed the landowner also deserved a share (albeit a reduced one) of the harvest. They said the landlord paid taxes, bought the land, made improvements and was 'still a person who needs to survive.'

Residents in the guerrilla zones support the revolution in other ways. They pay taxes and membership fees, and make donations. In the village with the converted pasture, the movement collects the mass organizations' membership fees, an agrarian-reform tax from the beneficiaries of the land seizure, contributions from a support group (consisting of the village's wealthier residents) and allies in town, taxes on 'class enemies' (landlords who still rented out some rice, corn and coconut lands), landlord donations, 20 per cent of the total *barangay* funds from the national government, and a staggered individual income tax (2 per cent from poor and lower-middle peasants, and 5 per cent from middle-middle and upper-middle ones).

Local cadres and residents said they encountered no difficulties in collecting or paying taxes in the village, but a CPP member described the total collected as small because of the village's poverty. A finance officer also said he encountered problems in collecting donations from 'allies' in towns and other population centres influenced by priests, businessmen, professionals, politicians and government officials. He said they were 'still willing to give Cory a chance.'

Complaints about taxation occur where the government extends its influence, where CPP authority breaks down or is abused, or where large corporations operate. But in the guerrilla zones even companies (which are usually in logging, mining and transport) pay their taxes to the movement. A colleague once described how on a bus trip through northern Luzon the bus would occasionally stop long enough for the driver to hand over an envelope to a man carrying a clipboard. His seatmate had casually described the man as an NPA tax collector.

While support for the movement in the Bicol village had grown out of economic gains and the guerrillas' willingness to side with and fight for people who claimed that outside forces, including the government, had previously ignored them, the comrades did not ignore the political side of organizing. Members of mass organizations, the support group, the local militia and (in one village) the 17-member CPP cell learned the party line through an array of courses on sectoral issues, national democracy and Marxism-Leninism. Residents felt committed to the revolutionary movement despite their lack of political depth. They chuckled as they called Generoso (a peasant in his mid-60s) the local Marcos loyalist when he stood as a CPP candidate during the 1986 presidential election.

'I voted for Marcos,' he told us, 'because I thought his economic recovery programme was better. And besides, I thought he would finally have so much power that he would do something for the little guy.' A neighbour and comrade sheepishly admitted to doing the same thing. The CPP had advocated a boycott of the election, but many of its supporters had voted for Cory Aquino in the hope of a change. Backing Marcos was out of the question. Shortly after the election Generoso became a full party member. 'We still have a lot of education work to do,' admitted an embarrassed Al Cortez not long after translating Generoso's comments. 'We have to be more careful. I think people wanted Generoso in the party because of his role as a community leader.' Organized peasants in the Bicol guerrilla areas — some of the poorest in the country — strongly support the armed aspect of the revolutionary movement. This stems partly from their own experience and partly from the strong emphasis placed on armed struggle by movement organizers. When Saturino Ocampo, a now imprisoned CPP leader, visited a Bicol village during ceasefire negotiations in 1986, he found himself hard pressed to explain the logic behind a ceasefire. Later, when the ceasefire was in place, rural cadres and supporters from places like Bicol pushed for a resumption of armed struggle.

We were fortunate. During our stay in the guerrilla zone we never encountered government forces and only saw troops marching along the highway as we returned to town. But the day after we left troops raided one of the villages we had visited. A few days later a police officer had killed one of our hosts in a market. And two months after that government troops had killed Al Cortez and two other members during a dawn raid on a house in which they had been sleeping. The turncoat who had fingered them was found dead a few days later.

A bloody battle is being fought in the Philippines. In 1988 the AFP (Armed Forces of the Philippines) and NPA were losing an average of three to four fighters a day. Government and CPP officials are being killed. Civilians caught in the cross-fire or targeted by one side or the other are dying. This is one reason why so many Filipinos want peace and why so many people placed so much hope in the 1986/7 peace talks staged by the government and the NDF.

But statistics fail to convey the human side of this tragic story. Al had loved the movies and his wife. He had recalled with such joy a day spent resting at a friend's house watching videos. He had spoken about his difficulties with his aging and beloved parents, and his inability to tell them about his life and work. Francisco had joked about not knowing how to shoot straight with the M-16 rifle he had been carrying during our visit. He had never participated in a battle and was not a guerrilla fighter. But he had accepted his role as a combatant and the fact that he might die without witnessing the victory of the revolution for which he lived. Other victims are not combatants. They are the men, women and children who have become victims of human rights abuses.

Cory Aquino emphasized human rights during her bid for the presidency and her early months in Malacanang Palace. That emphasis vanished during her second year in office. Malou Mangahas, the Malacanang correspondent for the *Manila Chronicle*, noted in a mid-November 1987 column that:

> Armies of all kinds, including the government's own, have taken the law by the nozzle of the gun, coups and mutinies have been mounted, spates of murders of cops and soldiers committed, massacres of civilians and rebels by lawmen carried out.... It saddens the heart and boggles the mind why, until now, government officials have not spoken out on human rights.[3]

What price do Filipinos pay for their government's total war on the rebels? Task Force Detainees, a left-wing human rights organization established by the Association of Major Religious Superiors, counted

312 cases of torture, 141 cases of 'salvaging' (extra-judicial executions) by government forces and 43 disappearances in 1989. It also claimed that the government had arrested at least 2,000 individuals for political reasons during the same year. Human rights organizations, which had originally applauded Aquino when she released all but a handful of political prisoners after coming to power, called 1987 the worst year for human rights in the Philippines since 1978.[4]

Two developments particularly alarmed human rights advocates — government support for anti-communist vigilantes and a series of assassinations of leaders and activists belonging to legal left-wing groups in Manila. Vigilantes proliferated throughout the country with the support of military officers, local politicians and elements of the national government. In some places, they acted as right-wing death squads.

During the year starting in November 1986, gunmen killed labour leader Rolando Olalia and an aide, political leader Leandro Alejandro, lawyer Alex Marteja, journalist Manny Sanchez, educator Dan Sibal and the brothers of two activists. Former guerrilla leader Bernabe Buscayno, university president Dr Nemensio Prudente and several others escaped with gunshot wounds. These incidents took place as the NPA stepped up its left-wing attacks on police, military and local government officials in Metro Manila.

This new violence brought fresh attention to the perilous nature of life in the city. The violence, however, tells only part of the story of the archipelago's overcrowded urban centres. Only 30 per cent of the nation's population lives in cities, but more than 8 million Filipinos crowd Metro Manila, and the number of people in the cities grows as life in the countryside becomes more tenuous. With close to 109,000 individuals per square mile, Manila is one of the most crowded cities in the world. In 1982, workers of only five of the world's 73 major cities earned less than Manila's workers. Construction and textile workers, toolmakers, engineers and teachers earned far less than their counterparts elsewhere in the world. And this does not take into account the legion of unemployed and semi-employed scavengers, beggars and street vendors in the metropolis.[5]

Corruption makes matters worse. Public servants and utilities demand grease money before processing forms or providing services. Traffic police stop motorists for minor or imagined violations and release them only after collecting bribes. Taxi drivers overcharge customers and jeepney drivers fail to give the correct change.

Profit-mad transport companies show little regard for safety, consistent service or the environment. At best this results in inconvenience, at worst in disastrous accidents. Drivers ignore rules and common sense alike. Poorly maintained buses and trucks emit billowing clouds of thick black smoke as they hurtle recklessly down crowded streets. As a matter of course, drivers pass on blind corners and ignore traffic lights. The *Manila Chronicle* used the city's anarchic traffic as a window on the country. 'The traffic congestion and behaviour of our people on the road are a microcosm of national behaviour which portrays us as a madly disorganized and ill-disciplined people.... We do not have a common notion of a corporate nation having a common purpose. Each one of us puts self-interest above that of the entire nation.'[6]

It is Manila's poor and middle classes who must deal with these problems. In contrast, the rich spend their days in air-conditioned offices, dine in fine restaurants, travel in comfortable cars, and live in palatial homes in luxurious walled suburbs. Maids, drivers and houseboys serve their needs. Armed guards keep the riffraff away while tens of thousands of city dwellers seek shelter where they can find it.

Manila hosts South East Asia's largest slum, Tondo. Thousands of urban Filipinos stay in tiny shacks or makeshift shelters in sprawling shanty towns. Others live in small, crowded squatter communities which pop up wherever there is an unguarded vacant lot. Slums spring up on the edges of rubbish dumps, on stilts above swamps and alongside rivers carrying industrial and human waste. Environmental health hazards (dirty water, poor waste disposal and insect-breeding swamps) make mere survival a struggle.

Almost all slum dwellers risk violent eviction. Community organizers, including some sympathetic to the government, hold it responsible for their plight. 'At this moment, we believe the Aquino government wants peace,' Eddie Guanzon, a Tondo resident and chairman of the Urban Poor Solidarity Committee told me in 1986, 'but there is violence everywhere. There will come a time when there is a violent confrontation. The government does not listen. It has its own interests.'

Violence takes on many forms in Manila's crowded districts. Robberies, beatings and gunfights occur frequently enough to support a slew of sensationalist tabloids. Notorious criminal gangs recruit bored and jobless youths. Shootings break out between rival bands of police and soldiers after late-night drinking sessions. Much of the violence is self destructive. This report from the daily *Malaya* is not unusual.

> A truck driver was hacked to death Sunday night in Pasig by a co-worker at the height of an argument over the real date of Christmas. The victim, Eddie de la Cruz, 21, a native of Quezon province, was hacked to death with a jungle *bolo* in the neck by Fernando Masa, 21, also a native of Quezon.

Witnesses said de la Cruz was insisting that Jesus Christ was born on 26
December while Masa said it was 25 December.[7]

Some of the violence has a class character. Resistance to eviction and
shanty-town demolition often turns into bloody confrontations between
stone-throwing slum dwellers and rifle-toting soldiers. Less heroic forms
of class conflict also take place. Reports of violent robberies of
employers by employees frequently make the front pages of the tabloids
— such as houseboys, maids and drivers plunging knives into their
masters' chests when caught pilfering jewels or cash boxes.

Class politics in the cities (and rural areas) usually occurs outside the
parliamentary arena. In Manila and other industrial centres, workers
apply pressure through strikes, demonstrations, individual criminal acts
and, at times, blatant political violence. The left-wing PNB (*Partido ng
Bayan*, or Party of the People) ran a slate during the 1987 congressional
elections, but found traditional politicians dominant in that arena. The
old formula of 'guns, goons and gold' and personality-oriented politics
won out over the 'new politics' of the left.

Like business tycoons everywhere, the Manila élite's primary concern
is to make money. Justice is not a priority. Business organizations apply
pressure to advance collective class interests and wealthy individuals
back candidates unlikely to pursue radical reform. Right from the start of
the revolution they applied pressure on the Aquino government to control
a restive labour force and to pursue right-wing economic policies of
privatisation and deregulation. Bitter conflicts also flare up within the
élite. Dissident groups sometimes resent policies that favour one business
sector over another, but more commonly the disputes involve power,
with those out of power plotting coups, developing elaborate schemes for
seizing power, or spending large amounts of money on getting elected.

Nationalism is the one ideological issue that enters élite political
discourse. The élite generally lacks a healthy sense of national pride —
illustrated, for example, by the behaviour of many of Marcos's cronies
who, instead of investing the profits of the dictatorship in the Philippines,
poured their money into assets abroad. The subsequent scandal rocked
the nation, but the practice did not represent an anomaly in the way
Filipino executives conduct business.

Filipinos and foreigners alike decry the lack of national pride and
culture. Some nationalists point to the long history of resistance to
foreign domination, but many of the revolts they mention were localized,
small or betrayed by affluent leaders. Today, as we shall see, US
influence is the greatest obstacle to developing a positive national
identity. It appears in all aspects of Philippine life — sport, fast foods,
films and clothing. It affects political, economic and cultural beliefs and

is protected by US political, economic and military power and by a captive élite. 'It boils down to who wields political power,' Bonifacio Gillego once reminded me. 'This is where you do not need clandestine or even overt efforts to influence the present crop of Filipino leaders. There seems to be a congruence of interest: "By protecting American influence, I am protecting my influence."'

Many politicians pay lip service to nationalist ideals, especially when a foreign scapegoat serves to deflect attention from their own failings. Likewise, segments of the business community rely on nationalist arguments to counter foreign competition but fall back on colonial ways when foreigners offer funds or partnerships. Only a small number of officials, editors and intellectuals bring nationalist thought into élite discourse. In fact the only significant nationalist force is the left and it finds its home, not amongst the élite, but in poor communities and on some college campuses.

The roots of this lack of a healthy national identity lie in the past. The colonial mentality and a system that guarantees domination and poverty did not spring from nowhere during the Marcos era — neither did dissent, resistance and rebellion. To locate the birth of both oppression and struggle, and to find out why the February revolution which swept Cory Aquino to power failed to solve the nation's problems, we must turn to the past.

2

Colonialism and an Emerging Nation

Ferdinand Magellan made a fatal mistake soon after leading the first European voyage to the Philippines in 1521. The famous explorer violated the orders of his sponsor, King Charles of Spain, and went ashore on the island of Cebu. A local chief, Humabon, welcomed him and his crew and, to seal their friendship, Magellan agreed to engage Humabon's enemy, Lapu Lapu of Mactan, in battle.

Lapu Lapu wasted no time with the fair-skinned intruders. Native warriors slew Magellan and forced his troops back to Cebu. Angered by the defeat, Humabon drove the remaining Europeans from the archipelago. This postponed Spanish conquest and gave birth to an important tendency in Philippine history — resistance to foreign domination. Time and time again village chiefs and entire communities would rise against the *conquistadores*. More often than not these conflicts ended in defeat for the heroic, but outgunned and isolated defenders — sometimes because of the treason of a chief or community leader.

It was not until 1565 that the Spanish conquest actually began. In that year Miguel Lopez de Legazpi set up the first European settlement on Cebu. The Spanish viceroy in Mexico had charged him with establishing a foothold in the East and finding a route to Mexico for ships carrying the wealth of the Orient. But Legazpi's settlement in Cebu failed to prosper and, seven years later, he moved to Manila to continue the search for wealth. On his death in 1572 the Spaniards had neither discovered any great wealth nor decided what to do with their Asian colony. Legazpi had, however, set in motion a second major trend in Philippine history — conquering and exploiting the native population and its resources for foreign profit.

In 1587, only 15 years after the Spanish had seized Manila, two chiefs built one of the first broad-based anti-colonial alliances, but before the rebels could act, a traitor exposed the plot. Anxious to set an example and stave off future uprisings, the Spanish authorities reacted swiftly and brutally. They executed some leaders, exiled others and seized their lands.

This uprising gave birth to yet another trend in Philippine history — betrayal. Collaborators invariably emerged from the native ranks to conspire with the colonial power. In time they gained wealth and power in the emerging class society and some tried to use their newfound strength to advance personal agendas in the name of the public good. They sought to replace the Spanish as landowners and rulers of the population, or at least to share power with the colonial state. To advance their cause, they had to mobilize the masses, but the disparity of interests repeatedly led them to betray their followers. The ramifications of conquest and resistance, élite leadership and betrayal still influence Philippine society. The roots of many characteristics of Philippine life can be found in the colonial past.

Prior to the Spanish conquest, there was no real nation on the Philippine archipelago. The descendants of waves of aboriginal, Malay and Indo-Chinese settlers lived in scattered coastal and riverside villages, or further inland in the mountains. Historian Renato Constantino describes these pre-colonial villages as 'primitive economic units with a system of subsistence agriculture which provided them with barely enough for their needs.' Some coastal communities practised small-scale trade with passing Chinese, Indian and Arab seamen.[1] Communities included leaders, freemen and debt peons. The emerging class structure was most advanced in the Muslim areas of the south. Constantino notes: 'There is every probability that the Muslim societies were already at the threshold of class society. They were evolving an Asiatic form of feudalism where land was still held in common but was private in use.'[2]

Had Spain not conquered the Philippines, it might have become an Islamic nation. Arab traders and Islamic missionaries had introduced Islam to the southern Philippines five or six centuries before Spain's arrival. By the 16th century there were some scattered Muslim communities on Luzon, including one in Manila. Spanish conquest reversed Islamization and, as Constantino notes, the trend toward indigenous development: 'Instead of a more developed society expanding its (the south's) influence over the others and diffusing its culture and social organization throughout the less-developed ones, Spanish conquest aborted this historical trend, developed the other regions and froze the evolution of what had once been the more advanced society — the Muslim south.'[3]

While Spain used military, political and economic power to dominate the country physically, to establish cultural hegemony it turned to the Roman Catholic Church. At the time of the conquest the non-Islamic natives believed in an array of gods. To control them the colonizers needed a more powerful set of beliefs, which Catholicism's God conveniently provided. Acceptance did not come immediately, but demanded a blending of Catholic dogma with native traditions. Still, Catholicism ultimately provided a powerful weapon for controlling the population.

Spain did not limit the role of the Church to the spiritual or cultural realm — it played a central role in politics and economics as well. Its friars eventually came to symbolize the evil of Spanish rule. From this emerged one of the ironies of Philippine history: as the population became more and more Catholic in its religious beliefs, it developed a strong anti-clerical streak.

Spain itself had begun a social and economic transformation not long before the conquest of the Philippines. Capitalism replaced feudalism as Spain's dominant economic system during the 16th century. Spanish capitalism followed a mercantile path. This led to an aggressive colonial policy as Spain sought new markets and, more important, new sources of riches (precious metals, spices and silk) for its European trade.

Until the late 18th century Spain did little to develop the Philippines. On failing to discover wealth equal to that of Latin America, it had actually considered abandoning the area even before Legazpi moved from Cebu to Manila. But other factors prevailed. Entranced by dreams of an Asian empire and embroiled in regional wars with European competitors (Holland, Britain and Portugal) Spain wanted the Philippines as a military outpost.

Spaniards also used the Philippines as a base for the galleon trade between China and Mexico. Pressure from Spain's domestic textile interests (which were opposed to unlimited shipments of Chinese silk) limited the galleon trade to one round trip a year. This provided enough wealth to enrich Manila's small Spanish community (including the religious), but not enough to pull the Philippines into the modern world. Historian Alfred McCoy notes how:

> The archipelago's integration within the world economy was slow, uneven, protracted and largely non-cumulative. After the Spanish landing in the 1560s, Manila became the remotest outpost of Spain's Latin American Empire, marginally linked to Europe through the trans-Pacific galleon trade. The Philippines offered few incentives for an intensive exploitation of local resources. The archipelago was too remote for bulk trade, produced neither pepper nor spices and was too lightly populated for mines or plantations (580,000 people in 1606 versus Mexico's 11 million in 1519). Manila was, however, well situated to serve Spain in its brief bid for an Asian trading empire in the first half of the 17th century. Responding to dislocations in the

global silk market, Manila became an entrepôt re-exporting Chinese silks and luxury goods to Europe via Mexico.[4]

The Philippines developed unevenly in the first half of the Spanish era. Great wealth was concentrated in Manila, where the Spaniards built a European-style walled city. Some reached the nearby provinces, which supplied the inhabitants of the capital with food and other basic necessities, but most of it found its way into the hands of Spanish religious orders, Chinese merchants and native administrators. Some of the more distant settlements were partially integrated into colonial society through religious missions, Spanish conscription of soldiers and labourers, and taxation and tribute collection, but the remote mountain tribes and Islamic Moros remained relatively free of colonial control until much later.

Spain had started to establish instruments of control even before the galleon trade became a priority. The original *conquistadores* needed a source of income and profit. Later Spain needed to fund the colony's government without hurting the Spanish traders or religious orders. It also had to provide its colony with food, shelter and labour. Throughout the period it therefore required tools with which to pacify the native population. These factors motivated Spain to establish a series of institutions, which brought the partial integration of the islands and great suffering.

The first programme, the *encomienda*, allowed the early *conquistadores* to enrich themselves while asserting Spanish authority in the archipelago. *Encomenderos* were empowered to collect tribute from residents of their domain. Labour conscription, slavery, the torture and murder of chiefs who failed to collect sufficient tribute and similar abuses proliferated until the last of the private *encomiendas* disappeared sometime after 1721. The end of the private *encomienda* system did not, however, mean the end of abuses. Residents of Crown *encomiendas*, administrative districts run by colonial officials called *alcaldes mayores* (the rough equivalent of provincial governors), also suffered regular abuses. Along with the *encomenderos*, other Spaniards entered the countryside. According to American historian Dennis Morrow Roth, some 120 Spaniards received land grants for vacant lands within a 100 km. radius of Manila.[5] But more significantly, the religious orders entered the countryside as *encomenderos*, missionaries and landowners.

The colonial authorities asked the friars to help them integrate the native *barangays* into the Spanish administrative structure by consolidating the population into fewer and larger villages. Using enticements and threats and exploiting their growing spiritual influence, the friars attracted native chiefs and their followers into their settlements.

Resettlement brought the priests into regular contact with large numbers
of natives and simplified the process of Catholic indoctrination. But the
priests were not simply interested in saving souls. Economic incentives
had lured many young Spaniards into the priesthood and had fuelled the
fervour of virtually all the religious orders, which now participated in all
aspects of economic life. Quietly and illegally at first, then with
government sanction, they joined the galleon and other trades. But their
biggest impact was in agriculture. By the time Spanish rule ended in
1896, the religious orders held sprawling tracts of farm land (called friar
estates) in several provinces near Manila.

The emergence of the friar estates led to a concentration of valuable
agricultural land in the hands of a few. Small non-commercial farmers
found themselves working much harder for less. As tenants they faced
exorbitant rents, arbitrary increases in rents and other charges, eviction
and demands for their labour and personal services. Friar abuses
(including new estate taxes, whippings and sexual abuse) increased their
suffering. But the friar estates did not create a full-blown hacienda
economy. They only served the wealthy but relatively small community
of Spanish-born administrators, Spanish and mestizo descendants of
earlier settlers (then known as Filipinos), Chinese traders and native
collaborators. The economy remained unevenly developed with Manila
at the centre, the friar estates concentrated nearby, and the outlying areas
linked only by the demand for labour and a few products.

As the urban élite's demand for products of the countryside grew,
small-scale, Chinese-dominated domestic trade emerged. The Chinese
also controlled the Asian barter trade which kept the Spanish community
stocked with luxury items. This trade attracted many Chinese to the
Philippines and contributed to the growth of the archipelago's Chinese
and later Chinese-mestizo population.

The nature of Philippine society began to change in the 18th and 19th
centuries when, mainly through the efforts of British and Chinese
merchants, the Philippines entered the global economy, thereby forcing
the Spanish rulers to open the country to outside trade and to develop
agriculture for export. During this later period of Spanish rule, the
Philippines began to develop a rudimentary national economy and
identity.

Britain became the dominant force in world trade. In the early 18th
century British-controlled trade between Manila and Madras, India,
prospered despite legal restrictions limiting the Asia trade to Asian
merchants. British traders took advantage of the opportunities the galleon
trade provided. Indian cotton and other goods passed through Manila on
the way to Mexico, while Mexican silver, Chinese-made gold plate and

pearls, skins, tobacco, leather and horses gathered by Chinese traders in the Philippines went the other way.

This clandestine trade brought the archipelago into the emerging global economy as a minor supplier of agricultural and animal products. Eventually, after a brief occupation of Manila (1762-4), the British found Spanish allies in the battle for economic integration. In 1778, Governor José de Basco y Vargas began to promote commercial agriculture and the trade of tobacco and sugar, which brought new riches to the landowning and trading élite. In 1815 Spain suspended the galleon trade and, shortly afterwards, opened the port of Manila to other Western traders. As Mariel Francisco and Fe Maria Arriola write:

> The growth of capitalism in Europe, with free trade as [a] key concept, induced Spain to open the Philippines to world trade in 1834. Manila became one of the busiest ports in the Orient. Banks opened as the barter economy was replaced by a money economy. British and American merchant houses financed the production of Philippine sugar, tobacco, hemp and coffee for export to distant markets. At the same time Western consumer goods - from cheap British textiles to French champagne - flowed into the country.[6]

The domestic economy still resembled a patchwork of different forms of production, class peculiarities and foreign relations, but a common thread held the different patches together. Since the developing commercial economy centred around agriculture for foreign and colonial markets, the government tobacco monopoly (which survived until 1880), the Bicol-based hemp trade, commercial rice farming in Central Luzon and the development of a sugar-based economy in Negros and Iloilo fitted, albeit awkwardly at times, into a single whole.

Some historians emphasize the heterogeneity of social change and economic development during the 18th and 19th centuries. McCoy, for example, declares that:

> The origins of national disunity spring from the very processes of transformation during the 'long' 19th century. The Philippines did not develop as a unitary colonial economy oriented towards a single satellite entrepôt at Manila. Instead, the archipelago emerged as a series of separate societies that entered the world economic system at different times, under different terms of trade and with different systems of production.[7]

Other historians, most notably Constantino, claim that this period gave birth to a national economy. While not denying the diversity referred to by McCoy, Constantino and like-minded historians emphasize the commonality of experience and the emergence of the first nationalist thinkers. Parts of the truth may be found in both approaches. Economic diversity certainly flourished, but within a framework of serving foreign needs. And, while nationalist thought and identity evolved in educated sectors of the élite, it did not gain a wide following beyond Manila and surrounding provinces. Identity remained rooted in regional or local experiences.

The coming of global trade did not always bring economic development. In at least one case, that of Iloilo and Negros, British interests actually reversed an indigenous trend towards industrial development by redirecting capital from an emerging textile industry into sugar production.

In 1856 a British consul, Nicholas Loney, started to promote cheap British cottons as a substitute for local products. At the same time Loney promised high profits to traders and to sugar planters trading with Britain's Manchester-based textile producers. He encouraged Iloilo's manufacturers to shift from textiles to sugar and from industry to agriculture. Iloilo's textile industry collapsed while the Chinese industrialists carved sugar plantations from the plains of neighbouring Negros. Iloilo became a sugar entrepôt and the families that still control Negros today established their foothold on that island.

British economic interests accelerated the class transformation that had begun with the coming of the Spanish. At the time of the Spanish conquest much of native society lacked a distinct class structure. To assert control and divide the native communities, the Spaniards promoted a native élite (or *principalia*) from the ranks of the traditional chieftains. These people gained their power and wealth by collecting taxes and tribute and by providing draft labour. They quickly learned to collect more than Spain demanded and to skim off a proportion for themselves. In addition, while the Spaniards had introduced the concept of private property primarily to benefit their own clergy and colonials, the native collaborators took advantage of this new and alien concept to claim ownership of communal lands. Though more powerful than other natives, the early *principalia* were still distinctly second-class residents of the islands. They could serve as town officials, but higher offices stayed in Spanish hands.

Changes to the class structure in the 18th and 19th centuries completed the metamorphosis of the Philippines into a highly stratified society. The process created a self-consciously Filipino élite, which gave birth to élite nationalism as a political force in the archipelago. This new national élite reflected the changing nature of the population. Instead of just Spanish, Chinese and natives, the islands now housed *peninsulares* (government officials and other Spaniards born in Spain), *insulares* (full-blooded and mestizo descendants of earlier Spanish settlers), Chinese mestizos, the urbanized native *principalia*, and the provincial *principalia*

— in addition to the peasants, fishermen and labourers who made up the vast majority of the native population.

The new élite class was structured along racial lines. *Peninsulares* held the top government and religious posts and had the largest share of the Philippines' wealth. Though rich and powerful compared with everyone else, the Philippine-born *insulares* were less well off. Next in social status were the Chinese mestizos, who combined Chinese-based wealth with native integration. These mestizos, usually the descendants of Chinese fathers and native mothers, suffered little of the official discrimination directed against the Chinese. Catholicized, hispanisized and accepted in native society, they took advantage of the Chinese community's disadvantage. When the Spanish authorities expelled the Chinese from the colony in the mid-18th century, the mestizos successfully assumed their role as middlemen in the economy. When the Chinese returned 100 years later, the mestizo community, attracted by profits to be made from the new export-oriented agriculture, shifted to lucrative landownership. They would become the leading *hacienderos* and ancestors of such notable Filipinos as Cory Aquino.

An urbanized native *principalia* also evolved and absorbed a number of Hispanic values. No longer dependent simply on its functionary role, it accumulated riches through owning land and engaging in export-oriented agriculture, but remained excluded from political power. Members of the new *principalia* (along with the Spanish and Chinese mestizos) gained notably better access to education than had previous native élites. This made the injustice of colonial rule and the concentration of political power in foreign hands even less acceptable. Time had opened the Philippines' college, university and seminary doors to members of the native élite. Scions of the wealthiest families even studied in Spain or other European countries where new liberal ideas caught their attention. This new educated élite took the name *ilustrados* and became the liberal ideologues of the emerging landed and commercial classes.

For the poor, the social transformation often meant new suffering, as Constantino describes:

> In the countryside, perhaps more than in the city, economic progress had depressed the living standards of the masses, both absolutely and relatively....
> Land rentals were increased from year to year; tenants forced by landowners to concentrate on cash crops were no longer sure of their food supply; cottage industries, principally weaving, which augmented farm income were destroyed by competition from imports. But above all, the export-crop economy increased the value of land and the desirability of owning as many hectares as possible. The religious orders and other Spanish landowners, the native *principales* and the rising class of Chinese mestizos all took advantage

of the various land laws, the mortgage law, and the *pacto de retroventa*, to dispossess ignorant and poor peasants of their small plots.[8]

These social transformations during the final century and a half of Spanish rule had a lasting impact on the course of Philippine politics. The local élite — natives, mestizos and Philippine-born Spaniards — resented Spanish control and joined in liberal dissent. They sought to replace Spain's power and the power of the *peninsulares* with their own, but they did not want to threaten property interests. The wealthier members of the new Filipino élite were conservative and prone to capitulation and collaboration with Spain. But to offset Spanish power, the Filipino élite, especially the native and mestizo elements, had to appeal to the lower classes and lead them in struggle and sometimes revolt.

For their part, peasants wavered between anti-colonial revolt (often élite-led and directed towards the friars as well as the local Spanish authorities) and rudimentary class struggle aimed at rich Filipinos. They (and other poor natives) also wavered between periods of revolt and long stretches of painful acquiescence.

3

From Rebellion to Revolution

Rebellion broke out early in the colonial era. There were over 200 recorded uprisings during the Spanish period. In the early years revolts were limited in geographic scope and awareness, for no one imagined a Philippine nation until much later. Aside from pitting natives against foreigners, the early revolts often pitted nativist religion against Catholicism. The old beliefs gave the rebels strength to fight the *conquistadores* and their strange new God.

As the natives became Catholic and the first *principales* appeared, the colonial experience entered a second phase. Members of the native élite frequently led the local revolts which, even when the rebels were railing against the friars, were coloured with Catholic trappings. Nationalist unrest, especially among the *ilustrados*, emerged in Luzon in the 19th century. But broad national unity, involving Visayans, Moros and others, remained elusive.

The Church became an early focus for Philippine nationalism. The spread of Catholicism encouraged numerous members of the non-Spanish élite to enter the priesthood and, when the authorities evicted the Jesuits in 1768, these native priests prospered. After a brief period in which the native parish-based Church flourished, authority reverted to the *peninsulares*-dominated religious orders. As Constantino writes:

> Like other sectors of the local élite, the native priests were finding that their own advancement was being impeded by the Spaniards. They, too, reacted with resentment at the injustice and discrimination they were subjected to. This sharpened their awareness of their separate national identity, a consciousness which was transmitted to their native parishioners. The demand for Filipinization became one of the rallying cries of the steadily growing sentiment of nationality.[1]

The Cavite mutiny of 1872 highlighted the convergence of religious and secular dissent and created three martyrs for the Philippine national movement. Workers in the Fort San Felipe arsenal rebelled against the Spaniards' suspension of their exemption from tribute and forced labour.

The government suppressed the mutiny within a day, but then overreacted to an imaginary broad separatist conspiracy.

Powerful friars accused a Spanish mestizo, Fr José Burgos, and native clerics, Frs Mariano Gomez and Jacinto Zamora, of leading the conspiracy. The administration agreed, and tried and executed the three. It also jailed or banished numerous other prominent dissidents. After a period of banishment in the Mariana Islands, Spain allowed some of the victims of the Cavite crack-down to settle in Spain. There they formed the Propaganda Movement in the 1880s, which advocated integration with Spain on a basis of equality. They did not seek independence, but representation in the Spanish parliament.

Many leading Philippine intellectuals joined the reform movement. None shone more brightly than student and future medical doctor, José Rizal, who secured his place in Philippine history with the publication of *Noli Me Tangere*, a powerful study of Philippine colonial society. Though the colonial authorities banned the novel, it became a classic in Philippine literature. Rizal held moderate, reform-oriented opinions. After returning to the Philippines in the early 1890s, he formed *La Liga Filipina* in Manila in 1892 which, while keeping the reformist thrust of the Propaganda Movement, broadened its base by recruiting 'common' folk.

A few days after having launched the League, Rizal was arrested and banished to the provinces. The League then fell on hard times until Andrés Bonifacio, a remarkable commoner who had helped found it, sought to revive it. But the absence of the towering figure of Rizal hastened the inevitable split between the conservative reformist élite and the plebeian and lower middle-class rebels around Bonifacio. During the next few years, while the élite sought compromise with its colonial masters, Bonifacio and his followers built the first revolutionary nationalist organization. The secret *Kataastaasang Kagalang-galangang Katipunan ng mga Anak ng Bayan* (Supreme Exalted Society of the Children of the Nation), known as the *Katipunan* (Society), caught on among the small urban working class. It also attracted the support of middle-class nationalists.

Bonifacio differed radically from other prominent Filipinos of his time. He had finished only two years of high school when he began to work as a pedlar, messenger, salesman and warehouseman, but read vociferously about revolution and politics. Other *Katipunan* leaders shared his class background and limited education, but the new rebels failed to develop a coherent ideology and this left a tragic opening for the conservative *ilustrados* to exploit.

The *ilustrados* were an ambivalent social stratum. Constantino observes how:

> Their grievances impelled them to relate to the people, but because they regarded themselves as the social superiors of the masses they also related to the ruling power. They were willing to join the *peninsulares* if some of their political and economic demands could be granted, but at the same time they identified themselves with the people in order to secure the maximum concessions from the colonial establishment.[2]

As for the general population, Constantino writes, they:

> readily accepted many of the teachings of the *ilustrados*. They themselves, though tempered in the struggle of the centuries, did not yet have the capability to integrate their experiences. Their articulate *ilustrado* compatriots gave expression to their thoughts, feelings, and aspirations, and the masses quickly responded by giving their enthusiastic support to these leaders who crystallized for them the injustices they had been subjected to for hundreds of years.[3]

The ambivalence of the *ilustrados* surfaced repeatedly during the course of the struggle with Spain and later the US. As a rule the wealthiest Filipinos, who were often of Spanish descent, collaborated after being offered minimal concessions. The native élite held out for more, though often in the form of personal rather than national or communal advancement.

Between 1894 and 1896 Bonifacio and his comrades quietly but quickly built up their underground organization. Rapid expansion brought eventual betrayal. On 18 August 1896 a Manila printer exposed the *Katipunan* to a loyalist priest. Four days later Bonifacio summoned his co-conspirators. He and Emilio Jacinto, editor of *Kalayaan* (Freedom), the *Katipunan's* short-lived newspaper, called for an immediate armed struggle, even though they knew the *Katipunan* could not match the colonial power. Soon battles and armed uprisings broke out in the towns and provinces around Manila. People rallied to the *Katipunan's* simple call: 'Long live the Philippines!'

Spain reacted swiftly and brutally. The colonial authorities executed *katipuneros* and suspected rebels and an orgy of blood and horror swept the islands. No one seemed immune to the wrath of Mother Spain — not even the moderate, José Rizal. From his prison cell in Manila's Fort Santiago, Rizal had urged his former followers to seek change peacefully, but the Spaniards still charged him with being the revolution's principal organizer and he was sentenced to death.

The revolution continued to spread. Often armed only with *bolos*, or machetes and spears made from pointed sticks, people attacked Spanish outposts in Nueva Ecija and Bataan. Rebel sentiments surfaced across Luzon. In many places the *Katipunan* won the hearts of the people, but Spain scored on the battlefield.

Bonifacio also had political problems — rebellious *ilustrados* refused to accept the leadership of a man they considered 'beneath' them. Bolstered by local military victories, in Cavite, just south of Manila, a faction led by the young Gen. Emilio Aguinaldo (the mayor of Kawit) sought to seize control of the revolution. In 1897 Aguinaldo established a revolutionary government as an alternative to the *Katipunan* and ordered Bonifacio's arrest and execution.

Bonifacio's murder led to the collapse of the *Katipunan* but not to the elimination of revolutionary fervour. Despite reversals on the battlefield, Aguinaldo pressed on to establish a new republic. On 1 November 1897 his supporters approved a constitution and set up a Supreme Council headed by Aguinaldo. At the same time he was negotiating with the Spaniards and, in December, signed the pact of *Biak-na-Bato* with them. Spain agreed to pay Aguinaldo 800,000 pesos and, in return, he called on the people to lay down their arms before leaving for exile in Hong Kong. The first draft of the agreement cited Filipino demands for reforms and called for their enactment within three years. The final draft dropped all mention of reform.

Aguinaldo's exile did not end the conflict. Revolutionary leaders and grassroots rebels continued fighting Spanish authority. Meanwhile a new factor, in the form of incipient conflict between Spain and the US over the former's remaining colonial possessions, entered the scene.

As the turn of the century approached the US came to a crossroads. As its Indian wars and conflict with Mexico drew to a close, its conquest of what would become continental US was completed. Agreements with Mexico and Britain ended the possibility of expanding to the north or south and left the country's new industrialists looking abroad for new markets and raw materials.

The capture of Hawaii whetted the appetite of America's budding imperialists. Spain's crumbling empire provided an easy opportunity. Cuba, Puerto Rico and the Philippines were among its last vestiges. They were troubled colonies, plagued by native uprisings. Expansion-minded Americans saw sprawling plantations, untapped forests and mines, and cheap native labour.

As would be true throughout the history of its involvement in the Philippines, the US, even its economic and political élite, lacked a unified approach to the situation. Conflicts between interest groups — old-style colonialists versus visionary 'neo-colonialists,' agriculture versus industry — shaped the course of Philippine—US relations. In the late 1890s the expansionists held the upper hand and, when the Spanish-American War broke out, they made sure the US government took advantage of the situation to capture new territories.

On 1 May 1898 Commodore George Dewey's modern fleet sailed into Manila harbour and sank all seven of Spain's decrepit vessels. It was the first US naval victory against a foreign power since the war of 1812 and sparked a wave of jingoistic pride and visions of a new empire. The US needed help to gain control of the archipelago and so turned to Aguinaldo. But corrupt as he probably was, Aguinaldo could not be persuaded to return simply to fight for the US. US representatives had to offer him naval support and cheap weapons with which to 'resume the revolution.' To Aguinaldo's queries about what would happen after the Spanish left, the Americans told him: 'Our Constitution does not allow us to take colonies.'

On 19 May 1898 Aguinaldo and 13 comrades disembarked in Cavite from a US ship. Five days later he proclaimed a dictatorial government with which to lead the revolution. His proclamation demonstrated his ignorance of US motives: 'as the great and powerful North American nation has offered its disinterested protection to secure liberty of this country, I again assume command of all the troops in the struggle for the attainment of our lofty aspirations.'

Despite the animosity many Filipino patriots held towards Aguinaldo, the youthful general (not yet 30) again captured leadership of the revolution. With Spain's days numbered, Manila's *ilustrados* flocked to the rebel side. The speed with which events developed testified to the weakness of Spanish authority at the moment of US intervention. Within a month of Aguinaldo's landing, Philippine troops, having captured virtually all of Luzon, had Manila surrounded. On 12 June 1898 Aguinaldo and 97 others signed the Declaration of Independence 'under the protection of the Mighty and Humane North American Nation.'

By this time US troops had started to arrive in large numbers. By 31 July the US had more than 11,000 men in the Philippines. US commanders cajoled the Filipinos into not entering Manila's walled city and, on 13 August, Spanish and US forces staged a mock battle for control of the city. The next day Gen. Wesley Merritt announced the establishment of a military government for the islands. The Spanish-American War ended on 10 December 1898 with the signing of the Treaty of Paris. Spain had surrendered the Philippines to the US for $20 million.

Eleven days later US president, William McKinley, issued the Benevolent Assimilation proclamation. We come 'not as invaders or conquerors, but as friends,' he declared, before ordering his military commanders to extend US sovereignty throughout the islands by whatever means necessary.

A little less than a year later, McKinley offered his version of the decision to keep the Philippines:

> When I realized that the Philippines had dropped into our laps I confess I did not know what to do with them. I sought counsel from all sides — Democrats as well as Republicans — but got little help. I thought first we would take only Manila; then Luzon; then other islands perhaps also. I walked the floor of the White House night after night until midnight; and I am not ashamed to tell you, gentlemen, that I went down on my knees and prayed Almighty God for light and guidance more than one night. And one night late it came to me this way — I do not know how it was, but it came: (1) That we could not give them back to Spain — that would be cowardly and dishonourable; (2) that we could not turn them over to France and Germany — our commercial rivals in the Orient — that would be bad business and discreditable; (3) that we could not leave them to themselves — they were unfit for self-government — and they would soon have anarchy and misrule over there worse than Spain's was; and (4) that there was nothing left for us to do but take them all, and to educate the Filipinos, and uplift and civilize and Christianize them, and by God's grace do the very best we could by them, as our fellow men for whom Christ also died.

While McKinley was wrestling with his conscience and pondering the Christianization of the Catholic Filipinos, Aguinaldo and other Filipino leaders were busy preparing for the inauguration of the new Philippine Republic. That event, a formal and oddly European affair (complete with French-language menus), took place on 23 January 1899.

The republican constitution reflected the ideas of the most progressive Filipino *ilustrados*, but still concentrated power in the hands of the élite. 'The electoral laws of the revolutionary government,' writes Constantino, 'limited suffrage even in local elections to the leading citizens of the towns. This meant the *principales* would be voting the *principales* into local office as well as to Congress.'[4] The leaders of the new republic (mainly affluent, conservative, Manila-based élites) did not want to fight the Americans — they actively sought compromise. For most autonomy would serve as well as independence, but the US refused an armistice. Betrayed again and backed into a corner, Aguinaldo had no choice but to prepare for war, to save his dignity and to hold onto his last chance of power.

After months of mounting tension, on 4 February 1899 fighting broke out between Philippine and US forces. The Filipinos won a few skirmishes, but mostly fell under the heavy onslaught of the better-equipped and more enthusiastic US army. With his forces using guerrilla tactics, Aguinaldo retreated into the mountains until he reached the small fishing village of Palanan, Isabela, on 6 September 1900.

Palanan, which is at the mouth of a bay on the north-east coast of Luzon, with the soaring peaks of the Sierra Madre surrounding the village and protecting it from the outside world, made an ideal sanctuary. Aguinaldo remained there for six months. The end came on 23 March 1901 when Gen. Frederick Funston, using pro-US Macebebe scouts disguised as rebels, entered Palanan and captured Aguinaldo. On 1 April Aguinaldo swore his allegiance to the US.

But the war did not end. Guerrilla armies, some commanded by Aguinaldo's officers, others by old *katipuneros*, and others still by local chieftains, fought on. It was a horribly bloody conquest. US forces destroyed countless villages and killed an estimated one-sixth of the archipelago's population. 'The present war is no bloodless, fake, opera bouffe engagement,' wrote a correspondent of the *Philadelphia Ledger*.

> Our men have been relentless; have killed to exterminate men, women, children, prisoners and captives, active insurgents and suspected people, from lads of 10 and up, an idea prevailing that the Filipino, as such, was little better than a dog, a noisome reptile in some instances, whose best disposition was the rubbish heap. Our soldiers have pumped salt water into men to 'make them talk,' have taken prisoner people who held up their hands and peacefully surrendered, and an hour later, without an atom of evidence to show that they were even *insurrectos*, stood them on a bridge and shot them down one by one, to drop into the water below and float down as an example to those who found their bullet riddled corpses.

Even as the violent conquest continued, the US took steps to consolidate its rule and ensure the collaboration of the native élite. In February 1900 McKinley established a Philippine Commission and charged it with implementing limited self rule. On 4 July 1901 Cmdr William Howard Taft established a civilian government. One year later, despite ongoing fighting and the US needing 120,000 soldiers to keep the peace, President Theodore Roosevelt declared the insurrection over.

4

The Road to Independence

Resistance to the US invasion continued until the second decade of the next century, by which time the new colonizers had developed new and effective techniques of domination. The gun kept dissidents in line, but far more sophisticated methods were used to pacify the leaders of Philippine society. So successful were these methods that, when the Japanese attacked during the Second World War, many Filipinos were ready to fight and die for US as well as Philippine interests. Not all Filipinos, however, so readily accepted foreign authority during the American period.

In 1916, after a bitter debate between various US interest groups, the government promised the Philippines 'eventual' independence and began to work for an independent Philippines loyal to US interests. The US found willing accomplices within the Philippine élite.

The US colonial authorities hid the dark side of their rule behind a façade of goodwill. They provided new schools for a fairly broad swathe of society, expanded public health care and built roads and infrastructure. Colonial-minded Filipinos still see this as proof of their benevolence. But the US period was also marked by class and foreign domination. US-style democracy strengthened the position of the domestic élite, while the literacy and property requirements of the colonial election laws limited popular participation. For example, in 1907 only 1.4 per cent of the population were eligible to vote for the first Philippine Assembly.

The Americans transferred police power to US-commanded Filipinos and, when peasant unrest broke out in the 1920s and 1930s, the PC (Philippine Constabulary) took responsibility for the pacification campaigns. The PC had virtually become a private army in the hands of the agrarian élite, which controlled the provincial governments.

With economic policies tailored to suit an export-oriented agriculture, the government opened the Philippines' doors to an influx of US manufactured goods. Free trade spawned a taste in things American. Instead of confiscating them, the US allowed the friar estates to be taken over by large private interests. This concentrated property in the hands of the Philippine élite, which came to depend on US markets, trade and investment for much of its wealth. English-language education, the teaching of US history, US-style politics, Western religion, economic dependency and consumerism, all helped to create a colonial mentality.

With the Philippine élite firmly entrenched in its US orientation, the US could now move towards granting independence. Though influential economic interests in the US favoured independence because it would bring relief from Philippine competition and this hastened the drive for change, other powerful interests (Manila-based Americans and US corporations investing in and exporting to the Philippines) wanted to protect their position, so held out for continued US involvement.

A compromise was reached whereby in 1935 the Philippines were granted limited self-government as a Commonwealth, with a promise of independence in 1946. The US president would continue to control currency and foreign affairs. The Philippines would allow free entry of US goods and would export sugar, coconut oil and abaca to the US in accordance with new restrictions laid down in the 1934 Tydings-McDuffie Act, which also mandated the preservation of US military bases.

The first three decades of the 20th century had already witnessed the establishment of political parties, trade unions and peasant organizations, as well as new churches, schools and other modern institutions. This period also saw the rise of class conflict, involving home-grown socialists and communists, and the emergence of a class of sophisticated native politicians.

Though the original *ilustrados* opted for naked collaboration with the US, this position proved unpopular, even with the small electorate allowed to participate in the early elections. The *Partido Federal* quickly faded away and was replaced by the Progressive Party, which supported gradual independence. The more successful *Nationalista* Party used the rhetoric of immediate independence, but also collaborated with the US colonial authorities. Its leaders included Sergio Osmena, Manuel Quezon, Claro M. Recto and Manuel Roxas. Quezon and Osmena, both born in 1878, entered the Philippine Assembly in 1907 (and subsequently the Senate when it was created in 1922) and balanced, with particular skill, the popular dream of independence and the élite's desire to protect its economic standing through collaboration.

The pre-war period gave rise to some of the worst aspects of modern Philippine political culture. As Constantino notes:

Since the Filipino politicians did not really run the government, since practically all were from the élite class and, finally, since electoral survival required that everyone demand independence, the parties that contended for control of the Assembly had no real ideological differences. Affiliation was based on affinities of blood, friendship, and regionalism as well as on personal expedience. Under these circumstances, patronage was vital to the retention of [a] political following, a fact which induced party leaders time and time again to barter the country's long-range interests for short-term bonuses for the party in power.[1]

The sugar block, a powerful element within the élite of the US era, took advantage of access to the US market to amass enormous family fortunes. Planters controlled the sugar-rich provinces of Tarlac and Negros and used their wealth to influence politicians in other parts of the country. Their wishes were normally at odds with those of Philippine nationalists and advocates of social justice. They wanted to maintain their close ties with the US and were prepared to fight to defend the hacienda system. Little wonder Quezon and Osmena resisted the forces trying to put immediate independence on the agenda.

The élite was not, however, the only player in the colony's political life. Struggles during the Spanish era had created the beginnings of a politicized mass. Class conflict had its roots in the peasant uprisings of the late Spanish era, in betrayal by the *ilustrados* and in the emergence of small labour unions as foci of nationalist dissent during the restrictive early years of US rule. Though founded and originally led by nationalist *ilustrados*, the unions gradually began to assume a distinct class base when the *ilustrados* started to join liberal political parties.

Identifiable left and right labour tendencies also developed. Leaders of the labour left, most notably Crisanto Evangelista, broke with the *Nationalista* Party in 1924 and, in 1930, founded the PKP (*Partido Komunistang Pilipinas*), which the government banned two years later. The PKP continued to be outlawed until 1937 and the labour movement, with its fairly small working class, remained relatively weak.

Class conflict in the countryside, by contrast, became much more visible in this period. Peasant unrest first broke out on the broad plains of Central Luzon, where conditions had been difficult for small farmers ever since the Spanish first tapped the region to feed Manila some centuries earlier. When paternalism started to break down, tenant farmers began to complain about usurious loans, ill-treatment and a shrinking share of the harvest.

Nativism resurfaced in the 1920s and 1930s in Central Luzon and southern Tagalog (east of Manila). Demagogues led many peasants into accepting illusions of strength, but socialists and communists were also active in attempting to give the peasants more scientific guidance. A pro-Japanese demagogue, Benigno Ramos, whipped up a mass frenzy through the pages of his weekly Tagalog-language paper, *Sakdal*. The paper raged against the colonial authorities, Quezon and his lackeys, oligarchs, the PC, the Church and other enemies of the poor.

The *Sakdalistas* performed well in the 1934 elections. Their simple slogans — 'down with oppressors,' 'reduce land taxes,' 'remove corrupt officials' — appealed to impoverished Filipinos. After the election Ramos dropped demands for immediate independence, but a group of his followers launched an abortive uprising in protest against the new Commonwealth constitution and postponement of independence. The rebellion was crushed, but 57 peasants lost their lives and 500 were gaoled.

The *Sakdal* then fell apart, as did much of the peasant movement in southern Tagalog. In Central Luzon the outcome was different. Most of the leaders belonged to the SP (Socialist Party). For the most part they were poor, ill-educated farmers, but there were exceptions, such as Pedro Abad Santos. The son of a wealthy Pampanga family, brother of a supreme court justice, lawyer, turn-of-the-century guerrilla and member of the Philippine Assembly, Abad Santos, appalled by the corruption of the colonial political culture, cast in his lot with the peasantry. He spent most of the 1920s and 1930s providing legal assistance to the poor, lending his skills to emerging peasant unions and, after founding it in 1929, building up the SP in Central Luzon. According to James Allen, a US communist active in the Philippines in the 1930s, 'his Socialist Party was not of the social democratic type familiar in Europe. Because of its peasant base it might be compared in some respects with the socialist revolutionaries of tsarist Russia, and it also had some resemblance to the anarchist trends in Spain.'[2]

Abad Santos attracted some of the brightest young men of Central Luzon (including future guerrilla leader Luis Taruc) into the SP. In the late 1930s his socialists scored numerous victories in municipal electoral contests. He himself fell just short of becoming governor of Pampanga, despite laws disenfranchising more than half his potential supporters.

The peasant movement's demands were quite simple. Farmers wanted a better share of the harvest, an end to usury, and fair treatment from landlords. They also wanted an end to PC and private army harassment. They were not yet demanding land redistribution. In 1937 the SP and PKP merged and this eased the CPP into legal status. But it did not radically change the pattern of struggle in Central Luzon, nor did it create the ideological conformity and iron discipline so common in Leninist parties. The growth of the peasant movement elicited a swift response from the élite. *Hacienderos* used private armies against generally unarmed peasants. The government sent in the PC to suppress strikes and to force evicted peasants off the land. Religious corporations, which still owned sizeable tracts of land, actively courted fascist support. Unlike the *Sakdal*, which looked to Japan, the élite looked to mother Spain and formed a local version of the Falange.

Ever the wily politician, Quezon, who was by now president of the Senate, played both sides of the fence. To the plantation owners he offered the PC. To the poor he promised a programme of social justice. 'Social justice,' he declared, 'means justice for all, labourers and employers, the poor and rich alike. Over and above the interests of class or group is the interest of the people.' To the rich, he added:

> If you know what is good for you, you [had] better improve the conditions of your tenants. You do not have enough sons for the army so we must conscript soldier from the poor. We can not put guns in their hands and teach them how to use them. If you are not careful they will use those guns against you. If you want to save what you have, give them 10 per cent of it or they will take it all.

Critics saw through Quezon's two-faced rhetoric. 'Quezon was a supreme cacique, a benevolent despot well aware of the complaints of the peasantry and the dangers of social unrest,' wrote James Allen after a lengthy meeting with the president. 'Some attempts at ameliorative legislation were made to improve the lot of the peasant tenant and small landowner but they were ineffective in the face of local control by the big landed proprietors.'[3]

As the 1930s came to an end labour and peasant movements continued to mount militant protests and strikes. Only when a more frightening enemy appeared did the left seek to cooperate with the Quezon government. The landing of Japanese ground forces in December 1941 overtook the growing class struggle, but did not end it. Like the Spaniards and Americans before them, the Japanese used unabated violence to conquer and control.

Defeat of the 80,000 Filipino and US soldiers who, under Gen. Douglas MacArthur, had retreated to Bataan and the capture of Manila left Filipinos with four options. They could collaborate with the enemy, avoid politics and try to survive, support the USAFFE (US Armed Forces in the Far East) and the exiled government of Quezon and Osmena, or resist through unofficial and often radical channels.

Many in the élite continued the tradition of collaborating with whatever foreign power occupied the country. For José Laurel, a pre-war supreme court justice, wartime opportunism and collaboration contributed to the spread of corruption in Philippine society. Small merchants and petty professionals sold goods and services to the Japanese. Those with ties to the Japanese authorities peddled influence to their fellow countrymen. Others walked the fine line between collaboration and loyalty, outwardly supporting the Japanese while passing information to US forces. But the most heroic had to be those who joined the USAFFE or the guerrillas.

The most important unofficial anti-Japanese guerrilla group sprang up in Central Luzon as a result of the united efforts of the peasant organizations and the PKP. The *Hukbo ng Bayan Laban sa Hapon* (People's Anti-Japanese Army) (*Hukbalahap*, or better known as the *Huk*), waged a guerrilla war against the Japanese invaders. Its fighters organized alternative village administrations, kept rice harvests from the Japanese and absentee landowners, infiltrated pro-Japanese organizations and ambushed Japanese soldiers. They also tangled periodically with US-supported forces, whose élite leaders hated armed peasants.

The CPP led the *Huks*. Luis Taruc, a PKP central committee member, served as commander-in-chief. But the PKP could not control the guerrilla army. Taruc and other *Huk* commanders responded to the demands of the peasants, but not always to the orders of the PKP.

The war generated new conflicts and polarized already contending forces. The heroism of US GIs on the Bataan Peninsula and MacArthur's posturing generated strong pro-US sympathies among many Filipinos. But the war also strengthened the anti-colonial left, for the *Huks* provided one of the few means by which rural people — especially from Central Luzon and the Bataan Peninsula in southern Tagalog — could resist the Japanese. In addition, the war divided the élite into pro-Commonwealth, pro-Japanese and fence-sitting factions.

The year 1944 saw the end of the war approaching and the longstanding promise of independence looming. But in the Philippines the victory over the Japanese was not translated into social peace.

5

From Liberation to a New Colonialism

In September 1944 tne US navy launched air raids against Japanese positions in the Philippines and Formosa. Adm. Chester Nimitz had proposed bypassing the Philippines, but MacArthur had convinced President Franklin Roosevelt that a return to the Philippines would prove beneficial for future US relations with Asia and for morale.

The invasion force (650-700 warships and supply craft and 200,000 troops) arrived off Leyte late on 19 October 1944. MacArthur was accompanied by Sergio Osmena, who had become Commonwealth president on Quezon's death two months earlier. On 20 October the two of them waded ashore. The US forces advanced in the Visayas, but the real prize lay in recapturing Luzon and Manila.

Troops landed on Luzon in January 1945 and swiftly advanced through Central Luzon, which was already largely cleared of Japanese forces. *Huk* and US-backed guerrilla resistance and the threat of a major US invasion had forced Gen. Yamashita to send the bulk of his forces into the hilly interior — out of reach of the navy's big guns. US forces advanced steadily towards Manila from several directions. Thousands of civilians died in the offensive and further casualties occurred as troops took the city in bloody street-by-street fighting. Even after the US had captured Manila, on 23 February 1945, fighting continued in outlying areas. It was not until 5 July 1945 that MacArthur declared the Philippines liberated.

Despite the destruction wrought by the returning Americans, many Filipinos welcomed the old colonial power with open arms. Individual soldiers captured Filipino hearts with simple acts of kindness and decency. The Americans, history says, came as 'liberators' and, to assure the Filipinos of this, the US kept to its promise of independence in 1946, but first it had to restore élite rule and protect what policy-makers in Washington decided were US interests.

Philippine components of the USAFFE (US Armed Forces in the Far East) and the PC (Philippine Constabulary) were integrated into Philippine armed forces. The US tried to disarm the *Huks*, arrested their leaders (whom they freed after strong protest) and refused to recognize *Huk* village administrations. MacArthur used his authority as military commander to exculpate certain members of the political élite. He directed Quezon to reconvene Congress, which had been elected in 1941, and this brought Roxas and other collaborators in Laurel's puppet administration back into government. Roxas's colleagues elected him Senate president. In August MacArthur freed a further 5,000 suspected collaborators.

The US government's next intervention was in the 1946 presidential elections, which would decide who would lead the newly independent Philippines. The elections pitted Osmena and the *Nationalista* Party against Roxas and his new Liberal Party. The Liberals called Osmena a tired old man, maligned his Chinese ancestry and redbaited him for accepting *Huk* support. Roxas fought the election over 'who was America's friend' and 'who could bring in more US aid.'

Though officially neutral, the US responded positively to Roxas's rhetoric. The army, with MacArthur's approval, allowed him access to its Philippine radio network. The new US high commissioner, Paul McNutt, joined in the charade by charging Osmena's supporters with terrorism. It was little wonder that Roxas won. It was little wonder also that, under Roxas, the Philippine government convicted very few collaborators. Many even claimed seats in Congress or local and national government. Others formed fake USAFFE units at the end of the war and went on to collect US military benefits.

What happened can be understood in terms of US resolve to restore a government loyal to itself and of Roxas promising to do just that. The only other serious presidential candidate, Osmena, also favoured the US but had too often crossed swords with MacArthur. At the end of the war there was some confusion over what the US wanted from the Philippines, and contending interest groups tangled with the issue. While Congress sought special relations with the Philippines, the State and Commerce Departments feared that such ties would disadvantage the more lucrative trade with the United Kingdom and other European powers.

Congress won. The US forced the Commonwealth government to accept its terms on trade and property relations and tied delivery of $620 million in aid to Philippine acceptance of the Bell Trade Act. The Act required duty-free trade between the two countries throughout 1954 and set quotas on Philippine exports to the US. It provided for a slow increase of duties between 1954 and 1973 when full duties would be reached. It also gave the US president power to decide the value of the Philippine currency.

Parity, the most controversial clause of the agreement, gave US citizens the same rights as Filipinos to own property, industry and public utilities in the Philippines, but did not offer Filipinos the same rights in America. Though Roxas and his Liberals supported these demands, a number of *Nationalista* Party members of Congress opposed the Act, as did members of the DA (Democratic Alliance), a left-wing coalition which dominated the election in Central Luzon. (Six DA candidates, including Luis Taruc and future PKP leader Jesus Lava, had won seats in Congress.) While the Bell Trade Act was passed in the Philippines by a simple majority, its parity provisions required amending the constitution and this needed a three-quarters majority of each house of Congress. Roxas knew he would have to subvert democracy to ensure that the amendment passed.

Congress opened on 25 May 1946. A Liberal proposed barring the six DA representatives, two *Nationalista* Party members and one Liberal Party member on the grounds that they had been involved in fraud and had brought terror to Central Luzon. That much of the terror emanated from the landowners' private armies seemed not to matter. The House voted to refuse seats to the DA and to the two *Nationalista* members and the parity amendment passed the House. Twelve days later the *Nationalistas* took their seats, but Congress still excluded the Democrats. Similar manoeuvres took place to ensure passage of the amendment in the Senate and again during a nationwide plebiscite.

Other bilateral relations were also being formed. In March 1947 the Military Bases Agreement gave the US control of Clark Air Base, Subic Bay Naval Base (including the town of Olongapo) and numerous smaller outposts. The Military Assistance Agreement gave the US a role in Philippine internal security. Through JUSMAG (Joint US Military Advisory Group), the US helped shape the AFP (Armed Forces of the Philippines), the PC and Philippine military policy. At this point the US government released $400 million of aid. Not surprisingly, the bulk of this was used to restore private property that had been destroyed during the war, thereby profiting the élite more than the others.

The exclusion of the DA from Congress angered the leftists, but did not drive them underground. PKP leaders continued to advocate parliamentary forms of struggle. Though in Manila the PKP leadership still looked to the urban working class, developments in Central Luzon were forcing the peasant movement and some PKP members to consider other avenues. Repressive taxes, unfair land tenancy, disenfranchisement, continued suppression of peasant organizations, economic crisis spurred by corruption and the refusal to grant the *Huks* the benefits given to other veterans of the anti-Japanese war had all helped to fuel unrest. Individual activists fled to the hills out of frustration and fear and it was there, as far back as late 1945, that the nucleus of a post-war peasant army was formed.

After the war Central Luzon's peasants grouped together in the PKM *(Pambansang Kaisahan ng mga Mabubukid* or National Peasants' Union). The PKM backed the DA and led mass peasant actions. This attracted the attention of the landlord-controlled Civil Guards and the PC (for a time renamed the MP, Military Police). 'The MPs and civilian guards just got worse and worse' after the April 1946 election, Alfredo Buwan, an elderly peasant, told Kerkvliet in 1970. 'Roxas took revenge against people in Central Luzon because they had voted against him.' Benito Santos added that: 'After that election, more PKM and *Hukbalahap* began to fight back.... I sure could not blame them. They had to defend themselves.'[1]

In mid-1946 representatives of the DA, the PKM, the PKP and the *Hukbalahap* met Roxas several times to try to arrange a settlement or truce. Hoping to resume parliamentary struggle and a peaceful life, they agreed to participate with Roxas in a pacification programme. Peasant leaders travelled with government officials and urged farmers to lay down their weapons. Government officials sought to calm mayors, landlords and MP commanders and asked for the disarmament of the civil guards.

Government officials, however, did not do their job well. Kerkvliet reported: 'Within days after the "pacification programme" had begun, Juan Feleo, Luis Taruc, and others protested that civilian guard and MP terrorism had already resumed.'[2] The arrest and harassment of peasant activists continued. The armed peasants, estimated by the MP at 10,000, defended themselves and, at the end of August, the truce collapsed. The MP's chief then threatened all-out war on the *Huks* and, that same day, Juan Feleo was kidnapped by uniformed men in a military vehicle as he was returning from a pacification mission. In September a newspaper reporter identified a headless body found floating in a river as his.

The death of Feleo, a prominent peasant and PKP leader, stunned his comrades. Within days, in a letter to President Roxas, Luis Taruc announced his decision to join the armed peasants:

> [Y]our blood-thirsty subordinates are already making an all-out punitive campaign against the peasants. The MP are shelling *barrios* and shooting civilians. They are even threatening to use bombs. Suspects they catch (and they pick up just anybody) are subjected to all despicable tortures. Together with the civilian guards, they are virtually in control of all government machinery, conducting a reign of terror worse than the Japs.... I respectfully inform you that I believe I will be of more service to our country and to our people and their government if I now stay with the peasants. In spite of every harm and

provocation done to them I am still confident I can help guide them in their struggle for democracy.

Taruc called attention to Roxas's earlier acceptance of the peasants' demands. These included:

1 Temporary right of the people to keep their firearms in view of their present insecurity. Registration of those firearms.

2 Stop MP raids.... The constitutional rights of the people must be protected.

3 Removal of Governor David of Pampanga, fascist municipal officials and MP officers.

4 Put into effect badly needed social welfare projects and agrarian reform.

Taruc's decision to join the simmering rebellion did not imply support from the whole of the PKP. While some of its members joined Taruc in the hills, the Party itself remained committed to peaceful struggle. Two factors contributed to this: the leadership's orientation towards the urban working class and its correct reading of that class's opposition to the peasant uprising, and a division within the Politburo between advocates of armed struggle and foes of it. Only in mid-1948 did the PKP officially endorse the armed struggle.

The peasants who flocked to what became the HMB (*Hukbong Mapagpalaya ng Bayan*, or People's Liberation Army) did not do so to overthrow the government or bring about the revolutionary transformation of society. They still had a simple vision of justice: a fair share of the harvest, the security of a subsistence living, freedom from landlord and military harassment, and the right to select their own representatives.

The rebellion reached its peak in the early 1950s. Thousands of peasants in Central Luzon and, to a lesser extent, southern Tagalog joined the HMB and PKP. Guerrilla skirmishes and larger battles ranged the well motivated *Huks* against the poorly disciplined PC. Abuses continued to drive peasants into the arms of the waiting *Huks*. Corruption and massive election fraud in 1949 further alienated the population. *Huk barrio* councils brought grassroots democracy to the region and strengthened the rebellion.

Change appeared inevitable. But when it came, it did not take the form the PKP leaders expected. A combination of the PKP's own errors and of state and military reforms conspired to defeat the insurgency. The PKP misread popular sentiment and failed to anticipate both the ability of the élite to change just enough to preserve its power and the willingness of the US to come to the rescue.

Though the PKP was correct to advocate giving 'land to the tiller' and transferring political power from an élite minority to a mass-based government, it failed to acknowledge the limited scope of immediate popular demands. As a revolutionary party it had a responsibility to lead the people from reformist to revolutionary consciousness. It failed to do this. Instead it turned its attentions to rapidly expanding its armed wing and preparing for a sudden seizure of power. Its expansion programme brought unreliable and undisciplined elements into the HMB and PKP and its attempts to extend the revolution beyond Central Luzon and parts of southern Tagalog were unsuccessful. The PKP leadership had failed to see the protracted nature of the revolutionary process until it was too late and the government had defeated the HMB.

It had also misread the enemy, which it saw as an assortment of crumbling domestic and foreign foes. The PKP believed that Elpidio Quirino, who became president on Roxas's death in 1948, was sinking in a swamp of corruption and that his regime would be unable to contain the growing rebellion. External factors also looked promising. The spectre of left-wing nationalism haunting foreign powers and domestic élites throughout South-East Asia encouraged the PKP to envisage the final defeat of imperialism and uncritically to accept the Soviet definition of the US economy as being on the verge of collapse. These predictions proved wrong. In the early 1950s the US helped defeat the *Huk* rebellion while at the same time consolidating pro-American power by combining reform and repression and promoting a little-known politician, Ramon Magsaysay.

In August 1950, a CIA operative named Edward G. Lansdale arrived in Manila to advise the government on counterinsurgency measures. The next month, under pressure from the US ambassador, President Quirino appointed Magsaysay, a former USAFFE guerrilla leader, secretary of defence. This popular Central Luzon-born politician came from one of his *barrio*'s most prosperous families which, apart from owning various firms, controlled a tenanted farm of over 1,000 acres.

Magsaysay and Lansdale ran the anti-*Huk* campaign. A US military report noted its good fortune in having a defence secretary 'with a genuine admiration and faith in the United States.' The two shared an office at the Defence Department and even Lansdale's living quarters in the JUSMAG compound. They cleaned up and revitalized the army. Magsaysay established the CAO (Civil Affairs Office) which, utilizing US resources, undertook a massive propaganda campaign. The CAO reached an estimated 1.5 million people in two years via thousands of meetings and millions of leaflets. It conducted anti-communist forums and essay contests in schools and universities, funded a national student organization, courted the pliable press and led anti-*Huk* demonstrations in Central Luzon.

Some of its psy-war operations had a devilish side to them. Lansdale boasted about turning provincial beliefs in vampires against the *Huks*:

> The psy-war squad set up an ambush along a trail used by the *Huks*. When a *Huk* patrol came along the trail, the ambushers silently snatched the last man of the patrol, their move unseen in the dark night. They punctured his neck with two holes, vampire-fashion, held the body up by the heels, drained it of blood, and put the corpse back on the trail. When the *Huks* returned to look for the missing man and found their bloodless comrade, every member of the patrol believed that the *asuang* [vampire] had got him and that one of them would be next if they remained on that hill. When daylight came, the whole *Huk* squadron moved out of the vicinity.

Reform of the AFP, and its expansion from 32,000 men in 1950 to 56,000 in 1952, resulted in increased combat effectiveness. With the Air Force using napalm against *Huk* bases and agricultural centres and the army pursuing guerrilla bands into the hills, Magsaysay soon had the *Huks* on the run.

In October 1950 José Lava and other members of the Manila-based Politburo were arrested. This forced the PKP to appoint a new Politburo, headed by Lava's brother Jesus, and allowed Magsaysay and his American colleagues successfully to pressure Quirino to suspend the writ of habeas corpus. When the government restored the writ two years later, it was holding more than 1,000 people in prison without charge.

Magsaysay's greatest success was to convince the masses of Central Luzon of the possibility of government-sponsored reform. Francisco and Arriola wrote: '[Magsaysay] offered the battle-weary peasants cash, credit, legal services, wells, health clinics and homesteads in Mindanao. Overnight, he became a legend as the saviour of democracy and hope of the masses.'[3]

That Magsaysay could not deliver on his promises made little difference. As Kerkvliet reported: 'Although modest and frequently superficial, these reforms were sufficient to improve the government's image and provide hope for those *Huks* and rebellion supporters for whom revolt had been a last resort in the face of government and landlord lawlessness. As most rebels were in this category, the government's actions did significantly weaken the HMB.'[4] Magsaysay's ability to communicate with the peasantry and his promises of further reform lost the HMB much of its support and, by 1952, the government had all but defeated it. In 1953 Taruc came to the conclusion that the

Huks no longer had the mass support they needed. Jesus Lava and a majority of the PKP leadership continued to argue for a protracted armed struggle, but the old alliance between the PKP and the socialist agrarian reformers had collapsed. In 1954, after two years of arguing for negotiations, Taruc surrendered and, despite promises to the contrary, was gaoled.

The PKP and HMB splintered and lost most of their historical significance. Before his arrest ten years later in 1964, Lava had tried to salvage the PKP and had had some success. In the early 1960s the Party began to recruit a new generation of radicals, with people like José Maria Sison and other future leaders of the left joining it. But with the demise of the struggle, the HMB lost direction entirely. It broke into roving bands and local factions, some of which became social bandits. The *Huks*, however, still attracted young dissidents anxious to fight against reprehensible conditions in Central Luzon. One such man, Bernabe Buscayno (Kumander Dante), grew frustrated with the criminality of his comrades and eventually, at the end of the next decade, led his followers into a second and more successful alliance between militant peasants and urban leftists.

The big winner in the conflict was Ramon Magsaysay. With strong financial support from US and Philippine business, with backing from the Catholic hierarchy and with considerable CIA involvement, Magsaysay swept into the presidency in 1953, defeating his former boss, President Quirino, by a large margin. He surrounded himself with bright young professionals and, under the guise of reform, led an essentially conservative regime. 'It was also a period of intense Americanization,' wrote Francisco and Arriola. 'In his first State-of-the-Nation address, Magsaysay affirmed his adherence to the principles of private enterprise, and welcomed foreign capital. His whole programme of government, which emphasized rural community development, was laid out by his American advisers, and supported by USAID funds.'[5] Magsaysay placed US advisers in all government departments, and Filipino intellectuais flocked to US schools and training programmes.

With the *Huks* on the run and the PKP in disarray, the main threat to US supremacy in the Philippines became élite nationalism. Nationalist sentiment spread among would-be manufacturers who felt their options limited by free trade and parity. Pre-war political leader Claro M. Recto gave shape to these nationalist demands. He rejected dependent development, proclaiming colonialism to be at the root of the nation's problems, and advocated nationalist industrialization (the development of Philippine industry behind trade barriers) as best serving the cause of development.

In response, the US and Philippines decided to re-negotiate the trade agreement to 'better fit the changed circumstances of the 1950s.' Aside from offering Philippine manufacturers limited protection in the domestic market, replacing absolute quotas on many Philippine exports with declining tariffs, eliminating the link between the dollar and the peso and doing away with Philippine taxes on foreign exchange, what became the Laurel-Langley agreement revised the parity agreement. As a concession to Philippine nationalism, the US agreed to make parity reciprocal. Since Philippine capital obviously could not compete with American interests in the US, this could not hurt US business, but it did give the Philippine élite the illusion of equality.

The new parity agreement in fact benefited US economic interests. Whereas the previous agreement guaranteed parity only in the exploitation of natural resources and public utilities, the revised version opened up the whole economy to US business. As a result, by 1970 the US controlled more than 25 per cent of the industrial sector and 80 per cent of foreign equity. Its investment in the Philippines had an estimated market value of $2,000 million.

Recto loudly rejected the entire pact as a sham. To protect their interests, the US and its allies decided to isolate him with cold-war rhetoric. Hearing of his plan to run for president in 1957, Magsaysay shouted, 'He can run as the candidate of Mao Tse-tung and I will run as an enemy of communism and a friend of the United States.' But before the contest could take place Magsaysay's plane crashed into a Cebu mountainside. CIA agents discussed liquidating Recto, but decided against it. Instead they resorted to dirty tricks, for example, distributing defective condoms in packages bearing Recto's picture.

By focusing on Recto, the US had allowed a quieter nationalist to sneak in and Carlos P. García, the vice-president who succeeded Magsaysay, won the 1957 election. His 'Filipino First' slogan captured the nationalist mood of the time but fell short as a programme. García used the room provided by the Laurel-Langley agreement to construct protective walls behind which he hoped Philippine industry would prosper. García was neither a populist nor the head of an honest regime. His government enacted an anti-subversion law; the House Committee on Anti-Filipino Activities conducted a witch hunt against progressive Filipinos; and corruption in the economic management agencies spun out of control.

Neither did García's policies work very well. 'This much heralded "golden age" of import substitution did not last long enough to effect a meaningful redirection of the Philippine economy,' noted journalist Petronilo Daroy.[6] Dependence on imported capital goods and raw materials and a limited local market crippled import substitution. Manufacturing decreased from 13.5 per cent of the GNP in the first half of the 1950s to 6.4 per cent in the latter half. Survival instincts led many manufacturers to collaborate with their American partners, for they needed their technology and managerial know-how. His economic policies, modest as they were, had brought him enemies. His emphasis on industry had alienated the still dominant agricultural élite and his nationalist pretences had earned him the enmity of the US. In 1961 the US (and elements of the élite tied to foreign capital and trade) turned to the lawyer and economist, Vice-President Diosado Macapagal. Macapagal had been on the US payroll while vice-president and, after some dispute, the CIA funded and advised him during his presidential bid.

Macapagal won and, though an unimpressive president, his administration marked a turning point in Philippine political history. He ended the flirtation with vaguely nationalist economics and laid the groundwork for Marcos's rapid political rise. He was more a technocrat than a politician. When he looked to the countryside he saw the need for agricultural growth and modest agrarian reform. To pursue his vision and overcome a balance-of-payments deficit created by the manufacturing sector's dependence on imported supplies, he sought the support of the IMF (International Monetary Fund), the World Bank and various US agencies. He secured $300 million in public and private loans, promptly abolished import and exchange controls and allowed the peso to be devalued from 2.00 to 3.90 to the dollar. As Stephen Shalom wrote:

> The impact of decontrol and devaluation was disastrous for all save the traditional Philippine exporters and foreign investors. Consumers bore the main burden, having to pay sharply higher prices for food. Filipino manufacturers were unable to meet their foreign debts, which had been effectively doubled by devaluation. At the end of 1964, Filoil, a Philippine company with a minority share owned by Gulf Oil, was forced to sell out entirely to Gulf. At the beginning of 1966, close to 1,500 firms were near a state of collapse.[7]

Macapagal's failure set the stage for the Marcos era. Multilateral institutions like the IMF began to take a more active part in Philippine political and economic life. His policies created divisions within the élite (which would widen considerably over the next two decades) and precipitated an economic crisis, of which a demagogue like Ferdinand Marcos could so easily take advantage. Also, a new generation of educated Filipinos began to look again at the concepts of nationalism and class conflict, which the Americans and the dominant élite had hoped they had eliminated in the 1950s.

6

The Marcos Era

I saw a demonstration turn into a battle. The anti-Marcos revolution's disciplined foot soldiers collected stones as they watched their leaders negotiate with officers of the other side. The well-known and their hangers-on gathered in the front lines. The tough guys — workers and slum dwellers — stood next, ready to come to the fore. The battle broke out near the railroad crossing, where shanties lined the tracks. Fuelled by a mixture of rage and boredom, it carried on — rocks and bottles against bullets; citizens against the state; slum youths against the police. The people's warriors pinned the police against a wall, palpably fearful as they cowered beneath their shields. A shower of rocks fell and the people's warriors tasted the possibility of victory, only to find that hidden behind the buildings were brown-shirted helmeted police reinforcements, who were now approaching down the side streets to rescue their comrades.

The sound of riot batons thumping against shields brought new courage and panic. Shots rang out from hand-held revolvers. A man in a white T-shirt caught a bullet in his chest. He fell. His shirt turned red as rescuers carried him away. Police burst forth from their makeshift fortress. Their rescuers broke ranks and, charging hither and yon, indiscriminately flailed their batons at innocent bystanders and rioters. The scene shifted to the 'organized masses.' Patience on both sides was wearing thin.

A week earlier police and soldiers had used water cannons, tear gas and clubs to break up a demonstration and had injured several people. Automatic rifle shots had echoed in the air, but had hit no one. This police riot had, however, changed the rules of the game. From maximum tolerance, to tear gas, to Armalite rifles. A nation in crisis. An ultimatum given.

Now the marchers did not budge. The fire hoses failed to disperse the crowd — 86 year-old former senator, Lorenzo Tanada, stood his ground; 70-plus year-old former newspaper publisher, Chino Roces, knocked

50

down during the dispersal a week earlier, stood his ground. No one budged. Then came the tear gas. Then chaos. Rocks and bottles thrown from both sides. The explosion of homemade 'pill box' bombs. Gunfire. A bystander, watching the demonstration after leaving the nearby telephone company office, fell. Dead. A student activist fell. Wounded. The masses retreated. Tough guys put together Molotov cocktails and prepared to defend themselves.

This was the end of the Marcos era — the time of palace decadence, lavish parties and compulsive spending. Chaos enveloped the state, engulfing it in political and economic crisis. Demonstrations swept the city. From gritty downtown slums to the glitzy Makati business district, people marched against the government. Workers joined militant unions and went on strike. Peasants, the urban poor, students and women all joined forces. In the halls of Parliament oppositionists accused the dictator of crime after crime: the nation passed a verdict of guilty. Guerrilla war swept the countryside. The main guerrilla army was growing daily and bringing its message of liberation to millions.

But the dictator fought back. Like an aging boxer whose skills had been sapped by too many blows to the head, he swung wildly. Where he hit he caused even more anger. Cracks began to appear in the military and the US started its belated search for alternatives. Dissident voices began to emerge in the dictator's own party. His health began to fade, his pillars of support to crumble.

Few could have foreseen such a dramatic end to an era. Earlier presidents had served their single term and retired gracefully, often much wealthier than they had been when they had entered office. Even when Ferdinand Marcos had imposed martial law in 1972 and extended his term of office, nobody had really imagined that there would be so much popular discontent. Initial attempts to generate insurrectionary fervour had fallen flat. Marcos had survived and seemed set to rule until death or voluntary retirement. But the Marcoses' behaviour, patient organizing by the new left, the courage and sacrifice of the most prominent opposition leader, Benigno Aquino, Jr., and the dedication of some of the traditional opposition, ultimately managed to galvanize the festering discontent.

The overthrow of the Marcos regime ended an era in which, for more than two decades, a new oligarchy (represented by Marcos) had been fighting a two-sided battle with the old oligarchs and their political system (represented by Aquino) and with a new left. The era began in the early 1960s, with both Marcos and Aquino setting their sights on the presidency, and a new left starting to emerge from the ashes of its decrepit past.

Ferdinand Marcos had been eyeing the presidency from an early age. Gifted intellectually, he had developed an almost unnatural drive for power as a young boy in Ilocos Norte. Though he grew up on the fringes of the élite, the harsh outback surrounding his birthplace on the South China Sea produced people noted for their tenacity and frugality. Soon after Ferdinand's birth, on 11 September 1917, his father changed careers. Mariano Marcos the teacher became Mariano Marcos the lawyer and politician. He left his job to study law in Manila and, in 1924, returned to Ilocos Norte to run for the colonial Congress. He won. In 1932 he lost, but fought again three years later, only to lose again to his old rival, Julio Nalundasan.

Soon afterwards, a single shot killed Nalundasan and suspicion immediately fell on the Marcoses. At the time of the shooting young Ferdinand had been enrolled at the UP (University of the Philippines) where he belonged to a shooting club and often boasted about his marksmanship. Three years after the shooting police identified a UP target pistol as the murder weapon. On 7 December 1938 Marcos was arrested.

The events of the next few years became part of the Marcos legend. On 20 November 1940 Marcos learned that he had topped the bar examination with the highest score ever. That same day the court had found him guilty and sentenced him to 17 years imprisonment. He spent several months in prison preparing his own 830-page appeal which he presented personally to the Supreme Court. The court reversed the lower court's conviction. Despite the decision, many Filipinos considered the young lawyer guilty, but his intelligence, daring and victory none the less won him the nation's admiration.

The Second World War gave Marcos another opportunity for myth making. While fighting with US-backed forces on the Bataan Peninsula he was wounded and received a medal — in later years he referred to himself as the most decorated Philippine soldier in history. Also during the war his father, accused of business dealings with the Japanese, had been executed by guerrillas for collaboration.

In 1949 Ferdinand Marcos entered politics and, using his celebrity, claims of heroism and promises to bring a cash crop and new power to his Ilocos region, won the election. During his early political career he remained a bachelor — a charming and rambunctious young man who dated many young women and fathered at least one out-of-wedlock child. But he knew that extended bachelorhood would not serve his political career well. He needed a wife, one who would expand his appeal beyond his Ilocos bastion and win him entry into the world of Manila's 400, the national élite which included such prominent families as the Zobels, Aquinos, Cojuangcos, Sorianos and Roumaldezes.

Marcos met Imelda Roumaldez on 6 April 1954. Imelda's unauthorized biographer, Carmen Navarro Pedrosa, describes the encounter:

> The partnership that would pillage the Philippines for 20 years began when José Guevara, a congressional reporter, introduced Marcos to Imelda in the cafeteria of the Philippine Legislative Building on a balmy April evening. The beauteous Miss Manila had accompanied her cousin-in-law Paz to collect Danieling Roumaldez, then Speaker Pro Tempore of the House.... [Marcos] was immediately captivated by her beauty.... When Imelda stood up, Marcos took note that he was half an inch taller than she and without further ado asked her to marry him. She was taken aback by his boldness and did not know whether he jested. The wily congressman was not her ideal man. She liked her men tall, rich, and aristocratic. Marcos, the short *nouveau riche* congressman, was none of these.... Still, Imelda was eager for a secure marriage, and this made her vulnerable.[1]

Marcos vigorously pursued Imelda and, 11 days after meeting her, they wed in a civil ceremony: 24 hours later, on 1 May 1954, Marcos, a member of the Aglipayan Church, was baptized a Catholic. The couple were then married again before 1,000 guests in Manila's San Miguel Cathedral. President Magsaysay held a wedding reception for them at the Malacanang Palace.

In marrying Imelda, Marcos did not get everything he wanted. Though she belonged to the noble Roumaldez clan of Leyte and Manila, she was from the poorer branch of her family. In 1952, at the age of 23, she had moved to Manila and had spent her first few months there working in rather menial jobs — as a salesgirl in a music shop and clerk in a bank — before moving into society. Her big break came when she won a Miss Manila contest. Two years later she married Ferdinand Marcos.

At first Imelda had difficulty adapting to her life as a political wife. Marcos pushed her to 'be other than what she was — to be sophisticated, well-read, a woman with worldly *élan*,' wrote Navarro Pedrosa. 'He did not want a simple wife; she was a Roumaldez, an aristocrat, and most of all, a prized political asset.'[2] The demands on Imelda overwhelmed her. She suffered from painful migraines and countless self doubts. She sought psychiatric help in New York and emerged a changed woman — the political asset Marcos sought.

Marcos's political career advanced steadily and he showed no aversion to the deals, corruption and compromises necessary for his survival in politics. By making shady deals with wealthy businessmen he enriched his family and established himself as presidential timber in the minds of the power brokers. But the ambitious young politician had one serious obstacle — Macapagal. Throughout his early career Marcos had belonged to the Liberal Party and had supported Macapagal's run for the presidency. When, however, in 1963 Macapagal announced plans to run for a second term, Marcos broke with the Liberal Party and (at the invitation of the Laurels) launched an aggressive drive for the *Nationalista* presidential nomination.

The Marcoses travelled tirelessly to call on delegates in their own homes. During the convention, while Marcos was busy twisting arms and calling in old favours, Imelda shamelessly violated the unwritten rules by visiting delegates in their hotel rooms. On the second ballot Marcos won a clear majority of 777 votes. Having always held a strange belief in the power of numerology, he added the number seven to his lucky number eleven.

A vicious campaign followed. Macapagal raised the Nalundasan murder and charges of corruption. Some officials at the US Embassy quietly referred to Marcos as a scoundrel. The next year documentation revealing the extent of his corruption surfaced: he had hundreds of thousands of dollars in the Chase Manhattan Bank in New York, far more than he could legitimately have earned as a politician and lawyer.

But Macapagal lacked Marcos's political skill. Marcos could captivate audiences with his brilliant oratory and, besides, he had kept his 1949 promise to bring commercial agriculture to Ilocos. He also had a special advantage, the still young and beautiful Imelda, who would woo the audiences with her song and banter. If voters had questions about Marcos's integrity, they had none about his lovely wife. To Filipinos still enamoured with John F. Kennedy's Camelot, Imelda promised a Philippine version. She would play Jackie to Ferdinand's Jack.

Although Marcos won by half a million votes, he did not have the support of all the old war-lords, traditional politicians and other wealthy and powerful Filipinos. The new president wanted to co-opt or destroy all opposition. Despite its populist appeal, his railing against the oligarchs sought to capture the élite for his own advantage rather than to destroy it as a class. The Lopez, Cojuangco and Aquino families were among his targets. He shrewdly neutralized the Lopez family, which controlled a sugar empire, by persuading its patriarch, Fernando Lopez, against his better judgement, to put himself forward as Marcos's running mate for vice-president.

The leadership of the opposition fell to the young Benigno S. Aquino, Jr. Like Marcos, Ninoy Aquino had something to prove. He too had a family name to repair, for his father had served as speaker of the

Japanese-controlled National Assembly during the war. In other ways Aquino was everything Marcos was not. He belonged to a truly élite family. His grandfather had served as a general in the revolutionary army and his family owned significant farmlands in Central Luzon. Aquino rose quickly to prominence. In 1950, while still a teenager, he went to Korea to cover the war for the *Manila Times*. On his return President Quirino awarded him the Philippine legion of honour for meritorious service. Like Marcos, he was blessed with great intelligence, a way with words and a will to advance. After Korea he led an active life as a student, journalist and man about town. He met *Huk* commander Luis Taruc and later negotiated his surrender, for which he received a second legion of honour.

In 1954, the same year as the Marcos wedding, Ninoy married another daughter of the Tarlac and Manila élite, 21-year-old Corazon Cojuangco. Cory's family had amassed great wealth in the sugar trade and owned an important bank. Her father had used his wealth and stature to amass political power. Cory had spent her childhood in Tarlac and at exclusive Catholic schools in Manila and the US. She was not just a daughter of the sugar block, but a daughter of the socially and politically conservative pre-Vatican II Church. Though touched by suffering in later years she would never escape her past.

The young Aquino couple advanced quickly in Philippine society. Despite his own background and family ties, Aquino skilfully positioned himself between the *Huks* on the left and the conservative landowners on the right. Using populist rhetoric, family ties and traditional political methods, he advanced from mayor to governor and finally, at the age of 35, became the youngest senator in Philippine history. Like other politicians, he built a private army and worked with existing armed bands — most notably the remnants of the *Huks*. He soon set his sights on the Liberal nomination for the presidency.

Throughout her husband's career, Cory remained in the background. She did not participate in political discussions, but instead served coffee to a never-ending stream of politicians and constituents who visited the young official. Though apparently content with her traditional role as wife and mother, she absorbed many lessons from her life in political households. And though, like Marcos, Ninoy had a well-deserved reputation as a womanizer, he did share his concerns and ideas with his wife.

While élite politics hogged the headlines in the early 1960s, important developments were taking place in the subterranean world of radical politics. Francisco Nemenzo, who had belonged to the PKP in the 1960s, wrote that after the defeat of the *Huk* rebellion in 1957, Jesus

Lava, secretary general of the PKP, had 'urged Party members to "return to civilian life" [a euphemism for surrender] and to conduct the parliamentary struggle through nationalist and reformist organizations.... In order to minimize exposure and arrest under the Anti-Subversion Law, members were freed from obligatory membership in Party collectives. Every Party member would operate individually, maintaining contacts with no more than two other comrades.'[3] With this so-called single-file policy in place, the PKP desisted from recruiting new members. Party leaders believed that only government agents would join the Party during such a difficult period. But by the time of Lava's arrest in 1964, the PKP had once more changed its policy. Student protests and the spread of anti-US nationalism on campus had convinced the Party to reopen its doors.

Few of those who participated in the protests of this period were, however, political radicals. 'We started out being social rebels,' recalls Behn Cervantes of his group of UP friends. 'We were soul brothers, and at that time beatnik was in and we were beatniks. We tended to be different already, and so we were open to civil liberties.' The serious politicos, by contrast, attached far more significance to the demonstrations. Youth leader José Maria 'Joema' Sison, for example, became very excited when the students marched on Congress during an Un-Filipino Affairs Committee hearing in the House. Cervantes remembers it quite differently: 'That big march that Joema wrote about as a breakthrough when students climbed the walls of Congress, we were part of that, in fact I fainted because it was so dull.'

It quickly became less dull though when the state started to react to these new assaults by élite and middle-class children. At this early stage the leaders of the old left were suspicious of these young people, including the young revolutionaries at the core of the student movement. It was only when an Indonesian communist studying at UP vouched for them that the PKP welcomed Joema and the most radical elements of his small crowd into the party. These initial recruits into the old party were campus revolutionaries already attracted to Marxism as an appropriate response to imperialism and other forms of oppression. Though well educated, the new recruits lacked the old cadres' links to peasant or labour movements.

José Maria Sison was typical of the new recruits. A poet and English instructor, he became involved in activist causes while a student. He joined the PKP soon after it opened its doors, bringing with him the *Progressive Review*, which he founded in 1963, and the KM (*Kabataang Makabayan*, or Patriotic Youth), which soon became the most important new left organization. Sison also brought an embryonic attraction to

Maoism, which the Lava dynasty within the PKP and its pro-Soviet faction did not share. Nevertheless, Joema quickly became head of the PKP's youth commission and a member of the central committee.

The seeds of a radical revival were also sown off campus during this period. In 1963 the leaders of left-wing labour and peasant groups, including *Masaka* (the Free Association of Peasants), formed a legal political party called the LM (*Lapiang Mangagawa*, or Workers' Party). Both old-time labour leaders and young radical upstarts were included in its leadership. Sison held the position of vice-president for education. Though factional disputes eventually destroyed the new party, it none the less marked the rebirth of dissident political action by a labour movement still reeling from the *Huk* catastrophe.

Marcos served his first term against a backdrop of growing social conflict. The élite was split into pro- and anti-government factions, modernizers and agrarian interests, nationalists and pro-Western 'internationalists', old money and new. Corruption intensified as Marcos planted the seeds of his own brand of capitalism. Students protested against the war in Vietnam, imperialism and the threat of fascism. The labour and peasant sectors became increasingly restive. More young radicals gravitated towards the KM and, even, the PKP. Radical Christians established their own organizations, while moderates formed alternative groups which, though anti-communist, were becoming increasingly militant. The seeds of a Muslim rebellion began to sprout on college campuses and in the deep south.

There were numerous demonstrations in the late 1960s. Some of the rank and file wanted to adopt a more radical stance. Sison and his followers were battling with their elders for the heart and soul of the movement. In 1967 Sison gave up the leadership of the KM to concentrate on fighting to change the direction of the Communist Party. He believed that the PKP had repeatedly erred in the past and that José Lava had been guilty of left opportunism in launching the party's bid for power in 1950. At the same time he charged Lava's brother, Jesus, with right opportunism for 'liquidating' the party after the *Huk* defeat and for pursuing an exclusively parliamentary policy. Sison thought that the party should recognize its past mistakes and conduct a protracted people's war. These differences came to a head in 1967. As Nemenzo puts it:

> It was a seemingly trivial incident that triggered an open split. Some over-zealous KM activists from UP visited a *Masaka* village in Central Luzon in 1967. With Mao badges prominently displayed on their shirts, they brandished the little red book like revivalist preachers and loudly espoused armed revolution. This behaviour shocked the old peasant cadres who at once

lodged a protest with the provisional central committee. The Lavaists readily saw in this a precious opportunity to mobilize *Masaka* against KM. Once they convinced the peasant section that Guerrero (Sison) might be an *agent provocateur*, the Lavaists hurriedly and arbitrarily enlarged the provisional central committee, ostensibly to increase peasant participation in policy making. Then assured of a firm majority, they issued a warning to the KM National Council that adventurism must be curbed. Sensing a neatly woven conspiracy, Guerrero and his loyal followers in the Youth Section declared their intention to defy a 'mechanical majority'. Guerrero then took decisive steps to eliminate PKP influence in the KM, the *Progressive Review* editorial board and the Philippine council of the Bertrand Russell Peace Foundation.[4]

The split imposed a considerable strain on the left. The old party, despite its many problems at the time, kept more of an organized following, even among its young people. In addition the KM had its own problems. Its leaders were finding it difficult to organize off campus and its initial attempts to recruit workers, slum dwellers and peasants had failed. On campus it had to contend with a splinter faction that was even more embittered by its personal conflicts than by its ideological differences.

Joema and his colleagues pushed on. In early January 1969 Sison and 11 comrades gathered in a small Pangarinan village to hold a Congress of Re-establishment of the Communist Party of the Philippines. The village itself was the home of one of Sison's comrades. The founders called their party the Communist Party of the Philippines (Marxist-Leninist) (CPP). In the media, the new Party came to be known by its English name and initials, while the old Party continued to be called by its Tagalog name and initials.

The participants at that first meeting recall the sense of uncertainty, adventure and daring of knowing that not only the state, but also the leaders of the old PKP, wanted to eliminate them. Here they were, promising to launch an armed struggle with neither an army nor any real organized connection to the masses. Fate, however, was on the side of the young rebels. In much the same way as Sison and his comrades had grown weary of the old PKP, Bernabe Buscayno was now tired of the lack of direction within the remnants of the old HMB (*Hukbong Mapagpalaya ng Bayan*, People's Liberation Army). Buscayno (nicknamed Kumander Dante) was also in his twenties, but his experiences had been quite different from Sison's. He was part of Tarlac's rural population. In the early 1960s he had joined a hold-over band of the *Huks* and quickly assumed a leadership role. But disgusted by the Angeles City-based *Huks*' drift towards gangsterism and the lack of direction from the PKP, Dante found himself in command of a small, perhaps 30-member, guerrilla army looking for a political movement. Hearing of Sison's break with the PKP and his formation of a new party,

Dante, who had already become enamoured with the works of Mao, met Sison and, on 29 March 1969, the CPP announced the formation of the NPA (New People's Army) with Kumander Dante at its head.

Meanwhile Marcos continued to excel at traditional pork-barrel politics. In 1969 he revealed his political skill by becoming the first Philippine president to be re-elected, but only after having spent between $50 and $100 million in public (some from foreign sources) and private funds. The money bought newspaper space, broadcasting time, goons and votes. It also went into high visibility projects like irrigation and roads in vote-rich areas. Over 200 people had died in the pre-election violence and Marcos's opponent, Sergio Osmena, the previous Commonwealth president's son, did not stand a chance.

Despite Marcos's political success, the crisis got worse. Election spending sparked a balance-of-payments crisis. Marcos sought IMF relief. The IMF demanded devaluation of the peso. Marcos consented. Commodity prices soared. And corruption continued unabated as Marcos and his cronies took a share of virtually every important business-deal cut in the country. This created fertile ground for the dissidents. Between the 1969 election and the declaration of martial law in 1972, competition among the upper classes spiralled, radical protest mounted and the domestic élite and Manila Americans became increasingly insecure. Nationalism reached new peaks of fervour.

Marcos set his annual State-of-the-Nation address for 26 February 1970. Political forecasters expected him to focus on the Constitutional Convention (the Con Con), which was scheduled to draft a new constitution in 1971. Members of the élite hoped it would lay the foundations for resolving the nation's problems. Student activists of all political persuasions, however, had little faith in the politicians' ability to reform the system. The moderate NUSP (National Union of Students of the Philippines) called a demonstration outside Congress Manila to demand a non-partisan Con Con. Radical students, workers and peasants flocked to it with their own demands. By the time Marcos arrived at the Congress building to speak in the late afternoon, over 20,000 protesters had gathered outside in the blistering heat. 'Marcos puppet! Marcos puppet!' shouted the students. '*Rebolusyon! Rebolusyon!*' shouted the radicals.

When Marcos emerged after his speech, the throngs surged forward with a cardboard coffin representing the death of democracy, a green cardboard crocodile representing greed, and an effigy of the president. Marcos grabbed Imelda and pushed her into a waiting limousine. The car sped away leaving a riot in its wake. 'Things got so confused at this point that I cannot honestly say which came first: the pebbles flying or the cops charging,' wrote journalist José Lacaba in the *Philippines Free Press*. 'I remember only the cops rushing down the steps of Congress, pushing aside the demonstration leaders, and jumping down the streets, straight into the mass of demonstrators. The cops flailed away, the demonstrators scattered. The cops gave chase to anything that moved, clubbed anyone who resisted, and hauled off those they caught up with.'[5] This was what became known as the First Quarter Storm. And it soon assumed the local significance of May 1968 in Paris or of the Prague Spring. Well into the 1980s student activists were still basking in its reflected glory and seeking to emulate its participants.

The storm clouds gathered again on 30 January when the moderates led by Edgar Jopson of the NUSP attended a rally outside the presidential palace. The militants led by the KM were demonstrating outside Congress. Marcos ushered Jopson and a few other leaders into Malacanang Palace for a talk, but the belligerent president was rude to the student leaders, especially to Jopson, an intelligent and thoughtful representative of his generation, whom he belittled for being a 'grocer's son.' In later years Jopson moved steadily to the left and eventually died a hero of the revolutionary movement.

As dusk approached, the militants began to march from Congress to the palace. Tensions mounted. A fire-engine advanced to disperse the students. The students charged the fire-fighters, beat those whom they captured and commandeered the truck. Then, using the truck as a battering ram, they broke through the gates of the palace grounds. 'They had apparently come prepared for the assault,' reported Lacaba. 'They lobbed Molotovs and pill boxes into the Palace grounds; the flames spread down the road.'[6] The presidential guard's battalion responded by firing bullets into the air and tear gas into the crowds. With rifle butts and night sticks, they beat up any demonstrators unfortunate enough to fall into their clutches. But the demonstrators refused to give up and the battle spread into the neighbouring 'university belt.' Demonstrators held firm with rocks, bottles and a homemade arsenal. The palace guards responded with army reinforcements. The 'Mendiola massacre,' which raged until dawn, had claimed six lives.

The events horrified the nation. Some of the richer and more powerful residents started to stash money abroad. Academics and government opponents were appalled by the military's brutal response. Marcos alleged that it had all been a conspiracy to topple his government and Philippine democracy.

The heated rhetoric failed to stem the tide of protest. The Parliament of the Street had established the MDP (Movement for a Democratic Philippines) to coordinate mass action, but it too had failed to reconcile the divergent tendencies. The Maoists continued to denounce the independent Christian left as clerico-fascist and the old-line communists as traitors. The moderates derided the radicals for their totalitarian impulses. The PKP continued to launch frenzied attacks on José Maria Sison and his CPP, even though its participation in the protest movement was fast coming to an end. Party leaders called for sobriety and denounced the CPP-led groups. The MDP expelled the PKP.

Still the storm raged on. Dissidents held teach-ins, marches and demonstrations. Many turned violent. Demands grew more and more militant. The call for revolution echoed through the balmy Manila night. The protest spread beyond the ranks of students, with jeepney and mini-bus drivers going on strike to force the government to increase fares. Other sectors of society expressed their support for the struggle in quieter ways. 'I hate the violence and fighting,' Gloria Dian Sena, a vendor of fried bananas, told a *New York Times* reporter who visited her 'garbage-strewn street' in March. 'A revolution would be a terrible thing for the Philippines. But I have ten children to feed. Prices keep going up but not the money my husband brings home. If it takes a revolution to feed my children, then I say let's have it.'[7]

Like all other storms, the First Quarter Storm passed. By the end of March the students were packing their bags to return home for the summer. But though the storm had passed, its impact lingered on in the hearts and minds of its participants. Nelia Sancho recalls how:

> The ferment at the time influenced me to look at social and political issues.... The entire university was kind of a classroom.... Seeing big demonstrations and having classmates who are activists discuss the issues, these are the things that start you asking questions: Why is this happening? What is this demonstration for? Why is there graft and corruption in government?

The First Quarter Storm had launched Sancho on a trajectory from beauty queen to radical activist. She journeyed to the countryside, joined demonstrations and later became a community organizer, semi-underground activist, political prisoner and feminist. Her trajectory was dramatic, but not unusual. Many veterans of the storm occupy leading positions in the legal and illegal left of today. Others hold positions of prominence in the media, business and even government.

The rising tide of protest also had an impact on traditional politicians. Marcos's opponents sought to harness the protest movement for their own purposes. One activist remembers collecting donations from Benigno Aquino and other anti-Marcos politicians to fund mass action. Another activist, a founding member of the new Communist Party, says politicians in Central Luzon offered logistical and financial support to the NPA in its early days, hoping to use it as they had used the *Huks*.

The rising tide of nationalism also forced elected officials to react. Many adopted a strong nationalist posture and started pushing for reform. As Nemenzo notes:

> Senators and Congressmen, probably the best political barometers, suddenly turned into champions of civil liberties.... Never before in Philippine history did the left make such a powerful impact on the law-making process. The system of constitutional oligarchy seemed to move in the direction of greater democracy because the masses, hitherto mute and submissive, were organizing themselves and learning to articulate their grievances and aspirations.[8]

A 1970 Senate committee report on the First Quarter Storm called for far-reaching changes, recommending land reform, tax adjustment and more relief and social welfare programmes. It also condemned the 'colonial nature of our economy' and called for the abrogation of existing trade agreements, the termination of the Military Bases Agreement, strict implementation of the existing investments code and expansion of relations with other countries, including socialist and Asian nations. The following year, 1971, Congress was scheduled to consider 23 bills aimed at Filipinizing the economy. A Supreme Court ruling soon cancelled US property rights.

The chaos of the late 1960s and early 1970s tore élite society apart. Reformists, many of them members of the civil service and industrial élite, found themselves at odds with the old oligarchs of commercial agriculture. Manila Americans and transnationalists felt pressure from the nationalists. Yet they still had common interests. Very few in the élite wanted to surrender their power to the unwashed masses and student activists. Everyone wanted to see a restoration of peace and order but disagreed about what mix of reform and repression was needed.

In the eye of the storm sat Marcos. He belonged to no camp but his own. He was neither nationalist nor internationalist, reformer nor reactionary. Marcos sought what was best for Marcos, not what was best for the nation, any particular class, or foreign interests. His goals included the co-optation or neutralization of all potential alternative centres of power. He was already building a coterie of loyal cronies and a strong military, and was moving in and out of alliances with various sectors of the élite. Though the US did not fully trust him, he knew enough not to pursue a nationalist course except rhetorically.

The countdown to martial law had started and 1971 would be a critical year. In January a sharp fuel-price rise sparked off a jeepney strike and students and workers supported the striking drivers. In the

Diliman section of Quezon City, the students barricaded themselves into the main UP campus and established what became known as the Diliman Commune. They seized the campus printing press and radio station and began churning out (often turgid) propaganda.

But the students' activities were not all serious. Shortly before the new round of protests broke out, Ferdinand Marcos had engaged in an illicit love affair with a curvacious American actress — Dovie Beams. Imelda heard of the affair and had her husband deport the would-be starlet. But before leaving, Beams held a press conference at which she played a tape of herself and Marcos in the bedroom — the students obtained a copy. The campus radio station played the tape repeatedly. Over the airwaves came the sounds of the president singing an Ilocano love song, squeaking mattress springs, squeals and orgasmic shouts. Marcos was outraged by the broadcast and sent in the troops. But upon hearing the tape, even his most loyal soldiers had a good laugh before carrying out their duty and breaking up the commune.

The year 1971 also witnessed an increase in guerrilla activity. The tiny NPA guerrilla army had expanded slightly and moved to the mountains of Isabela, a province in north-eastern Luzon. There, in surroundings more conducive than Central Luzon to guerrilla warfare, the rebels established a base amongst the impoverished peasantry. At the end of 1970 the NPA scored a victory of sorts when a young AFP lieutenant, Victor Corpus, defected to its ranks after raiding the Philippine Military Academy's arsenal. Corpus later told me of his disgust with Marcos and traditional politics:

> It was a series of incidents that got me disillusioned with the armed forces finally. There was the Jabidah affair in which most of those involved were my intimates in the PC Special Forces so I got to know the details of that incident.* I also had some bad experiences with some powerful politicians. When I was in Cavite during one of the local elections, I had to disarm some of the goons of some local politicians, one politician happened to be a relative of the president, and he threatened to destroy my career.

The NPA still only had a few hundred members at most, but it was growing more sophisticated. Some of its members had undergone training in China and the Chinese had sent them about 1,000 weapons. With Sison's political skill, Buscayno's guerrilla experience, Corpus's military training and the assorted talents of various other leaders, the CPP and NPA presented a potent force.

---

* The Jabidah incident occurred when government forces murdered young Muslim Filipinos originally recruited to participate in an aborted invasion of Sabah. For more details, see Chapter 21.

In 1971 attention again focused on traditional politics, for a contest was underway for eight Senate seats. Aquino's Liberal Party was pitted against Marcos's *Nationalistas*. Filipinos elect their senators on a nationwide basis, with voters casting ballots for individual candidates rather than for party lists. The eight with the most votes would make it to the 24-member Senate. Many considered the 1971 Senate election a dry run for the 1973 presidential election. Though not running, Ninoy Aquino took an active role in the campaign. Pundits considered him a prime candidate to succeed Marcos.

Marcos and Aquino traded barbs throughout the campaign. Since the Jabidah scandal in 1968, Ninoy had become a leading critic of the militarization of Philippine society. Marcos retaliated by accusing the Liberal Party of conspiring with the CPP. To some extent Marcos had a point. Liberals and communists did meet and cooperate from time to time, but not as part of a grand conspiracy designed to alter the whole nature of Philippine society. As politicians, the Liberals, who had the same general world view as *Nationalistas*, hoped to use the NPA and the mass movement against Marcos. The CPP viewed the Liberal Party and Marcos as part of the same evil system and simply sought to use the Liberal Party to sow divisions within the ruling class.

The Liberal Party planned to close its campaign on 21 August with a giant pre-election rally in Plaza Miranda in downtown Manila. That night there were thousands of supporters packed into the small square in front of an old Spanish church. At 9.13 p.m. a bomb exploded near the stage. Filipinos watched the carnage on television. Nine spectators died, 98 were injured — many seriously. All eight of the candidates had to be treated in hospital. One lost a leg. Fate saved Ninoy Aquino. Prior to the rally he had been attending a birthday party for his goddaughter, the child of *Nationalista* senator, Salvador Laurel, and had been delayed.

Though there is speculation about who bombed the rally, there is no doubt about its political impact. Marcos moved swiftly to curtail civil liberties. He suspended the writ of habeas corpus and his minions invaded the offices of radical groups, arrested activist leaders and held them without trial. Such moves in turn sparked the eventual growth of a civil liberties movement involving prominent jurists, journalists and political figures. Marcos failed to sway voters with his claims of a Liberal-Communist conspiracy and seven of the eight opposition candidates went on to win the election. The next slap in the face came when the Con Con (Constitutional Convention) decided that neither he nor a relative could run for the presidency in 1973.

After the Plaza Miranda bombing the march towards martial law gathered momentum. Marcos wanted to consolidate his power and turn the public against his foes. He also wanted to create a climate of fear in which a final step towards authoritarian rule would be welcomed as an alternative to anarchic democracy. All communications between him and the opposition broke down. He forced the Con Con to approve a parliamentary system that would allow him to retain power as prime minister at the head of the majority party. Shortly after revealing left-wing plans to sow terror, bombings struck the capital city. At this point even the US believed that Marcos's agents were responsible. On 4 July 1972 a fishing vessel (apparently carrying Chinese arms to the rebels) was captured. The government took advantage of the incident to drum up more hysteria.

On 21 September, 30 anti-Marcos organizations held a rally in Plaza Miranda to protest against creeping authoritarianism. The next day the car of the defence secretary, Juan Ponce Enrile, was ambushed by unidentified gunmen. Enrile, who had played a key role in developing and administering plans for martial law, was fortuitously riding in a security van behind his own car. Years later, after breaking with Marcos, he admitted that the ambush had been staged by the government's own men.

The next day Marcos imposed martial law. In the ensuing hours the military arrested over 100 people (mainly opposition politicians, newspapermen and intellectuals) including senator and former secretary of justice, José Diokno, publisher of the *Manila Times*, Chino Roces, and Ninoy Aquino. The authorities closed down newspapers and TV and radio stations not controlled by the government. Marcos declared his intention to save the Republic and to build a new society. He gave no hint of the darkness that was to come.

7

Dictatorship

Shortly after the declaration of martial law, journalist T.J.S. George wrote that:

> For a city under military control, Manila is remarkably free of troops. This is one case of martial law without tanks. There are soldiers guarding installations, and the presidential palace is completely cordoned off, but, by and large, troops are conspicuous by their absence. One night my car was stopped twice by troops looking for private firearms; they did not seem to realize that the man sitting in the driver's seat like a humble chauffeur was a wanted political worker.[1]

Ninotchka Rosca describes the situation differently. She spent two weeks in hiding before falling into the Marcos regime's clutches. She wrote many years later:

> Those two weeks had not been reassuring. Despite the overt political crisis — radio and television stations went dead, newspapers disappeared, and the city of Manila, normally the noisiest in the world, was abruptly quiet — no one wanted to acknowledge that there was one. In public buses and jeepneys, passengers sat in the new silence and avoided one another's eyes. When a building surrounded by barbed-wire and guarded by soldiers in combat fatigues came into view, they shifted restlessly and looked askance on the scene. No one ventured a public reaction.[2]

Marcos did not suddenly become a mindless brute set on imposing his will by force. He remained the consummate politician. He claimed constitutional authority in imposing martial law, promised the sometimes contradictory reforms demanded by different sectors of society and ordered his military to avoid harassing civilians. Playing on people's fears of violence and chaos, he banned private hand-guns, strikes and political demonstrations. When corruption became an issue, he, the most corrupt of all, dismissed countless petty officials thought guilty of graft. To solve the agrarian problem in the countryside he declared the whole country a land-reform area, but, being reluctant to challenge the power of sugar and other export-crop producers, restricted the reform to rice and corn lands.

But the smiling face of martial law hid many evils. In the first few years an estimated 67,000 Filipinos were arrested on political grounds. With Congress suspended and only controlled newspapers allowed to operate, how could people speak out? The façade of constitutionality and civilian supremacy soon faded. Aquino and other political prisoners faced trial before military tribunals, not civilian courts; generals and colonels grew considerably more powerful than governors and mayors.

At first a general quiescence settled over the city. Some oppositionists had courageously tried to resist martial law before it happened, but mass arrests effectively neutralized them. The underground left grew fast, but found itself cut off from the mass movement it had once led. A former KM leader remembers his disappointment at the mass reaction. 'We expected an insurrection. We did not expect people to allow martial law to pass so easily.' CPP leaders seemed less disappointed than their comrades in the city. Martial law did not change their expectations of a protracted people's war — it brought them new recruits.

Most of the support for martial law came from the élite, the military and Manila's American community. The élite, for all its differences, hoped it would bring peace, order and business as usual. As if to demonstrate its new-found confidence, the Manila stock-market broke a two-year slump just days after it was declared. Manila's Americans applauded it. In a telegram to Marcos on 27 September, an organization representing US businessmen in the Philippines proclaimed: 'The American Chamber of Commerce wishes you every success in your endeavours to restore peace and order, business confidence, economic growth and the well being of the Filipino people. We assure you of our confidence and cooperation in achieving these objectives. We are communicating these feelings to our associates and affiliates in the United States.'

Though denying it, the US knew about martial law in advance. An agent in Marcos's inner circle had told Ambassador Henry Byroade about it on 17 September. The US was unlikely to have encouraged Marcos — it did not entirely trust him and there was no agreement on the appropriate response to the crisis. None the less, it soon acquiesced and continued to treat Marcos as an important ally in South East Asia.

With the Vietnam war, the military bases at Clark and Subic and Philippine business interests uppermost in their minds, US policy-makers continued to offer the Philippine government extensive economic and military assistance. Between 1970 and 1972 the US sent $60.2 million in military aid. The figure rose to $118.8 million between 1973 and 1975. In the year between 1972 and 1973 military aid leapt from $18.5 to $45.3 million. But Marcos knew that he could not count on continued US acquiescence. In a self-serving interview with T.J.S. George on 28 September, he expressed his commitment to change: 'Reforms will have to be drastic — some egalitarianism in property ownership, a degree of welfare society, creation of a middle class rather than only rich and poor, land reforms, restructuring of the education system, which now produces misfits from top to bottom.[3] Marcos laid the foundations of his dictatorship under the guise of creating a 'new society.' Its legal framework would be the constitution drafted by the now tightly-controlled Con Con. Enacted in 1973, it allowed Marcos to retain power as both president and prime minister and to rule single-handedly until 1978 when an interim National Assembly would be elected.

Economic conditions favoured Marcos at this time. A boom in the prices of the country's main commodities, sugar and coconut oil, lasted until 1975 and forestalled opposition from the élite and, to some extent, the masses. The construction of a new oligarchy was essential to his plans. At its centre would be members of his and Imelda's families, loyal soldiers and those who became known as 'the cronies.' Some of these belonged to the old oligarchy — Cory Aquino's cousin Eduardo 'Danding' Cojuangco for one — others were outsiders not unlike Marcos and Imelda themselves.

Marcos used state power to build his system of 'crony capitalism'. He created monopolies to control the trade and processing of basic export commodities which, rather than leave to flounder in the old feudal way, he wanted to develop along capitalist lines. The coconut planters (generally relatively small businessmen) at first supported Marcos's modernization and supported a coconut levy to fund marketing, research and processing through a United Coconut Planters Bank. Smaller planters therefore went along with the reforms, even though Cojuangco and his partners, including Juan Ponce Enrile, were increasing their share of the industry's profits. It was only much later that significant numbers of coconut planters felt sufficiently squeezed to join the opposition.

The following events provide an illuminating example of the growth of crony capitalism. In 1975 Cojuangco gained control of the First United Bank by arranging for the Philippine Coconut Producers' Federation to buy it out from Cory Aquino's side of the family. He took a 10 per cent share as his commission and attained a contract with which to manage it. Thanks to favourable treatment from Marcos the renamed United Coconut Planters Bank grew in wealth and power. The president imposed a levy on coconut products and ordered the money to be deposited in interest-free accounts in the bank. The levy gave Danding Cojuangco control over an estimated $500 million. But coconut planters had never posed a serious threat to Marcos. They lacked the clout of the wealthier sugar barons, whose political power Marcos wanted to neutralize without causing a showdown — hence his deliberate exclusion of sugar lands from the land-reform programme.

Marcos's first step in this direction was to eliminate the influence of the leading sugar clan represented by his estranged vice-president Fernando Lopez. He confiscated the family's media and industrial holdings and gaoled one of its members on flimsy charges. Lopez and numerous other members of his family went into exile in the US. Marcos then launched a two-pronged attack on the sugar industry. He fought a propaganda war against the sugar oligarchs, which even went so far as supporting sugar workers' demands for wage increases in 1973 and 1974. And he restricted the planters' ability to fight back by increasing his control over their purse strings. In 1974 he established Philex (Philippine Exchange Company) and gave it a monopoly over buying and exporting sugar.

The high price of sugar in 1973 and 1974 benefited planters and government alike. Philex cornered the bulk of the profits by selling sugar on the world market for over three times what it had paid for it. For the time being high prices and reliable credit kept the planters quiet, but disaster soon struck. In late 1974 Philex refused to sell two million tons of sugar on the grounds that its officers were expecting another price rise. Instead the price plunged from 67 cents a pound in December 1974 to 20 cents in May 1975 and to 10 cents in 1976. Had Marcos been a lesser politician the collapse of the international demand for sugar, the expiry of the Laurel-Langley agreement guaranteeing the Philippines an important share of the US sugar market, the extension of a monopoly over the industry, and the cronies' increasing control of the milling process could well have generated widespread dissent among the oligarchs. But Marcos protected his flank by getting US refineries to agree (in 1976) to buy 75 per cent of the Philippines' sugar over five years. Many of the traditional planters applauded his action.

'By and large, the Philippine sugar élite in the early years of martial law supported the dictatorship,' reported business correspondent Roberto Tiglao, and 'that support was a major factor in its consolidation.'[4] Moves to modernize the sugar and coconut industries also appealed to the segment of the urban élite in favour of industrialization. Marcos saw this segment as a potential source of support and moved to please it. He sought foreign funds to expand the country's infrastructure and to build new dams and power plants. He also cracked down on labour unrest, which pleased various sections of the urban élite and made other restrictions on political activity acceptable.

During the early years of martial law Marcos skilfully manoeuvred the contending interests of domestic producers, exporters, international finance and Manila Americans. So long as money was easily available he could maintain the delicate balance between élite factions. He thus kept many of the protective barriers demanded by local industry while at the same time welcoming technocrats into his government as representatives of international capital. He supported the export-oriented sector by establishing export-processing zones, bonded warehouses and tax privileges.

Marcos needed US support so he moved to protect US business interests. He circumvented laws restricting foreign ownership of land and expedited extended lease agreements between agribusiness corporations and his government or private Philippine corporations. Companies like Dole and Del Monte, under threat from a 1972 court ruling outlawing foreign ownership of land, even enlarged their agricultural empires in Mindanao. In addition, Marcos's new constitution allowed foreigners to sit on the governing bodies of Philippine corporations and to control 40 per cent of companies engaged in the exploitation of natural resources.

To maintain the growth he needed to balance the interests of various segments of the upper classes, Marcos launched the nation on a massive borrowing binge. Debt-powered growth and easy money helped to consolidate his political power for a while, but the growing debt burden became a time bomb which exploded before his regime fell. Marcos knew he could not focus all his efforts on winning the support of the wealthy. The growth of mass activism had radically altered the nature of Philippine political life and he had to appear to make some concessions to the poor if he hoped to quell the growth of radical dissent.

No one was surprised by Marcos's proclamation on 21 October 1972 of a nationwide agrarian-reform programme. With a flourish of populist rhetoric he promised at last to free the peasants from their bonds of feudalism. But his programme was doomed from the start. Not only did he exclude all but rice and corn lands, thus sparing the richest landowners the impact of redistributive justice, but he demanded payment for the land. This put the beneficiaries in the precarious position of having to pay off loans or lose the land to their creditors — the state. But despite its flaws many rural Filipinos initially supported the agrarian-reform programme. In 1974 the PKP opted to reconcile itself with the government — it had already ordered its militants to stop challenging the government's authority. While condemning the excesses of martial law, the PKP declared the Marcos faction the more progressive segment of the bourgeoisie. This surrender further eroded the PKP's influence.

In wooing the US and building a modicum of popular (crony-led) backing, Marcos started to build two pillars of support upon which he would depend for the rest of his term in office. A third — the military — was already in place and gaining strength, with its budget increasing as rapidly as the size of the AFP (Armed Forces of the Philippines). Between the declaration of martial law and 1985 the AFP (including paramilitary troops) grew from 60,000 to 250,000 men.

Despite salaries of less than 5,000 pesos a month, numerous generals bought fabulous multimillion peso homes in Manila's best neighbourhoods. Some acquired their money in fairly open business transactions; others in more nefarious ways. One AFP commander, for example, earned himself the nickname of 'General Carnap' for running the country's largest motorcar-theft ring.

By 1975 corruption, dependency, debt, militarism and favouritism had started to conspire against Marcos. The radical left was now firmly established in the countryside with its urban underground preparing the way for future militancy. While some Church people had joined the underground, others were setting up BCCs (Basic Christian Communities), or helping task forces established by heads of religious orders work on issues such as human rights abuses and poverty. Other Christian activists, mainly moderates from the protest movement of the late 1960s, emerged with the new ideology of social democracy and built links with the old élite opposition in Manila and with the Muslim rebels in the south. As the commodity market collapsed even members of the élite started to bridle at the regime's ill-conceived programmes. But the urban workforce was the first to break its silence. Marcos had thrown bones to other segments of the poor, but had always ignored the urban workers' demands. Their real wages had fallen steadily during the early 1970s.

Throughout this period, the CPP maintained an active core in Metro Manila. Its rural forces had taken a beating in Isabela, but this had not resulted in widespread disillusionment. Instead, the party had learned from its errors and, dispersing its forces throughout the archipelago, had built a number of solid political bases under decentralized operational leadership in preparation for resumed military offensives.

The urban left had suffered no such setback. Throughout the early years of martial law the CPP and the new underground alliance it led, the NDF (National Democratic Front), had been quietly building a network of members and allies on college campuses and in work places. In late 1975 leftists in the labour unions launched a minor offensive which gave

birth to a new culture of dissent and rebellion. This happened in October,
when more than 5,000 workers at La Tondena Company had walked out
in defiance of the no strike law. A handful of priests, nuns and students
had joined the picket lines, thereby providing the labourers with a
middle-class shield against harsh repression. Workers at 26 companies
soon followed the example.

In 1976 and 1977 leftists continued to hold demonstrations. These
were often frightening experiences for the participants. Generally small
groups would gather quietly in a crowded part of the city and wait on the
pavement for a signal from the local cigarette vendor to group together
and start chanting anti-Marcos slogans. 'It was so scary,' one activist told
me of her first demonstration:

> The firetrucks and firemen came and started spraying us with water. We were
> lying on the street, and they started spraying us with water coloured pink so
> they could identify us. We had to run to the market to buy new shirts so they
> would not know who we were. It was really scary because they were shooting
> behind us — I do not know if they were shooting at people or in the air —
> but it was frightening.

Activism continued despite the arrests of most of the movement's
original leaders. José Maria Sison, Bernabe Buscayno, Victor Corpus,
ex-journalist Saturino Ocampo, rebel priest Ed de la Torre, KM boss Nilo
Tayag and others fell into government hands in the early and mid 1970s.

The 1977 arrests of Sison and Buscayno forced the CPP to reorganize
its highest organs, which it did with surprising success. Its new leaders
came from the CPP's regional affiliates. Though many belonged to the
generation that spawned the protest movement of the 1960s and early
1970s, their experience in the field had turned them into more practical
revolutionaries than some of their predecessors. Maoism still weighed
heavily on the minds of the party leaders, most of whom still regarded
the countryside as the bastion of revolutionary potential, but they were at
least prepared to build a distinctly Philippine movement. The opening up
of ties between the Chinese and Marcos governments during this period
hastened the move away from China.

The growth of crony power now began to irk those elements of the
industrial and rural élite not belonging to Marcos's inner circle. As the
economic pie shrank, bickering between cronies and non-cronies,
industry and agriculture, nationalists and transnationalists resurfaced.
The middle class and some members of the élite once again began
listening to opposition criticism of martial law.

The year 1978 was to be a crucial one. Since 1976 US President
Jimmy Carter had been badgering Marcos about human rights; now the
plight of Ninoy Aquino, who had been sentenced to death by a military

tribunal in 1977, was of special concern. Under Carter US relations with Marcos were strained, but, though less close than with other Republican presidents, both in the past and the future, each needed the other's tolerance. Though the Military Bases Agreement was not due to expire until 1991, its terms were due for review in 1979. Both sides manoeuvred for position. Carter prodded Marcos on human rights. Marcos threatened to evict the Americans.

Marcos scheduled elections for the Interim National Assembly for 7 April 1978. The election posed no real threat since the opposition was either gaoled or in disarray. Marcos's newly formed KBL (*Kilusang Bagong Lipunan*, or New Society Movement) would be the dominant force. Besides, he would continue to hold dictatorial power through martial law.

At first the opposition opted to boycott the election. Then, at Benigno Aquino's initiative, decided to contest the 21 seats available in Metro Manila. Opposition groups had few illusions about winning in rigged elections, but believed the campaign would stir anti-Marcos fervour. Aquino headed a ticket called *Lakas ng Bayan* (Strength of the Nation). The opposition slate, commonly known by its acronym *Laban* (Fight), included traditional politicians like Aquino, social-democratic activists and militants nominated by the local CPP.

Marcos waged a dirty campaign. His defence minister, Juan Ponce Enrile, accused Aquino of both communist ties and CIA connections. Aquino had to campaign from his gaol cell while Cory and their daughter, Kris, then seven years old, represented him on the campaign trail. On 10 March the government granted Aquino 90 minutes of television time to respond to Enrile's charges. For the first time since Marcos had imposed martial law, his most flamboyant and popular foe appeared before the public. Aquino admitted to having worked with the CIA with the Philippine government's approval, but denied having belonged to the CPP. He tore into Enrile and Marcos and left audiences gasping at his audacity.

As election day approached the momentum mounted in favour of the opposition. At 7 p.m. on 6 April, Filipinos poured out of their homes in a massive show of support for the opposition. Car hooters blared, pots and pans rattled, whistles blew and fireworks exploded. Despite the opposition's evident popularity, Marcos's candidates swept to victory in Manila. Fraud was obvious. Still, the campaign had given the opposition new life.

The campaign had, however, presented the anti-Marcos forces with problems. Apart from anything else it had created turmoil within the radical left and demonstrated the difficulties of working in alliances. The

CPP's Manila-Rizal commission had been in favour of participation, but the central committee had intervened and ordered a boycott. Other opposition groups faced a more serious tactical dilemma. What course would they follow? An agreement in 1976 had briefly united the main social-democratic organizations in a single party. The social democrats had exercised considerable influence within *Laban*, but the fraud and defeat of the election had forced them to reconsider their tactics. In 1979 they adopted a policy of waging a protracted people's war but this never really got off the ground.

Frustrated members of the élite favoured dramatic action and, in 1979, started burning effigies. The Light-a-Fire Movement torched targets like Imelda Marcos's prized floating casino. 'Most of the participants in the Light-a-Fire Movement were frustrated members of Manila's business community,' Gaston Ortigas told me in 1988. Ortigas himself went into exile after being implicated in plots against the Marcos government. 'It was important that upper middle class people make a statement. To be a powerful statement, risk was necessary, the action had to be illegal and it had to not be in the traditional form of terrorism. Attempts had to be made to avoid occupied targets.'

In December agents at Manila International Airport arrested a courier who revealed the names of the movement's leaders. On 6 May 1980 Ninoy Aquino suffered a heart attack. It provided Marcos with an opportunity to get rid of a persistent thorn in his side. Aquino's execution or death in a Philippine hospital would give the opposition a martyr Marcos had no desire to create. His release would give the opposition too prominent a leader to rally behind. Sending Aquino abroad for medical treatment seemed an ideal alternative.

Ninoy Aquino was an intriguing politician. Though he never bent over backwards to compromise with the dictatorship — he languished in gaol while others, like Salvador Laurel, joined the KBL — he did veer between militant anti-Marcos struggle on the one hand and the search for compromise and reconciliation on the other. For all his anti-Marcos activities, he none the less understood the dictator and his motives. What he feared most was the post-Marcos era — a takeover by Imelda and subsequently the military, or by a CPP-led revolutionary movement, both of which would render politics as Filipinos knew it obsolete. In the early 1980s he started searching for a way of making the traditional opposition more relevant. The old forms of political activity no longer worked, but the armed struggle alternative posed by the communists and now the social democrats did not appeal to an old-time politician like Aquino. He did not reject violent struggle, but neither did he embrace it.

To recover from his operation in Houston, Aquino travelled to San Francisco, where he soon began to mix in opposition circles. Some members shared his background in traditional politics, others were exiled businessmen and political activists of a variety of hues. Among them were men and women involved in establishing the April 6 Liberation Movement. This group borrowed much from the social democrats' Christian-based ideology, but, unlike mainstream social democrats, they were in favour of a dramatic burst of urban guerrilla activity. They planned a series of explosions.

On 4 August 1980 Ninoy Aquino broke his silence and warned Marcos of the consequences of refusing to dismantle the martial law regime and step down: 'If martial law is not lifted soon there will be an escalation of rural insurgency. Worse, some elements have completed plans for massive urban guerrilla warfare.' He proceeded to detail the plans of the urban guerrillas.

> I have been told of plans for the launching of massive urban guerrilla warfare where buildings will be blown up, and corrupt presidential cronies and cabinet members assassinated along with military officers who have engaged in warfare and rampant tortures of political prisoners.... There are plans to disrupt tourism. Also to kidnap the children of corrupt aliens who have exploited the people mercilessly and who have profited immensely from the palace connections. Business is also on the target list: Banks and companies linked with the Palace and which have cornered the bulk of government credit and/or guarantees, as well as multinational corporations that have entered into joint ventures with the ruling clique. All these actions are intended to bring the Marcos regime to its knees. The guerrillas are well educated, articulate young men and women who have patiently studied the latest tactics in urban warfare.

The political atmosphere in the early 1980s certainly seemed ripe for an explosion. Economic hardship was squeezing the nation. Non-crony members of the economic élite were suffering from restricted markets, low commodity prices, pro-crony favouritism and monopoly control of various sectors of the economy. After a period of relative quiet, the armed left had moved way beyond its traditional confines of Luzon and was preparing to initiate tactical offensives on a variety of far-flung islands.

The pillars of support for the dictatorship were weaker than before, but seemed stable. Marcos still had the support of his cronies, of KBL politicians, of the war-lords and their followers, and of his fellow Ilocanos. And, as members of the April 6 Movement pointed out, he had successfully created a new oligarchy which was totally beholden to him.

In the late 1970s Imelda Marcos was asked why so many of the president's relatives and friends had fared so well economically under martial law. She replied: 'Some are smarter than others.' A group of opposition business executives took that quote as the title for a study circulated surreptitiously in Manila in 1979.

> In spite of his often repeated promises of reforming the oligarchic structure of society, Mr Marcos's policy toward the traditional élite has in no way been consistent; he has been very selective with regard to whose wealth he chooses to 'reform' in contrast to whose wealth he chooses to fortify and extend. For example, Mr Marcos had the military 'sequester' all the corporations of the Jacintos, but he has shown favour to the Elizaldes. These are two traditional families — the difference being that one is in active collaboration with him, while the other opposed him during his bid for re-election in 1969. Marcos has created a new [oligarchy] out of his cronies. Disini, Cuenca, Silverio, and Villafuerte stand out as cronies who were formerly ordinary employees or small textile merchants but are now multi-millionaires who were able to become rich only upon the imposition of martial law.

The military still appeared to be solidly behind the regime and the US fell in line. In 1979 the Marcos and Carter governments concluded their review of the Military Bases Agreement, with various amendments accepted and a US government promise to do its best to deliver $500 million in military and economic aid by 1983. Carter had stopped criticizing Marcos once Aquino was released.

The April 6 Liberation Movement launched its offensive on 22 August 1980. Bombs went off in nine crony- or government-owned buildings in Manila and continued to shatter the complacency of Manila throughout the rainy season of 1980. On 19 October, soon after Marcos had finished addressing delegates to the American Society of Travel Agents' convention in Manila, the bombers detonated a powerful explosive which went off 50 feet from Marcos's seat on the podium and, despite advance warnings, wounded 18 delegates.

But the period of terror quickly fizzled out. Marcos's troops arrested many of the direct participants and, among others, blamed Ninoy for the movement's activities. Aquino almost certainly approved of the campaign, for he had hoped the bombings would push Marcos to the negotiating table. He was still trying to reconcile the contending forces in Philippine society so that an orderly transfer of power from Marcos to a democratic regime could be arranged. But Marcos's harsh response to the bombers and his refusal to compromise made the campaign's US-based sponsors question its appropriateness and they let the movement die. However, Ninoy and other members of the traditional opposition continued to seek relevance in the wake of the April 6 Liberation

Movement's campaign. Turned off by the Nicaraguan and Iranian revolutions and discouraged by the prospects of using violence as a principal tool of struggle, Ninoy then began the search that would end with his fateful decision to return to the country in 1983.

Back in the Philippines traditional politicians formed a new opposition alliance in September 1980. The group, which eventually became the United Nationalist Democratic Organization (Unido), brought together longstanding oppositionists, members of the pre-martial law Liberal and *Nationalista* parties, and former Marcos supporters like Doy Laurel, Ernie Maceda and (later) Luis Villafuerte. Originally centrist in orientation, it moved steadily to the right when Doy Laurel took control.

The next year another group of opposition politicians, this one led by the mayor of Cagayan de Oro City in Mindanao, Aquilino Pimentel, formed the PDP (Philippine Democratic Party). Its founders wanted a new type of party that combined electoral machinery with mass organizations and ideological commitment. Members of the banned democratic socialist organization, *Kasapi*, were among its instigators. Pimentel himself had been influenced by Raul Manglapus's Christian Social Movement. In 1983 the PDP merged with *Laban* to form the PDP-*Laban*. The new party adopted the PDP's democratic, socialist, nationalist and theist programme.

While the opposition was reorganizing and considering new directions and tactics, Marcos was busy developing an ideology and adjusting the political system. His 'Filipino Ideology' and 'New Republic' were to be his legacy to the nation. Both were, in fact, shams. The Filipino Ideology was a confused hodgepodge in which commitment to a nationalism bordering on jingoism contrasted with the reality of close cooperation with a foreign power. Platitudes about love, beauty and spiritual strength conflicted with the violence and brutality of martial rule. His New Republic was no less of a fraud. On 17 January 1981 he lifted martial law. Pope John Paul II was scheduled to arrive in the Philippines a month later. Marcos also wanted to make a political gesture towards newly elected US President Ronald Reagan, whose close relationship with him would be more acceptable in the US if Marcos could clean up his image.

The New Republic only came into being after Marcos had won a fresh six-year term in elections boycotted by even the most conservative elements and after he had protected his dictatorial powers. Amendment Six to the 1973 constitution granted the president power to legislate by decree. The Public Order Act and the National Security Code allowed the state to detain suspected subversives indefinitely without trial. US Vice-

President George Bush attended Marcos's inauguration on 2 July 1981 and toasted the dictator: 'We stand with you, Sir,' the future US president said. 'We love your adherence to democratic processes, and we will not leave you in isolation.'

Despite Marcos's attempt to reclaim the lustre of his earlier years, by the beginning of the 1980s the pendulum had started to swing against him. An economic crisis spurred by bad policy, poor management, corruption and debt accumulation forced him to turn to technocrats and international financial institutions, notably the IMF and World Bank, but their export-oriented, free-market solutions failed to save the economy from collapse. Economic pressure spurred political dissent as those elements of the élite not supported by the state saw their share of a rapidly shrinking pie all but disappear. The sugar élite, hurt not only by the general economic decline, but by its own failure to diversify and modernize, found an easy scapegoat for all its many problems in Benedicto's Philippine Sugar Commission monopoly and Marcos's support for it.

Unrest was also spreading amongst the urban poor. On 1 May 1980 radical unions formed the KMU (*Kilusang Mayo Uno* or May First Movement) to provide workers with an alternative to the US-backed, pro-government TUCP (Trade Union Congress of the Philippines). By the early 1980s Marcos's appeal to the rural poor had worn thin. His agrarian-reform programme had failed miserably. Less than 25 per cent of the targeted beneficiaries had received any land and less than 17 per cent of the targeted land had been redistributed. In addition the green revolution had created a dependence on fertilizers and pesticides. Debt and crop failures drove many poor farmers under. The CPP took advantage of the crisis in the countryside to consolidate and expand the revolutionary movement. More and more farmers found common ground with the CPP's anti-feudal, anti-landlord appeal. All that remained was for a catalyst to spark off a more generalized revolt.

Back in the US Aquino settled into Boston and academe. At Harvard and MIT he continued to search for a political alternative to his mounting fears about the post-Marcos situation. Reports of the president's fading health had reached America — despite his feeble denials to the contrary Marcos had serious kidney problems — and Aquino felt the need to act before either the CPP or the military captured the future. Believing there was no other option, he decided to return home to campaign for the National Assembly, lead a non-violent struggle, and once again urge Marcos to restore political competition.

Aquino landed at Manila International Airport on a China Airlines flight from Taipei at 12.45 p.m. on 21 August 1983. Soldiers surrounded him and escorted him down a metal staircase towards the runway. Within seconds a single shot rang out. Ninoy fell from the stairs. Four more shots sounded. A man in blue sprawled dead on the runway. Soldiers leapt from a van. One pumped another volley of automatic rifle fire into the still body of the man in blue. The commandos threw the bodies of Ninoy Aquino and Rolando Galman, a small-time criminal, into the blue van and sped away. Ninoy Aquino was dead.

Outside a reported 20,000 people had gathered to greet him. Doy Laurel and Agapito 'Butz' Aquino, Ninoy's younger brother, climbed aboard a truck. Doy spoke emotionally: 'Ninoy, our beloved, is back. But you might not be able to see him. Eyewitnesses say he has been shot.' A New York-based Japanese reporter telephoned Cory Aquino in Boston. Could she confirm what had happened in Manila? Cory said no. Later she told the nation that she had cried as she gathered her children around to break the news.

Marcos blamed Galman for the killing. He called him a communist hitman. The official version lacked any credibility. How could a lone gunman penetrate the airport's especially tight security on that day? Later evidence proved Ninoy had been shot from behind while on the stairway. Clearly a soldier had shot him. Clearly there had been a cover-up, but this time it neither swayed the nation nor saved Marcos. The public blamed Marcos, believing that either he or his underlings, Gen. Ver and Imelda Marcos, had ordered the killings. So did the Aquinos.

Despite his ill health (he was recovering from a kidney transplant), Marcos took steps to control the damage. An initial investigating panel had resigned over the lack of credibility and a second panel spent a year investigating the incident and, after months of deliberation, reached a split decision. The head of the board, Justice Corzaon Agrava, charged six Aviation Security Command soldiers and their commander with killing Aquino. A four-member majority saw a broader conspiracy. It implicated Gen. Ver, two other generals, two colonels, four other officers, 16 soldiers and a civilian in the conspiracy. Marcos reluctantly granted Ver and the others leave of absence. Lt-Gen. Fidel Ramos became acting chief of staff. Ver and the others stood trial before a special court. By the time the court acquitted them at the 2 December 1985 conclusion to a farcical trial, the legal drama had been relegated to sideshow status. The main events were taking place not in the courtroom, but on the streets, in the halls of parliament and in the rural areas. The tide turned decisively against Marcos the moment his soldiers shot Ninoy. In death Aquino accomplished what he had failed to achieve in life. He rallied a 'fed-up' nation. He catalysed a general uprising against his longtime foe.

The uprising began with Ninoy's funeral. More than 800 family friends, diplomats, opposition members and journalists filled the Santa Domingo Church near Aquino's home in Quezon City. Jaime Cardinal Sin and Cory Aquino delivered the homily and eulogy. Sin, who wavered between opposition and critical collaboration, picked up Ninoy's call for peace and reconciliation before Cory quietly approached the podium, the crowd standing and clapping. Few really knew Cory Aquino at the time. She had none of Ninoy's spark or showmanship. Unlike her husband she did not enjoy crowds or politicking, but she had a mission and her simple ways — which led many to forget her patrician background — captivated the nation. From the moment she first spoke in her soon to be familiar monotone, the public was with her.

She told of Ninoy's commitment to return home despite warnings that he would not be allowed into the country. She told of Ninoy's love of the Filipino people. She told of her own disbelief at the outpouring of support from people, strangers from all walks of life, who filed past Ninoy's coffin during the wake. She thanked 'all the Filipino men and women who have demonstrated that Ninoy did not die in vain.' Cory's talk left the audience in tears. As pallbearers carried the coffin to the head of the funeral procession, red and yellow banners fluttered in the air. Voices lifted in patriotic song.

Hundreds of thousands of Filipinos marched from the church to the cemetery, through Manila, past the US Embassy. Workers, matrons, businessmen, students, slum dwellers walked together. A storm of yellow confetti filled the air. Yellow had become the colour of courage and before Ninoy's return activists had tied yellow ribbons around trees and on chain-link fences. Their motive, the song lyric: 'Tie a yellow ribbon round the old oak tree. Its been three long years, do you still want me.' At nightfall the rally split and most of the people went on to the cemetery outside Manila. Elsewhere in town a battle raged. Several thousand militant students and other young radicals broke from the crowd and headed to Mendiola Bridge and the approach to Malacanang, where they greeted waiting riot troops with insults and stones. The sound of exploding pill-box bombs and gunshot soon echoed through the night air. One student died.

Despite the violence and the death, many Filipinos no longer feared the Marcos regime and new organizations proliferated. First, JAJA (Justice for Aquino, Justice for All), then CORD (Coalition of Organizations for the Restoration of Democracy) emerged to coordinate the Parliament of the Street. Business executives and professionals in the Makati business district formed their own groups, such as Jaycees for Justice, and the Society of Professionals for the Advancement of

Democracy. Militant labour organizations also continued to grow and the leftists consolidated the Nationalist Alliance. Organizations of lawyers, women and health workers seemed to appear overnight. An epidemic of marches and other political activity broke out. Business executives staged protest runs. Employees fed old Yellow Pages into office shredders to make confetti. Street kids collected bags of used confetti to sell back to the affluent protesters. A new dissent culture arose in the affluent districts to supplement the burgeoning rebelliousness in the slums and factories. Mass action spread throughout the country. In Davao City, yellow banners appeared alongside the radicals' red. In Bacolod, sugar planters joined their impoverished employees in denouncing the dictatorship. In the Cordillera mountains, tribal leaders and urban activists from Baguio City pushed through with plans to form an opposition alliance.

An alternative media prospered as new activists led a boycott of the crony media. The government suppressed the weekly, *We Forum*, but could not quieten its publishers and editors who went on to launch the first opposition daily, *Malaya*. The publisher of the women's magazine, *Mr and Ms*, started a weekly special edition dedicated to covering the Parliament of the Streets. The Catholic Church offered its support to *Veritas*, another alternative weekly. Radio Veritas, an established Catholic station, brought news of Aquino's funeral and other opposition events to an eager public.

Marcos tried to launch a political offensive of his own. His backers organized a Thanksgiving Day rally on 20 September to commemorate the birth of the KBL (his New Society Movement). A pathetic 2,000 marchers strode down Ayala Avenue in support of the beleaguered president. With more and more people joining opposition organizations and demonstrations, leaders of opposition groups found themselves confronted with a series of tactical decisions. The communist-led left commanded the largest organizations and entered the various alliances — such as JAJA and CORD — from a position of strength. The CPP maintained its policy of waging a protracted people's war with the rural areas as the principal battleground. But it was in the urban centres that the radical left really took off after Ninoy's death.

The CPP's influence spread with the growth of the Parliament of the Street. New activists were impressed by the CPP-led NDF's discipline and ability to mobilize students, workers and slum dwellers for demonstrations and rallies. But people were also scared of the CPP and some members of the new middle-class opposition sought alternatives to the NDF. Butz Aquino and his colleagues in ATOM (the August 21 Movement) became influenced by the social democratic movement, which then grew despite its lack of a solid party. Social democratic forces then spurred an early attempt at unity with the new Makati-based organizations and, in January 1984, delegates gathered for the Congress of the Filipino People (*Kongreso ng Mamamayang Pilipino — Kompil*). Its leaders included former government officials, judges and politicians, as well as the representatives of various political movements in the country. From his prison cell, former CPP chairman José Maria Sison called for the broadest anti-fascist united front. The delegates elected Sison an alternative leader.

The organizers sought to map out the future of the anti-Marcos movement. The most divisive question focused on what to do about the coming National Assembly election. Neither the social democrats nor the radical left saw much use in participating. The CPP called the election a sham. The NDF, most social democrats, and the independent nationalists pushed for a boycott. But the politicians found themselves caught in a bind. Many hoped to use the election to save the traditional opposition from irrelevance, to gain a toe-hold in government and to position themselves for the eventual transfer of power. Originally, everybody had agreed to issue a call for meaningful elections. 'Boycott unless...,' they proclaimed. The opposition demanded a series of reforms from Marcos, including the abolition of Amendment 6, amnesty for political prisoners and a series of election reforms by 14 February. Cory Aquino joined the politicians and activists in signing the letter.

Marcos refused to give in. His rejection of the demands split the opposition. The traditional politicians, led by Doy Laurel's Unido, opted to participate. The radical left, most social democrats and the old nationalists chose to boycott. The left wing of the old Liberal Party, led by the exiled Jovito Salonga, also boycotted. PDP-*Laban* faced an internal crisis. Its mass activists favoured a boycott; its politicians favoured participation. Finally, PDP members hammered out a compromise. Though officially pro-boycott, the party would allow local units to act independently. Cory Aquino, the symbolic leader of PDP-*Laban*, struggled with her own demons before deciding to support the opposition candidates running for the *Batasang Pambansa*. She publicly concluded that the election might provide a final opportunity to avoid a civil war. Following Cory's decision, many of PDP-*Laban*'s previously undecided locals decided to join the campaign. PDP's participation meant that a number of left-of-centre reformers, men like Augusto 'Bobbit' Sanchez and Aquilino 'Nene' Pimentel, would be candidates for office.

8

The Fall

I arrived in Manila on a hot sultry April day in 1984. As the plane came down I noted the shanties abutting the runway and the skyline of the city in the distance. An air-conditioned car took me past beggars and peddlers to my hotel in Manila's tourist district. Prostitutes, barkers and money changers jostled foreigners on street corners. Tattered political posters cluttered walls and utility poles. Local papers blazoned hosannas to the president and first lady. Truckloads of heavily armed soldiers passed along city highways. Periodically soldiers manned checkpoints looking for weapons and subversive materials, but the city did not have the feel of an armed camp. Sex-obsessed escapism was far more apparent than militarism. Virtually every street corner housed a brothel disguised as a bar. Beer houses and night clubs, many offering nude models and live sex shows, lined several major thoroughfares. At dusk prostitutes, young women and transvestites took over a stretch of Ayala Avenue near the Hotel Intercontinental in the heart of the capital's main commercial district. Government money supported the production of sex films through an experimental cinema project.

A political storm was raging. On 1 May I attended my first political rally in Manila and watched tens of thousands of workers pouring into Liwasang Bonifacio. They carried red banners, thrust clenched fists skyward, sang a Tagalog version of the *Internationale*, and chanted anti-Marcos and anti-US slogans. Leaders exhorted them in fiery Filipino to boycott the elections and continue the struggle for nationalism and democracy. Filipino journalists and activists translated speeches for me and explained the origins of CORD (Coalition of Organizations for the Restoration of Democracy) and the boycott movement. At times they spoke bitterly of the politicians, but generally veered away from condemning the moderate and left-leaning opposition candidates. The point they made repeatedly was that the people rather than the politicians would free the nation.

A few days later I joined a small group of local journalists and a representative of Namfrel (National Movement for Free Elections) who

83

were visiting Central Luzon to take a close look at a particularly nasty Assembly election campaign. The campaign pitted a popular young incumbent against Marcos's minister of political affairs. The incumbent, Carlos Padilla, had belonged to Marcos's KBL, but when Marcos threw his support behind Leonardo Perez, he decided to run as an independent.

Padilla's campaign contained many of the elements of the opposition's campaign against other Marcos-backed candidates. Perez represented the Marcos machine and had the resources of the state and the looming threat of violence and cheating at his disposal. Padilla presented himself as a fresh alternative. With Padilla we visited a small farming village not far from the main road. Farmers walked from distant fields to attend. They shared their problems and listened intently as Padilla addressed their concerns about irrigation and marketing before asking for their votes. Padilla's populist campaign contrasted dramatically with Perez's style. Perez campaigned in the town centre where a rock band attracted quite a crowd to his rally. A comedian joked in Ilocano. Finally Perez appeared to speak. The crowd grew restless as he droned on in Ilocano and English. Some drifted off, others waited to see what entertainment would follow.

Earlier Padilla had expressed a concern that was common to members of the local élite. The NPA (New People's Army) had recently entered the province and had gained some influence among peasants in the mountainous border areas. He thought that the state's rejection of a popular mandate would only increase the appeal of the guerrillas. Throughout the country similar localized campaigns were being pitted against the Marcos machine. The opposition could not match the Marcos camp's election spending, nor could it expect fair treatment from the crony press, but what it lacked in resources it made up for in spirit. With Cory Aquino travelling around the nation, adding her increasing moral standing to the opposition campaign, a surprise seemed possible.

Many of the politicians refrained from attacking the boycott movement, but some right-wingers could not prevent themselves belittling the left. In Doy Laurel's plush Makati office I met Ernesto Maceda, a former member of Marcos's cabinet and now in the Unido opposition. 'The left amounts to nothing,' he sneered. 'They say they represent the people, they say they can bring 100,000 people to a demonstration, they are lucky if they can bring 5,000. The real representatives of the people are running in this election.' Maceda had a point of sorts. The left could mobilize the most active and reliable core of the opposition, but by far the largest number of anti-Marcos activists saw the election as a chance to express their sentiments and did not want to boycott it. Besides, elections held a fascination for most Filipinos. They provided the sporting core of Philippine political culture.

The boycott movement played an educational role, however, for while most politicians were focusing their rage on Marcos, the boycotters were raising questions about the system. Just before election day I joined a caravan organized by the boycott movement in Central Luzon. Boycott partisans would travel from town to town and stop to hold rallies in municipal squares. During these rallies, political activists, labour leaders and peasant organizers would speak about economic injustice, US imperialism, human rights violations, militarism and élite domination. Many of those who were standing in the sun listening to them would agree with what they had to say, but would still vote for the opposition because they simply wanted to use whatever means were at hand to bring about a change.

But Marcos could still manipulate a vote to get the results he wanted. The opposition and the Church-backed, pro-democracy poll-watching organization, Namfrel, charged the regime with widespread cheating and, in mid-1984, the struggle against Marcos was resumed on a number of fronts — in the hills and on the streets, as well as in parliament, where the opposition now held one-third of the elected seats. The broad left continued to take to the streets, periodically joined by members of the traditional opposition and by the business community. Weekly (sometimes daily) demonstrations took place in old Manila and modern Makati. Though not altering its strategy, the revolutionary movement was experimenting with new tactics. Insurrectionary thinking took hold among underground and legal left leaders in Manila and other urban centres, where people's strikes (*welgang bayans*) were being organized.

The left's biggest urban advance, combining mass action with armed struggle, took place in the sprawling southern city of Davao where sparrow units (three-member teams of urban guerrillas) would emerge from the slums to terrorize the police and military forces. Davao's largest slum, Agdao, became known as Nicaragdao, another neighbourhood, Ma-a, as Ma-anagua. Small homemade banners, red paint on empty rice bags, flapped from many an Agdao shanty. Slum dwellers flocked to underground organizations; some out of political conviction, others to belong to something exciting. Unknown to most, the movement attracted scores of infiltrators who would cause it serious harm in 1986. But in 1984 and through much of 1985 the left seemed in command in Davao City. Left-wing labour unions led numerous strikes. Even businessmen and politicians reached accords with the left-wing mass organizations.

The military and the left alike saw Davao as a laboratory. Lt-Gen. Fidel Ramos had told reporters that the left regarded it as a model of urban insurrection. I met the leader of the NDF in Mindanao and asked him about this. The wiry 32 year-old who introduced himself as Lucas Fernandez explained:

> In the past, cities played a passive or secondary role in the revolutionary movement. After Nicaragua and, more important, after the Aquino assassination, we began to reassess this way of thinking. We developed a greater understanding of urban potential. Adjustments had to be made to the strategy of surrounding the cities from the countryside. As early as 1975 or 1976, Davao City began experimenting with sparrow units. At first they were based in the countryside. They would carry out an operation in the city then run back to the hills. We learned that we could establish a base of support and operation in the city. The lesson will be propagated in other cities throughout the country.

On 21 May 1985 gunfire erupted in a residential area in Quezon City. Some 200 military men surrounded an apartment building and opened fire. Its occupants returned the fire. But they, six members of the NPA, somehow slipped away. Afterwards, one soldier lay dead.

The first Manila attack by the NPA's ABB (Alex Boncayao Brigade) took place in May 1984. Guerrillas killed a general who had been responsible for anti-labour violence, then were quiet. In 1985 it prepared for action in Metro Manila. Top NPA commander and organizer of Davao's partisans, Rodolfo Kintanar, slipped in and out of Manila to plan an early 1986 urban offensive. In 1984 and 1985, demonstrations had been the left's main form of activity in Metro Manila. Now tear gas, pill-box bombs and police or military gunfire reverberated throughout the city.

On 21 August 1984 hundreds of thousands of Filipinos had gathered beneath red and yellow banners in Manila to commemorate Ninoy's death. Cheers welcomed most speakers, including members of parliament who picked up the nationalist and populist rhetoric of the left, but large sections of the crowd greeted representatives of the opposition's right wing with hoots and catcalls. For a time attempts at organizational unity and cooperation in the opposition and in the Parliament of the Street moved forward. Self-described national democrats (members of the communist-influenced left), social democrats, independent nationalists and leftists, and some left-leaning politicians sought a united front as they moved towards a showdown with the regime.

The *Bayan* (People), or more fully the *Bagong Alyansang Makabayan* (New Patriotic Alliance) was launched in May 1985. Hundreds of workers, peasants, lawyers, feminists, nuns and priests (radical and moderate) spent two days in a sweltering Quezon City gym at its founding congress. All were agreed on the need to oust Marcos, to change the country's relationship with the US and to initiate a social and cultural transformation, but sectarian differences blocked unity. For example, social democrats fought for inclusion of an article alluding to God, which the national democrats resisted. The issue was not really important — Filipino Marxists had long shed their anti-Christian baggage — but the moderates wanted to make their last stand on an ideological issue. The far more numerous national democrats won to the extent that they expanded their influence within the *Bayan* leadership, but the social democrats walked out and formed their own group, *Bandila* (Banner), or *Bansang Nagkaisa sa Diwa at Layunin* (A Nation United in Thought and Purpose). The split between *Bayan* and *Bandila* tore apart the Parliament of the Street. The two groups rarely cooperated. *Bandila* worked with the progressive members of parliament and of the political parties, while *Bayan* continued its drive to organize a people's strike.

Meanwhile the party political opposition engaged in its own attempts at unity and two paths emerged — the Convenor Group's 'fast-track' and the NUC's (National Unification Committee's) coalition of political parties. The Convenor Group had been conceived of in 1984 by a group of professionals, businessmen and Jesuits who foresaw the need for a quick reaction in the event of a snap presidential election. The group asked the opposition's grand old man and future chairman of *Bayan*, Lorenzo Tanada, the president of Benguet Consolidated (one of the nation's largest corporations), Jaime Ongpin, and Cory Aquino to act as its conveners.

Cory had already started to come into her own by the time the Convenor Group was formed. Filipinos respected her courage in the face of suffering, but politicos and activists were still unsure about her leadership capabilities. The conveners also selected a group of potential standard bearers for a snap election. The list included Butz Aquino, José Diokno, Teofisto Guingona, Eva Estrada Kalaw, Salvador Laurel, Raul Manglapus, Ramon Mitra, Ambrosio Padilla, Aquilino Pimentel, Rafael Salas and Jovito Salonga. All but Aquino, Ninoy's younger brother, and Salas, a technocrat working for the United Nations, held or had held elected office. Cory was not on the list. On Diokno's insistence, the group developed a Declaration of Unity which included plans to remove the US military bases.

Meanwhile the political parties advanced their own scheme. They proposed selecting an opposition presidential candidate through a convention organized by the NUC, which was overwhelmingly dominated by the political parties. Seeing the differences as self-destructive, Cecilia Munoz Palma, a member of parliament and of the

NUC, and Cory Aquino sat down to hammer out a compromise, but the whole process was thrown into chaos when Marcos called a snap election.

This was precipitated by the appearance of cracks in two of Marcos's main pillars of support — the military and the US. In the early 1980s a group of young military officers had formed RAM (Reform the Armed Forces Movement). Among their grievances were that their careers were being blocked by Marcos's propensity for extending loyal generals' tours, that there was widespread corruption within the AFP and that Marcos was losing the all-important battle for the hearts and minds of the people. RAM gained a benefactor in Juan Ponce Enrile when the ambitious defence secretary fell out with Chief-of-Staff Fabian Ver and Imelda Marcos. Enrile's aides spearheaded the formation of RAM's Core Group. In 1985 the Core Group had been hatching plans for a *coup d'état* when Marcos's call for a snap election forced the plotters to change their minds. In the US as well, foreign policy specialists were looking to a future without Marcos. The government's official position appeared in a November 1984 National Security Study Directive (NSSD).

> While President Marcos is part of the problem, he is also necessarily part of the solution. We need to... try to influence him through a well-orchestrated policy of incentives and disincentives to set the stage for peaceful and eventual transition to a successor government whenever that takes place. Marcos, for his part, will try to use us to remain in power indefinitely.

The directive represented a compromise. Foreign policy professionals, in Washington and in the US Embassy in Manila, generally saw Marcos as more of a problem than a solution. An internal report on the growth of the communist-led insurgency had struck fear in their hearts. They started courting the non-communist opposition, and the National Endowment for Democracy, a government-funded organization that channels money to private (generally conservative) organizations abroad, had quietly sent an estimated $3 million to the Philippines to fight communism and cultivate political leaders.

Ideologues and politicians in Washington were less quick to respond to reality. Reagan, Defence Secretary Caspar Weinberger and CIA chief William Casey still favoured Marcos. Back in Manila another powerful institution struggled to find its place in the charged political atmosphere. The Catholic Church walked a fine line between opposition and collaboration. Many priests and nuns had joined one or another faction of the opposition. Some bishops came to be identified as opposition prelates, others as Marcos loyalists. The majority, however, while socially and politically conservative and committed officially to the policy of critical collaboration, had been appalled by the government's recent acts. The CBCP (Catholic Bishops Conference of the Philippines) did not officially break with Marcos until after fraud in the snap election became painfully obvious. Privately, however, bishops advised the opposition. The CBCP also supported Namfrel in its stand for free and democratic elections.

Growing popular discontent accelerated the drift away from Marcos in the military, the US government and the Church. Though ideology and tactics divided the opposition, anti-Marcos organizations belonged to the same broad popular movement committed to the replacement of Marcos with some form of democracy. During the final years of the anti-Marcos struggle the opposition's efforts on many fronts — on the streets, in the halls of Congress and in the hills — combined to weaken the dictator. Members of the opposition in the National Assembly (*Batasang Pambansa*) fought valiantly for reform and even for Marcos's impeachment. Guerrillas also weakened the regime. The NPA's guerrilla war had drained the AFP of its morale and fighting spirit. Fear of the NPA had made many traditional politicians, the US, and members of the military search for alternatives to Marcos and, as 1985 drew to a close, this search strengthened the conservative anti-Marcos forces.

On the evening of Sunday 3 November I sat relaxing in front of my television watching a basketball game. A message appeared on the screen: Marcos would make an important announcement at 11.50 p.m. The broadcast would change the course of Philippine history.

By calling an early election — election day was set for 6 February — Marcos was trying to take advantage of opposition disarray and at first seemed to be succeeding. Aside from the NUC and Convenor Group, a Cory Aquino for President Movement had materialized. Much to the dismay of Doy Laurel and Eva Estrada Kalaw, Cory for President banners had appeared back in August at a rally commemorating Ninoy's death. Cory received thunderous applause as she addressed the rain-drenched crowd from the back of a flat-bed truck in the centre of the financial district. She coyly ignored the call for her nomination, but while the traditional politicians were jockeying for position, her supporters were preparing a draft. Cory had set two preconditions to running: Marcos had to call a snap election and her supporters had to gather the signatures of a million citizens supporting her candidacy. In November her conditions were met.

On 10 November Cory prayed in a local convent while the Convenor Group endorsed her candidacy. On 13 November she had a meeting with Doy Laurel, Unido's presidential candidate. He still hoped to become the NUC candidate, but the NUC was divided. The next few weeks saw intense in-fighting between Laurel's camp and Cory's supporters. On 18 November the newly formed *Laban* (*Lakas ng Bayan*, or Power of the People) coalition of opposition parties and cause-oriented groups endorsed Cory. On 30 November she told Doy, 'the public perception is I can gather more votes than you.' The next day Cory appeared at the Santo Domingo Church where she had first addressed the nation as Ninoy's widow. More than 4,000 people jammed the church and its grounds for the presentation of the million signatures that had now been gathered. Excitement and nervous tension filled the cavernous church as Cory walked to the podium.

'If I were a traditional politician I would be very happy standing before you tonight,' Aquino told the hushed audience. 'But I am not, and so I am very nervous when I think of the days that lie ahead.' She finished just short of announcing her candidacy: 'I assure you, you will hear what you want to hear.' The soon to be familiar chant of 'Cory! Cory!' erupted. The multitudes filled the broad boulevard outside the church and marched by candlelight to Cory's nearby home. Something palpably new had surfaced in the atmosphere. A sense of victory now joined the festive atmosphere common at anti-Marcos demonstrations.

On 3 December Cory's supporters and journalists packed the auditorium of a Makati office building for the announcement. Cory called herself 'the exact opposite of Marcos.' She answered questions with little trouble. She explained she would postpone her decision on the US bases until 1991, seek economic justice and a peaceful solution to the insurgency, and would continue talking with Doy about a joint ticket. Neither Cory nor Doy wanted to run together. Aquino and many of her backers distrusted Laurel, and Laurel's ambition and sexism stood in the way of compromise. Aquino's camp, fearful of playing into Marcos's hands, compromised first and offered Laurel the vice-presidential slot on Cory's ticket. Laurel resisted. Finally a group of anti-Marcos businessmen, including Namfrel chairman, José Concepción, asked Cardinal Sin to intercede.

Sin had a meeting with Cory on 10 December, the day before the final deadline for filing candidacy papers. He convinced her to run on Laurel's Unido ticket. He then sat down with Doy for the more difficult conversation. Run with Cory, Sin said, and you will win, run alone and you will lose. Doy unhappily accepted the cardinal's plea. Close to midnight he changed his application of candidacy to that of vice-president.

Aquino and Laurel launched their campaign with a motorcade to Batangas, the home of the Laurel clan. The night before, Laurel's supporters had hung banners hastily changed from 'Laurel for President'

to 'Laurel for Vice-President.' Unido was out to make a strong showing
in its bastion of support. But Cory captivated the audiences that day.
Even in Laurel's home town she provided the drawing power. As would
be the case throughout the campaign, Laurel spoke first, whipping up the
audience with his fiery rhetoric, before Cory softly spoke about her life
with Ninoy, her family's suffering and her absolute commitment to replacing Marcos's tyranny with a new age of democracy. 'I am not the
only victim of Marcos's rule,' she would say. 'I am only the most prominent victim.' It was a statement with which the nation identified.
Filipinos everywhere listened intently to Cory's speeches, straining to
hear her every word. Aquino's slogan: *'Tama Na! Sobra Na! Palitan Na!'*
'Too Much Now! Enough Now! Change Now!' captured the popular
sentiment.

I travelled with the Aquino campaign on several trips. In Baguio City
in the north and Davao City in the south, in farming towns and urban
centres, people reacted in the same way — lining the streets as Cory's
motorcade passed, waiting for hours to catch a glimpse of the Joan of
Arc who would lead them to salvation.

A whole new style of electoral politics emerged during Cory's campaign — part electoral circus, part popular movement, part religious
crusade. In Davao, members of left-wing organizations broke organizational discipline to support Cory. One labour leader told me he expected
90 per cent of his unions' members to vote for Aquino. I did not have to
travel far to find evidence of his prediction. That evening I met a local
opposition politician in the cafeteria of a small hotel in the centre of
town. A worker and activist in a union affiliated with the KMU soon
joined us. His enthusiasm for Cory's campaign bubbled over. He wore a
yellow T-shirt and a yellow headband with Cory's name printed in red. I
asked him about the boycott his union advocated. 'Everyone I know is
voting for Cory,' he said. He saw no sense in the boycott. 'That is something the leaders are talking about, but I do not think anyone takes it too
seriously.'

The consequential blunder to boycott the election had come only after
much painful debate in left-wing organizations. The snap election had
caught the CPP off guard. In early discussions the party had considered
supporting Aquino, but by the end of December had decided in favour of
the boycott. CPP leaders decried the election as a 'mask for the US-
Marcos dictatorship' — they had failed to recognize the uniqueness of
Aquino's campaign. Instead of looking at the campaign as a popular
movement, the CPP focused on Aquino's weaknesses and the obvious
flaws in the electoral process. The same thing happened on the legal left.
'It is our responsibility to raise the issues,' José Castro, a *Bayan* official,

explained. 'We have to lead the people away from their fixation with personality-oriented politics. We cannot support candidates who are not running on a nationalist and democratic platform.'

This position was so obviously wrong. Cory's campaign was becoming the high point of a broad democratic movement against an often brutal dictatorship. The left could best advance its cause within the ranks of Cory's crusade, or so many believed. Social democrats, small Marxist groups, independent nationalists and individual members of *Bayan* and the underground organizations supported Aquino. *Bayan* lost some of its most prominent allies and leaders to the Aquino campaign. I later learned that several underground leaders had also broken Party discipline and cast their ballots for Aquino. Movement sources in Davao surprised me by telling me that even some NPA units urged followers to vote for Cory. They hoped her victory would lead to peace. 'The best thing that could happen is Cory wins,' University of the Philippines political scientist Alex Magno told me at the time. 'If that occurred it would create a democratic opening. This is unlikely, however. The next best thing is for us to force Marcos to cheat.' He added perceptively, 'we are not so concerned with what happens on February 7, but with what happens on February 8.' Who was best placed to lead the popular movement after election day and Marcos's expected fraudulent victory? The mainstream left was counting on the fact that, having boycotted a fraudulent election, it would be in a good position to assert itself when the prolonged nature of the struggle became obvious. But it failed to take into account the insurrectionary fervour which was mounting as Aquino's roadshow swept the nation.

While Aquino put tremendous human energy into the campaign, the ailing Marcos counted on his machinery to deliver the vote. 'The machinery will make the difference,' presidential assistant Gualberto B. Lumauig told me. 'This is the most important aspect. We have a system of people checking on other members of the community.' KBL officials in Davao City described how the machinery worked by distributing funds to *barrio* officials, teachers, individual voters and local reporters. One Davao opposition politician told me of how his cousin, a KBL *barrio* official, had received 150,000 pesos to distribute to his lieutenants, but had lost half of it betting on a cockfight. 'How am I supposed to compete with that?' asked the opposition politician. 'Here is a guy earning 150 pesos a month — you have that in the slums — you give him 500 pesos and he'll die for you.'

Marcos himself campaigned almost exclusively in Metro Manila. On the stump the strongman appeared, but a shadow of his former self. On several occasions he had to be carried onto the stage by his bodyguards.

Attempts to make it appear as if enthusiastic supporters were spontaneously carrying him failed. The only spontaneous thing about Marcos's campaign was the evidence of his medical problems. Blood-stained bandages masked needle marks on his hands. Once he passed out on the platform.

The dictator used his powers to entice the voters. He decreed rises for government employees, released funds for rubbish collection and other public services, and ordered a decrease in interest rates. At a meeting with members of the Makati Business Club he had signed several pro-business decrees, yet the executives received him far more coolly than they had received Cory the previous day. Marcos tried to take advantage of his foe's inexperience. He redbaited Cory, belittled her intelligence and cast doubt on a woman's ability to run the country. He lambasted her for failing to present a coherent platform. Marcos's rhetoric combined with Cory's early mistakes had some impact on public opinion. A taxi driver in Manila told me he would vote for Marcos because of Aquino's 'communist ties'. But many more felt the communist issue either bogus or unimportant. The key issue was Marcos. And many Filipinos believed, as one small businessman told me, that 'a pig could replace Marcos, and we'd be better off.'

Aquino's campaign problems did not last long. She quickly became more adept at dealing with the press and more conservative in her position *vis-à-vis* the insurgency. Her media campaign improved with the introduction of a team of US and British advisers. Aquino addressed the communist question before an audience of conservative, though generally anti-Marcos, business executives. 'The present regime, in desperation, has been dishonestly drumming into the consciousness of our people the accusation that I will sell our nation to communism,' Cory said.

> Let me reiterate my stand on this. I am not a communist. I never was and never will be. Moreover, I will use the power of the state to fight any force, whether communist or not, that will seek to overthrow our democratic government or destroy our cultural heritage, including our belief in God. But I will respect a communist's right or anybody's right, for that matter, peacefully to sell his ideas to others. I am confident that under a government that enjoys the confidence of the people, ideologies that run counter to our cultural and religious values will be rejected without bloodshed.

Cory Aquino did not rely solely on anti-Marcos broadsides and on defending herself against the dictator's charges. In a series of policy speeches she mapped out her position on economics, social justice and political democracy and tried to keep her appeal sufficiently broad to include the various factions of the anti-Marcos movement. To the economic élite she promised to destroy the monopolies and crony capitalism of the Marcos era; she also promised privatisation, clean government and free enterprise. To the masses she promised agrarian reform, the right to organize labour and peasant unions, an end to corruption, and peace. To the military reformers she promised to dismiss 'overstaying' generals and to purge the ranks of men who were a discredit to their uniforms.

Violence and tension mounted as election day approached. At least 14 campaign workers, ten belonging to the opposition, died during January. By 10 February, three days after the polls closed, the death toll had climbed to 93. Bribery and intimidation increased as the race reached the finishing line.

Both sides assiduously courted religious support. Marcos won the backing of the indigenous autocratic *Iglesia ni Kristo* (Church of Christ), with its block of perhaps a million votes. Mainline Protestants and Catholic religious orders continued their courtship with the opposition. The most important religious organization in the country remained the CBCP (Catholic Bishops' Conference of the Philippines). The bishops walked a fine line between neutrality and reflecting popular disgust. A week before the election, the CBCP issued a pastoral letter calling for clean and honest elections. Cardinal Sin went a step further and issued a personal endorsement of Aquino two days before the voting. '[She] will make a good president,' said the portly prelate. 'I am tempted to ask: Is this a presidential election or is this a contest between good and the forces of evil, a fight between the children of light and the children of darkness?'

US interest in the election ran deep. The US government supported Namfrel and other organizations working for free and fair elections. Pro-Marcos forces in Washington hoped this would add legitimacy to the old regime. More realistic policy-makers knew their efforts would favour the opposition. This they felt would enhance the US's standing in the country and make the political defence of the US military presence easier. Marcos's forces resisted US efforts to influence the election. Marcos agreed to the presence of official US and unofficial international observer teams, but unleashed the latent anti-Americanism among some of his supporters. His daughter led a youth demonstration outside the US Embassy decrying US intervention. Other foreigners and I endured the chants of 'white monkey' as we passed a picket line set up by the young fascists of *Kabataang Barangay* (Village Youth).

Semi-official US pressure increased when, a week before the election, an anti-Marcos Democrat congressman, Stephen Solarz, opened an investigation into Marcos's 'hidden wealth.' There had been a scandal the previous year when US newspapers revealed that Marcos and his cronies had been illegally taking money out of the country to purchase property in the US and elsewhere and that they had opened secret Swiss bank accounts. The scandal quickly spread to the Philippines. It would have been bad enough if the accused had taken much needed private money out of the country, but they had also looted the nation's treasury, including foreign aid. More than two years after Marcos fell a New York court indicted him and his wife for using $200 million in Philippine government funds to buy property in Manhattan and other items for themselves. In total the Marcoses and their associates were accused of stealing up to $10,000 million.

On the eve of the election a handful of colleagues and I flew to Cebu City, where we had planned to spend part of election day with a team of volunteers from Namfrel. On reaching Namfrel's headquarters we encountered a knot of angry volunteers, who had just visited their polling station only to find their names missing from the electoral register. They would not be allowed to cast their ballots despite having registered to vote. Similar doctoring had taken place in many other parts of the country.

Before sunrise the next morning we left for Davao. We drove along the coastal road to the north with Namfrel attorney, Manual Go, and special action team leader, Domingo Juan. The turquoise waters and palm-shaded beaches spread a deceptive calm. Reality struck when armed PC (Philippine Constabulary) soldiers met us just outside town. After a short, tense delay, they escorted us into Davao.

Regional KBL chief Ramon Durano, then 80, ruled Davao City for Marcos with an iron fist. His name was associated with the manufacture of illegal hand-guns. At the time of our visit Durano's son was serving as mayor and assembly-man. 'This is a terrorist city,' a former teacher told us as we passed the town church. 'There is an opposition here but we are afraid. Yesterday they arrested two Unido members. We have not seen them since.' No Davao residents volunteered to serve as opposition or Namfrel poll watchers. Only five of the 60,000 to 70,000 residents of the city dared become Namfrel volunteers in any capacity and they refused to watch the voting. 'I do not know if I will live tomorrow,' said Leanardo Capitan, one of the local Namfrel volunteers. Capitan left Davao before election day. We met him in Cebu City.

Tough-looking men in dark glasses carrying walkie-talkies lingered outside the polling stations. Men in jeeps followed the Cebu City-based Namfrel volunteers around town. The Comelec (Commission on Elections) supervisor refused to let the volunteers from Cebu City serve as poll watchers. He also refused to let the US observer team led by Republican Jerry Lewis of California near the polling stations. Amidst the furore a US consul and his mysterious colleagues set up a communications centre using a tiny satellite dish to beam messages to Manila. They sent frequent reports to their superiors. Such teams had fanned out throughout the country to keep the embassy updated.

An hour or so after we arrived the Comelec registrar received an order to allow us to view the polling. Harassment of the volunteers continued. Cameras were stolen. Polling stations on the outskirts of the town still closed their doors to the volunteers. At 10 a.m. Domingo Juan decided to pull his team out of town. 'This is fraud. We will not be a part of it,' he said. 'We will consider the results here null and void.' Further evidence of fraud surfaced in our conversations with a few frightened but courageous Davao residents. On election eve, the KBL chief had invited the local teachers to his house and had them prepare ballots with votes already cast for Marcos. Some teachers quit their jobs as official poll watchers and refused to sign the fraudulent ballot summaries. One of them spent election day in the plaza church, crying and praying.

We left town with Namfrel and hurried to the airport where our pilot was waiting to return to Manila. He wanted to be back in time to vote. We also wanted to see what was going on in the capital and to hear about what was happening elsewhere.

Election day chaos was sweeping Manila. Armed goons were invading polling stations and trying to remove ballot boxes. Namfrel volunteers and opposition supporters were surrounding the buildings in an attempt to stop the goons leaving with the ballots, and violence was breaking out in several places. Scrambled voting lists had disenfranchised between 30,000 and 300,000 voters in Metro Manila and other opposition strongholds. In Marcos bastions, such as the Ilocos region, Juan Ponce Enrile's Cagayan Valley, and Davao, the KBL had put Operation Zero into effect.

The KBL had promised cash bonuses to the leaders of precincts in which Aquino received no votes. Later Enrile revealed the extent of cheating in his bailiwick. 'In my own region, I know that we cheated the elections to the extent of 350,000 votes,' he told reporters after breaking with Marcos. Others had detected the cheating long before Enrile's admission and it had shocked Namfrel leaders, US observers, Church leaders and press reporters. 'The level of anomalies compared with the 1984 assembly election is much higher,' said Namfrel's José Concepción. 'Large-scale harassment of Namfrel volunteers and voters has been reported.'

Comelec, KBL officials and the government-controlled media accused Namfrel of working with the opposition to sabotage voting results. The opposition, Church officials, and the official US observer team headed by Republican Senator Richard Lugar, rejected this contention. Lugar and his colleagues returned to Washington to condemn Marcos's conduct and the fraud he and his supporters had perpetuated. So did unofficial reports filed by the hundreds of foreign correspondents and members of an international observers' delegation. But they failed to move President Reagan. 'Well, I think that we are concerned about the violence that was evident there and the possibility of fraud, although it could have been that all of that was occurring on both sides,' Reagan told a White House press conference on 11 February.[1] A day earlier Reagan had said: 'We want to help in any way we can, that once the election is over that the results of the election can go forward and the two parties can come together to make sure the government works and we can retain the historic relationship we have had with the Philippine people and the Philippine islands.'[2]

Reagan's administration was mainly interested in the military bases and early statements from the White House revealed little or no concern for the aspirations of the Filipino people. As an unidentified US official told the *New York Times* in Washington, 'the main thing is that we have a strong and stable Filipino ally in the Pacific for the US.'[3] How Filipinos voted did not matter, only that they did vote. This was not lost on Aquino's aides who felt bitter about such remarks. Reagan's foolishness had forced the US team in Manila to resort to damage control — to try to calm an outraged opposition — while the foreign policy professionals in Washington went to work on Reagan.

In the Philippines post-election events moved at a dizzying pace. On 8 February Aquino declared herself the winner (based on results garnered by her own poll watchers and by Namfrel's Operation Quick Count). The next day 29 computer operators involved in the official Comelec tabulation walked off the job, claiming the posted results differed from their tabulations.

Four days later the CBCP (Catholic Bishops Conference of the Philippines) issued a powerful statement stripping the Marcos regime of its little remaining moral legitimacy. 'The people have spoken,' proclaimed the bishops, 'or have tried to. Despite the obstacles thrown in the way of their speaking freely, we, the bishops, believe that on the basis of our assessment as pastors of the recently concluded polls, what they attempted to say is clear enough.' The bishops condemned 'systematic disenfranchisement of voters,' 'widespread and massive vote-buying,' 'deliberate tampering with election returns,' and 'intimidation, harassment, terrorism and murder.' They urged the people to wage a non-violent struggle for justice. 'According to moral principles, a government that assumes or retains power through fraudulent means has no moral basis,' they declared. 'If such a government does not of itself freely correct the evil it has inflicted on the people then it is our serious moral obligation as a people to make it do so.'

On 15 February the Marcos-controlled *Batasang Pambansa* (National Assembly) declared the dictator the winner during an opposition walk out. Official results gave Marcos 10,807,197 votes and Aquino 9,291,716. Namfrel's count, based on 69 per cent of the vote, gave Cory 7.5 million votes and Marcos 6.8 million. A leaked CIA projection gave Aquino 58 per cent of the votes cast.

Cory responded immediately by staging the first of her post-election anti-Marcos rallies. At least half a million people jammed Manila's sprawling Rizal Park. Once again the yellow-clad hordes joined with the red-banner brigade, although this time the radicals hung back, somewhat chastened by their experiences during the boycott campaign. Aquino declared her intention to lead a non-violent campaign of economic boycott and civil disobedience. The campaign would start with a boycott of government and crony-controlled banks, media and corporations. A groan went up when Aquino called for a boycott of San Miguel beer! Consumers were also asked to delay payment of their utility bills. In time, the campaign would escalate to include tax boycotts and other protest measures. Cory also called for a nationwide general strike on 26 February, the day after Marcos had planned his inauguration. Had the popular movement been the only player, Cory's campaign might have gone further. The left might even have reasserted its leadership in the broad democratic movement. The CPP still had plans to bring partisan warfare to Manila and some of Aquino's backers were talking of re-newing a terrorist campaign along the lines of the Light-a-Fire Move-ment.

But the people were not alone in conspiring against Marcos. When Marcos called the snap election RAM's Core Group postponed its coup plans and used the cover of the campaign to broaden its base of support. It organized a campaign within the military for fair elections and developed links with the Aquino camp. The Core Group still saw a coup as the best way of getting rid of Marcos and Enrile's boys, who dominated it, expected Enrile to emerge as the most powerful member of the junta. RAM's plotting was thus resumed in earnest after the election-day debacle. RAM planned to move on 23 February with a quick strike at Malacanang Palace. The rebels would kill Ver and force Marcos to resign.

On 22 February, however, it became clear that an informant had revealed the plan to Gen. Ver. The government arrested three plotters and moved quietly against troops of suspect loyalty. Upon hearing of this Enrile and the Core Group retreated to Camp Aguinaldo. A phone call got Gen. Ramos to establish a second dissident base across E. de los Santo Avenue (EDSA) with his own troops. The rebellion started with fewer than 400 soldiers in the rebel camps. Cory Aquino was in Cebu when the rebellion broke out. She reacted with caution. Though aware of parts of RAM's plans, she did not trust the military rebels or Enrile. She spent that first night praying in a Cebu City convent before flying back to Manila.

On returning from dinner with friends I found a message about the events at Camp Aguinaldo. I hurried to the darkened camp in a taxi. A small clump of rebel supporters stood outside. With the help of a soldier I crawled through a guard-house window and entered the camp. Inside, amidst palpable tension, soldiers were setting up defensive positions and worrying about a possible artillery attack. Enrile, Ramos and members of the Core Group conferred in a command centre. No one knew what to expect.

Fortunately Gen. Ver panicked. By telephone he and Enrile agreed to a one night ceasefire. The ceasefire played into the hands of the rebels who lacked the capability of defending the two camps. In addition, what would become people power was a rather pathetic sight that first night. Only a few thousand brave souls had responded to the pleas of Cardinal Sin and Butz Aquino.

In Camp Aguinaldo tension rose as dawn approached. Dawn, the soldiers said, would be the prime time for an enemy attack. We all tried to convince ourselves that Marcos would not use artillery on a camp set in the centre of a crowded residential area. When the sun rose we breathed a collective sigh of relief. But the coup had already failed and the situation called for a different approach. Enrile now denied having plotted a coup. He declared Aquino the winner of the presidential election and he and Ramos called on Marcos to resign. As the news spread early the next day, thousands upon thousands of Filipinos flocked to EDSA, thereby creating what Ramos called a revolution of the people.

Ver and Marcos had spent Saturday night planning an attack on the rebel strongholds. Marcos appeared on television at 12.30 p.m. on Sunday and hinted at an artillery strike. An hour later a frightened Enrile brought his troops across the highway from AFP headquarters at Camp Aguinaldo to the much smaller Camp Crame. He and his troops crossed the street to chants of 'Johnny! Johnny!' By that time, organized groups of civilians had established themselves on EDSA and were preparing for the long haul. Sandbags blocked the street. Banners fluttered in the air. Vendors hawked cigarettes, soft drinks and yellow headbands.

At 3 p.m. Aquino reached Manila and went into hiding at the home of a wealthy pro-opposition socialite. At the same time, pro-Marcos marines, with their tanks and armoured personnel carriers, came to a halt about one kilometre from Camp Crame. Tens of thousands of civilians flocked to the intersection of EDSA and Ortigas Avenue. The column ground to a stop as the people pressed forward. Nuns knelt in front of the monstrous vehicles.

The tanks turned, the people cheered, the tanks turned again and broke through a cinder block wall into a vacant field used for carnivals and fairs. There they sat for hours. People flocked to the scene, some watched from the tops of buses, others climbed over the walls or through holes to surround the tanks and heavily armed men. Military helicopters circled above. Opposition leaders and military officers negotiated and pleaded. Communications between the field and loyalist headquarters filled the airwaves. Finally, after dark, orders came to retreat. The Marcos loyalists would have to try a different plan of attack. The people had tasted victory. But Marcos and his men were not giving up yet.

At 6.30 p.m. armed men destroyed the transmitter belonging to Catholic Radio Veritas. The station had been broadcasting news of the rebellion and appeals of the opposition and the mutineers. At 7 p.m. Ramos pledged to respect the orders of the 'newly constituted authorities.' The presence of Doy Laurel made it clear whom he meant. Negotiations between opposition representatives and the military rebels had succeeded.

On Monday morning, however, Marines loyal to Marcos used tear gas and clubs to disperse an anti-Marcos barricade near the camp. The Marines took up a position inside Camp Aguinaldo and levelled their artillery at Camp Crame. At 7 a.m. radio reports claimed Marcos had left the country. Enrile and Ramos went outside the camp to announce the victory. The jubilation, however, was premature. Marcos appeared on television two hours later and proclaimed his determination to push through with his inauguration. It was a strange broadcast. Marcos declared a state of emergency and threatened the use of small arms against the crowd. Ver interrupted his commander-in-chief and excitedly recommended the use of artillery. 'We are ready to destroy them, sir,' the sweating and hyperventilating Ver declared. No, said Marcos, we will use small arms. But Ver was right. At that very moment the marines had their heavy guns trained on the rebels.

Col Braulio Balbas, commander of the marines at Camp Aguinaldo, procrastinated. He did not want to fire on his comrades and on the civilians holding Camp Crame, but he also did not want to disobey orders. Fortunately the rebels acted pre-emptively. A force of five helicopters that had just joined the rebels leapt into action. One attacked Villamor airbase destroying loyalist helicopters there. Another swooped down on Malacanang and let loose a barrage of six rockets. The rockets left the Marcos family cowering inside. Orders quickly came to allow Balbas to withdraw from Camp Aguinaldo.

Even before the attack on Malacanang rebels scored an important victory. As Marcos spoke, rebel soldiers attacked the government television studio and pulled the plug on Marcos. His image disappeared from the screen. When Government Channel 4 returned to the air four hours later, it was run by the opposition. A crude sign identified it as People's Television.

At 2 p.m. Aquino appeared at the barricades for the first time. Euphoria swept the crowd as she declared victory and led in the singing of a religious hymn. By this time rebel civilian and military forces controlled much of the city.

That evening President Reagan finally came around and called for Marcos's resignation. Reagan had been under pressure ever since his statement a fortnight earlier which held both sides responsible for the election fraud. Support for Marcos had crumbled in the US Congress, with both Democrats and pragmatic Republicans threatening to introduce legislation to cut off military aid to the Philippines. Secretary of State George Shultz, the most astute of Reagan's foreign-policy advisers, impressed upon Reagan the truth of the situation in Manila. Marcos, in Shultz's mind, was a goner and an obstacle to stability.

Reagan responded by changing his earlier statement and shifting the blame for the fraud onto Marcos. But he stopped far short of calling for his friend's resignation. Instead he sent veteran diplomat Philip Habib to Manila to assess the situation. He still wanted to see if Marcos could be saved. During Habib's trip pressure continued to mount in Washington. On 19 February the US Senate voted 85 to 9 to condemn Marcos for corrupting the electoral process and Shultz assailed fraud in the strongest public statement by an administration official to date. The next day a House sub-committee voted nine to nil to place military aid in a trust fund until Filipinos established a legitimate government.

Habib arrived in Manila on the day the *Batasang Pambansa* confirmed Marcos's election. He met Marcos, Aquino, Enrile and more than 100 other individuals before leaving on the day the mutiny broke out. Despite rumours to the contrary, Habib never asked Aquino to form a coalition government with Marcos. He was also reportedly impressed by her intelligence and ability. When Habib returned to Washington, with the rebellion underway, he joined others in trying to convince Reagan to break with Marcos.

A series of intense meetings now took place in Washington. Habib (whom Reagan trusted) and Shultz forcefully argued in favour of Aquino. Adm. William Crowe, chairman of the US Joint Chiefs-of-Staff, joined in calling for Marcos's dismissal. But Defence Secretary Caspar Weinberger, CIA Chief William Casey and President Reagan still held out. Raymond Bonner, who wrote the definitive history of US relations with the Marcos regime, notes that 'support of Marcos was still the official policy of the US government' until 24 February.[4] But by then events had moved irreversibly against Marcos. He appeared that night on television and declared his intention to fight 'to the last drop of our blood.' People ignored the curfew he imposed and erected barricades around the city. The next day, Tuesday, the Marcos era came to an end.

Cory Aquino was sworn in as president at 10.50 a.m. Enrile and the RAM boys had wanted to stage the ceremony at Camp Crame, but Aquino refused. She did not want to appear captive to the military mutineers. Instead she held the ceremony at Club Filipino, an élite social club with a nationalist heritage. She and Laurel motored peacefully to the club, which demonstrated the lack of control Marcos held over the city. She and Vice-President Laurel were sworn in by Supreme Court Justice Claudio Teehankee. Before a crowd of affluent supporters and journalists, she named Enrile defence minister, Ramos chief-of-staff of the New Armed Forces of the Philippines and Laurel prime minister. The audience was hushed as she delivered her inaugural speech.

> It is fitting and proper that, as our people lost their rights and liberties at midnight 14 years ago, the people should formally recover those lost rights and liberties in the full light of day. Ninoy believed that only the united strength of the Filipino people would suffice to overturn a tyranny so evil and so well organized. The brutal murder of Ninoy created that unity and strength that has come to be known as *Lakas ng Bayan* — people power. People power shattered the dictatorship, protected those in the military that chose freedom, and today, has established a government dedicated to its protection and meaningful fulfilment of our rights and liberties. We became exiles, we Filipinos who are at home only in freedom, when Marcos destroyed the Republic 14 years ago. Now, by God's grace and the power of the people, we are free again.

Following the inauguration I took a taxi to Makati where I filed my report for an American radio network. The operator who connected me to New York told me that the Marcos government was planning to shut down the telephone lines to the outside world — the threat never materialized. Marcos lacked the power to carry out even this simple threat. By the time I had finished it was too late to go to the palace for Marcos's rival inauguration ceremony. So I hailed a taxi and drove around town. Makati's business district was empty. In some parts of town tyres burned as people continued to man barricades. Tanks guarded the bridges near Malacanang, but otherwise troops loyal to Marcos were invisible. Insurrectionists gathered at the Mendiola Bridge approach to Malacanang.

Inside the palace a pathetic scene was being enacted. The Marcoses appeared before a crowd of Ilocanos, lumpens and other loyalists chanting 'Martial Law! Martial Law!' between bites of food from boxes of free lunches. Marcos urged his supporters to come to the palace and bring their guns. Pro-Marcos thugs threatened journalists and others who did not seem to belong. But it was already all over for Marcos. Crowds now stretched from the shopping district of Cubao to Makati on EDSA, a distance of about ten kilometres. Other crowds were already heading for the palace.

People Power had also become a national phenomenon outside Manila. Though most of the decisive events occurred in and around Manila, civilians in Baguio City, Davao and elsewhere staged their own supportive actions by surrounding military camps and taking to the streets. Soldiers elsewhere also joined the rebellion. Some flew to Manila, while others liberated their own provinces. The military mutiny, itself a reaction to popular unrest, had turned into a generalized uprising. When the military and the US withdrew support from the dictatorship it crumbled, but it was the mobilized populace that provided the decisive element in determining the fate of the dictator. The military rebels were not strong enough to pursue their vision of a civilian-military junta.

When Tuesday dawned negotiations between Marcos, Enrile and the US were already underway. Marcos made a last ditch effort to preserve his pride. He called US Senator Paul Laxalt at 3 a.m. to ask if the US could mediate a deal giving Aquino control of the government while allowing him to remain president until his original term expired in 1987. Laxalt consulted the crisis committee and received a firm no. At 9.05 p.m. four US helicopters left Malacanang and headed towards Clark Air Base. Ferdinand and Imelda Marcos, their children, Gen. Ver and other close allies were on board.

I joined the crowds inching towards the palace. People walking, talking, smiling. People clogged the streets heading towards Malacanang from all directions. For 14 years most Filipinos had not been allowed to approach the palace. Military guards turned back all those without a reason to visit. Now the gates were swung open. People surged through. Those who could not wait clambered over the walls. As we entered the palace grounds, many people turned to the first building they saw. It was the administration building. They had no idea where the actual palace was. Seeing me, clearly a foreign journalist, striding in the opposite direction many followed. When we arrived people surrounded the palace. From a second-floor balcony revellers tossed pictures of the dictator and his family to the ground. Framed paintings and photos of the former first couple were smashed by young people joyously wielding clubs.

Earlier arrivals had managed to breach the inner sanctum of the Marcos clan. Some had bolted down a meal waiting on a dining-room table. Others had searched for souvenirs. Books about the Shah of Iran lay near Marcos's bed. Books on and by an array of political strongmen lined his library shelf. Medical equipment had been left in his bedroom. Tom Lansner of the London *Observer* discovered a handbook for renal transplant outpatients, confirming what we all suspected to be the cause of Ferdinand Marcos's ill health. By the time I arrived, soldiers had secured much of the building and were searching it for hidden bombs and explosives. I made it only as far as a first-floor study. My only souvenir — stationery from the president's office.

9

Why Change?

Cory Aquino became president with a mandate to change Philippine society. Her movement appealed to popular demands for democracy, peace and justice, but it also contained disaffected elements of a powerful but divided élite. Neither her nation nor her supporters shared a common vision for the future. Superficially, at least, some changes were desired by Filipinos of all classes, regions and interests. None defended corruption, cronyism or privilege based on political connections. Everyone talked of the need to break the trap of underdevelopment and poverty. All advocated democracy and respect for human rights. The desire for peace was apparent everywhere, especially in the countryside.

But these points of unity masked the great divide between classes and ideologies in the country. They also obscured the fact that corruption and greed reached Aquino's movement. Debates over economic policy, differing views on the protection of human rights and the nature of democracy, and corrupt practices would continue to haunt the nation long after Ferdinand Marcos fled. Many of the negative aspects of Philippine life remained in the Aquino era.

The pro-Aquino élite demanded change for reasons very different from those of the great mass of peasants, workers, slum dwellers and religious and tribal minorities. It was also divided. The aspirations of the nationalists contrasted dramatically with the desires of the pro-Western transnationalists. Some of Cory Aquino's supporters simply sought a change in the country's moral order, while others sought structural changes. Still others hid a naked desire for power and riches behind their lofty rhetoric. 'The big problem with EDSA,' said Maris Diokno, historian and sometime Aquino government official, 'was it wasn't the product of a single ideological or philosophical orientation. You had a mass of people there who were against Marcos the dictator, but perhaps not necessarily against certain structures of the dictatorship.'

As a group, the pro-Aquino élite tended to see the nation's most serious problems in terms of personalities rather than systems or structures. On rare occasions when members of the élite criticized structures, they spoke only of those set up by Marcos to benefit selected industries, partners and cronies. Many affluent Filipinos had suffered through Marcos's use of state power for his own advantage. Such powerful families as the Lopezes and the Jacintos had lost their holdings during martial law to the Marcos government and to the president's relatives and cronies. There were strong arguments in favour of nationalizing these families' strategic holdings — which included the country's only integrated steel plant — but only if the government used them for the public good. It did not. Instead it discredited the notion of public intervention in the economy and eventually turned some of the nation's most powerful clans into enemies of Marcos.

Herminio Disini's behaviour provides one of the best examples of crony capitalism. Once a mediocre small businessman, he parlayed his personal links with Ferdinand and Imelda Marcos into a conglomerate worth an estimated US$1,000 million. The president's golfing partner controlled an empire with stakes in the tobacco industry, banking, property and computers. He had also acted as a middle man in negotiations between the Westinghouse Corporation and the Marcos administration. Westinghouse had won a contract to build a nuclear power plant despite an array of unanswered safety questions and a more credible offer from its arch-rival General Electric. Disini had allegedly pocketed millions of dollars for facilitating the deal. He had been able to build this empire because his cigarette filter business received a tremendous boost in 1975 when President Marcos imposed a 100 per cent duty on imported filters, while exempting Disini by allowing him to pay a paltry 10 per cent tax.

By creating marketing and processing monopolies for his cronies and relatives in the prime agricultural export industries, Marcos eventually drove some of the most backward economic forces in the country — coconut and sugar planters — into the arms of the opposition. Another segment of the élite, the producers of manufactured goods for the domestic market, found cause for dissent when the World Bank forced the government to accept the Structural Adjustment Program. Liberalization forced many smaller manufacturers out of business.

While Marcos's policies affected different sectors of the non-crony élite in different ways, there remained significant overlapping interests between the various sectors of capital. Lines between the transnationalist élite and the nationalist big bourgeoisie became blurred. Groups like the Ayala Corporation, Concepción Industries and San Miguel started out producing commodities for the domestic market, but in the 1960s and 1970s entered into licensing and franchise agreements or launched joint ventures with Japanese and American concerns. By 1971 only one-third of the Philippines' top 250 corporations were entirely Philippine owned and many of these were controlled by the state or the cronies.

Transnationalists and remnants of the big national capitalists found room for agreement on many economic issues. President Marcos's abuse of state power, coupled with a free enterprise ideology, had made many dissidents in the business community yearn for right-wing economic reform. Privatisation became their mantra, state intervention their villain. Business organizations demanded that government get out of business (while demanding that the same state maintain strict controls on organized labour). Collectively, the élite expressed concern about economic recovery, not redistributive justice. With some exceptions, the pro-Aquino élite spoke of justice in the old and largely discredited trickle down manner. The basic economic reforms demanded by all factions of the élite failed to address the serious problems facing the majority of Filipinos.

The mid-1980s were not, however, the late 1960s. New problems could not be ignored. A national debt in excess of US$26,000 million had to be considered. The interests of emerging industries — such as electronic assembly and garment production for export — competed with those of traditional commodity exports and the older manufacturers producing for domestic consumption. New militancy on the part of labour and the peasantry created increased pressure for either reform or repression. These factors contributed to disputes within the élite. Some voices called for the partial repudiation of the foreign debt. Producers for the domestic market tangled with importers and exporters over questions of import liberalization, tariffs and taxes. Disputes arose between elements of the urban élite favouring a moderate agrarian-reform programme to develop domestic markets and bring peace to the countryside, and their rural counterparts resistant to land redistribution.

In his drive for control Marcos had sought to limit democracy in both parliamentary and extra-parliamentary spheres. Aside from turning electoral politics into a sham, the dictatorship enacted controls on labour unions and the right to strike, squatters' activities, political demonstrations and the media. These controls broke down under pressure from the rising popular movement in the late 1970s and 1980s. But not everyone in the opposition shared a common commitment to expanding the extra-parliamentary democratic space. Participation in the broad anti-dictatorship movement led the mainstream of the anti-Marcos élite to take a rather liberal view of political demonstrations. But Marcos's wealthy foes found no need to extend the democratic space to cover labour's right to strike, the urban poor's need to squat and the peasants' desire to plant fallow land. For the élite opposition the goal of restoring formal democracy and competition for government position did not require the legitimization of extra-parliamentary democracy. As the politics of the street reverted to the poor and outcasts after Aquino assumed power, the élite democrats once again looked down upon such activity.

During the Marcos period Filipinos had experienced the close link between human rights abuses and the disappearance of democracy. In 1984 Amnesty International expressed its concern 'that the pattern of serious human rights violations established in the earlier years [of martial law] showed no sign of changing. The organization received frequent reports of the torture and ill-treatment of detainees, often while undergoing interrogation in incommunicado detention, "disappearances" and extrajudicial executions.'[1] The largest number of victims belonged either to the underground left or to the poor rural communities where both the AFP (Armed Forces of the Philippines) and the NPA (New People's Army) concentrated their forces.

Visitors to guerrilla zones and AFP areas of operation, myself included, noted stark differences during the Marcos period in the behaviour of the troops of the two armies. Strong motivation and high morale characterized the NPA in most regions. Guerrilla forces made efforts — at least in the presence of visitors — to pay for the food they ate, the transport they used and the cigarettes they smoked. The military showed less discipline and a lower morale. Poorly-paid soldiers expressed uncertainty about their cause and complained of loneliness on islands far from home. In 1984 I spoke with an army sergeant stationed in a combat zone in the mountains of the northern Philippines. He longed for his home on the southern island of Mindanao and expressed confusion because local women would not talk, joke or flirt with him. Government troops contributed to their poor reception by stealing chickens, refusing to pay for rice and harassing *barrio* folk.

Lack of legal services, difficulty in gaining access to the media and isolation from centres of political and economic power aggravated the human rights problem in the countryside. So did the attitude of many in the rural upper classes. Planters, landowners, money-lenders and local officials wanted to preserve a subservient underclass. Many human rights abuses were in fact committed by paramilitary groups and private armies loyal to members of the local élite. Perhaps the most bloody example of the state and the rural élite combining to abuse the rural poor came when government troops and members of the locally-recruited paramilitary, the CHDF (Civilian Home Defence Force), fired on between 5,000 and 10,000 protesting sugar workers in Escalante, Negros Occidental, on 18 September 1985, killing 27. Armando Gustillo, a crony sugar planter, summed up the callous feeling of the pro-Marcos planters when he told a local radio audience that, 'the issue is between anarchy and order, between democracy and communism. The issue to my way of thinking is not whether people were killed or not.'

Left-wing human rights groups did their best to defend victims of abuse. Filipino priests and nuns, and some foreign missionaries spoke out courageously for impoverished victims. But for the most part the poor were left to fend for themselves. Three times in 1984 I joined fact-finding missions to the countryside organized by human rights groups. In Cagayan province we visited a village evacuated by its residents after a series of military operations. After hiking for several hours along slippery narrow paths we found the villagers camped deep in the forest far from their fields. Makeshift bamboo shelters provided little protection from the night-time chill and the many insects. The villagers, rice and pineapple farmers, told of their woe. Unseen gunmen had shot at two of their neighbours as they travelled downstream to market. Soldiers constantly stole *carabao* (water buffalo), chickens, firewood, appliances and household items. Threats, arbitrary arrests and shooting incidents had driven these farmers into their forest sanctuary.

In Quezon province scores of men, women and children, some dressed in the black of mourning, walked from their mountain *barrios* to meet us in a dusty schoolhouse. We met a young girl whose father had died at the hands of three soldiers he had fed earlier. A young man showed us the scar where his neck had been sliced, he said, by a military man who proceeded to suck his blood like a vampire. We heard other tales of summary execution, mauling and torture. In Cagayan, Quezon, Kalinga-Apayao and later other parts of the country, I heard countless tales of such abuses. Surely some of the victims belonged to banned organizations. Some may even have been members of the NPA. But many victims were simply poor farmers who had the misfortune of living where the NPA and AFP fought their war.

For the poor, the need to stop human rights abuses became a basic issue in this élite-dominated society. Aquino unfortunately brought only limited relief. To many of her middle-class and wealthier supporters the demand to protect human rights became secondary to counter-insurgency. By 1988 the human rights groups of the Philippine left, a handful of prominent individuals and numerous international organizations were once again expressing grave concern. Dictatorship, military influence in government, limited élite democracy and human rights abuses were standing in the way of popular empowerment. This lack of empowerment is also an obstacle to change. Without a broad democracy the poor either have to seek favours from the powerful or use extra-parliamentary and sometimes illegal means to pursue their goals. Most of these goals relate to economic concerns.

A visitor to the Philippines cannot avoid witnessing its overwhelming poverty. In 1988 the World Bank drafted a startling report to the effect that between 1975 and 1985 'an additional 12 million persons had been recruited into the ranks of the absolutely poor.' The report went on to say that, 'The Philippines has one of the most unequal income distributions among middle-income countries: in 1985 the top 10 per cent of the population had more than 15 times the income of the poorest 10 per cent.' And it exposed the fallacy of simply depending on growth as a response to poverty: 'while rapid economic growth will help alleviate the poverty problem, alone it is not sufficient to solve the problem.'[2]

Mrs Aquino's personal wealth did not blind her to the aspirations of the poor during her campaign. She capped her appearance in Davao City with a well-received speech outlining her social justice programmes and Marcos's failures.

> He promised you land reform; he sent you landgrabbers instead and he protected the landgrabbers with the guns of the unsavoury elements who have infiltrated the military. He promised you better housing; but with the aid of goons willing to disgrace the military uniform he hamletted you instead. He promised you that his government would be close to the people; yes, close enough for his bullies to be able to bludgeon you to submission with their guns. And so today, instead of an abundance of the fruits of a rich land, you have an abundance of bloodshed.

Aquino's critique of Marcos focused broadly on the causes of discontent amongst the poor. Her promises highlighted their aspirations. She pledged consultation with the people and popular organizations, 'efficient utilization and equitable sharing of the ownership and benefit of the land,' 'repeal of repressive laws and dismantling of economic structures which keep workers in a state of quasi-slavery,' 'the creation of work opportunities and self-contained communities outside the crowded urban centres,' 'adequate urban housing,' equal rights and autonomy for Muslim and tribal Filipinos, 'adequate health care,' accessible education as 'an instrument of liberation and not indoctrination,' and reform of the armed forces.

The candidate received prolonged applause when she promised to pursue peace with justice. She said:

> The social and economic reforms I propose will go a long way towards solving the insurgency problem. Beyond social and economic reforms, however, should you elect me president, I will, as I have repeatedly promised, immediately declare a ceasefire with the rebels and release political prisoners and thereafter enter into a dialogue with the insurgents in

order to afford the new administration the opportunity to redress their legitimate grievances.

Some of Aquino's liberal and social democratic supporters joined other leftists in proposing sweeping changes to the Philippine political, social and economic system.

They opposed the ability of the IMF, the World Bank and other foreign institutions to influence and even impose economic strategies in the Philippines. Maris Diokno recalled these common aspirations when we spoke two years into Aquino's presidency.

> I think we expected more than just a change in the persons on the top.... We wanted to see some basic social changes that we had expressed during the struggle against the dictatorship, as well as things the president herself had promised during her campaign speeches: Land reform, definitely, repealing all the repressive decrees, a serious reconsideration of our debt problem, a change in the thrust and orientation of our foreign relations, removal of the US bases.

Representatives of the NDF (National Democratic Front) put their particular twist on this in public statements after the fall of Marcos. 'We think there should be a clear-cut and definitive approach that would solve the problems of mass poverty and foreign domination,' NDF representative Carolina Malay told members of the media during the 1986/7 ceasefire. 'This would involve very basic issues, such as land reform and industrialization and a genuine human rights policy.' When I interviewed the chairman of the NDF, Antonio Zumel, he elaborated on the need to free the country from foreign domination. 'We would like the national interest of our country to be asserted finally after more than 400 years of direct and indirect rule by foreign powers.'

Nationalist issues appeal to the country's intellectuals and politically-aware workers, peasants and slum dwellers. But the main concerns of the masses are economic. Identifying the source of poverty and then educating and organizing people into overcoming it traditionally provides the basis for the politics of the left. Leto Villar, vice-chairman of the KMU (*Kilusang Mayo Uno*), told me:

> We have to educate workers on their right to have a decent living in our society. This is why we have an economic struggle. But also, we have to teach them the reality that unless we change the present social structure, meaning economic, social and political structure, wherein only élite groups control the economy and the political affairs of the country, that even if we get the best collective bargaining agreements, we are still slaves.

To national democrats like Malay, Zumel and Villar, Philippine society is 'semi-feudal and semi-colonial.' According to CPP founder José Maria

Sison, the three basic problems of Philippine society are 'feudalism, imperialism and bureaucrat capitalism.' Sison, writing under the pen-name of Amado Guerrero, defined these problems in his early legal work entitled, *Philippine Society and Revolution*. On feudalism, Sison writes that:

> The semi-feudal character of Philippine society is principally determined by the impingement of US monopoly capitalism on the old feudal mode of production and the subordination of the latter to the former.... In Philippine agriculture, the old feudal mode of production persists side by side with capitalist farming chiefly for the production of a few export crops needed by the United States and other capitalist countries.[3]

On imperialism he argues that, 'domestic feudalism is the social base of US imperialism.... The present reactionary state cannot be expected to solve the basic problems of the Filipino people because it is in the first place a creation and puppet instrument of US imperialism and feudalism.'[4] And on bureaucrat capitalism he says that, 'the bureaucratic capitalists would rather pocket the spoils from their government offices and seek concessions from their foreign and feudal masters than fight for the national and democratic interests of the Filipino people. Bureaucratic capitalism is the social basis of fascism.'[5]

Accepting Sison's formulation led the national democratic movement to several important political positions. The first was to emphasize the priority of the rural struggle over all other forms of political action. The second was to define the ruling class as big landlords and the comprador section of the bourgeois or capitalist élite. Other elements of the business, professional and landowning classes are considered potential allies of the masses and revolutionary movement, owing to varying degrees of oppression under the existing system. The third result of the formulation was to fight for national democracy and a democratic coalition government rather than socialism.

Despite the NDF's pledge to fight for democracy, not all left-wing Filipinos have confidence in its commitment to democratic procedures. This doubt stems from questions about the relationship between Leninism and democracy and the CPP's vanguardism and periodic sectarianism. The smaller non-national democratic left tends to emphasize formal political democracy far more actively than the NDF. It has not, however, ignored issues of class and social transformation. They are at odds with the national democrats, however, about what the system is that needs changing. For most socialists and social democrats, the system is not semi-feudal and semi-colonial, but dependent capitalist with certain remnants of feudal society. 'We think that from the time of President Garcia, there has been a definitive shift in social power from the feudal sector to the domestic capitalist block,' Fr Romeo Intengan, a leader of the democratic socialists, told me. 'If you look at the power of the sugar block, for instance, they are more powerful than the ordinary landlords, and the sugar block is not feudal, it's basically rural capitalist.'

No left force denies the existence of both capitalism (generally dependent) and feudalism. What they debate is which dominates the country's economic and political life. Each argument has some merit. For example, big-time, Manila-based capitalists dominate the executive branch of government, but agrarian capitalists and feudal interests control the House of Representatives and many local government bodies. In the rural economy, the capitalist sector is the most advanced and profitable segment; however, many rural poor Filipinos rely on a feudal landlord-tenant relationship for at least part of their income. As the World Bank observed: 'The majority of crop-farm poor families do not own the land they till.'[6]

Despite many dissimilarities, the common ground on the broad left is far greater than the differences. All agree that to eradicate poverty, to assert national sovereignty, to promote the rights of national minorities and of women, and to empower the impoverished majority, the Philippines must undergo a radical restructuring. The political, economic, social and cultural problems confronting the Philippines present a daunting challenge to those hoping to create a just, strong society. With its endemic corruption and abuse of state power, the Marcos era exacerbated existing problems and stunted the political development of the nation. The advent of a strong opposition and its ultimate success with Cory Aquino's accession to power gave Filipinos cause to hope for a brighter day.

10

New Era

Euphoria and pride swept Manila as the city returned to work on Wednesday, the day after the Marcoses had fled. Within days enterprising vendors were hawking an array of yellow T-shirts celebrating the revolution. 'I stopped a tank,' proclaimed one. 'Need to stop a tank? Call a Filipino,' declared another. 'Veteran: Philippine Revolution of 1986.' 'People Power!'

President Aquino and her aides faced a terribly difficult task. They had to build some sort of democracy on the shell of the vanquished dictatorship. They had to construct a government out of the unwieldy alliance that had swept her into power. Not only did Aquino have to deal with her own diverse supporters and Vice-President Laurel and his wishes, but the military wanted its role recognized and a share of power.

Cory sat down to work in the family-owned Cojuangco Building in Makati. Until Malacanang was secured, Cory would live in her Quezon City home and work in her Makati office. She wasted no time in getting down to business and announced her first cabinet appointments on 26 February. Aside from Laurel and Enrile, they included two former members of Marcos's cabinet, Ernesto Maceda and Luis Villafuerte. There were veterans of the *Batasan Pambansa* (National Assembly) opposition, as well as of the Parliament of the Street, business executives and professionals. The key economic posts went to prominent members of the urban élite — Aquino adviser, Jaime Ongpin, and Namfrel chief, José Concepción. IMF fellow traveller José Fernandez remained as head of the Central Bank. The key posts affecting popular interests, labour and agrarian reform, were left vacant.

As Aquino filled out her cabinet it began to reflect the coalition that had swept her into office. Left-leaning politicians like Nene Pimentel (local government), Bobbit Sanchez (labour) and Teofisto Guingona (audit) sat beside human rights lawyers like Joker Arroyo (executive secretary) and Rene Saguisag (press), big businessmen like Concepción and Ongpin, academics like Solita Monsod (economic planning) and Lourdes Quisumbing (education), and older politicians like Jovito

Salonga (good government) and Ramon Mitra (agriculture). The new government reflected the upper layers of the coalition that had brought her to power, but failed to involve leaders of the mass organizations. *Bayan* leaders who also belonged to prominent political families — Wigberto Tanada, Silvestre Bello and Alex Padilla — received important sub-cabinet posts, but no labour or peasant leaders were given high government office.

Despite this limitation, conflicts soon emerged between the government's left and right wings and between advocates of different sectors of the economic élite. Cory Aquino's frequent failure to provide strong leadership gave an impression of chaotic government. A year after he had left the cabinet, I asked Bobbit Sanchez for his thoughts on that initial administration. 'Like everybody else, I had a lot of expectations,' Sanchez told me.

> We had envisioned a good future for our people, and the government could do a lot of things to achieve this. But one thing seems clear now, there was no central plan because government failed to come out with a vision of what it wants people to do. I was hoping Mrs Aquino would at least have a clear path to work on, but this did not happen.

Aquino took some early steps to restore democratic structures and fulfil her electoral promises. She started by freeing political prisoners, including such prominent leaders of the left as José Maria Sison and Bernabe Buscayno, and established a Presidential Committee on Human Rights headed by José Diokno. She promulgated a temporary freedom constitution — which abolished the *Batasang Pambansa* and placed executive and legislative power with her office until a new constitution was approved — and appointed a constitutional commission to prepare it.

Her most controversial early move was to pursue ceasefire talks with the Communist-led insurgents. Military officers and the far right instantly opposed the idea. Aquino initially harboured the naïve opinion that most of the rebels would simply lay down their arms once a sincere government took office. She established machinery for reconciliation or surrender by individual members of the revolutionary movement. She considered her government the legitimate representative of the people and felt no need to make concessions to the rebel leadership to bring about peace. She refused to consider the argument that the revolutionary movement represented a portion of the population. A majority of the government therefore came to see negotiations as simply one ploy in a counter-insurgency programme.

When it became clear that Aquino had no intention of introducing sweeping agrarian reforms, removing the US military bases, reducing the size of the AFP and sharing power with radicals, much of the military withdrew its opposition to the ceasefire and to the talks. By the time the ceasefire took hold nearly a year later, on 10 December 1986, the government had already adopted a counter-insurgency posture. The military used the ceasefire period to gather intelligence and prepare for future battles. The government used it to demonstrate its commitment to peace without seriously discussing the issues presented by the NDF representatives. The NDF also prepared for war, but it at least made serious proposals for a political settlement.

Another problem arose during Aquino's first year in office. Both pro-Marcos forces and members of Doy Laurel's Unido were against Pimentel replacing Marcos-era local officials. Laurel's complaints reflected the political rivalry which existed between his party and Pimentel's PDP-*Laban*, which were jockeying for position as the dominant government party during the first year of Aquino's presidency. Laurel also felt aggrieved because Aquino had abolished the post of prime minister. These political matters had little impact on the popularity of the Aquino government. She had a popular mandate, which was something Laurel and Enrile lacked.

Aquino wanted to keep the promises she had made to labour on 1 May, when she had pledged to free unions from the constraints imposed by the Marcos regime, but the reaction from the business community and conservatives within the government caused her to have second thoughts. When she finally signed a labour reform package nearly a year later, it reflected many of the concerns of business. Agrarian reform created tremendous conflict within the government. A significant majority of the population favoured redistributing farm land and militant peasants had staged a series of protests to demand the immediate enactment of an agrarian-reform law. But powerful landed interests, supported by bankers with money tied up in agriculture, resisted. The debate also focused on the relative roles of agriculture and industry. Those in favour of strengthening the agrarian economy as the basis for future development predominated. Advocates of state-supported industrialization were barely heard over the din of the agriculturalists and anti-statist private sector.

Nationalists and transnationalists clashed early on over a number of issues — the future of economic relations with the US, Japan and other foreign powers, how to respond to the burgeoning debt crisis, and what to do about the military bases. Conflict also erupted between the government and private sector. The dismantling of government and crony monopolies won the applause of the private sector, but members of the traditional élite feared the influence of mass-based organizations and 'leftists' in the government and questioned the competence of some government appointees.

A drift to the right became apparent within months of Aquino coming to power. In October/November 1986 I spent several weeks interviewing peasant, labour and urban-poor groups and found disillusionment already setting in. 'Since the time of Marcos we have been struggling for economic, social and political rights,' Josie Cabrerra, secretary of the Urban Poor Solidarity Committee told me. 'By economic rights, we mean the security of our homes. After the February Revolution, we were expecting new hope for the urban poor. Even after the revolution, the demolition of so many homes and communities occurred.'

Of all impoverished sectors of the population, peasants and farm labourers had the strongest reasons for despair. The government had ignored their demands. Twice in 1986 President Aquino had refused to meet peasant representatives who had marched on Manila. On 21 October troops prevented a march on the palace by 10,000 peasants who had travelled by foot and bus from distant provinces. All Aquino would do to appease them was to grant the peasants a single seat on the Constitutional Committee responsible for drafting the new constitution. 'The Aquino government is not prepared to break up the big farms, especially those controlled by the multinational corporations,' vice-chairman of the KMP (*Kilusang Magbubukid ng Pilipinas* or Philippine Peasant Movement), Felicisimo Patayan, told me. 'We don't have much hope.'

Emerging frustration turned to outrage when government troops shot dead 13 peasant protesters near Malacanang Palace in January 1987. But that was not the first violent assault on the legal left. On 13 November 1986 Rolando Olalia, head of the KMU, had disappeared along with his driver. Their mutilated bodies turned up the next day in a grassy roadside field just outside Metro Manila. Later evidence would point to renegade military men tied to the shadowy right-wing underground. Olalia's killing highlighted the growing tension between popular movements and the country's right. Tens of thousands of Filipino workers walked off the job on the day of Olalia's funeral and joined what became the largest left-led demonstration in Philippine history. At least 100,000 (some say 200,000) workers and sympathizers joined the day-long march through Metro Manila.

The KMU had been relatively quiet prior to Olalia's death. It had worked with the sympathetic labour minister in drafting new laws and ordinances. But the Olalia murder unleashed labour's pent-up anger and frustration with the slow pace of reform under Aquino. The KMU then revealed that 20 of its members had been murdered between Marcos's fall and Olalia's assassination. It held Aquino responsible for what it called the resurgence of fascism.

Frustration with the Aquino administration led some Filipinos to warn against two possibilities: the escalation of armed dissent or the emergence of a demagogue capable of leading a mass movement of the far right. 'If because of these harassments, threats, intimidations, violent attacks upon us, our ranks dwindle,' Alan Jazmines, secretary-general of the newly-formed PNB (*Partido ng Bayan* or People's Party) told a small group of reporters shortly after Olalia's murder, 'then I'm afraid that those who would otherwise have joined us will be joining the others in the hills.' Sr Christine Tan warned of the appeal of a Marcosian demagogue to the urban poor. Up to the very end many slum dwellers, she said, chose to believe Marcos's mixture of lies, half-truths and illusions. They refused to accept the stories people told about him.

The collapse of the Marcos dictatorship had not spelt doom for the Philippine right. As Aquino faced increasing dissent from the organized popular movement, she also faced tremendous pressure from the right. Marcos loyalists staged the first visible far-right offensive when diehard supporters of the generally unlamented dictator began to hold regular demonstrations at various points in Manila, including outside the US Embassy, where they set up camp and charged the US with kidnapping their hero. Former members of the *Batasang Pambansa* re-convened for a day, pretending to be the legitimate government.

On 1 May all hell broke lose when Marcos loyalists went on a rampage, clashing with fringe elements among the Labour Day marchers and with police in front of the US Embassy, which is located beside the park where Aquino was addressing the workers. By nightfall a full-scale riot had broken out in Manila's tourist belt. Far into the night battles between stone-throwing Marcos loyalists and the police raged. Authorities used tear gas and water hoses. I watched as they chased demonstrators into the district's numerous small hotels, girly bars and brothels and thumped them with riot batons. By morning the police had cleared the area of loyalists, but not of the stones and broken glass that served to remind early risers of the previous night's action.

Loyalists followed this up by staging a comic opera coup attempt at the Manila Hotel. Provincial politicians mustered their private armies and on Sunday 6 July joined renegade soldiers in seizing the majestic old waterfront hotel. They swore in Arturo Tolentino as acting president in the absence of Ferdinand Marcos. Soldiers under the command of generals José Zumel (the NDF leader's brother) and Jaime Echeverria mingled with the private armies of pro-Marcos war-lords.

The majority of troops remained loyal to the government. Some who had joined the coup surrendered less than 24 hours after the action started. Before dawn on Monday the military had the hotel sealed off. In the early evening Tolentino left the hotel, met with government representatives and went home — unpunished. The AFP welcomed the soldiers back with 30 push-ups for punishment. Some would participate in future coup attempts.

Questions arose about the role of Enrile and his RAM boys in the coup attempt. Certainly Enrile was already becoming a dissident within Aquino's cabinet. He began accusing the government of being soft on communism and riddled with left wingers. He opposed talks with the rebels and appeared at anti-Communist rallies where he lambasted the government. He and his followers wanted to control the government. At first, they hoped to grab actual political power while keeping the popular Aquino as a figurehead. Such was the nature of the God Save the Queen plot, RAM's first attempt to grab power since the fall of Marcos.

To the surprise of many, including the plotters, Aquino and Gen. Ramos had sufficient resolve to undercut the plot. Ramos mobilized a counter-coup, using his troops on the pretext of preventing an Enrile-led coup. Aquino fired Enrile on 23 November 1986. Ramos had strengthened his hand by suppressing Enrile's plot. He then joined Aquino's conservative backers in pushing to remove the leftists from her government. He argued that their presence destabilized the government by spawning distrust between the civilian and military branches and between the state and business.

Pimentel and Sanchez lost their jobs. Pimentel remained a ministerial-rank adviser, but lost the extensive power he had held with the local government portfolio. His replacement, Jaime Ferrer, took the lead in promoting military-backed vigilantes and civilian involvement in counter-insurgency. The concentration of executive power in the hands of the right and the growing influence of the military made the pursuance of a political settlement with the rebels an exercise in futility. On 10 December a 60-day ceasefire began. During subsequent talks the government failed to respond to the proposals of the left. It merely offered the newly drafted constitution — which did not address the economic or social concerns of the left constituency — as an alternative to the left's proposals.

Peace talks collapsed amidst renewed violence. Rebel leaders had decided the talks were going nowhere and privately decided to pull out at the most opportune moment. The military provided that moment when, as already mentioned, on 22 January troops fired on angry peasants marching on the palace. The violence and terror, generally absent during the ceasefire, returned with a vengeance.

In the face of these problems Aquino restored a structure of formal democracy, in which the old oligarchs shared power with those elements of the new élite not dragged down by Marcos during his final days — notably the urban business community linked to foreign capital and finance. The first phase of restoration involved drafting a new constitution. Relatively conservative members of the economic and political élite dominated the Con Com, but a nationalist or progressive block sought to influence the shape of the constitution. These included Jaime Tadeo, chairman of KMP, José Suarez, a *Bayan* officer, film director Lino Brocka, Sr Christine Tan, and others from such broad left groups as *Bandila* and *Kaakbay*.

'I was hoping the new constitution would address itself more to social justice and national sovereignty as well as to more effective government in general,' Con Com member Wilfredo Villacorta told me. 'But the Constitutional Commission was made up mainly of people from the upper and middle classes, many were lawyers and a substantial number of these lawyers worked for multinationals. Some were big landlords themselves, a lot were businessmen, the majority were US educated.' Lino Brocka became so frustrated with the process that he walked out before the Commission completed its work. Tadeo and Suarez signed the document, but noted their opposition to its ratification beside their signatures. The document was fairly strong on political and human rights but weak on issues of social or economic justice and national sovereignty. It included a far-reaching bill of rights, provisions for popular legislative initiatives and referendums, and a party-list system aimed at strengthening popular representation in the Congress. It called for a ban on nuclear weapons and for the implementation of agrarian reform, but left significant loopholes on both scores. In addition, it did not include a firm stance on the future of the US military bases.

The Con Com established a presidential system of government with power divided between an executive branch, a bicameral legislature consisting of a 24-member Senate and a much larger House of Representatives, and a judiciary topped by a 13-member Supreme Court. Provincial officials would also be elected, but the national government would control their purse strings.

Con Com members sought to limit military power. The constitution called for the separation of the PC (Philippine Constabulary) from the military command, the abolition of the CHDF (Civilian Home Defence Forces) and increased local control over a demilitarized police force. It also established a Commission on Human Rights. Finally it sought to limit the power of the president by establishing congressional oversight over the president's power to declare martial law or exercise emergency powers, and by limiting the chief executive to a single six-year term. Leftists reacted to the new constitution in different ways. Radical labour unions and peasant groups like the KMP and the KMU opposed ratification. Legal left alliances like *Bayan* and the PNB (*Partido ng Bayan*) wavered between a critical yes and opposition. The CPP opposed ratification.

During the referendum the government faced tremendous pressure from the far right. Enrile and his followers waged an all out war against ratification. Days before the 2 February 1987 plebiscite, some soldiers who identified with Marcos mutinied. They seized control of a Metro Manila television station but failed to capture strategic military and civilian offices.

The coup attempt generated chaos within the still young government. Anxious civilian officials urged the military to move swiftly. The military — divided between pro-Ramos, pro-Enrile and pro-Marcos factions — hesitated. Aquino's civilian supporters wanted victory over the mutineers. The military wanted to avoid the fracturing of the armed services. For Cory's supporters, the military put on a show of determination. During the night, flares filled the air as the military pretended to prepare for an offensive. But the real action went on elsewhere as negotiations plodded forward and eventually resulted in the honourable surrender of the mutineers.

To this day many people suspect that RAM had worked behind the scenes to encourage the mutiny. Enrile's public stance — that the new constitution would weaken the authority of the AFP and damage its ability to fight the CPP and the NPA masked his more devious goals. He and his military allies in RAM feared the stabilizing aspects of the constitution and their permanent exclusion from power. Democrats and many on the left saw the plebiscite as a simple referendum on democracy (no matter how imperfect) versus dictatorship or military rule. Cory campaigned for ratification on that basis. Voters approved the new constitution by a wide margin. The military mutiny had highlighted the urgency of restating popular support for the democracy Aquino represented.

The restoration of élite rule within a democratic framework moved forward with the 11 May 1987 election for the Senate and House of Representatives. Not only did the election result in a conservative Congressional majority, but it also paved the way for the consolidation of élite-oriented control of the cabinet. Aquino's executive branch moved further to the right when she announced her candidates for the Senate in early 1987. Several ministers left their posts to run for the Senate. The new cabinet members (now known as secretaries) were primarily technocrats who had worked for large corporations before joining the government. Only Health Secretary, Alfredo Bengzon, and Environment & Natural Resources Secretary, Flugencio 'Jun' Factoran, had had any real connection with the old Parliament of the Street.

The new constitution restored the old way of electing senators and representatives. Each Filipino voter could vote for 24 Senate candidates (all of whom ran on a national basis) and a district representative for the House of Representatives. Future Senate terms would be staggered to allow for smaller fields, but in 1987 voters had to fill all 24 slots with men and women who would remain in office for six years. Four major parties or alliances entered slates: Aquino's *Laban* coalition, Juan Ponce Enrile's GAD (Grand Alliance for Democracy), the remnants of Marcos's KBL, and the ANP (Alliance for New Politics), a coalition of *Bayan*, the PNB (*Partido ng Bayan*) and the VPD (Volunteers for Popular Democracy). The ANP only entered seven candidates and endorsed two of Aquino's: Bobby Tanada and Bobbit Sanchez. Scores of independents filled the field. Like the constitutional plebiscite, the Senate election became a referendum on Cory. The KBL and GAD ran entirely negative campaigns lambasting Aquino, questioning her legitimacy and ability, and harping on the anti-communist theme.

Aquino's slate swept to victory as Cory once again demonstrated her personal allure. The right-wing opposition lost badly. Only two GAD candidates won Senate seats, including Enrile who barely squeaked in, just beating Bobbit Sanchez for the last seat. The Aquino ticket's Senate campaign was generally devoid of issues other than that of restoring democracy. Her candidates represented a wide range of interests and ideas. Her ticket included left-leaning lawyers and activists, traditional politicians, big businessmen, academics, a pro-US labour leader and others to whom she owed a debt of gratitude. Given the make-up of the slate, it would have been impossible to have run a comprehensive, issue-oriented campaign. Instead most of the candidates opted to run simply as 'Cory's candidates.'

Sanchez lost, but half a dozen left-leaning candidates backed by Aquino won. Leftists running independently of Aquino performed quite poorly. After the election the pro-Aquino progressive senators had their power checked not only by their more conservative colleagues, but by a House that was far more conservative on many basic issues. Cory Aquino had supported many members of the old oligarchy in their race for seats in the new Congress. She had also supported a relatively small number of left-leaning activists who had backed her campaign for the presidency. But as with the Con Com, Aquino had picked people from the walks of life she knew best: the landed élite, politicians, professionals and members of the business community. GAD and the KBL also supported oligarchs (old and new) and war-lords. The ANP (Alliance for New Politics) (Alliance for New Politics) (Alliance for New Politics) (Alliance for New Politics) supported human rights lawyers, labour and peasant leaders and mass activists.

Local factors and personalities joined the Aquino factor in determining the outcome of the House election. Old-style elections took place in much of the country. Candidates of the traditional parties made use of 'guns, goons and gold' in running for office. The military played a role by terrorizing supporters of the PNB and the ANP. Aquino-backed candidates won an easy majority in the Lower House, but here traditional conservatives far outnumbered progressives. Close to 70 per cent of the members of the new Congress belonged to landed or traditional political clans, another 15 per cent belonged to the professional, industrial or commercial sectors of society. According to House records made available in 1989, at least 152 members of that body were worth more than one million pesos, four held more than US$1 million in assets. Only two members of the PNB won seats in the Congress.

But the House did occasionally act in ways out of keeping with its reactionary reputation. It was not immune to grassroots pressure and intellectual turmoil on such issues as labour's wage demands. In most areas, however, it remained rooted in conservative politics. It rejected a sweeping agrarian-reform programme, failed to consider seriously bills that would give meaning to anti-nuclear sentiment and neglected constitutional provisions calling on the state to give budgetary priority to education. In 1989, for example, the debt service portion of the budget approved by Congress was four times that of the budget for education. Some analysts have described the 1987 congressional elections as the restoration of the old oligarchy. This analysis is partially correct, but the old oligarchs did have to contend with surviving members of the Marcos-era oligarchy (cronies and transnationalists) and some democrats.

Local and *barrio* elections held in 1988 and 1989 continued the trend started with the national elections. Members of the traditional élite gained control of the majority of elected local offices. Democrats and leftists gained only a toe-hold in the government and Marcos loyalists and Enrile supporters remained a force in particular regions. After the elections politicians moved to consolidate their political machinery. Traditional politicians in the Aquino coalition broke with PDP-*Laban* and established the LDP (*Lakas ng Demokratikong Pilipinas* or Strength of Philippine Democracy). Progressives held out in the PDP, the Liberal

Party and the smaller parties and cause-oriented groups. After finalizing his break with Aquino, Laurel came together with Enrile and they consolidated their forces in the old *Nationalista* Party.

People power eroded under these circumstances. Aquino did nothing to bring popular organizations into active participation in the political system. She became dependent on a narrow base — the military, the élite and foreign powers. The gap between the government and the governed grew wider. Violence and suppression made life difficult for members of the legal left and other advocates of popular democracy. The assassination of Lean Alejandro in September 1987 and the attempted killings of Bernabe Buscayno, Nemensio Prudente, Leto Villar, José Castro and other less prominent activists put a damper on the activities of those working towards expanding the democratic space. New anti-communist actions forced *Bayan* to curtail dramatically its activities in early 1989. A coup attempt in late 1989 and the subsequent declaration of a state of emergency led some *Bayan* leaders to seek refuge abroad.

Perhaps the best example of the erosion of people power can be drawn by looking at the government's response to the 28 August 1987 coup attempt by Lt-Col Gregorio 'Gringo' Honasan and other RAM leaders. Instead of mobilizing the public to resist the coup, Aquino counted on the military to put it down. No massive demonstrations of support for the government occurred. Instead Ramos used forces loyal to the chain of command to suppress the coup.

That Aquino felt beholden to the military could be seen in her moves after the coup was suppressed. Quickly the government responded to military demands for higher pay, better supplies and a closer relationship with the state. Gen. Ramos became secretary of national defence and other military men gained control of numerous, though rarely strategic, government offices. The government also placed even greater emphasis on counter-insurgency. Its support for military operations, civilian anti-communist organizations and a reorganized paramilitary gave rise to new complaints about human rights abuses. None of this was enough to stave off future trouble with the military. Dissidents within the AFP — believers in a militarized state — continued to fight for the hearts and minds of the men in uniform. Aquino's new dependence on the military opened the doors for mutinous soldiers to have an impact far beyond their numbers.

The economic and political élite formed a second pillar of support for Mrs Aquino. The private sector, however, complained about competence. For example, the government had failed to utilize the resources at its disposal and by mid-1989 had about US$3,500 million in unallocated foreign aid.

Corruption re-emerged as an issue early in Aquino's term. Even such strong supporters of Mrs Aquino as Cardinal Sin and Joaquin 'Chino' Roces criticized corrupt practices in her government. No one accused Aquino of personal corruption, but various top officials and relatives were charged with misusing government power for personal gain. Roces, a courageous cancer-stricken old man, gently criticized the new government's performance upon acceptance of the Legion of Honour award on 26 July 1988 at Malacanang Palace:

> Please allow me to remind you, first: That our people brought a new government to power because our people felt a need for change. That change was nothing more and nothing less than that of moving quickly into a new moral order. It was not rice, roads, bridges, water, electricity and such other mundane [things] that people expected of us. It was, and is, much more: A moral order led by you Cory, and by you, my friends now gathered here. To our people, I dare propose that new moral order is best appreciated in terms of our response to graft and corruption in the public service. We cannot afford a government of thieves unless we can tolerate a nation of highwayman.

Roces, who died soon afterwards, alluded to what much of the nation sensed: despite a general belief in Cory's honesty, she had failed to control the grafters in her government and, even, in her own family.

In the first quarter of 1989 researchers reported 25 major cases of alleged graft and corruption involving six cabinet members, five relatives of the president, ten members of Congress and an assortment of elected and appointed local, national and military officials. Thus, deep into the Aquino era graft and corruption remained the issue it had been during all the country's previous presidencies. For the economic élite this provided an attractive complaint. By blaming the nation's problems on illicit activities, the élite could ignore many of the structural concerns raised by the left. But, by sustaining government inefficiency, crippling efforts by honest officials to serve the public and attracting to government office men and women ill-suited to public service, graft and corruption caused problems for all Filipinos. As Roces noted:

> We must insist that public service — first, last and foremost — place a premium on one's record of commitment to the common *tao* [people] of selflessness and dedication versus the all-too-common self-aggrandisement and service to vested interests, relatives and friends.... Somewhere out there are many honest, hardworking, selfless, God-loving Filipinos who may not be a doctor or master of something, or rich or connected by relation, but just the same Filipinos who will labour for love of country and fellow Filipino. They are waiting to be called to serve. Open the door and let them in.

Cory did not heed Roces's advice to open her government's doors to broad popular participation. Instead her government continued to drift away from its democratic and independent roots.

With this happening, the US government effectively courted Cory and her government. Secretary of State George Shultz appeared in Manila with a Cory doll pinned to his lapel soon after Cory came to power. Economic and military aid flowed into the Philippines. After much debate, the Philippine cabinet rejected appeals to renege on payment of part of the foreign debt contracted during the Marcos years, and the government actively sought fresh loans from the IMF, World Bank and the like. By March 1988 the foreign debt had climbed to US$28,600 million.

The government also prepared a liberal investment policy aimed at drawing fresh investments from the US, Japan and other countries. It agreed to an import liberalization programme recommended by the foreign financial institutions, despite opposition from sectors of domestic capital. When members of the US Congress spoke vaguely of developing a multilateral Mini-Marshall Plan modelled on the US assistance programme offered to Europe after the Second World War, official Manila salivated. Pursuit of the increased aid became a primary goal of Manila's financial and foreign-policy establishments.

The executive branch rejected the left and nationalist alternatives to a dependent relationship. Likewise, it rejected plans to infuse the manufacturing sector with direct state support. When the government finally presented its plan for industrial development in 1989, it relied on export-oriented light manufacturing and private sector initiative.

Some members of the business community had begun to criticize the Aquino government soon after it came to power. Though these disputes involved real issues of contention, they must be considered within the proper context. Unlike disputes between the basic masses and the state, disputes between the private sector and the government were not between excluded classes and governing institutions, but between members of the same class.

Many of the new government's policies slashing income tax and dismantling monopolies favoured the private sector. Having abandoned its early flirtation with organized labour, the executive branch nakedly favoured management in labour/management relations. The package of labour law reforms signed by Aquino stopped far short of those promised on Labour Day. The government retained its power to declare strikes and picket lines illegal and to order arbitration.

In response to demands from her élite constituencies, Aquino dismantled the crony sugar and coconut monopolies and restored much of the old sugar oligarchy's economic power. The sugar industry even experienced a brief boom. Profits increased and planters planted more sugar. But dependence on a shrinking export market slowed the industry's recovery. That many planters invested their profits abroad did not help matters.

Aquino also moved to privatize the numerous state-owned corporations. The government sequestered corporate assets worth an estimated US$4,000 million between February 1986 and April 1990, which it claimed were the ill-gotten gains of the Marcoses and their cronies. It ordered the Presidential Commission on Good Government to privatize the corporations it seized. Privatisation, however, moved too slowly to satisfy the private sector. This could be partially traced to the failings of the private sector itself. Qualified buyers simply did not appear for many government assets: especially those termed non-performing assets. But government officials also held partial responsibility. Some officers in charge of state-held corporations enjoyed the financial benefits of corporate leadership and resisted privatisation.

The economy began to grow for the first time since Ninoy Aquino's assassination in 1983. By 1988 the gross domestic product was growing at about 6 per cent per annum. Other indicators also pointed to economic growth. Between April 1988 and April 1989 the value of Philippine exports increased by 24.4 per cent to US$1,800 million and imports by 20.7 per cent to $2,270 million. These rates were lower than neighbouring Malaysia and Thailand, but dramatically better when compared with Marcos-era stagnation.

But this did not necessarily justify dependence on the private sector, nor did it guarantee long-term economic health. Economist Orville Solon told me that the government rather than the private sector had provided the principal impetus for development. Expansion of the economy had grown out of consumer spending, which in turn resulted from higher government and political spending. Solon cited election spending on emergency programmes to repair and expand the infrastructure (roads, bridges, ports) and to create jobs, wage rises to government employees and increased military spending as examples. What is more, in the late 1980s the government drew more than 30 per cent of its budget from loans. Debt-fuelled growth again became part the Philippine reality, raising questions about the stability of the economy.

The infusion of money into the economy led to the expansion of trade, commerce and construction, but not to dramatically increased investment in manufacturing and agro-industry. More imported items appeared on the shop shelves. Construction picked up as Filipinos built houses and commercial centres. Unemployment and underemployment abated slightly, but the underlying causes of economic hardship remained. Instead of addressing the economy's structural problems, the Aquino government opted to borrow and spend its way out of immediate trouble. Government policies did not encourage productive investment, nor did they address the maldistribution of wealth or the debt question.

For some in the urban élite, disillusionment set in and had tragic consequences. Jaime Ongpin had been one of Aquino's earliest and strongest supporters in the private sector and she had rewarded him with a post in her cabinet. The former chief executive of Benguet Consolidated seemed eminently qualified for his job as finance minister. But while few questioned his professional qualifications, he provided a lightening rod for nationalist dissent. He represented the sector of Philippine capital closest to international finance and markets. He argued persuasively for ties with the IMF and World Bank and rejected appeals for debt repudiation.

But Ongpin was not simply a representative of transnational capital. He also believed in good, efficient government. Disputes within the government dragged him down. He grew frustrated with Aquino's apparent inability to bring the government out of its mire of corruption and inefficiency and soon found himself embroiled in a heated battle with Aquino's powerful executive secretary, Joker Arroyo. As a human rights lawyer and former member of the Parliament of the Street, Arroyo provided an easy target for the business community which, along with the media and much of the public, wrongly identified him as a leftist. Arroyo's real problems with Ongpin and the business community, however, arose over questions of competence. His office became a bottleneck, as bills, proclamations, communications and budget requests lingered on his desk. He faced an overwhelming task, but many in the business community considered him not up to it. After the bloody 1987 coup attempt the private sector and the military called for Arroyo's head. With genuine regret, Aquino conceded. But Arroyo brought Ongpin down with him. Aquino unhappily accepted Ongpin's courtesy resignation as well. To bring stability to her government she had had to dismiss two of her strongest supporters.

Slowly Ongpin slipped into despondency and, on 7 December 1987, he shot himself. His tragic suicide galvanized right-wing criticism of the Aquino government, especially in the Western media. Most of these critics, however, failed to note the observation made above, namely that despite the tension between the private sector and the government, the government remained dominated by officials drawn from the private sector. Ongpin's departure from government opened the door to a new offensive by the advocates of debt repudiation. Activists from a variety of political tendencies, various senators and the head of the National Economic & Development Authority, Solita Monsod, joined to try to sway the government away from what they saw as a subservient stance towards foreign finance.

The battle pitted the freedom-from-debt coalition against advocates of strong ties with Western-dominated financial institutions, most notably Vicente Jaime (finance secretary) and Fernandez (governor of the Central Bank). Monsod, a tough-minded academic economist, picked up the nationalist baton and carried it forward with surprising effectiveness. Economist John Cavanagh told me that Monsod had won support within the cabinet for a cap on debt-service spending. But Jaime and Fernandez — who had the ear of the president — went on the offensive. They argued that the country needed to bring more money in and that, to do so, it needed to preserve its good relations with foreign governments, multilateral financial institutions and private banks. A unilateral limit on the amount of money leaving the country to service the debt would displease creditors.

Aquino made her own position clear when she signed a letter of intent to the IMF in early 1989. Like most governments seeking IMF money, the Philippines agreed to an array of constraints aimed at keeping spending down and improving the business climate for export-oriented industries. The IMF also demanded belt-tightening measures. To cool the overheated economy and to attract investors, the government agreed to keep wages down. But placing the burden on impoverished workers did not sit well with the unions.

The unions were pushing for a 30-peso-a-day increase in minimum wages. Torn between the threat of a general strike and her pledge to keep wages down, Aquino supported a bill calling for a 15-peso-a-day rise in Metro Manila and a 6-peso increase elsewhere. On 29 May a general strike hit at least 169 companies, involving (according to the unions) half a million workers on Luzon alone. The full extent of the labour discontent became evident when the conservative TUCP (Trade Union Congress of the Philippines) joined the protest. The strikes led a nervous Congress to enact a compromise bill that gave labour much of what it demanded. Unions called off their campaign when Congress legislated a 25peso-a-day minimum wage increase.

The conflict between the nationalists and transnationalists picked up again after the round of strikes. The new bait offered by the transnationalists was the MAI (Multilateral Assistance Initiative) which, after a long gestation period, was expected soon to bear fruit. The government created the CCPAP (Coordinating Council on the Philippine Aid Programme). Aquino promoted Roberto Villanueva, former head of the US-Philippine Chamber of Commerce, to a cabinet-level post in order to head the CCPAP. Responsibility for coordinating all foreign loans and foreign-funded projects was quickly handed over to the CCPAP, taking from the National Economic & Development Authority its powers to develop medium- and long-term development plans. Monsod resigned her cabinet post in protest and was replaced by a conservative economist.

The new CCPAP development plan ignored the most glaring structural problems facing the Philippines — grossly inequitable distribution of farm land and wealth and a depleted resource base. Instead it emphasized infrastructure projects in five special economic zones, faster privatisation of public holdings and growth powered by more borrowing. Despite criticism abroad, foreign governments and institutions went along with it. At a meeting in Tokyo in mid-1989, the US, Japan, the European Community, the World Bank, the ADB (Asian Development Bank) and the IMF (International Monetary Fund) together pledged US$2,800 million for the fiscal year 1990. Among donor nations, Japan led the way with a pledge of $1,000 million plus $500 million in debt relief contingent on the Philippine economy meeting certain conditions. This led advocates of the plan to boast that in 1990 alone the Philippines would receive close to $3,500 million via the MAI.

But what you see is not what the Philippines gets. Monsod noted that the Philippines would only receive US$250 to $300 million in additional funds in 1990 via the MAI. Much of the money pledged had in any case been in the pipeline before the Tokyo summit. Monsod also pointed out that much of the money would be loans that would add to the country's debt burden. Nevertheless, the transnationalists won the immediate political battle. Reports of a huge influx of new money filled the Manila papers and deflected the critics' arguments. In addition, with Monsod gone, the government's economic portfolios were all in the hands of like-minded representatives of big business and finance.

Soon afterwards, and against a backdrop of festering corruption, poor economic planning, continuing class conflict and eroded popular support, Aquino faced the most serious threat to her rule and to her project of consolidating élite democracy. That threat came once again from the right-wing militarists who ideologically opposed even the limited democracy of the Aquino era. Unlike the left, which needed active popular participation in its struggle, the right (organized in the military by RAM and remnants of the Marcos leadership) needed a relatively small group to shake up and threaten the government. Thus, when several hundred well-equipped and motivated soldiers mutinied on 1 December 1989, they were able to demonstrate the weakness of the government and of Philippine democracy.

The mutineers forced Aquino to call on the US for military backing to suppress the coup. This raised questions about her ability to bargain with the US during the bases negotiations, which were set to dominate bilateral relations in 1990 and 1991. Later she had to call a state of emergency to deal with the festering economic and political problems which were contributing to the instability. Aquino abided by the constitutional requirement to seek approval from Congress for the emergency measures. Congress granted the emergency power, but this did not augur well for the development of a sound democratic order. It was no exaggeration to say that four years into Aquino's rule the Philippines remained a country deep in crisis.

11

Forces for Change: Cory Aquino's Left Wing

Cory Aquino's own limitations only partially explain the failure of her government to pursue structural and cultural change. The conservatism of her government reflects the balance of power within it and in Philippine political life. Radicals and reformers who at first felt that they would be able to work for change within the Aquino government soon realized their mistake and either left or found themselves pushed out of government office. They then returned to the political parties, mass organizations and other groups that constitute what Filipinos call the popular movement.

Though troubled by internal disputes and strategic uncertainties, this diverse popular movement is the driving force for change in Philippine society. Its activists are working to build a movement powerful enough to overcome the many obstacles to change in the country and to set the direction for the future. As Horacio 'Boy' Morales, a former NDF (National Democratic Front) leader now involved in the legal movement, told me.

> Basically, we are trying to develop the growing strength of the popular movement composed of farmers' organizations, fishermen's organizations, women's organizations and so on.... I think this is really one of the most potent forces in Philippine society today. This people's movement should be and right now is the leading group in the effort to democratize the whole country. We should not believe the government can do it.

Bringing together a popular movement made up of individuals and organizations with diverse convictions, contentious and distrustful factions, and legal and illegal components is no easy task. It includes reformers and revolutionaries, Marxist-Leninists of various hues, communist-influenced activists who call themselves national democrats, advocates of Philippine versions of social democracy and democratic socialism, self-styled popular democrats and non-ideological activists. None the less it

132

has periodically put aside its differences to march together for common goals.

In so far as the movement is made up of diverse tendencies, it also utilizes many forms of organization. Activists have created their own lexicon to identify the different types. The underground, for example, is composed of clandestine organizations supporting armed revolution. Sectoral groups include trade unions, peasant movements and women's organizations. Cause-oriented groups include sectoral groups and multi-sectoral alliances united around a common cause. Institutions or non-governmental organizations service the movement through human rights advocacy, research and fund-raising.

The movement also includes political parties. Left-wing groups like the CPP (Communist Party of the Philippines), the PDSP (*Partido Demokratiko-Sosyalista ng Pilipinas*), *Kasapi, Tambuli, Bisig*, the PNB (*Partido ng Bayan*) and an ever-changing array of smaller parties clearly belong to the popular movement. The parties in the left wing of Cory Aquino's ruling alliance — the PDP (*Partido Demokratiko Pilipinas*) of Nene Pimentel and Bobbit Sanchez, the LP (Liberal Party) of Jovito Salonga, and the NUCD (National Union of Christian Democrats) of Raul Manglapus and Bonifacio Gillego provide the movement with some allies in government.

But from the history of élite-led electoral parties in the Philippines, the future role of these groups is in serious doubt. Mainstream political parties have historically served simply as vehicles for personal political advancement; they only laid claim to the banner of change during the political unrest of the 1960s and early 1970s. The LP, in particular, used its strong opposition to Marcos to promote itself as an alternative force in society. Several of these parties shed their progressive façade with the advent of the Aquino government. A long-expected split tore the PDP-*Laban* apart in mid-1988. Pimentel supporters and the left wing sought to revitalize the PDP as a social democratic party. Others moved to rid their organization of its ideological baggage. They formed the new LDP (Strength of Philippine Democracy).

As the LDP slid towards old-style issue-free politics, the remaining parties of the old People Power alliance claimed the mantle of reform — the LP most successfully. The LP's long history of electoral success, its leadership in the Senate and its nationalist stance attracted numerous new recruits, including individuals from the ranks of *Bandila, Bayan* and other cause-oriented groups. Quietly, but true to its historical roots, the LP also recruited former Marcos supporters.

The PDP found itself a much smaller party after its split with *Laban*. It attracted left-wing socialists, left-of-centre reformers and staunch anti-communists personally loyal to Nene Pimentel. It retained members scattered throughout the government and strong roots in parts of the country, but it faced a major rebuilding effort.

The smallest of the three parties to back Aquino, the NUCD, is also the oddest. Its two most prominent members represented its ideological poles. Secretary of Foreign Affairs Raul Manglapus (an intellectual, playwright and jazz musician, as well as a career politician) favoured a traditional brand of Christian democracy. Bonifacio Gillego, a former army intelligence officer and secretary-general of the NUCD, advocated a radical brand of Christian socialism. Gillego may well be the only Marxist to lead a Christian democratic party anywhere in the world.

All three parties faced an uncertain future as the 1980s drew to a close. They cooperated in a loose alliance with *Bandila* within the ruling coalition and shared many common concerns. Logic called for their close and lasting cooperation, but logic has never governed Philippine politics.

Bobbit Sanchez and I discussed the situation facing the PDP after the split in 1988. He said: 'PDP was conceived as an ideological party. Even up to now, it seems it is the only party that has a vision.' The new PDP wants to build on a base of members who share an outlook rooted in a common ideology. But PDP members do not share an identical world view. Some, like Sanchez, cooperate with leftists, others, like the Ferrer brothers, staunchly oppose anything remotely identified with the CPP or with Marxist ideology.

Pimentel stands out among the Party leaders. Political observers often mention him as a potential presidential candidate. Imprisoned three times by Marcos, Pimentel describes his party's ideology as 'close to that of the Socialist International.' He has promoted progressive causes in the Senate and prior to that in the *Batasang Pambansa* (National Assembly). His social democracy may be described as steady reform-oriented politics.

Though it lost members to the LDP, the Liberal Party remains a potent political force, especially in the Senate. It built its public reputation on nationalism and reform, but seems stuck between old personality and patronage politics and new issue-oriented campaigns. Party leader Jovito Salonga commands the respect of many progressive activists, but they remain sceptical about the depth of the party's commitment to change. Bobbit Sanchez offered this criticism of the LP: 'It came out with a 15-point programme, but so far I think only Salonga understands this programme.' This may be an unfair assessment. After all, LP members in the House were the only representatives to vote as a block for real agrarian reform.

But the LP has a split personality. Serious questions have arisen over its recruitment of traditional local leaders (including some once identified with Marcos) and prominent politicians known more for their ambition than their vision. Ernesto Maceda, who served as Marcos's executive secretary, entered the opposition as an ally of Doy Laurel and grew wealthy practising law in New York, is one such example. Maceda gained new notoriety when, amidst rumours of corruption, Mrs Aquino dismissed him from his cabinet post. He had never identified himself with nationalism or reform, but, after the 1987 coup attempt, as chairman of the Senate Armed Forces Committee, he became a prominent promoter of the military interest. In the middle of 1988 the LP accepted his application for membership.

The LP's relationship with Maceda raises the question of what happens when progressive politicians come into contact with the Philippines' endemic corruption. In the House of Representatives, for example, some progressives used funds meant for their staff for other purposes and accepted questionable donations from wealthy interests seeking legislative relief. Charges of corruption even touched LP leader, Jovito Salonga, despite his reputation as Mr Clean and his posts as Senate president and former chairman of the Presidential Commission on Good Government. James Clad of the *Far Eastern Economic Review* reported: 'Numerous business and internal PCGG sources speak freely of moneymaking on the side by close relations of Salonga.... Even the most reckless of Salonga's political enemies hesitated to accuse Salonga himself of any lapse from strict personal probity though two commission sources said privately that he seemed to have "one or two blind spots about his family".'[1] Progressives tainted by corruption may continue to support certain reforms but are less likely to overhaul a system from which they prosper.

All three reformist parties are torn between the new politics of the cause-oriented movements and traditional politics. They can be pulled to the right by the promise of power and to the left by the promise of support from committed activists. For example, in 1989 the LP had been flirting with the idea of softening its stance on the US military bases and was moving towards accepting a short-term renewal of the agreement when opposition from its members pulled it back to its original anti-bases position.

As parties primarily interested in securing government posts, the LP, PDP and NUCD tend to allow a narrow stratum of leaders to make decisions. These reform parties include many who view the parliamentary arena as the centre of political activity and the primary source of change in the country. At best, they believe that parliamentary politics can lead to substantial reform. At worst, they simply use the reform parties, with their populist rhetoric, as vehicles for self-advancement. For these politicians, popular movements exist to help members of Congress promote causes, rather than Congress existing to promote popular demands and aspirations.

Historically, such a view has been proven short-sighted. In the past Congress has only become an avenue for reform when outside pressures have mounted. It did not act on agrarian reform until open revolt broke out in parts of the countryside and, even then, neither party discipline nor popular pressure could overcome the domination of Congress by landed interests. That no potential beneficiaries of agrarian reform sat in Congress was a poor reflection of the political parties claiming to speak for the people.

Another of the reform-oriented parties' shortcomings is their limited understanding of class conflict. Many reformers see class conflict as a Marxist creation rather than as a reality of Philippine society. Their pursuit of national unity blurs the distinctions between different classes behind the 'we're-all-Filipinos' rhetoric. They hold the idealistic belief that change can occur with a minimum of conflict or struggle. So they play down the importance of mobilizing the 'basic masses.'

Senators Orly Mercado and Joseph Estrada are good examples of this, for they top the list of politicians popular among low-income Filipinos. Both men gained attention through the media — Mercado by hosting a popular television and radio programme about community service and Estrada by starring in countless films portraying the often heroic common man.

One evening in 1988 I visited Estrada at his large suburban home. He sat in a spacious study surrounded by staff and family, with scores of constituents waiting outside to discuss their problems. 'I owe everything I have to the little guy,' he told me. 'It's the poor man who made me rich. The wealthy, they laughed at me, at my movies, but the little guy, I entertained him.' He added. 'Now, it's time I give him something back. I want to use my political career to serve the poor.'

Estrada and other politicians sympathetic to impoverished Filipinos may provide charity, they may vote for agrarian and urban land reform, but they do not challenge the political system on which poverty thrives. Of course there are exceptions — Gillego, Senators Wigberto Tanada and Agapito Aquino and a handful of others have maintained links with cause-oriented groups and the Parliament of the Street. They see their position as serving an organized movement rather than an amorphous mass grandly called the people.

If the government is to be used for reform then political parties must relate differently to the public. Instead of offering patronage and promises during elections, they must involve the public at all times, must institutionalize people power. As Butz Aquino put it: 'You know, this thing called "people power" can work both ways: It can prevent abuses, it can also act like "big brother," you know, "everywhere they're watching." So it deters anomalies. I am hoping we will have a political party loyal to this vision.'

Many advocates of this new type of party are found, not among the reform-oriented parties, but in small left-wing parties, like the PDSP and PNB, and in groups like *Bandila*, *Bayan* and *Bisig*. The PDP does, however, have some potential in this respect, its activists hope to use the party to educate and activate the public. As Sanchez reminded me:

> Elections will only be in 1992.... We need to have an ongoing approach to organizing and building the Party. In the building of the Party, education will play a vital role. When you talk of education you talk of educating people not only on the immediate issues, but on principles and on the basic problems of the country. This is a big, big task.

While some activists have joined reformist political parties in an attempt to gain access to political power, others dislike their limited agendas. This has led activists into organizing the PNB and PDSP. Pragmatism, however, makes them willing to enter alliances with the reformers. For social democrats,* this means permanent alliances to defend liberal democracy and promote reform. For national democrats, it means aligning with others only on an issue-by-issue basis.

The PNB won a great deal of attention when it was founded on 30 August 1986 by a group of former political detainees, activists and ex-CPP leaders. That José Maria Sison, the original chairman of the CPP, played a central role in organizing the PNB guaranteed its visibility. 'We hoped to be able to put up a viable party of the left and middle that could compete with the traditional politicians in the electoral arena, win seats

---

* The use of the terms social democrats and democratic socialists can be confusing in the Philippine context. The leaders of the small organizations all describe themselves as democratic socialists. They consider their version of democratic socialism the ideal form of social organization. However, all support a transitory phase described as social democracy. Thus, they operate in a broader movement described as the social democratic movement. When talking about the parties and party leaders, I have used the term democratic socialist. When discussing the movement I have used the term social democrat. The existence of the PDP as a larger organization that describes itself as democratic and socialist makes the situation even more complex as many democratic socialists do not view all PDP members as a part of the social democratic tendency. I have chosen not to include the PDP — though that does not mean that I do not consider it a social democratic party in the common international sense of the word.

and be able to project the nationalist and democratic aspirations of the Filipino people,' said Fidel Agcaoili as we drank coffee in his brother's law office. Agcaoili, an ex-detainee, had succeeded Rolando Olalia as PNB chairman soon after the labour leader's violent death. The PNB organized chapters throughout the nation and sent two members to the House of Representatives, but lost far more races than it won and sacrificed numerous candidates and activists to the guns of anti-communist vigilantes. Harassment, defections and other problems soon left it with only a skeletal organization and an uncertain future.

But we cannot discuss the PNB without first considering the national democratic movement as a whole. In fact the movement as a whole is far more potent than the PNB's meagre representation in parliament would indicate. The national democratic movement is the primary left force in the Philippines today. It commands the largest mass organizations and the bulk of the popular movement. Though the legal mass organizations are highly visible and involve far more people, the core of the movement is in its underground structure with the CPP at the centre.

12

Forces for Change: The Underground

In my time as a journalist I have reached guerrilla zones in different ways. During the ceasefire I rode in a bus to our rendezvous with the guerrillas, with rebel leader Tony Zumel and his bodyguards. On disembarking the guards pulled automatic rifles from tennis bags. Usually the trip was more onerous. In Bicol, two colleagues, an armed guide and I trekked for hours over rolling hills and along dry creek beds, hitched a lift on a country road and hiked for another couple of hours before scrambling up a steep hill to reach our destination. We spent the next several days hiking up and down hills and small mountains visiting the various rebel-controlled communities.

In Cagayan, I climbed off the crowded overnight bus from Manila in the wee hours of the morning. I waited in a small house not far from the highway where the government's army patrolled. In the early afternoon, four guerrillas arrived armed with hand grenades, small arms and a hand-held radio. They put their weapons down on a table and listened as the radio crackled with coded messages. We set out just before dark in a light rain that soon turned into a steady downpour. Two hours later — after having skirted rice paddies and climbed a third of the way up the first foothill of the Cordillera — we arrived at a small supply camp. We spent the whole of the next day walking into the mountains of neighbouring Kalinga-Apayao. Heavy rain turned the narrow paths into a slippery obstacle course. My escorts, who were carrying long arms and burlap bags full of supplies, moved swiftly along the treacherous route. On foot and in small boats we crossed rivers and streams before reaching the centre of the guerrilla front.

After a few days of observing revolutionary mass organizations and a municipal PRG (Provisional Revolutionary Government) in a fertile valley, I pushed on — this time to a guerrilla training camp situated in the thickly forested mountains. Again, the paths went straight up muddy mountain sides. We passed one valley where slash-and-burn farmers had cut trees and burnt the earth in preparation for planting. We ducked under fallen trees and used logs as downward sloping bridges to cross muddy

pits before pausing briefly to chew sugar cane and chat with the impoverished farmers.

We left the tiny settlement to embark on the final leg of our trek. We
soon departed from the noticeable trail and cut through the forest itself.
A barefooted guide from the settlement used a machete to clear a path for
us through the luxuriant foliage. We slid along over the slippery jungle
floor, grabbed trees to prevent ourselves falling and splashed our way
through rapidly rushing streams. Mosquitoes nipped at our skin. Lizards
scurried underfoot. Only after dark could we see the flickering lamps of
the guerrilla camp. We had to ford a final river — shallow enough to
cross on foot — before being greeted by the foot soldiers of the
revolution: members of the CPP (Communist Party) and NPA (New
People's Army).

The CPP, which directs the guerrillas I visited, is the most important
left-wing organization in the Philippines. Not only do as many as 30,000
to 35,000 activists, community and labour leaders and full-time revolutionaries belong to it, but it leads a network of legal and illegal groups
commonly referred to as the national democratic movement. Clandestine
groups, including the CPP, the NPA (which claimed more than 10,000
full-time guerrillas at the end of 1988) and at least 12 sectoral organizations (women, youth and so on), belong to the NDF (National
Democratic Front). Other national democratic groups operate — or try to
operate — openly. The important legal national democratic groups, with
the exception of the PNB (*Partido ng Bayan*), belong to *Bayan*, an
alliance that suffered severe difficulties in the late 1980s.

Conventional wisdom put the percentage of the population influenced
by the revolutionary movement at 20 to 25 per cent in the immediate
post-Marcos period, most of it in the countryside. In 1988 guerrillas were
operating in 63 of the country's 73 provinces. It is in the guerrilla zones,
such as those I visited, that the reality of war hits home. Military operations by both sides bring death to ordinary Filipinos. The sounds of gunfire and the sight of armed men and women surprise no one. Helicopter
gunships, tanks and armoured personnel carriers are the strange links of
rather primitive communities to the modern world. Yet a semblance of
life as usual goes on.

Within its rural zones, the CPP seeks to build stable guerrilla bases, a
regular army and the rudiments of a revolutionary government or dual
power. It organizes peasants, women and youth, introduces agrarian
reform and a harsh system of justice, and provides basic education and
political indoctrination. Here it conducts an escalating war against the
AFP, the private armies of landlords, the state, and other enemies of the
revolution. The CPP emphasizes rural work for two essential reasons.

First, the majority of oppressed and impoverished Filipinos live in the countryside. Peasants, the movement claims, provide the main force of the revolution. Second, it is here that the state is at its weakest. The government rarely provides rural people with sufficient services. Many communities go without schools, clinics, power and transport. In Bicol, we stayed in several of Guinobatan town's hinterland villages with members of the CPP's regional socio-economic staff — young graduates from the UP agricultural school who were working with the CPP's agrarian reform committee to improve the standard of living.

Filipino revolutionaries have a fairly standard way of organizing throughout the country. Outside organizers — either members of the NPA's Armed Propaganda Teams or the CPP's Semi-Legal Teams — start the process, but local people quickly join in. Local recruits form an organizing committee, which works with CPP or NPA members to build revolutionary mass organizations, a local CPP cell, a support group among better-off members of the community and, finally, a KRB (*Komite Rebolusaryong Baryo*) or BRC (*Barrio* Revolutionary Committee). Where neighbouring *barrios* have BRCs, the movement establishes rudimentary municipal PRGs. In time, the CPP hopes these organizations and structures will provide stable base areas for the NPA and a model for a new society.

In 1978, to take an example, an NPA Armed Propaganda Team entered the hinterland *barrios* of Guinobatan. The courtship between the revolutionary movement and the villagers began with a few contacts. David, a former member of the paramilitary CHDF (Civilian Home Defence Forces), became a member of the initial contact group along with two neighbours. Residents of a neighbouring village who knew David through volleyball matches and religious activities had both introduced and recommended him to the movement.

We met David outside his family's one-roomed farmhouse. My companions and I sat on the grass enjoying the first cool breezes of the evening while our hosts described our mission to the local communist leader. As we waited, an NPA squad stopped for a short break. Two teen-aged girls in the ranks giggled as they approached us before marching on. David invited us inside where he sat among some of his 11 children and recalled his experiences with the movement. 'In 1974, I met three comrades who infiltrated the CHDF,' David said. 'They invited me to join the movement, but could not explain well enough why they opposed the system.' He left the CHDF but did not join the movement. It was not until 1978 that organizers approached him again. 'I was invited to a nearby house for a short discussion,' he told us. 'At that first meeting some of my big questions were cleared up.'

After his initial contacts David took the NDF's 'basic mass' and 'peasant' courses. With the help of his contacts he conducted a social investigation and recruited two other *barrio* residents to form an official contact group. The new recruits underwent the same training and launched a more extensive investigation into the class background, economic situation and moral standing of the village. But David's group encountered problems. One of the original recruits became a heavy drinker and was a poor organizer. The other lacked propaganda skills. But David did not give up and, with fresh recruits, the initial contact group evolved into a *barrio* organizing committee. Its members took not only the basic mass and peasant courses, but more advanced ones in the 'revolutionary programme for agrarian reform' and in 'Marxist-Leninist instruction.' This group spawned additional organizations involving more *barrio* residents: a party cell, the sectoral organizations, a *barrio* militia and a support group.

When we visited, the support group was not fully organized, so there was no BRC yet in existence. Our hosts described the process:

> Before establishing a BRC there must be full-fledged organizations for peasants, women and youth; there must be a militia, a consolidated Party branch, and a support group. The support group must have gone through the Basic Mass Course and the NDF 12-Point Course. Once the basic requirements are met, there are elections for slots with the following breakdown of membership: Peasants (2), women (2), youth (1) for a total of five seats for the sectoral groups. The support group elects its (5) representatives and the higher Party organs designate their (5) Party members for the BRC (all of whom live in the community). These 15 then meet to elect the chairman and the five vice-chairmen who are designated to head the five sub-committees of education, organization, defence, health and economics/finance. Without the KRB — *Komite Rebolusaryong Baryo* — the Party is responsible for seeing that programmes are implemented at the *barrio* level.

In Kalinga-Apayao, the area I visited was considerably more advanced. Support groups, mass organizations and party chapters existed even in some towns of the plains of neighbouring Cagayan. The rebel strongholds, however, were in isolated mountain valleys, far from roads, government offices and military camps. Greater isolation, tougher terrain and more time had allowed the organization to grow stronger. The movement had established BRCs several years prior to my visit. One year before, in 1987, CPP organizers had pulled four neighbouring *barrios* together and drawn from their BRCs to create one of the nation's first PRGs.

The CPP District Committee, which covers several towns, appointed the PRG from among BRC and mass organization members. The PRG

Executive Council consisted of seven officers plus the heads of the four BRCs. Representatives appointed by the BRCs made up the larger PRG General Council. Party members played an important role.

The ordinariness of the community leaders and members of the revolutionary organizations struck me in both Kalinga-Apayao and Bicol. Certainly the leaders demonstrated special qualities — especially intelligence, courage and charisma — but their culture, lifestyle and concerns were much like those of Filipinos in unorganized communities. David worries about his family and — under pressure from his wife — thinks of cutting back on his movement responsibilities to take care of his family. Marin, the head of the PRG's finance committee, a middle-aged Jehovah's Witness, and his wife look after neighbours' children as well as visiting guerrillas. Henry, a liaison worker in a roadside village, tries to drum up business as an electrical repairman. Members worry about their crops and look forward to cock fights, fiestas and religious observances. This comes to mind whenever I hear people say that the Philippines will not go communist because the Christian Filipinos will not accept communism.

The PRG, in cooperation with the BRCs, took on many ordinary government responsibilities — taxation, defence and education. A month before my visit the PRG had organized a town meeting at which residents had gathered to vote on a series of local laws proposed by the PRG General Council. The laws governed property rights and responsibilities, penalties for minor infringements of individual and communal property, and the registration of animals and land. The voters (all residents of the valley over the age of 16 were eligible) had attended workshops on the bills prior to voting and had voted by a show of hands.

On national laws the PRG respects the NDF and CPP rules. But herein lies a contradiction. For the first time people in the countryside are receiving some empowerment — through the mass organizations established under CPP guidance. Yet the CPP also demands adherence to its own line and regulations and, more important, does little to encourage debate among rank-and-file members. It also limits their participation in shaping that line. In essence, the CPP promotes a degree of real grassroots democracy while also promoting an autocratic political culture. Organizers in the field certainly hope their efforts will result in a strengthening of the movement's democratic side, although few rural cadres actively challenge the top-down nature of party organization.

In coming years the members of the party I visited hope (through the BRCs and mass organizations) to stage elections for PRG offices. But nobody claimed to have a blueprint to follow. 'This is still somewhat experimental for the Party,' Rebo, an NPA member assigned to the area told me. 'This is the highest type of organization we've attained, and we're still in the process of learning how a provisional government is run, based on concepts we've studied.' She added: 'There's a big difference between theory and practice.' I asked Rebo, a 30-year-old daughter of peasants, what she found most significant about the PRG. She responded: 'We are the ones building what we like. Ours is a real experience in building alternative structures. We can now view the real direction of this revolution of ours. The people and their army are building the type of system we want to build up.'

Barrio-level mass organizations serve the movement in several ways. They provide tools for organizing the mass base. Through them peasants, rural women and youth become involved in the revolutionary war. They provide recruits for the NPA, financial and moral support, intelligence information and havens that are relatively safe from enemy infiltration. They also serve as experimental models and the basis of what rebels hope will be the national government.

Mass organizations and BRCs provide the rural foundation for a national united front, though here the gap between theory and practice often seems glaring. NDF publications, for example, describe BRCs as NDF *barrio* committees and mass organizations as components of NDF sectoral groups.[1] In practice, however, I have never encountered the NDF by name in a guerrilla zone. It was only discussed when I or one of my companions raised it, and then with little or no detail. In the guerrilla zones I visited, the mass organizations did not use the names of the NDF constituent groups. This reflects the underdevelopment of the NDF, which is still more of a cadre than a mass organization. 'We have set up some organs on the provincial level,' Jackie Peralta of the NDF-Cagayan told me. 'We have to establish more councils on all levels, from the lowest to the highest level. Right now, we're trying to build our organizations and councils on the provincial level.'

While the NDF provides the structure for a united front of classes and sectors (not political tendencies), the PRG emerges as a bottom-up governing structure in the most advanced rural areas. The CPP plays the leading role in the movement. This comes from its control of the NPA, its leadership in creating the sectoral organizations, its ability to recruit the most important community activists and leaders, and its control of the educational programmes through which all activists and mass organization members pass. This gives the CPP pervasive influence over the organs of the revolutionary movement; yet, at the same time, a new leadership grows within these organizations. This leadership is locally based, generally popular and dedicated. In the process, the Party itself becomes a local institution. District and front committees, though appointed by and responsible to higher organs and the Central Committee, draw their members from the grassroots.

Ring, for example, was a local farmer before joining the revolutionary movement. He had minimal education and limited exposure to the outside world. Yet the Party saw in him the potential to become a leader in his community. Even as 'mayor' and district committee member he continued to live in the village with the people who had been his neighbours since birth, and to work the fields for a living.

The day-to-day local leadership of the revolutionary movement thus passes from outside organizers to an intricate overlay of local leaders, committees and organizations. The CPP and NPA remain on hand to give guidance and overall direction, but also gain the freedom to work in unorganized areas. This combination of local leadership rooted in the community, widespread organization and regular mobilization of village people, and a presence of full-time cadres gives the revolutionary movement an advantage over the often distant government and more orthodox political forces. There are, however, exceptions to the standard organizing model. In some cases, for example, the underground takes advantage of existing organizations to develop its links with the community. This may mean working with an independent peasant organization, a BCC (Basic Christian Community), or an organization linked to the legal left. The goal, however, remains the same — to organize a stable environment for the revolutionary movement on a local level.

Solid organization does not guarantee permanence. A successful government military operation can break the revolutionary movement's hold on a locality. Where the government follows up that operation with social services and a development effort, the revolutionary movement faces a difficult task in re-establishing itself. The government, however, has an abysmal record of doing this. Its lack of a meaningful programme for redistributive justice hinders its ability to win the affection of the rural people.

The revolutionary movement's work becomes more difficult when it has either erred or been betrayed. In Davao City, for example, a violent purge of real and imagined infiltrators generated distrust. In Bicol, our hosts told us about a village where people hesitated if the movement tried to make a comeback because the original organizer had turned out to be an infiltrator who had subjected the community to the wrath of the army.

In other cases, however, military operations fail to break the hold of the revolutionary movement. The villages I visited in Kalinga-Apayao provide an example. In 1987 the villages came under heavy attack. Using helicopters and fighter planes, the Air Force strafed the area leaving burned-out skeletons of former homes in its wake. Ground troops poured in. The militia and the NPA initially put up a resistance, but losses and continuous enemy fire forced their retreat. Government troops occupied the *barrio* but could not break the people. Faced with hunger and the advent of the rainy season, the military abandoned the valley and the revolutionary movement resurfaced.

A variety of NPA units operates in the countryside: armed propaganda teams initiate organizing efforts; *barrio* militia and local guerrilla units act as police forces and local defence teams; partisan units operate in the towns and provincial cities; and main guerrilla units make war on the state and its army in the plains and valleys.

Revolutionaries want to regularize the NPA and build bases where 'remnants of the reactionary local government have very little or no capacity to challenge' in preparation for the 'strategic stalemate.' *Ang Bayan*, the CPP monthly, has noted: 'Base-building has become the most urgent task of the people's army as it strives towards further strengthening the active armed resistance of the revolutionary movement and the broad masses, and achieving the leap to the next strategic stage of the people's revolutionary war.'[2] The NPA General Command issued its own assessment of its goals in April 1988:

> At present, the central task of the people's army is the full maximization of guerrilla warfare along with the simultaneous and step-by-step development of the components and requisites of regular mobile warfare. This will mean establishing more companies and other bigger formations like battalions; fulfilling logistical requirements and upgrading military hardware; streamlining and strengthening command structures, systematizing large-scale recruitment and training; improving fighting techniques and tactics; improving the capacity to launch coordinated campaigns and counter-campaigns; and continuously strengthening the political and military discipline of the New People's Army.[3]

I observed some of the measures that were being taken to strengthen the NPA during my stay in its training camp in north-eastern Kalinga-Apayao. The camp was located on a muddy hillside across a small river from an open field used as a shooting range. The guerrillas slept in fairly comfortable bamboo and mud shelters. Larger shelters served as a classroom — complete with blackboard and home-made benches — and mess hall. Front commanders stayed in a hilltop shelter, which also stored month-old Manila newspapers, writing materials and their personal weapons and ammunition. In a neighbouring shelter, communications crackled over the guerrillas' modern radio equipment.

Gas-powered generators (carried in by foot and *carabao*) kept electric lamps glowing in this deep forest encampment well into the night.

Here a section of the NPA's Far Northern Luzon command prepared to continue its war. Platoons of experienced fighters, fresh recruits and mass activists underwent hours of military and physical training. They rose at dawn to exercise, scramble over obstacle courses and shoot carefully rationed bullets at distant targets. Political education classes punctuated the day and discussions continued until lights out. Songs, chants and friendly chatter kept morale high among the mostly young warriors. Camp commanders hardly resembled hardened military officers. Julian Sidari, a member of the front command, spent a great deal of time with me, discussing his background, goals and dreams.

Sidari had joined the NPA at the relatively advanced age of 30. Within three years he had become a commander of the north-west front which covers parts of Kalinga-Apayao and Cagayan. According to him, the NPA has several companies (each of about 100 fighters) in the region, but operates in smaller platoons. His Ilocano family had owned a small farm at the beginning of martial law, but had lost their farm to a pro-Marcos war-lord. His parents had packed up and moved across the mountains to the plains of Cagayan, where they had invested their savings in another small farm. Within a few years, however, they had lost this land to another crony, this time one linked to Juan Ponce Enrile. Sidari traced his rebellion to these events. He is a soft-spoken man who moved around the camp carrying a British-made 9mm Sterling machine pistol, a most unusual weapon in the Philippines.

In Kalinga-Apayao, I also met four new members of the NPA — three women in their early 20s and a man in his mid-30s. Most had been active in *barrio* organizations prior to joining the NPA. One had given Aquino a chance, serving as a *Kabataang Barangay* captain. Nilda, a member of a mountain tribe, summarized her feelings when she said, 'I came to realize that I'm more effective in the army.' Before my visit, the NPA had decided to develop a more comprehensive military leadership structure as part of its move to regularize its forces. Where the NPA relied on area commands and squad leaders in the past, it now saw a need for a dependable core of platoon and company commanders.

Sidari spoke with pride of his young officers. Despite their lack of formal education, he compared them favourably with the region's notorious but talented Rodolfo Aguinaldo, a former PC (Philippine Constabulary) commander turned governor turned outlaw. (In the aftermath of the December 1989 coup attempt Aguinaldo and his private army had gone underground after killing a general who had been loyal to Aquino, but had surrendered in mid-1990.) Sidari attributed the regularization to something more basic than revolutionary theory. He said the NPA opted to reorganize in response to the demands of the masses. 'The beginning of regularization was when the masses criticized the NPA,' he told me as we sat beneath the thatched roof of his quarters. 'They said, "you're always talking about serving the people, why are you not attacking the enemy formations more often?" We started regularizing in 1984 and the advantage is regular fighters were able to destroy enemy formations, giving the masses the courage to form political organizations.'

Everyone with whom I spoke in the guerrilla zone agreed that once the political structures (the party, the mass organizations and the BRCs) could provide leadership and organizational stability, the NPA's primary function became military. The NPA regulars, they said, concentrate on tactical offensives aimed at weakening the government's military and economic power and expanding the influence of the movement outside the guerrilla zones. 'The main thrust of our operations is in the plains,' Sidari said.

> If we are always conducting military operations in the interior lands, in the mountainous areas, the influence there is not so wide. Once you conduct a military operation in the town centres or on the highways, the political impact is already there. Then you can manage to organize the masses if you show to them you are fighting for their interests.

Rebel military operations take different forms. The ordinary operation involves a small unit attacking a military patrol or outpost. Occasionally the guerrillas mount larger attacks utilizing several platoons.

Virtually all military operations require some popular support. Most commonly members of underground mass organizations provide the NPA with intelligence on troop movements. On rare occasions, supporters of the NPA have actually joined the operations. Guerrillas in the north spoke proudly of times when community members cheered them on, carried supplies to the battle front and helped cart off state property once the battle drew to a close.

Guerrillas escalated certain controversial forms of warfare after the collapse of negotiations with the government in 1987. They sabotaged property in rural areas, and assassinated police and military officers (including a handful of US military men) in Metro Manila and other cities. The AFP's official mimeographed *Update of CT-Related Violent Activities (As of 30 June 1988),* noted that:

> There was a total of 1,709 communist terrorist (CT) related violent incidents reported nationwide from January 1 to June 30, 1988, of which 692 or 41 per cent were AFP-initiated operations (encounters, raids or ambuscade), 363 or

21 per cent were CT combat activities (ambuscade, attacks on installations, harassments or landmining), 654 or 38 per cent were CT terroristic activities (liquidations, disarming, sabotage, bombing or robbery) of which 349 or 20 per cent were perpetrated as liquidations.

Independent corroboration of the AFP claims does not exist. In all likelihood the AFP bloated certain figures to make the military appear stronger and the NPA more dastardly. It also claimed that the NPA was losing steam and thus adopting terrorist tactics.

The rebels defend these actions as legitimate steps in a revolutionary war. 'Within the framework of weakening and eventually defeating the unjust and violent ruling order, sabotage is but necessary and just,' wrote Celso García, an NPA political officer in *Ang Bayan*.[4] The destruction of four bridges in the Bicol region during military operations heightened the controversy surrounding sabotage in mid-1987. Severe delays in transport between Bicol and the rest of Luzon resulted. Ordinary travellers, including truck drivers bringing produce from the region to markets elsewhere, suffered as much as military and strategic transport. The NPA justified 'unpleasant effects on the people' in the cause of advancing 'the struggle.' 'Revolutionary sabotage operations are not terrorism, anarchism or plain destruction,' wrote García.

> We are conscious of what Lenin taught us: guerrilla actions 'must be ennobled by the enlightening and organizing influence of socialism.' There may be indirect, unpleasant effects on the people, as for example in sabotaging electric plants. But the people know only too well that the havoc and destruction wrought on their lives and properties by their oppressors are a thousand and one times worse than what they have to sacrifice to attain their national and democratic aspirations.[5]

Sabotage provides a vivid example of the NPA's often delicate situation when it perceives a need to heighten its armed struggle. Sabotage can do serious damage to the state, but it can alienate those who need to be won over and provide the military with a weapon to be used in the propaganda war.

Other examples of controversial acts include kidnapping and the meting out of the death penalty to informers and criminals in guerrilla zones. A former high-ranking CPP officer complained bitterly about such acts as we talked in a smoky Quezon City restaurant. He questioned the movement's holding of Korean engineers, local officials and rank-and-file military men as hostages. NDF sources replied that the captives had been involved in counter-insurgency.

Human rights groups, including Amnesty International, have noted the execution of captives. Many Filipinos have complained about the harshness of revolutionary justice. At times the movement acts as if all problems can be solved by the gun. The liquidation of suspected deep penetration agents in southern Tagalog in late 1988 and the massacre of members of a religious cult in 1989 in the south brought this problem into the open.

Sparrow or Armed City Partisan actions in the cities and towns also create controversy. In Metro Manila, for example, the series of liquidations that followed the temporary ceasefire, perhaps as many as 100 before the end of 1987, generated criticism from an array of generally sympathetic activists and human rights organizations. But criticism was not universal. Many of those killed by the ABB (Alex Boncayao Brigade) were guilty of criminal behaviour, harassment and other deeds that made them unpopular in slums and factories. I asked Sonny Reyes of the NPA's Manila-Rizal command: 'What is the purpose of the armed struggle in the city in terms of the overall revolutionary struggle?' He responded:

> First, we consider urban guerrilla warfare as an extension of the armed struggle, in the countryside. Second, we are of the view that political struggle or mass movements should develop together with a strong military component. And third, the presence of armed guerrilla units here in the city can tie down a great number of enemy forces, providing relief to the revolutionary forces in the countryside.

In response to criticism the ABB implemented several policy changes towards the end of 1987. According to Reyes and Marty Rojo it decided to offer perpetrators of minor offences the opportunity to reform and to target only 'some high-ranking officials in the military and police establishments which are mainly involved in counter-insurgency operations.' Reyes and Rojo had also told me of plans to attack foreigners involved in counter-insurgency a year before the NPA killed a US colonel in a daring Metro Manila attack.

Though military operations gained the most attention in Metro Manila, other activities continued. Partly because support for the revolutionary movement is often limited in the towns, the underground remained committed to developing its own sectoral organizations and working within the legal mass movement. Reyes described this as a way of building urban guerrilla bases. As he put it: 'A partisan base has, for it to be called an urban guerrilla base or partisan base, it has three requisites: An area must have a strong people's organization, second, it must have a strong or relatively complete unit of armed operatives and it must, the area must, have a party branch.' Some critics, however, see the movement's urban strategy as flawed. Francisco Nemenzo acknowledges the CPP's influence within the labour movement, but says it could be greater if the Party recognized the capitalist nature of Philippine society. He suggests the emphasis on combating feudalism relegates urban struggles to a secondary status and leads many of the best labour recruits to seek rural assignments with the NPA. Movement documents seem to confirm this criticism.

After a series of tumultuous debates and criticism of some of its violent acts, the CPP decided to put renewed emphasis on developing lower- and middle-level leaders, providing the membership of mass organizations and Party cells with appropriate training, recruiting new members, and rebuilding the open mass movement. The decision revealed a realization that its practice in recent years has been flawed, but not necessarily that the leadership has the answers.

13

Forces for Change: The Mass Movement

A sound truck rolled through a quiet residential neighbourhood in Davao City. Campaign jingles blared through the loudspeakers as campaign workers scurried from house to house handing out leaflets. The candidate shook hand after hand and chatted with potential voters. Scenes from an ordinary campaign? Hardly. The campaign marked the legal national democratic left's attempt to stage a comeback in its former stronghold. The candidate was Larry Ilagan of the PNB (*Partido ng Bayan*). Ilagan was hoping to convince voters of Davao City that the open movement was a legitimate part of the community and an ally in the struggle for democracy.

The legal movement provides the radical left with its public identity and exists alongside the underground. In a multi-faceted struggle, it is important to consider the relationship between the illegal and legal movements. Enemies of the national democrats draw a picture of a unified movement strictly commanded by the CPP. Some activists paint an equally misleading picture of completely independent movements. The CPP itself admits to influencing the legal left. 'Naturally, the Party is interested in and tries to develop links with progressive legal organizations,' said CPP spokesman, Julian Banaag, in a carefully worded 1988 *Ang Bayan* statement. 'We believe that all efforts must be exerted to strengthen the unity and cooperation of progressive forces. But in recognition of the legal status of those organizations and alliances, there are severe objective limitations to Party links with them.'[1]

The CPP exerts some of its influence through its members being placed in important positions in legal organizations. They sometimes even play a leading role in launching such organizations. In some cases the CPP infiltrates existing organizations, thus enabling it to exert an influence way beyond its numbers. In addition, communities organized by the underground provide the numbers and financial support for campaigns staged by the legal left. For example, when I visited a CPP-organized village in Bicol, residents spoke openly of the role their underground organizations played in campaigning for agrarian reform.

152

According to the farmers, after the underground had taught them about the campaign's demands, banned organizations had taken them to demonstrations in Manila.

What keeps some left organizations legal? The simple answer is that, while they include people who belong to outlawed organizations, they avoid formal links with the CPP and advocating violence. 'Our official position is that we do not condemn it if some people take that option, the option of armed struggle, then we respect their commitment, their choice,' PNB's Fidel Agcaoili told me.

The legal and illegal wings of the movement have a complex relationship. The legal left provides an option for individuals who support the goals of national democracy or socialism, but do not accept the primacy or even the correctness of armed struggle. These organizations give leftists the option of pursuing different paths towards radical social change. There also exists a dynamic relationship between radical reform and revolution within the legal left. While legal left organizations would certainly play a central role in an insurrectionary situation, and are preparing for that possibility, they also play an essential role in struggles for change within the existing system. Thus the KMP campaigns for agrarian reform, the KMU cooperates with moderate unions, and the PNB participates in election campaigns.

I asked Agcaoili whether he considered the PNB a reformist or a revolutionary party? He replied:

> I think it is still revolutionary in the sense that the ideas or the programmes it is pursuing are revolutionary. Better still, I consider PNB a progressive Filipino party. Progressive because its political programme is meant to carry the national democratic aspirations of the people. I draw a distinction between reformism and struggle for reforms. If we start saying that the road to power is only through the electoral struggle, then that is reformism. But when you say it is the people who are to decide exactly on how they would venture to push on, we are only agents in arousing and organizing and mobilizing them to attain their nationalist, democratic aspirations.

Developments underground affect the open movement. For example, in Davao City people identified the underground and open movements so closely together that when the armed left committed numerous excesses in 1986, both the legal and underground movements all but collapsed.

To take another example, when debates were raging in the underground after the success of Cory Aquino's election campaign and the failure of the left's boycott, they also moved into the open movement. Hard-liners sought to continue a militant struggle, while popular democrats favoured a more flexible approach to democratic tendencies within the Aquino government. Hard-liners found support particularly in the labour and peasant organizations. This first manifested itself in the plebiscite on the constitution. While multi-sectoral groups like the *Bayan* could not agree on a position and predominantly middle-class groups opted for a critical yes vote, the KMU and KMP opposed ratification.

Leto Villar of the KMU told me that frustration had emerged early with the Aquino administration: 'In the countryside and here, right here in Manila, the so-called democratic space was not felt by the workers. Even when there were changes in the local government, there was harassment in picket lines, killings, using military goons, continued.' Militants felt that their marches, dialogues and pickets were failing to move the government, which continued to destroy urban squatter communities, to enforce draconian labour laws and to waffle on about agrarian reform.

Such frustrations made militants harshly critical of the new regime, though their hard line did not always filter down to the membership. In early 1987 I encountered a KMU leader on a Manila street corner. He told me: 'We are attracting new members because of our work in the factories, because of our militancy on economic issues, but this does not mean they accept our political position. We have still got a long way to go on that.'

Despite the limited aspirations of many of its members, the KMU did call for radical reforms. It alone among the legal national democratic organizations openly advocated socialism. In 1986 it articulated its immediate demands and long-term goals in a series of papers expressing the leadership's desire for sweeping change and continuing political struggle. Its immediate demands included no surprises: restoring the unconditional right to strike; repealing anti-labour laws and drafting a new labour code; abandoning the IMF-World Bank wage-freeze policy; allowing government employees to organize; prosecuting policemen and soldiers for picket-line violence; and restoring maternity benefits.

The KMU went further than presenting its immediate demands. It also analysed the deeper problems confronting the nation and suggested some solutions: 'The basic structural defect of the Philippine economy is its underdeveloped productive capacity,' it noted. As an alternative to the free-market religion of big business and foreign finance, the KMU called for a mixed economy with state ownership or control of strategic industries, an anti-monopoly thrust, a progressive tax structure, and strictly limited room for foreign companies to operate.

Such demands reflected the wishes of its active core. Most KMU members joined the alliance's unions, not to fight for the transformation of society, but to win immediate concessions from employers and the government. In this lies a dilemma confronting left organizations with a real mass base. A majority of the members of left-led mass organizations do not fully appreciate the politics of national democracy or socialism. In addition, the majority of poor Filipinos remain unorganized and open to élite overtures. How then does the movement maintain the support of its radical core (and advance the radical propositions it finds necessary for justice), politicize its rank-and-file members and reach out to the unorganized?

Leftists find the answer in campaigns on specific issues. In August 1988 the KMU staged a general strike demanding an oil price reduction. Two months later union workers walked out demanding an across the board wage rise. And in 1989 members of the KMU and other labour federations forced Congress to ignore an agreement with the IMF and grant a major wage increase.

Though one of the largest Philippine labour alliances, the KMU still represents a relatively small percentage of the overall workforce — many of whom work in small shops or on farms. To mobilize effective campaigns, it needs to cooperate with generally less radical workers' organizations. The KMU pursues alliances at the local and national level. I spoke with Leto Villar about alliance work at the community level.

> Consolidating the labour movement can only be done by pursuing a new concept of organization work, meaning putting more emphasis on the territorial concept of organizing Filipino workers through municipal, district, city, provincial and regional organizing. Building alliances gives you the chance of inviting different local unions regardless of national affiliation. Very basic issues of salary and the dismantling of repressive labour policy can be raised. You could elevate the discussion in these alliances through the introduction of the KMU curriculum to workers from different unions and federations.

Shortly before having that conversation with Leto, I visited some KMU organizers in the industrial area of Valenzuela. Valenzuela is one of several industrial towns surrounding Metro Manila. It hosts scores of small factories manufacturing garments, weaving textiles and assembling electronics circuitry. It is a crowded, dirty town. Workers live in small houses in established neighbourhoods and shanties in hastily-constructed *barrios* bordering the factories. In Valenzuela, KMU organizers set about the task of building not only its own affiliated unions, but a local alliance of workers belonging to different unions. For a while Valenzuela claimed the title of strike capital of the Philippines.

Radical labour leaders also worked to build and maintain national alliances. The LACC (Labour Advisory & Consultative Council) emerged as the main national labour alliance in the immediate post-

Marcos era. It attracted all the labour federations except the US-backed
TUCP. Villar explained that:

> Actually, the LACC is a tactical alliance of different labour organizations.
> Within the LACC, aside from the KMU, one finds the FFW or Federation of
> Free Workers, WFTU (World Federation of Trade Unions, a Soviet-in-
> fluenced international organization) affiliates and the LMLC or *Lakas
> Manggagawa* (Workers' Power) Labour Centre. They have differences in
> ideological and political views, but they unite on specific issues.

Villar described the KMU's participation in the LACC as a sign of
maturity and the need to take a more active role in uniting the labour
movement. 'We are now the dominant labour centre and with that have a
greater responsibility to the labour movement in the country: that is to
unite workers as one,' he told me. Ironically, this leads the KMU into a
sort of uneasy cooperation with the very government and system it des-
pises. For, in its attempts to develop mutually acceptable policies, the
KMU participates with the LACC in the tripartite government, labour
and business committee.

The KMU is one of the two largest labour alliances in the country,
the other being the TUCP, and it sets the pace for the whole of organized
labour. But like other unions it represents only a minority of wage
earners in the Philippines. It claims to have more than half a million
members, though this may be an exaggeration. What is certain is that
collective bargaining agreements covered only 262,000 workers in 1985,
which is barely 3 per cent of all employees or just a little over 1 per cent
of the total workforce.[2]

Organizing workers into bargaining units reflects one side of the
KMU's role. But it also fights for socialism and national democracy.
Openly, KMU leads or joins public campaigns for radical reform.
Privately, some KMU leaders and members, who also belong to the CPP,
view their work as preparation for a revolutionary transfer of power.
These cadres use the KMU to recruit members to the underground and to
develop labour's insurrectionary potential.

The same duality faces other open left groups led by national
democrats, such as the peasant's KMP. KMP activities include advocating agrarian reform through land occupations and protest marches, including the one that ended with 13 deaths in 1987, as well as more
development-oriented activities. The KMP's local affiliates have taken
matters into their own hands by illegally seizing idle farm lands
belonging to Marcos cronies. Like the KMU, the KMP also belongs to a
broad alliance involving peasant groups of different political
orientations. The KMP joined the CPAR (Congress for a People's

Agrarian Reform) despite its being a social democratic initiative (see Chapter 22 for more on the KMP, CPAR and the peasant struggle).

National democrats also work in coalitions of fishermen, students, women, professionals and the urban poor. They join issue-oriented alliances tackling such concerns as the foreign debt and threats to civil liberties. The women's and students' movements are probably the most important sectoral fronts after those of the workers and peasants. Students have long catalysed other segments of the population. Recent years have not been easy for the national democratic student movement. In the aftermath of Marcos's fall many students simply grew tired of politics, especially in the élite universities (including the UP) which had spawned many of the radical and revolutionary movements' top leaders. Also, the national democrats, who long dominated campus political life, have been seriously challenged in recent years by social democrats and other political forces that offer an opportunity to combine political activism with a normal life.

Filipinos know the largest legal coalition in the radical women's movement as Gabriela. Aside from focusing on women's concerns, such as the exploitation of women in bars and brothels, mail-order brides and the high costs of running a household and feeding children, Gabriela tackles broader issues such as the debt, nuclear power and environmentalism. National democrats also participate in an array of more narrowly-defined women's organizations.

Two of the most prominent issue-oriented alliances of the post-Marcos era have been the Freedom From Debt Coalition and the National Movement for Civil Liberties. In the Freedom from Debt Coalition, national democrats work with radicals of various hues and generally moderate politicians. In the National Movement for Civil Liberties, prominent national democrats play only a secondary role, for organizers of the group have paid particular attention to limiting their influence.

For most of the late 1980s *Bayan* formed the core of the legal national democratic movement. It coordinated broadly-focused political campaigns involving groups like the KMU, KMP, Gabriela and other like-minded organizations. It also provided an outlet for independent left activists comfortable with the arguments of national democracy, but uncomfortable with the discipline required by underground collectives.

Bayan faltered during the presidential campaign leading up to the 1986 election and again after Cory Aquino came to power. Its boycott had alienated many sympathetic individuals, including some middle-class and affluent activists. Debates and defections slowed the group's progress after Cory came to power. *Bayan* then found itself at the centre of a violent attack on the left in general and on the legal movement in particular.

Rolando Olalia was the first prominent *Bayan* leader to be murdered. He would not be the last. In September 1987 unknown assassins took the life of *Bayan*'s charismatic secretary general, Lean Alejandro. Alejandro was still in his 20s when assassins pumped his body full of bullets. With him, the movement lost its brightest young leader and a symbol of hope. He had waged a valiant electoral campaign against Cory's sister-in-law during congressional elections earlier in the year. He symbolized *Bayan*'s appeal to young people, the middle class and nationalist politicians. He was articulate, soft spoken and likeable.

Attacks on *Bayan* and its affiliates did not end with Lean's assassination. Murder and mayhem drove many prominent activists into hiding, out of the organization or into exile. The situation became so bad that *The Economist* reported its demise in September 1989, two months before Alejandro's successor as secretary general sought refuge in Canada. 'The Philippines' defence secretary, Mr Fidel Ramos, has been accused of destroying legal front organizations as a way of undermining the rebels behind them,' wrote the magazine's Manila correspondent. 'Army surveillance and harassment, as well as kidnapping and assassination of more than a dozen officials finished off the largest communist-controlled political party, *Bayan*, last year.'[3]

Movement sources do not dispute *Bayan*'s troubles. One told me that the organization had stopped acting as it had when its staff could no longer function openly. But he said *Bayan* continued to exist as a skeletal organization and that activists hoped to rebuild it in the 1990s. The likelihood of this happening will depend as much on internal as external factors. For, as well as suffering from attacks from the military and police, *Bayan* suffered when the underground organizations debated the role of the open mass movement. Through much of the late 1980s, after the collapse of the ceasefire, the CPP laid emphasis on military work and the expansion of underground organizations.

In late 1989 the underground leadership of the national democratic movement announced plans to focus more attention on the mass struggle. Where the legal movement goes will tell us something about its success.

14

Forces for Change: The Debate

Radicals, especially in the CPP (Communist Party), faced tough choices following the fall of Marcos. No longer did they share a common enemy with a broad mass movement. Instead they confronted a government put in place by a popular uprising. The roots of the national democrats' difficulties lay in their boycott of the snap presidential election Marcos had held in February 1986. The boycott symbolized all that was wrong with the radical left and sparked off an intense debate which shook the very foundations of the movement. The CPP itself declared the boycott a mistake:

> For more than 17 of the 20 years... Marcos... was in power, the Communist Party of the Philippines had played a leading role in our people's anti-fascist, anti-imperialist and anti-feudal struggles. Yet, where the people saw in the February 7 snap presidential election a chance to deliver a crippling blow on the Marcos regime... the Executive Committee of the Party Central Committee (EC-CC) saw it merely as 'a noisy and empty political battle' among factions in the ruling classes.
>
> And when the aroused and militant people moved spontaneously but resolutely to oust the hated regime last February 22-25, the Party and its forces were... in large measure... on the sidelines, unable to lead or influence the hundreds of thousands of people who moved with amazing speed and decisiveness to overthrow the regime. This was because of the Party's official policy enunciated by the EC-CC to launch an active and vigorous boycott campaign *vis-à-vis* the election, a policy that was based, as the events showed, on an incorrect reading of the political situation.[1]

Dissent and debate spurred by the boycott debacle brought fresh intellectual life to a movement that often seemed more centralized than democratic. Debate flourished. Position papers circulated. Groupings favouring popular democracy and insurrection challenged advocates of the traditional protracted people's war.

Middle-class allies, many of whom accepted Party leadership during the anti-Marcos struggle, questioned the infallibility of the revolutionary leadership and the propriety of armed struggle against a popular regime. One prominent middle-class activist, a businessman, met his underground contacts after Aquino's rise to power. They asked him to join a new united front effort. He accepted, but insisted on the CPP respecting the independence of the new alliance. When it did not, he left the new alliance and it collapsed.

Another issue added to the growing distance between the movement and its middle-class allies. The movement refused to accept the wisdom of participating in electoral politics. 'We have had experiences of government officials, even at the local levels, who had sentiments for the people,' Jackie Peralta of the NDF in Cagayan told me.

> But if you are in a bureaucratic form of reactionary government, you are forced to enforce the bureaucracy's law and order, and that is where the contradiction comes in. The aim of the government is to break the structure of the revolutionary movement, while the aim of the revolutionary movement is to break the structure of the bureaucracy. So, as much as possible, we do not encourage people to run.

This distrust of the electoral process finds its roots in the early history of the CPP. The founders of the re-established Party rejected the right opportunism of the old Communist Party's turn to parliamentary politics in the 1950s. Amado Guerrero's 1974 *Specific Characteristics of Our People's War* reiterated the rejection of the parliamentary road:

> To have a few seats in a reactionary parliament and to have no army in our country is to play a fool's game. Any time that the enemy chooses to change the rules of the game, say the constitution, he would be able to do so at the people's expense. Between armed struggle and parliamentary struggle, the former is principal and the latter is secondary.[2]

The CPP continued to denounce elections as 'props for counter-revolution' and a 'reactionary circus,' adding harsh words for 'those elements who spread the illusion that parliamentary processes can serve to effect fundamental change.' Nevertheless, the Party gave a green light to legal national democratic organizations that, after Aquino came to power, wanted to join in both congressional and local elections.[3]

National democrats envisioned the PNB (*Partido ng Bayan*) as the primary vehicle for radical electoral activities. But PNB leaders knew what difficulties they faced. Candidates who ran for office under the PNB did not always get the support they expected from movement resources in their districts. Mass organizations were fickle in delivering support. In some areas the traditional stance of boycott reigned.

Two candidates in Metro Manila complained to me about the unreliability of the movement's support for their campaigns. As dedicated activists in the Parliament of the Street and as businessmen, they opted to run with movement support. One candidate told me of the on-again, off-again support from organized labour and slum dwellers in his district. As he put it:

> One woman in particular really liked me and wanted to support me. She lived in one of the slum communities and kept coming back even after her organization cut off its support. But then she came to me in tears and said she could not work for me any more. I understood. She could not afford to alienate them. But it was one more alienating experience for me.

Questions about the wisdom of urban terror fuelled the problem. In the past, many middle-class activists had swept their disenchantment under the rug of anti-dictatorial unity. Now they had other options. Some joined the government or the Liberal Party. Others gravitated to the emergent independent left or the dissident popular democratic tendency within the national democratic organizations. A few opted to play an independent role within issue-specific alliances. Others, embittered by their experiences, chose to drop out of politics.

Not all middle-class elements left the mainstream movement. Many, like Agcaoili, remained in important positions. However, questions lingered even amongst those loyal to mainstream national democracy about the movement's appreciation of their involvement. I spoke with one long-time activist in his comfortable old suburban home about his involvement, which stretched back to the 1960s, and about some of the difficulties he had encountered. He said: 'I think there's really a disdain for the middle forces, for the bourgeoisie, from the point of view of the basic masses and even the leaders.'

Many radicals expect the best middle-class activists to return to the fold once 'Aquino's failure becomes clear.'[4] Certainly few progressive Filipinos, even those working within the government, voice satisfaction with the regime. But many will not return to the national democratic movement unless they see some real changes in the way the movement presents itself and deals with allies' criticisms. They demand a far more democratic and flexible movement than the one they have worked with in the past. At times the movement has responded to middle-class complaints. In 1988, for example, partially because of public complaints by middle-class progressives, the NPA's Manila-based partisans announced plans to proceed with greater caution. In 1989 they announced their renewed emphasis on alliance building.

Why have we discussed middle-class activists at such length when their numbers have always been small? Why discuss a group considered less important than the workers and peasants? Just what role do the middle classes have to play in the struggle? Theoretically and practically, the middle classes — small businessmen, professionals, university students and small landowners — do play an important role in the movement for change. Even 20 years earlier, José Maria Sison had noted in *Philippine Society and Revolution* that: 'The petty bourgeoisie deserves our close attention because its support for and participation in the people's democratic revolution is decisive in shifting the balance of forces against the national and class enemies of the Filipino people.'[5]

Middle-class Filipinos have played an important role in both spreading and opposing revolutionary ideas. The middle class includes the men and women who write newspapers, produce radio and television programmes, preach in churches, run government offices and political campaigns, teach in schools and universities, and lead community and civic organizations. They are people with influence far exceeding their numbers.

Sison ignored another middle-class role — that of building alliances with different political forces. His having overlooked this function is, however, understandable. He viewed alliances only in terms of multi-class cooperation based on acceptance of a national democratic programme. It was much later that some national democrats began working for multi-tendency alliances.

As middle-class alienation with the left grew, an intense debate over theory, strategy and tactics swept the revolutionary movement. Advocates of popular democracy and insurrectionary struggle, who sought stronger alliances with other political forces, wanted to rectify a Party long guided by policies shaped by experience but grounded in Mao's vision of a protracted people's war. The debate's intensity can be seen in the following passage from *Praktika* by Carol Victoria:

> Placing the boycott error in the proper strategic framework must be stressed. We have to remove the blinders obstructing our view of the complex issues concerning strategy and tactics. In this context, the assertion [made by the Central Committee] that 'experiences have confirmed the correctness of the general line and overall practice of the Party' would sound gratuitous. Certainly, the experience of being left out in the cold while the dictatorship was being overthrown is no confirmation of correctness.[6]

During its short life-span, *Praktika* became the main vehicle for analysing the boycott and other party errors, drawing on the experiences of revolutionary movements in other countries, and propagating the urban insurrectionist line of thinking. 'The Party has adhered to the "strategic principle of encircling the cities from the countryside",' wrote Victoria:

The February uprising, however, is the most visible evidence that urban insurrection is a most decisive and dynamic method of struggle. This is to say
that its success is not entirely tied to the armed offensive from the countryside. It is of course incorrect to make a dichotomy between rural armed
struggle and urban insurrection. What must be stressed is not to subordinate
or append the insurrection to the *ex cathedra* 'principle of encircling the cities
from the countryside.' Both play complementary roles and their combination
is most lethal.

She continued:

The boycott error merely manifested our fetishism of protracted armed
struggle as the principal means to overthrow the dictatorship. Because of this
fetish, the Party subsumed its tactics into a three-year plan for a 'strategic
counter-offensive.' The concept of the strategic counter-offensive as the
highest sub-stage of the strategic defensive is primarily, but not exclusively, a
military strategy. Its implication: the military struggle was the centrepiece of
the three-year plan. It was the lynchpin in the plan to intensify the struggle
against the US-Marcos dictatorship....

Since 1968 [when the CPP emerged], profound, drastic changes have swept
Philippine society and revolution. Our strategy and tactics cannot turn a blind
eye to these crucial changes. At all times, the theory and principles embodied
in the line must apply to the ever-changing conditions.... Taking into account
the new concrete conditions, three special tasks must be the Party's utmost
concern. These are the following: (1) according the political struggle a much
bigger role, (2) building a popular democratic front and (3) mastering the art
of insurrection. Insurrection is a lever of strategy. It is a most decisive form
of struggle to respond immediately to a revolutionary situation. It is
particularly forceful and effective to frustrate any sudden outbreak of
counter-revolution like a *coup d'état*. An ultra-right putsch is logically
possible. This should impel us to move double time and learn the art of insurrection.[7]

In their attempt to develop a comprehensive revision of Philippine revolutionary theory, the insurrectionists drew on their own experiences in the
country's urban centres, on the experiences of revolutionary movements
in Central America, Vietnam and Thailand, and on the experience of the
February revolution. They also drew upon the insights of the popular
democrats.

Unlike the insurrectionists, the popular democrats, most of whom
worked in the open rather than underground movement, stopped short of
presenting a comprehensive revolutionary strategy. Advocates of popular
democracy included those who saw it as complementary to the armed
struggle and others who felt political violence should be rejected by the
left.

Leading popular democratic theorist, Ed de la Torre, described it as a 'conscious effort to overcome sectarianism and hostility among different left tendencies.' He said that popular democracy encouraged the institutionalization of people's power through 'new structures of direct democracy like people's councils and new modes of political intervention like recall, initiative and referendum.'[8]

The chief NDF representative during the ceasefire talks, Satur Ocampo, told me that one of the main debates within the movement in 1986 was over the nature of the Aquino government. Popular democrats and insurrectionists saw the government as one of the élite, but with strong progressive and democratic tendencies. They were eager to strengthen positive tendencies within the government and made efforts do so. The rural-based protracted people's war group tolerated these efforts but viewed the reactionary faction of the ruling Aquino coalition as dominant. In their analysis, the February revolution had not altered the nature of class rule. The ebb and flow of this debate shaped the CPP's line and the movement's behaviour towards the Aquino government during the first phase of her rule.

Because of her popular mandate, the Party could not simply attack Aquino as it had Marcos without alienating a broad section of the population it sought to influence and lead. On the other hand, it could not spread the illusion that the success of the February revolt meant the end of the struggle. The opening of a democratic space had put additional pressure on the Party to alter its practice. The people's crusade had created an opening for political activity and many Filipinos wanted to enjoy this victory. This space gave the left, especially the urban left, room to advance its views. Pressure to utilize the democratic space came from urban sectors of the Party, middle-class allies and the non-national democratic left.

At the same time, however, there was mounting pressure in the Party to continue the armed struggle. This came not only from ideologues, but from the countryside where peasants politicized by the CPP saw little in their situation to justify abandoning the armed struggle.

Meanwhile, the movement was experiencing organizational difficulties in some areas. In the Cordillera, Conrado Balweg, an ex-priest and full-time guerrilla, led a faction out of the CPP and NPA (see Chapter 21). His group, the CPLA (Cordillera People's Liberation Army), was seeking a regional solution to the problems of the northern mountain tribes and an accommodation with the government. A festering split in Negros (where a top leader had broken with the CPP following the collapse of the ceasefire) and serious complications in Mindanao added to the problem.

The Mindanao difficulties stemmed from a widespread and high-level infiltration of CPP, NPA and movement organizations by deep-penetration agents of the AFP. The movement discovered these towards the end of 1985 and immediately launched a purge, which involved some inexcusable excesses. In late 1988 regional officials in southern Luzon discovered a similar problem with infiltrators and reacted in an almost identical way. These incidents and others, including the massacre of members of a religious cult in a bizarre confrontation in Mindanao, grew out of a tendency within the movement to solve problems with a gun. Movement leaders had promised to punish those responsible and their own policy of executing informants, cattle rustlers and other criminals had set the stage for local excesses.

When the NDF started negotiating with the government in 1987, neither the debate nor the problems in Davao, Negros and the Cordillera had been settled. The consensus at the time was to pursue negotiations without sacrificing the movement's strategic goal — to establish a democratic coalition government and a national democratic state.

Negotiations collapsed during the ceasefire because of a fundamental disagreement over the grounds for a political settlement. Fighting resumed as the military responded to Aquino's earlier threat to 'unsheathe the sword of war' and guerrillas resumed their 'tactical offensives.'

Harsh criticism of the Aquino government followed the collapse of negotiations. In the February 1987 edition of *Ang Bayan*, the CPP for the first time denounced the 'US-Aquino regime.' 'It is indeed an illusion to hope for peace under the reactionary rule of the US-Aquino clique that is hell-bent on imposing its oppressive and exploitative powers.' And it described the Aquino group as 'the dominant faction at the centre of the neo-colonial state.'[9]

In mid-1987 representatives of the movement's various regions met clandestinely to discuss policy. Prior to the meetings, Manila buzzed with rumours of an impending showdown. Sources who attended, however, say it never took place. Amidst increasingly strong anti-communist rhetoric from Aquino and her government, the representatives decided to continue the protracted people's war. The consensus, which was reached amongst regional organs and not ideological tendencies, did not eliminate debates, but set the direction for the immediate future.

Comments published in *Ang Bayan* and *Liberation* provided insights into the movement's strategy:

> Against the effort of the reactionaries to impose their will on the people is the revolutionary struggle for national liberation advancing the strategy of people's war. The strategy calls for an all-out mobilization of the people for

various revolutionary activities. It combines military and political actions; armed and unarmed operations; guerrilla, regular and partisan warfare; general strikes and mass uprisings; indigenous, home-made and modern weapons; etc.[10]

And from a *Liberation* interview with a member of the NPA general staff:

Q. Has there been a shift from the strategy of protracted people's war, encircling the cities from the countryside, to urban insurrectionary strategies? AFP propagandists suggest that disagreements regarding which strategy to follow is one cause of rifts within the CPP-NPA.

A. As Amado Guerrero has pointed out in 'Specific Characteristics of our People's War,' our people's army should develop from being small and weak to being big and strong. We do this by capitalizing on our strengths and taking advantage of the enemy's weaknesses. The enemy is weaker in the countryside, so that is where we started, and where we developed our strength. Now that our people's war has made tremendous advances, the role of political and military struggles in towns and cities has also grown. But this does not mean that we have abandoned the countryside and are now concentrating our efforts in the urban areas. On the contrary, we are at present creating bigger NPA formations and launching bigger military offensives in the countryside. This we will continue alongside the stepped-up development of our mass base and political struggles in the countryside and cities. The development of urban partisan operations, insurrectionary forms of struggle and the like do not indicate a change in strategy, but merely indicate the advances in and growing sophistication of our comprehensive people's war.[11]

I asked numerous underground activists and leaders to assess the popular democratic and insurrectionist tendencies and received representative answers from two members of the Manila-Rizal NPA command.

'There were some intensive discussions regarding policy towards the Cory government,' said Marty Rojo. 'Some thought that critical collaboration would work and that we could even win over Cory and implement some basic changes, social changes, but later, it was, I mean an illusion was there.' 'A lot of interest was generated by the prospects of an insurrectionary policy, especially after the EDSA revolution,' added Sonny Reyes, a guerrilla since 1970 and former member of the NPA general command.

[An] insurrectionary approach is valid in the sense that there are specific periods or developments in the revolutionary process where insurrection can be applied. But these are times when the revolutionary situation is having a flow and that really happened during the 1986 EDSA revolution. Had the leadership prepared for that kind of development, we could have pursued the insurrectionary approach for that particular period, but that opportunity has passed. Had we adopted that approach and were able to seize power, I do not think we could have sustained or maintained at that point. At that time, the revolutionary movement was not yet in the position to hold power.

The Philippine military called the policy of protracted people's war a hard-line approach. They attributed its importance to ideologues. But support for a hard-line approach also came from the very core of the movement's support: the politicized peasants and workers who face daily suffering and are less involved in inner-party debates than urban intellectuals and college-educated cadres. Their perception that nothing had changed encouraged them to reject a modified line, since the changes that did take place after the fall of Marcos had little impact on their lives. The movement's teachings provided a second source of mass support for the hard-line. Most of the organized workers and peasants had received all their political education from the revolutionary movement, which had hammered home the need for an armed struggle to bring about change. Experience, especially in the countryside, has supported this argument. Many peasants only received land, lower rents or higher pay, and a sense of empowerment, when the armed left entered their lives.

But the movement had another priority. It had to rebuild its leadership following the arrest of numerous key CPP, NDF and NPA officials in the late 1980s. The arrests of the CPP's chairman, Rodolfo Salas, the secretary-general, Rafael Baylosis, an NPA commander, Rolly Kintanar (who later escaped), Satur Ocampo and Carolina Malay created obvious problems. The military viewed these arrests, and the seizure of important documents at the same time, as potentially decisive blows against the revolutionary movement. But CPP officials reacted with less panic than one might have expected. 'In 1974-6, there was also a series of arrests of leading cadres, including Sison and Dante no less,' noted a Party official in a letter written after the 1989 arrests of Ocampo and Malay. 'But this failed to stem the tide of growing revolutionary forces. I am confident that today's level of strength and experience of the Party, the people's army and organized masses is enough to withstand the enemy onslaughts.'

Much of this optimism was founded on a faith in the second-tier leaders who would replace the gaoled officials. During my stay in the Philippines, I met numerous regional and second-tier revolutionary leaders. Most had entered the movement in the early 1970s and struck me as intelligent, talented individuals and often flexible strategic thinkers. In fact many of the leading advocates of insurrectionary politics come from this stratum of leaders, who may well have been involved in the movement's renewed discussion of united front work in 1989.

The CPP's determination to expand its army led it belatedly to try and extend its contacts with communist parties and liberation movements throughout the world. This came at a time when many communist parties, especially ruling parties, were looking inwards and going through a period of tumultuous change — which says something about the CPP's limited grasp of international developments. The primary goal of this ill-fated attempt was increased material and diplomatic support. Former CPP chairman, José Maria Sison, noted this when he wrote: 'Increasing the NPA's automatic rifle strength from 10,000 to 25,000, thereby allowing the NPA to operate effectively in 1,000 municipalities, can bring the people's war into the stage of strategic stalemate.'[12]

This emphasis on the strategic importance of weaponry created some tension within the movement. Flor S. Eugenio, a member of the NDF-affiliated CNL (Christians for National Liberation), complained in a letter published in *National Midweek*: 'Suddenly, rifle strength and weaponry — including the seeking of anti-tank and anti-aircraft weapons — have become the focal points. What happened to such Maoist principles as "politics in command" and "the people, not objects will decide".'[13]

With the movement suffering from internal criticism, alienated allies, a shortage of arms, an absence of international support and serious leadership problems, as the 1980s came to a close it reconsidered the importance of political struggle, alliance building and a broad united front. One CPP representative told me that the immediate task would be to consolidate the mass organizations led by national democrats and to strengthen the issue-specific alliances. He thought that an attempt to build a broad alliance — such as *Bayan* had originally been envisioned — would not take place immediately, but would be possible in the future. Critics can be excused for viewing this assertion with scepticism. When in the past national democrats had tried to form a broad front with social democrats, liberals and independent leftists, the CPP's sectarianism had stood in the way. Denigrating social democrats and democratic socialists for being 'clerico-fascist,' characterizing the PKP as reactionary and expressing fears that the 'petty bourgeois reformists [might] pose a threat to the Party's ideological political line' do not set the stage for successful alliance work.

While the movement may be making tactical adjustments to suit current conditions, it has not changed its overall strategy, despite the problems it confronted following the fall of Marcos and rise of Aquino. It has not abandoned its concept of fighting a long-term revolutionary war. Nor has it reassessed the impact of its vanguardism on alliance work.

It will not be easy to re-emphasize open, predominantly urban politics. Apart from its internal problems, the radical movement faces tremendous external pressures. Not only has the military openly targeted legal left organizations, but it has also put tremendous pressure on underground activists working in the city.

The future of the revolutionary movement, however much it has become an institution in the modern Philippines, is not assured. Its policies, tactics and strategies and even its survival are not cast in stone. Its future will depend not only on its response to an ever changing political situation, but also on the actions (successes and failures) of other forces — the government, its military, foreign powers and the host of other political organizations struggling to set the course of the nation's history.

15

Other Left Forces

An independent left reaches beyond the middle-class activists who work with the national democrats and the leftists in the mainstream reform parties. It includes social democrats and democratic socialists, environmentalists, left-leaning nationalists, some intellectuals, disillusioned members of various tendencies and religious activists. The independent left is primarily middle class but includes some labour leaders and their followers.

The independent left lacks a sizeable mass base, but includes numerous prominent individuals belonging to an array of organizations. Collectively they have a strong intellectual pull and play a central role in heterogeneous alliances such as the Freedom From Debt Coalition, the National Movement for Civil Liberties and movements against the US military bases and nuclear weapons.

A number of independents gravitated to *Bisig* (*Bukluran sa Ikauunlad ng Sosyalistang Isip at Gawa*, or Movement for the Advancement of Socialist Ideas & Action), which various independent Marxists, disgruntled national democrats and social democrats, and ex-members of the PKP (the old Communist Party) had formed after the fall of Marcos. Its core came from the Independent Caucus, a group originally within *Bayan*. Its leadership was provided by a pair of UP (University of the Philippines) professors — Francisco Nemenzo, who broke with the PKP in the early 1970s and subsequently led the small Marxist-Leninist Group, and Randy David, who gained fame as the host of a popular television programme in the wake of the anti-Marcos uprising.

Bisig, which regarded dependent capitalism as the Philippines' basic problem, proposed a Philippine version of socialism that would utilize various forms of public and cooperative ownership of economic enterprises governed by workers' councils. 'In the case of individual enterprise, the informal business sector and petty commodity producers, the state must encourage cooperatives rather than resort to the imposition of socialized systems.'

In the political sphere, *Bisig* sought to counter the self-conscious vanguardism of the Communist Party. *Bisig* noted:

> Socialism in the Philippines will encourage the presence of multiple parties, each one with its own perspective on the correct path to socialism.... Unlike the much misunderstood and sometimes abused concept of the vanguard party, socialism in the Philippines will encourage the interplay of forces and perspectives on socialism, each aspiring for the vanguard role. The vanguard role, therefore, is not one that is bestowed on any party or political force. It is a role that is dependent upon the support of the majority for a party's policies and programmes.

B*isig*'s most important function has been to offer intellectual alternatives to the sometimes stuffy and dogmatic thinking of the CPP. *Bisig* members promote new ideas and alternative approaches for the Philippine left. Its members include some of the Philippines' more creative thinkers, but *Bisig*'s mass support does not match its intellectual powers. The group does pursue mass work, and Nemenzo told me in mid-1988 that, contrary to public opinion, it had more worker and peasant members than intellectuals. Still, *Bisig* asserts itself more through ideas than mass mobilization. Its political strategy has been to take advantage of the democratic space to promote socialism.

In an attempt to influence the NDF (National Democratic Front), *Bisig* members have worked with the more independent CPP and NDF members. One intellectual close to *Bisig* told me that he had worked with some of the *Praktika* writers before becoming frustrated anew with the mainstream left's bureaucracy. *Bisig* has also courted other progressive groups. It cooperated with social democrats and independent left supporters of Aquino's government in promoting people power and in organizing anti-fascist events. It also supports long-term efforts to unite the socialist and popular democratic left.

Other forces on the left merit attention. Female activists — liberals, socialists, independent-minded national democrats and others — launched a novel experiment and formed the country's first all-women's political party before the 1987 congressional elections. *Kaiba* succeeded in having one of its members elected to Congress, but its ideological diversity and lack of party discipline work against it.

The PKP still retains an influence within some labour and peasant groups despite the critical support it offered Marcos through much of the martial law period. It has attempted to regain some of its lost prestige but remains marginalized.

The main force on the independent left is the social democratic movement. Compared to the national democrats, the social democrats are organizationally small and weak. In 1986, for example, the largest of the groups claimed 1,200 members compared with 30,000 for the CPP. But in the post-Marcos era they have shown some signs of life. 'We have an advantage over the Communists and the national democrats now,' Fr Romeo Intengan of the PDSP (*Partido Demokratiko-Sosyalista ng Pilipinas*) told me. 'We are completely legal. Our organizers can work in most places without harassment or with minimal harassment.' In 1987 the party proclaimed that:

> The attainment of national liberation through the establishment of a demo-cratic socialist Philippine society requires a sequential approach. The sequential approach is necessary because of the presence of three structural evils of Philippine society — imperialism, dependent capitalism and feudalism. This sequential approach is reflected in the two periods in the ongoing Philippine revolution: first, the social democratic period of the revolution; and second, the democratic socialist period of revolution.

Dividing the process into two stages allows the movement to involve people with different politics. Fr Intengan points out that many prominent politicians, notably members of PDP and *Bandila*, describe themselves as social democrats while not adhering to the full programme of the PDSP. *Bandila* leader, Butz Aquino, is one such individual. I asked him to define social democracy. 'To me, that means making available the very necessities of life,' he responded. 'Of course, food, shelter, health, education and employment opportunities.'

Democratic socialist intellectuals have a more detailed idea of how the transformation should take place. Mar Canonigo, a government official now trying to build a social-democratic tendency within the Liberal Party, described his vision of democratic socialism while he was still a leader of the PDSP:

> We want a society wherein the primary means of production, the basic indus-tries, etc., are owned not by the state, but by the people. When we say by the people, we are speaking of the working people — the workers, the peasants, the basic masses — but we will not exclude what they call the bourgeoisie or petit bourgeoisie. They will be part of the working people because we are all brother Filipinos.

Intengan told me that he had drawn some of his inspiration from Yugoslavian experiences with workers' management. But he emphasized the need to retain political democracy while developing a socialist economy. Some members of the social-democratic tendency work within existing parties, notably the PDP (Philippine Democratic Party). The desire to press for reforms has also led the social democrats to join alliances working for agrarian reform, freedom from debt, environmental sanity, and closure of the bases.

But one ideological factor has had a serious impact on the politics of the social-democratic movement — anti-communism. Canonigo told me that Philippine-style social-democratic ideology grew out of a search for an alternative to Marxism-Leninism. Many of the early social democrats were religious activists opposed to the materialism of the Marxist-Leninists and the main national-democratic organizations. Fr Intengan, who became the leading theoretician of Philippine social democracy and democratic socialism, told me that his own experiences within the KM (*Kabataang Makabayan*) had led him to seek an alternative. He objected to that youth group's emphasis on dialectical materialism.

Canonigo explained the social democrats' alternative to the materialism of the left:

> Man is not a purely material being, but man is body, mind and spirit. If we work for the liberation of man, we should work not only for the liberation of his temporal order, but towards the fulfilment of his spirit. In other words, it is not only important for man to be given food and shelter, etc., but it is also important that his basic rights be respected and given full expression in all fields of life — political, social, economic, etc.

Fr Intengan described the principal conflict of the post-Marcos era as being between democrats and non-democrats rather than between left and right. He told me that from the simple standpoint of survival, the PDSP and many other social democrats support conservative democrats against left-wing 'totalitarians.'

Their limited mass base creates serious problems for the social democrats who, unlike the national democrats, failed to build a significant base (especially among workers and peasants) during the years of Marcos's dictatorship. After several particularly difficult years in the early 1980s, when the government gaoled or forced into exile numerous party leaders and the movement attempted to build an army, in 1985 and 1986 the PDSP and other democratic-socialist groups once more began to gel. Some oppositionists, alienated by attempts to cooperate with the radical left, established *Bandila*. *Bandila* members played leading roles in Aquino's campaign. The advent of Aquino's government led the social democrats to shift from armed to legal struggle — though not to disband their small armies. Given strong links with the Liberals, the Aquino family and others close to the president, some social democrats expected a golden era for their movement, but new difficulties were to surface.

Mrs Aquino tapped numerous members of social-democratic organizations for government positions. Butz Aquino, Tito Guingona, Mar Canonigo, Noel Tolentino, Emmanuel Soriano, Alfredo Bengzon and other leaders of *Bandila*, entered government as either elected or

appointed officials. But this failed to strengthen the movement. The new
government officials found themselves captive to their duties and unable
to give the movement much time. Some found it more practical to join an
established electoral party, such as the Liberal Party, rather than stick
with a struggling small movement. By the latter part of 1988, Intengan
told me, the movement had lost many of its best people to government
service and other political parties.

Two years into his sister-in-law's reign, Butz Aquino discussed
Bandila's difficulties, suggesting that the political situation favoured
political parties and sectoral groups (like labour unions) rather than a
multi-sectoral alliance. 'Multi-sectoral, cause-oriented groups try to bite
off more than they can chew,' he argued:

> When you are multi-sectoral, you are already talking of several issues and
> sometimes you dissipate your energies. For instance, in *Bandila*, we have
> several issues — agrarian reform, urban land reform, urban poor problems,
> fisher-folk problems — you know, these are national problems. Since this is
> strictly a voluntary organization with the problem of funding to begin with...
> [Aquino let his sentence fade as he shook his head]. To be effective, we must
> have a permanent staff and sometimes, just to maintain a small staff, is some-
> thing the organization can not afford, so it is a problem.

But not all *Bandila*'s problems come from a lack of resources and time.
The organization and those of its leaders who are in the government have
conflicting interests. Social democrats working in the government find
themselves in the delicate position of serving two masters.

Many social democrats have worked to give their movement renewed
energy. Grassroots activists, organizational leaders and intellectuals have
struggled to build organizations and alliances. They became notably
more visible in peasant struggles as organizers of the CPAR (Congress
for a People's Agrarian Reform). They have also been playing a key role
in trying to launch the Green Forum, an alliance of leftists and newly
active ecologists. But in the other key sector, labour, social democrats
face glaring weaknesses.

A short cut being taken is to form alliances with existing organizations. Attempts to court Conrado Balweg's CPLA (Cordillera People's
Liberation Army) and the MILF (Moro Islamic National Liberation
Front) have produced uneven and still uncertain results. Another dal-
liance involves the TUCP (Trade Union Congress of the Philippines).
The PDSP, through its chairman, Norberto Gonzales, has been talking
with TUCP president, Democrito Mendoza.

The TUCP represents the most conservative trend in Philippine
unionism. Founded in 1977, when militant unions faced tremendous
repression, it became known as Marcos's house union. Militants

denounced it as a yellow union in the days before yellow came to symbolize opposition to the dictatorship. Vehement anti-communism and strong support for the US dictate TUCP politics.

American support fuels TUCP anti-communism. The Asian-American Free Labor Institute, an organization controlled by the right wing of the US AFL-CIO, channels US government, labour and private sector funds to the TUCP. The birth of the KMU (*Kilusang Mayo Uno*, or May First Movement) and growing labour militancy forced the TUCP leadership to shift direction. Just before Marcos's regime fell apart the TUCP stopped inviting the dictator to its Labour Day celebrations and began talking vaguely of socialism. By that time the more astute of the TUCP's leaders, especially US foreign-policy makers and Philippine military officers, had seen that the Marcos government was crumbling and did not want to fall with it. The TUCP now pursues a reformist line, supporting agrarian reform and a repeal of the most controversial anti-labour laws, while opposing communism, the KMU and class struggle.

I asked TUCP president, Mendoza, 'Is there any place in this society for a labour party or some sort of political vehicle?' 'They are coming out with that,' he responded. 'In fact, the chairman with the political party is outside waiting to talk with me. This is a political party we believe has identical or shares most aspirations, purposes and goals with the labour movement.' 'What party is that?' 'The PDSP. This is democratic socialist.'

The TUCP and PDSP share certain aspirations for change and justice, but the TUCP's programme is nowhere near as comprehensive or radical as that of the PDSP. For example, the PDSP calls imperialism a basic problem facing the Philippines while the TUCP receives support from the US government. In addition, the TUCP has an ugly tradition of collaboration with the worst elements of Philippine society. While social democrats suffered in jungles, prison and exile, along with other forces opposed to the Marcos regime, TUCP leaders worked within the system — gracing Malacanang and applauding Marcos's revolution from the safe havens of suburban Manila.

Aside from the PDSP's desire for a ready-made mass base and the TUCP's drive for political respectability, the courtship rests on a common negative impulse. Anti-communism unites the two groups, both of which feel pressure from the left. Deep cooperation between the TUCP and PDSP is by no means assured, but what would happen if the relationship were to develop beyond a tentative courtship?

At best the PDSP would pull the TUCP to the left, cut its ties with the US government and reduce the likelihood of collaboration with anti-democratic forces. The chances of this happening, however, are bleak. More likely, the TUCP would pull the PDSP to the right. The TUCP retains a far greater mass base and access to many more resources than does the PDSP. A relationship grounded on anti-communism would open the door to collaboration with various forces, many of them strongly opposed to the radical restructuring of society, in the name of anti-communism and the defence of democracy.

The essential factor in strengthening the social democratic movement lies in building its own forces. This calls for building mass organizations and reuniting the social democratic tendency on a programmatic and organizational level. Intengan says that his and other organizations see this as a priority. But it has not happened yet and does not appear likely in the near future. Yet it is essential if the social democrats are to play a role in transforming Philippine politics and society.

How much success have the social democrats had since Aquino came to power? According to Intengan, the movement has a larger mass base than at any time in the past. He suggests his movement's advocacy of liberal democracy conforms to the aspirations of the Filipino people. This is certainly a factor that cannot be overlooked as many Filipinos, especially middle-class ones, hope that positive change might come without the trauma of civil war.

Overall, the social democrats remain numerically weak. Their mass organizations exist, but command limited support. And questions about the quality of their leadership remain unanswered. At present, social democrats, *Bisig* members and other advocates of alternative left-wing futures inject a healthy amount of intellectual and political energy into Philippine life. In the long run they may do much more. Stronger alternative lefts could contribute to the construction of a broad left committed to both radical change and a pluralist grassroots democracy. Some argue that such a left, a popular democratic left, will be needed to save the existing left from itself, its enemies and political marginalization.

16

Popular Democracy

Lean Alejandro died at the age of 27. Mourners flocked to the small hall on the UP campus. Alejandro's comrades from *Bayan* and other radical groups passed by his coffin and tried to console his wife, the mother of his six-month-old daughter.

Prominent social democrats, Liberal Party stalwarts and others not identified with Alejandro's faction joined the mourners. As so often before, it took a tragedy for people to demonstrate, in some small way, the common bond between different forces fighting for change.

Despite the common bond, unity between various change-oriented factions is elusive. Though some see it as essential to building a just and democratic Philippines, it unfortunately remains a distant and perhaps idealistic vision. Deep-seated differences, born of ideology, past conflicts and failed attempts to build a popular front, stand in the way.

The shortcomings of *Kompil* and *Bayan* provide examples of the kinds of obstacles facing advocates of broad left unity. *Bayan* especially demonstrates the deep distrust between the main left tendencies and the organizational weakness of the non-national democratic forces. But the failure to establish *Bayan* as a united command must be considered within the context of national democratic and social democratic attitudes towards alliances.

Both factions see the basic alliance as one of classes rather than of tendencies. The national democrats want an alliance between the working class (as the leading force in the revolution) and the peasantry (as the main force in a united front with middle- and upper-class adherents to the national democratic programme). Social democrats support a triple alliance between workers, peasants and the petty bourgeoisie, with the workers and peasants at its core.

Filipino social democrats and communists also share certain vanguardist tendencies — which does not help cooperation between these two largest left forces. Sectarianism, particularly on the part of the CPP, is another problem. At times, it reaches foolish proportions. A former activist provided an example: 'Did I ever tell you about Happy Feet sandals?' she asked me. 'When I was at UP, we were told by our political officer not to buy Happy Feet sandals because the social democrats owned the franchise.' The editors of *Praktika* offered their own critique of CPP sectarianism: 'Many a time since the Aquino assassination, the proletarian revolutionaries displayed sectarianism... due to their dogmatic insistence on the national democratic line and, also, due to unreasonable assertion of domination of the national democrats in legal democratic alliances.'[1]

Praktika's position reflected a tendency in the Party that has long fought for cooperation with other progressive forces. This position surfaced several times during the Marcos period, but always lost out to those who argued that united fronts must 'uncompromisingly be based on the wholehearted acceptance of nothing less than the... programme of the NDF.'[2]

For a time in 1986 the CPP appeared to be resisting its sectarian past, but after the collapse of peace efforts, old-style rhetoric resurfaced with a vengeance. National democrats, however, did not create a fractious left on their own. The social democratic programme frowned on cooperation with the 'extreme left,' putting, in political analyst P.N. Abinales's words, 'unreasonable constraints on the extent [to which] the social democrats can have relations with the national democrats.'

Both sides were responsible for the collapse of *Bayan's* founding congress, for both engaged in a series of arcane debates and very real power plays. Since the social democrats were unable to challenge the radical left on grounds of political support, they could do battle only on an ideological level.

The *Kompil* fiasco revealed another impediment to forming a broad progressive movement. What to do with the politicians? *Kompil* had ultimately failed to resolve the differences between traditional politics and the Parliament of the Street. Its agreements broke down when many of its politicians, including some progressives like Bobbit Sanchez and Nene Pimentel, decided to run in the 1984 *Batasang Pambansa* (National Assembly) elections, which most social democrats, the national democrats and other leftists were boycotting.

Polarization had made 1986 an unlikely year to start a new broad-front project, but that is just what Ed de la Torre, Boy Morales and a handful of former political prisoners, intellectuals and activists did when they launched the VPD (Volunteers for Popular Democracy). The VPD and the people around it became active participants in debates and discussions about the left's future. 'Popular democracy,' de la Torre wrote, 'represented a conscious effort to overcome sectarianism and hostility among different left tendencies and to promote dialogue and mutual respect, while recognizing that differences will not be resolved quickly.'[3]

Popular democracy and the NDF (National Democratic Front) have very different theoretical underpinnings. The NDF is a worker-peasant based, multi-class alliance under the leadership of the vanguard party, the CPP. Its theoretical principles are found in the works of José Maria Sison and Mao Zedong. The popular democratic front, on the other hand, represents a coalition of left-wing forces rooted in the experience of the anti-Marcos struggle. 'Within this movement there seemed to be two distinct tendencies,' de la Torre told Lester Edwin J. Ruiz in a *World Policy Journal* interview:

> It was not simply that the traditional opposition was anti-Marcos but not anti-imperialist, while the new opposition was both anti-Marcos and anti-imperialist. What the traditional opposition wanted was a strictly election based approach; essentially, these people were seeking to restore pre-martial law élite democracy. The new opposition, on the other hand, advocated a broader approach, including pressure politics, that would create a new form of democracy, which we called popular democracy.[4]

De la Torre discussed his vision of the coalition line in a pamphlet published by his Institute for Popular Democracy:

> Some elements of this coalition line are quite clear. All left tendencies are anti-fascist and anti-imperialist. All are also anti-feudal in so far as feudalism exists, although they differ in their assessment of its extent and dominance. In varying degrees, they prefer a socialist perspective, while accepting some form of transition. They also accept the need for waging all forms of political struggle to set up a left-led coalition government.

> On the basis of these identifiable elements of a shared coalition line, some activists from various left tendencies have proposed the following basic attitudes towards one another: (a) mutual recognition as left and democratic forces; (b) mutual stake in one another's expansion and growth; (c) mutual restraint in recruiting from each other's organized forces.[5]

De la Torre noted the presence of non-national democrats in the original popular democratic formation. But he did not reject his own political heritage. Instead, he argued that popular democracy could be a component of national democracy.

In essence, he argued that, in several of its components, popular democracy corresponded to national democracy — in the organization and empowerment of workers and peasants, in the development of a national unity based on a common opposition to imperialism, fascism and feudalism, and in the establishment of structures with which to transfer power from the élite to the masses. Critics have questioned the sincerity of popular democrats who are rooted in a national democratic tradition precisely because many remained within national democratic organizations while promoting popular democracy. But the whole object of popular democracy is not to replace existing left organizations, but to pull them together.

The popular democrats failed to create the broad left front they sought in the immediate post-Marcos period. They did, however, create the theoretical framework for such cooperation while organizing support for the concept within the various left tendencies. They kept the possibility of broad popular unity alive in the most difficult of times. Cooperation on an issue-by-issue basis has now given popular democrats reason to believe that their vision has a future. Tactical alliances on agrarian and labour reform, freedom from debt and anti-bases and anti-nuclear campaigns have survived faction fights and, though constantly in danger of collapse, have built the foundation on which broader future cooperation might be built.

Is such cooperation needed? Is a popular democratic front essential to social transformation? The two main left forces, the national democrats and the social democrats, sometimes say no. But in practice the factions must respond to a situation that does not always coincide with their theoretical view of the world.

For the social democrats, a vanguard role in the struggle for change appears to be a pipe dream. The national democratic movement would have to be destroyed for the social democrats to have a chance at hegemony within the broad movement. For the national democrats, leadership of the struggle for power and social transformation cannot be so easily ruled out. The NDF has a sizeable base, yet developing its capacity depends on several factors. These include improving its own ability to attract ever broader support; responding better to changing circumstances; the government's failure to provide viable alternatives; and the continued weakness of other left forces. These are formidable challenges and they make broader alliances attractive.

In the past, the national democrats have viewed broad alliances as a way of strengthening their own movement. When the CPP and NDF have felt the need to cooperate with other left forces, they have adjusted their tactics and rhetoric. 'We call on all forces fighting the dictatorship to firm up their unity,' proclaimed *Liberation* back in 1984. 'This unity, to be more stable, should be set on the basis of a clear-cut anti-fascist, anti-imperialist and anti-feudal position. We are willing to unite and cooperate with members of the parliamentary opposition and even some independent-minded members of the ruling party.'[6]

The period following that statement was marked by cooperation between the progressive anti-Marcos forces. That cooperation peaked with the agreement on *Bayan*'s programme and policies and collapsed with the fiasco at the *Bayan* congress. Two years later, in the wake of the February 1987 uprising, the radical left once again made overtures to other political forces.

Some national democrats have pushed for cooperation that goes beyond immediate tactical considerations. Boy Morales, who later emerged as a leader of the popular democratic tendency, was asked 'Will the coalition government [a left idea that surfaced prior to the fall of Marcos] adopt the NDF's programme?' Morales responded that, 'since the coalition would include quite a mixture of forces, we cannot expect any outright adoption of a proposal by a single group, or even of an alliance as formidable as the NDF. But the main lines of democracy and national-ism should not be difficult to accept.'

The agreement to enter substantial negotiations with Cory Aquino's government demonstrated a degree of responsiveness to sentiments out-side the NDF on the part of the CPP and the national democratic move-ment. NDF proposals demonstrated a willingness to compromise on something less than its programme. What of the other tendencies? Would they be open to a popular democratic front? The independents, always anxious to avoid marginalization, have sought cooperation with other forces. But recent experiences have strengthened the independents' resolve to avoid domination. Thus their participation, so essential to building alliances, demands diplomacy and respect.

Bisig also seeks cooperation with other left forces. Given the ideological differences, it would probably seek to maintain some sort of organizational integrity in a broad left front. The social democratic cum democratic socialist axis provides the most problematic factor in discussing cooperation among existing left groups. Their involvement may depend on how they grow. If growth means being pulled to the right by the TUCP, then the prospect of a popular democratic front incorporating the largest independent left tendency is dim. If, however, the social democrats grow on the strength of their own programme and commitment to the struggle for social transformation, then the possibility of popular democracy increases, provided the social democrats feel able to avoid domination.

This brings us to the final group available for a broad left or progressive alliance — the reform-oriented politicians. Elite democrats who believe change can come through purely parliamentary means and those out to protect their careers in government are unlikely to join in a broad coalition tainted by left participation or leadership. But men and women honestly committed to the values they profess are likely to co-operate.

How, then, might a broad left emerge and cooperate in gaining power and transforming society? Two possibilities come to mind. The first would be for the legal left to strengthen itself and, perhaps through the PDP and Liberal Party, win increased access to government; in other words, build a powerful movement for justice and peace within the framework of the constitutional system. That social democrats and independent leftists have cooperated in the Coalition for Peace, which advocates peace based on justice and negotiations, demonstrates the basic appeal of a compromise solution to the non-national-democratic left.

Were these tendencies to gain strength, they might force the government to respond to calls for negotiations issued by the Church. The obvious and possibly overwhelming obstacle to the pursuit of a compromise political settlement, however, is opposition from the military, as well as from those who benefit from the status quo and certain foreign powers. Another alternative would be for non-national-democratic forces to grow disillusioned with both the government and the system. The likelihood of an opposition popular democratic front would increase dramatically if the government closed off the democratic space. To some extent, this has already been happening. Still, for all the reasons discussed above, popular democracy may not be the most likely path for the Philippines to follow in the 1990s. But it could well be the best. For popular democracy could combine socialism's positive thrusts towards justice and equity with grassroots democracy and the checks and balances provided by a pluralist political system.

But whether we talk about national democracy, communism, social democracy, socialism or popular democracy, the movement for change has its work cut out for it. For the left to bring about the social transformation it envisions, it must overcome its own internal demons and defeat numerous and powerful enemies who redbait progressive politicians, sow intrigues between different progressive forces, and resort to repressing progressive political movements.

17

Obstacles to Change

Talk comes cheap in Philippine political circles. I have heard executives in Makati's glass and steel office blocks, planters on Negros's sprawling plantations, government officials in their comfortable homes and offices, military officers in countless camps, diplomats at after-office parties, and politicians from various parties praise their own efforts and blame others for the nation's problems. I have never heard anyone face up to and claim responsibility for failure. For those who benefit from the status quo, it is never the 'system's' fault. It is always uppity workers, a disruptive opposition, ineffective government, scheming foreigners or obstructionist nationalists.

Part of their skill lies in sounding sincere and convincing. It is hard to find someone you simply do not like in the Philippines. I enjoyed my chats with the planters who shared their midday snacks with me, with the military officers who told exaggerated but exciting tales of adventure, with government officials who prattled on about their grandiose plans, and with political operatives who flashed wads of cash as we drove along country roads. I even enjoyed the hospitality of an anti-communist vigilante leader as we roared around Davao City in a car overloaded with gun-toting thugs. But all these people must share the blame for the Philippines' continuing plight. Foreign powers, right-wing military forces, segments of the Catholic Church, and a conservative culture all present obstacles to change, but none more than the various segments of the domestic élite.

The rural élite forms the most reactionary stratum of Philippine society. Its feudal wing resists all change; its capitalist segment favours modernization, but not change aimed at building a truly diverse economy, and certainly not change premised on social justice, equity and popular empowerment. Anti-Marcos segments of the local élite fought for an end to the favouritism bestowed on Marcos's cronies, and little more. Landed families flocked to Aquino's movement as their problems mounted. But once empowered, these families opposed all attempts to redress the grievances of the rural poor population.

The traditional families and war-lords, local politicians who built private armies to win power, have continued under Aquino to use 'guns, goons and gold,' traditional rural culture and economic domination of the countryside to win control of local government and the House of Representatives. The government's failure to pursue agrarian reform forcefully demonstrates the tremendous power held in the post-Marcos era by the rural élite.

The urban élite is more complicated. At best its members advocate reform as part of a modernization drive. At worst they succumb to the demands of the more conservative élite groups. They usually behave through self-interest rather than for the public good. The priorities and complexities of the urban upper crust were revealed during the build-up to import liberalization. Some lined up alongside progressive nationalists in opposing tariff reductions, the elimination of quotas and other forms of import protection and prodded leaders of the Philippine manufacturing sector to establish the BPMM (Buy Philippine Made Movement).

The movement, which grew from 80 to 150 members in the first half of 1988, set out 'to raise the level of quality of Philippine-made products and ultimately make the Filipino consumers change their buying preferences from imported to local products.' But the movement became so broad that it lost much of the nationalist thrust it had had at its inception. Leading Filipino industrialists actually welcomed foreign firms with Philippine subsidiaries into the movement. These firms employ only about 1 per cent of the nation's workforce and transfer little technology to local partners or firms. In addition, their profits do not remain in the country. In 1986, for example, the Securities & Exchange Commission reported that foreign firms sent US $100 million in locally-earned profits abroad. This money could have been used to build an industrial base and to create more jobs.

Many leaders of the urban élite advocate liberal investment policies to attract foreign capital. Such policies allow tax holidays for new investors, repatriation of profits and full foreign control of selected industries. They also advocate paying low wages and limiting labour rights.

Mainstream business organizations even went so far as to criticize the country's liberal Omnibus Investments Code for offering fewer incentives to foreign investors than neighbouring countries. The Makati Business Club claimed that Singapore, Brunei and Indonesia placed far fewer restrictions on multinationals than the Philippines, while Malaysia and Thailand offered more incentives. The Club called on the government to 'correct these deficiencies in our Code or we lose the investment drive by default.' Many in the Manila and Makati business communities support this type of development. And why not? Ties with foreign investors mean increased profits and greater wealth for themselves, even if the cost includes low wages for workers, a reduced public revenue base and repatriated profits.

Opening Philippine doors to foreign investment is but one example of the outward-looking view of the nation's urban élite. Growing involvement in the export sector provides another example of Philippine capital's integration into the global market. For many Philippine firms and foreign firms operating in the country, Filipino consumers provide only a secondary market. The big money is made selling on the regional and global markets.

Firmo 'Boy' Tripon is one of the few businessmen I know who puts the national interest ahead of his own in actions as well as words. He left a successful career with a large corporation rather than be part of an anti-labour management team and took charge of his family's foundering dental laboratory. Unable to prosper on the impoverished local market, Boy faced a choice between closure and export. Wisely he chose export. Boy would be a rare bird in any society. In the Philippines he is exceptional. Thoughtful members of the business community recognize the importance of enlarging the local market, but even they find themselves torn between short- and long-term goals, between protecting existing markets or creating new ones, and between capitalist and feudal values. The urban élite's vacillations over the issue of agrarian reform are an illuminating example.

Initially, many members favoured land redistribution as a way of strengthening the domestic market and bringing political stability to the countryside. But when I met Victor Lim, then president of the Philippine Chamber of Commerce & Industry, in early 1988, I was surprised by his negative view. He spoke of the 'chaos' wrought by the battle over agrarian reform and complained of it 'hampering recovery' as landowners lost interest in 'putting money into the land.' He thought that agrarian reform should aim to 'increase income' rather than simply transfer control over the land. He suggested that the government 'go slow' by implementing the Marcos-era programme before going any further.

One reason why the urban élite withdrew its initial support for agrarian reform can be traced to the influence of banking interests in the city's economic life. According to economist Orville Solon, banks that had extended loans to agrarian interests feared the ramifications of far-reaching agrarian reform. On an ideological level, many members of the urban élite had never felt comfortable about the redistributive aspects of agrarian reform; they ran counter to the sanctity of private property.

The ideological leanings of most rich people in Manila were manifested even more bluntly over other issues. Leaders of the private sector argued forcefully for unrestrained freedom of business, limits on government intervention, a trickle-down approach to social justice and tight controls on the labour force. Manila's business mandarins measure the nation's economic success in terms of growth rates and profit margins. Equity and justice are secondary.

The reactions of mainstream business organizations to attempts to extend the rights of organized labour under Aquino demonstrated the primacy of self and class interests. Opposition to progressive labour laws united the business community more than any other issue. Producers for export versus the national market, importers, bankers and others in the urban élite may have bickered over the details of the nation's political and economic agenda, but were united in their opposition to pro-labour reforms.

As soon as President Aquino pledged to protect workers' rights to organize and strike in May 1986, the urban élite let out a howl of protest. The well-organized business community used its access to government officials, its control over several cabinet posts and its economic power to force Aquino's hand. Businessmen reminded Aquino that she herself, not the government or organized labour, had called the private sector the engine of development and had demanded the dismissal of the minister of labour, Bobbit Sanchez. Though the business sector won the initial skirmish — Aquino issued a much emasculated decree and dismissed Sanchez — a series of industrial and general strikes in 1986 and 1987, slow progress on privatisation and other complaints again stirred discontent in the business community. Right oppositionists attempted to exploit this discontent, but failed. The vast majority of the business community stuck by Aquino. 'For the most part businessmen feel there is no alternative to Cory Aquino,' Victor Lim told me in 1988, 'despite her inadequacies. She is the personification of many Filipino virtues that are being lost.' He added: 'If there are deficiencies that she cannot overcome by herself, then we have to help. That is the conviction of many businessmen.'

Aquino responded to the complaints of the business community far more quickly than she did to the grievances of other sectors. I asked Bobbit Sanchez for his reaction. 'Obstacles to change?' he repeated. 'Well, aside from the United States, big business people, local big business people. Most of them are concerned with profits only. What they cannot understand is that you cannot have real or full economic development without justice for labour.' Many businessmen do speak of the need to attack widespread poverty. But their way of fighting poverty has nothing to do with popular empowerment through labour unions, cooperatives and political change. They see the solution in increasing profits, charity and population control. Theirs is a classic combination of social engineering and trickle-down social justice.

An examination of the urban élite's agenda reveals the amazing strength of discredited economic models. These people have an almost religious belief in free enterprise and deregulation. Advocates of export orientation still accept the no longer applicable aspects of the NIC (newly industrialized country) model: production for a now more restricted and competitive global market. They choose to ignore the state's contribution to the success of this model. Yet, as Walden Bello pointed out, NICs grew during periods of massive state economic intervention:

> Mainstream interpretations of the NIC model convey an image of economies that have successfully harnessed the two engines of capitalist development: free markets and free trade. In fact, Taiwan and South Korea — the NICs most often cited as models of industrial development for the rest of the Third World — built up highly protected domestic markets at the same time that they were mounting a massive export drive to take advantage of the relatively open US market in the 1960s and 1970s. Moreover, both the Taiwanese and South Korean governments are interventionist states *par excellence*. In South Korea, an authoritarian state, working closely with huge monopolistic conglomerates called *chaebol*, targeted for development promising manufacturing industries like steel, electronics, and cars, and supported them with a variety of direct and indirect subsidies.[1]

Filipino business organizations argue that the state should limit its role to infrastructure development, carefully considered protectionism and other steps that can help the private sector play its leading role. Regulation, public investment and efforts aimed at directing the private sector should be avoided.

The private sector objects to government intervention in such areas as occupational safety and health, environmental and consumer protection, minimum wages and other areas where the state can regulate private industry in the public interest. Even when the state does try to enforce existing regulations, industry howls.

The shipping industry provided a tragic example. Though shipwrecks occur with frightening frequency in the waters of the Philippine archipelago, none brought home the ugliness of deregulated Philippine corporate life quite like the *Dona Paz* catastrophe. Late one night, shortly before Christmas 1987, the MV *Dona Paz*, an inter-island passenger liner, and the MS *Vector*, a cargo ship, collided off the coast of Mindoro.

Thousands died in what many believe was the worst peacetime maritime disaster in world history.

The *Dona Paz* had set sail with as many as 2,000 more passengers than its legal capacity of 1,800. The shipping company kept selling tickets while the coast guard looked the other way. Subsequent investigations revealed further irregularities: malfunctioning navigational equipment, drinking among crew members, shortages of safety equipment and so on. Yet, instead of accepting responsibility, the companies involved fought tooth-and-nail to avoid paying indemnity to the few survivors and the victims' kin.

Aside from demonstrating the callousness of the corporate world towards the public, the *Dona Paz* case brutally reveals the conflict between a deregulated market and the public interest. Without regulation, industry exploits the market to the greatest degree possible with concern only for maximizing profits. Advocates of deregulation and privatisation can point to a real problem with state control as practised during the Marcos era, when the state gained control of numerous enterprises not for the good of the public, but for the private advantage of the Marcoses and their cronies. Critics say this use of state control for personal gain continued under Aquino. 'We have witnessed the privatisation of government,' Lim said. He accused officials in charge of government corporations of using them as they would private enterprises, but without the risks inherent in the private sector.

The private sector's solution to a real problem does not, however, consider the public good. Instead it focuses on turning public sector reform into a push for private sector gain. Filipinos could have considered other options after the fall of Marcos, but the economic élite so dominated the discussions on economic policy that such options were not seriously thought about. As Rep. Bonifacio Gillego put it:

> So you have a constitution, a legal system that is so biased in favour of free enterprise, capitalism, private property, private initiative, there is an aversion to the public sector, to the role of the government. So, every time you talk about the government, they react — 'ah that is corruption, that is nepotism' — without ever realizing that at this stage in our economic history, it would require the active intervention of government to really do something important and substantive to uplift our people. Look at this privatisation thing, we have something profitable, so you give it to private enterprise, good heavens! I cannot believe it!

I asked Gillego for his reaction to the business community's enthusiastic response to Aquino's October 1987 anti-labour and pro-private sector speech.

'Yes, but what is that talk, it is all on privatisation, it is all on free enterprise, it is all "you guys, do it", but do any of them respond to social responsibility or to a basic needs approach?' he asked. 'What they want is "clear the way so we can make more money."' And that is the essential point. While the urban élite prattles on about structural adjustments or economic reforms, it opposes efforts to change the basic class structure, to challenge the very nature of a highly skewed social order, or to enhance the role of the state as a public advocate.

But the situation is even more tragic. The urban élite has failed to come up with a practical and visionary economic programme with which to rescue the nation from the morass of poverty. No Keynes, no Franklin Roosevelt, no creative thinker of the NIC variety has emerged from the élite to chart the course of anything even resembling development. In its place, a mishmash of ideas, part technocratic solution, part import substitution, part export orientation, emerged from Makati's high-rise buildings and government offices. The need to please various segments of the élite and the power of conservative thinkers drove many promising officials out of government and discouraged many critical thinkers.

Through an array of business clubs and fraternities, through their access to government posts and through their political use of economic power, members of the economic élite hold a tremendous amount of political power. They support traditional politicians and parties. Their money buys influence.

Most of the leaders of the traditional political parties today started with a particular regional base. Clark Soriano, a researcher with Ed de la Torre's Institute for Popular Democracy, carried out a study of the May 1987 congressional election and found that 129 of 200 elected representatives belonged to long-established regional political clans. This has led some analysts to point to a resurgence of 'bossism' as an important factor in the Aquino period. According to the *Far Eastern Economic Review*, many of the bosses converted economic power, built through farming, business and logging, and also illegal activities such as gambling, into political power by buying votes, intimidating citizens and making generally unfulfilled promises.[2]

'Bossism' provides the base for the traditional political parties. While the Marcos-era KBL (New Society Movement) and the Aquino-era LDP (Strength of Philippine Democracy) differ in some regards, one feature they have in common is that regional bosses give them their strength. With this base, it is not surprising that the major political parties follow a very conservative path. Their alternatives have nothing to do with constructive change and everything to do with changing the names and faces of the individuals running the government.

'Marcosism' without Marcos lived on in the faltering KBL. Its members initially refused to recognize Aquino as the rightful president of the Philippines. Following the departure of its leader, however, it fell on hard times. To all intents and purposes it has become a regional party led by a bunch of elderly politicians from the far north. By the time of Marcos's death in September 1989, it had become totally emasculated.

The groups identified with Enrile and Laurel, which came together under the Nationalist Party banner in 1989, offer more serious opposition to the ruling alliance and to social change. Enrile and Laurel do not suffer from total identification with the old regime, but they have damaged their credibility by courting Marcos loyalists and forming links with military conspirators. They also offer very little by way of an alternative. They are good at attacking the Aquino government, redbaiting and hate mongering, but refuse to be pinned down on specific policies. Unless they pull off some sort of violent manoeuvre — such as an assassination that would put Vice-President Laurel in Malacanang Palace — the best they can hope for is a post-Aquino revival. Neither man has much credibility, leaving the far right to continue its search for a saviour into the 1990s.

In the post-Marcos atmosphere, it is the conservative pro-Aquino parties (which use the rhetoric of the February revolution but seek to preserve much of the status quo) that provide the most formidable political opposition to change. The LDP emerged as the principal party of this type in late 1988. Five senators and 158 House members led by the president's brother, Rep. José Cojuangco, brother-in-law Paul Aquino, speaker of the House, Ramon Mitra, and speaker pro tem, Antonio Cuenco, joined the new party, leading many observers to declare it the new ruling party. President Aquino attended its founding convention, but cautiously stopped short of joining, warning against dividing democratic forces into permanent hostile camps.

If the LDP's emergence was inevitable, so too was the return to the old style of political organization. The LDP quickly became an alliance of opportunist politicians and regional bosses united, not to advance a common cause, but for access to power and patronage. It has proven a rather fragile alliance, with members moving in and out as their interests demand, but an essentially conservative one in that its members have a stake in the existing system.

Most of Aquino's supporters in the Senate — independents, the Liberal Party and Nene Pimentel's wing of the PDP — made no attempt to hide their distaste for the new party. Pimentel noted: 'We are happy that those who are not comfortable with the PDP—*Laban* in its pristine form have now transferred to the LDP. Apparently they have no ideological direction.' Rep. Gillego went further in an interview with the *Manila Chronicle*. 'How can the formation of the LDP be a positive development when in the eyes of the people it is nothing but a recycled KBL which feeds and sustains itself on the old traditional politics?'

The LDP's founders attempted to refute these arguments by describing the new party as the legitimate heir of the February Revolution and the alliance that had formed behind Mrs Aquino's campaign. Mitra described the new party's objectives as 'to consolidate, not break up, all forces supporting President Aquino.' Immediately after forming the LDP, Mitra and Cuenco moved to assert the LDP's status as the majority party in the lower House. They purged a handful of progressives in leadership positions. Liberal Party Rep. Raul Daza lost his post as assistant majority floor leader, Gillego surrendered the chairmanship of the Agrarian Reform Committee and Rep. Nikki Coseteng, a member of *Kaiba*, the small feminist party, lost her job as head of the Committee on Human Rights.

The LDP's performance on agrarian reform is an indication of the bankruptcy of this so-called centrist party. In enacting a new agrarian-reform law, Congress, especially the LDP-dominated House of Representatives, was much more responsive to the demands of the landed than to the needs of the far more numerous peasants and farm workers. Yet even an LDP majority can act in surprising ways when there is enough pressure and when the interests of their key constituents — the rural élite — are not at stake. In 1989 a panicked Congress approved a significant wage increase in response to a spreading campaign by organized labour (see Chapter 10), even though the move outraged President Aquino who had agreed to keep wages down to please the IMF.

The LDP is roughly at the centre of the current Philippine political spectrum. Unlike the parties of the far right, it does not advocate an autocratic state with a politically powerful military and minimal commitment to civil liberties. Even after the very serious 1989 coup attempt, when the LDP-dominated House joined the Senate in granting President Aquino emergency powers, it did so for only six months and continued in session.

Conservative or traditional politicians from the country's upper classes cannot continue to dominate the nation's politics without a compatible political system and political culture. During the early days of the Aquino government, left-of-centre activists and new-style democrats made concerted efforts to expand Philippine democracy beyond its traditionally limited confines. The new constitution reflected their efforts, but this turned into a hollow victory for progressives. The government put little or no effort into encouraging the growth of popular organizations. Prominent individuals in government instead opted to form traditional parties. And the government and the governing class used red-scare tactics to limit the scope of political democracy.

The political culture of the Philippines goes a long way towards explaining the élite's ability to limit Philippine democracy. This culture presents an obstacle to change. The voters' fixation with prominent individuals, the prevalence among ordinary people of *utang na loob*, or feeling a deep debt of gratitude to members of the local élite, and their inability to resist the influence of 'guns, goons and gold' provide fertile ground for traditional politicians.

In the immediate post-Marcos era, however, Cory Aquino herself provided the key obstacle to change. Her popularity, and the legitimacy she brought to an outmoded system, stood in the way of those who sought to organize a struggle for a radical renewal.

But her popularity declined as time passed and her inadequacies began to show. Neither she nor her successors will reclaim the tremendous popularity she held during her first years in office. This will help movements for radical change, but it will not guarantee their victory. The élite classes and regional bosses will fight to hold on to their wealth and power. And in this struggle they will be defended by an array of other conservative forces in Philippine society, including the army.

18

A People's Army or the Strong Arm of Reaction?

Two vintage Second World War 'tora-tora' planes circled overhead, suddenly fell towards the enemy target firing rockets at a burning building, then climbed skyward again. Tanks blasted holes in cement walls, troops poured through the gaps and the sound of cannons echoed off nearby buildings. For a day war seemed to have come to Manila.

Early morning machine-gun and automatic-rifle fire tore apart the silence of the night and claimed at least 50 civilian lives. Marines fought army renegades near Malacanang Palace forcing a retreat to Camp Aguinaldo where the mutineers gained control of AFP headquarters. The Air Force swung into action joining ground troops in attacking the camp housing the offices of the military's top brass and the Department of National Defence.

The coup attempt, which shook the nation on 28 August 1987, brought to the surface long-simmering disputes within the military over strategy, leadership, and its role in society. It, like previous attempts and the one that came two years later in 1989, revealed an ongoing battle for the hearts and minds of the nation's soldiers — a battle between those outwardly loyal to the existing order and a clique committed to replacing civilian authority with that of the military.

Coup attempts expose Manila's residents to the fact that Philippine politics partly revolves around armed power. In much of the country the AFP is fighting a counter-insurgent war against a poor people's army. It is a dirty war that claims scores of civilian lives and limits the scope of Philippine democracy. It is a war that is fought in most of the country's provinces, with the heaviest fighting in a few key regions where the guerrillas have strong forces and the AFP concentrates its fire.

Negros is one such place. On Negros the collapse of the sugar industry in the early 1980s fuelled poverty, rapid growth of the NPA (New People's Army) and a popular movement centred on a militant farm workers' union and dozens of BCCs (Basic Christian Communities).

Early in the Aquino period, the AFP command decided to make Negros, along with eight other provinces (out of the country's 73), an example and testing ground of its counter-insurgency expertise.

Operation Fishnet was put into play in early 1989 to a rhetoric about winning public support and using special operations teams to service communities and to counter the left's *barangay*-based mass organizations. But the reality was often very different. War came to Sipalay town in April that year. The military called it Operation Thunderbolt. It was to be a quick strike against the enemy, but it brought terror to the area's residents. 'We launched the operation after our detachment was attacked by members of the New People's Army,' explained Major Edgardo Cordero. 'They killed five of our soldiers.' Before retaliating, Brig.-Gen. Raymundo Jarque radioed Sipalay's mayor and advised her to evacuate the residents of outlying villages. Those who stayed behind were to regret their decision.

Sikorsky helicopters bombed what were believed to be the insurgents' sanctuaries. Soldiers searched, burned and looted houses. At least 25 people suspected of aiding the NPA were killed. The military failed to capture a single rebel. By the end of Operation Thunderbolt an estimated 30,000 refugees had moved into an evacuation centre near the town's schoolhouse. They soon faced epidemics of measles, pneumonia and malnutrition. By the end of their four-month exile, an estimated 300 children had died.

Peace remains elusive in the Philippine countryside. A dirty war fought by an army that promises to serve the public and punish the scoundrels in its own ranks, that holds a tremendous amount of political power in the post-Marcos Philippines, rages on. A self-styled military reform movement had played a central role in ushering out the Marcos dictatorship. Gen. Fidel Ramos had been quick to tag the AFP the 'new armed forces of the people.' Yet most of the old colonels and generals remained in charge and it was only a matter of time before fresh accusations of human rights abuses, corruption and incompetence surfaced. Meanwhile, the advent of a popular government promising serious reform under Cory Aquino appealed to many Filipinos tired of almost two decades of fratricidal strife. The idea of a 'political settlement' with the communists gained currency as an alternative to counter-insurgency.

Many factors contributed to the failure of the peace campaign, one being military opposition. The military mustered all its might to oppose concessions to the rebels, no matter how just their demands. Though senior officers spoke of political and social responses to the guerrilla war, they did so within the framework of counter-insurgency. They sought victory not compromise. Ironically, despite being less disciplined and more divided, the AFP managed to assert itself. Three main factions emerged — pro-Marcos officers, RAM (the Reform the Armed Forces Movement close to Juan Ponce Enrile), and forces loyal to the new chain of command. The first two would collaborate on occasions, as in the 1989 coup attempt when pro-Marcos and pro-Enrile forces tactically united to oust Aquino. The dissidents launched countless plots and sometimes bloody coup attempts. All factions opposed communists, i.e. anyone fighting for radical structural and social change.

On becoming president, Aquino had hoped to unite a reformed AFP. In early 1987 she said:

> As for the Armed Forces of the Republic, it is admitted that the military has been demoralized and dishonoured by the Marcos regime. I assure you, however, that there are among the military a restlessness and a desire for the restoration of the honour and prestige which the profession once possessed. My leadership will lend support to the restoration and revitalization of the military ideal.

At the time Mrs Aquino had thought she would be able to reform the military with the cooperation of reform-minded officers who respected her authority as commander-in-chief. But these officers had other ideas. They were thinking about seizing power through a *coup d'état*, or, failing that, turning their pivotal role in the success of the anti-Marcos revolt into a basis for attaining new power. Enrile (and RAM members loyal to him) hardly veiled their thirst for overt power and influence. Gen. Ramos and other 'professional' officers demonstrated greater political acumen in using Aquino's fear of the military's armed power and instability to influence the new government.

The military's politicization had begun in earnest with the advent of martial law in the 1970s. Its mission became the defence of a particular administration, not of the nation or constitution. Marcos offered top command posts to officers who showed loyalty but not necessarily competence. Gen. Fabian Ver, Marcos's cousin and former driver, came to exemplify and lead the military cronies. With limited training and no combat experience, he passed over several more qualified candidates to become chief of staff. Such promotions created tensions in the AFP (young professional officers found their careers blocked by Marcos loyalists) which mounted rapidly when Enrile fell out with Ver and Imelda Marcos and began to recruit bright junior officers to his staff.

These junior officers, who formed the core of RAM, rejected corruption and incompetence, but not the politicization of the military. In fact they saw themselves as the final arbiters of the nation's political life. Seeing this led one of the country's most respected military men to reject

RAM's anti-government plots. 'February 1986 was like opening Pandora's box,' Marine Brig.-Gen. Rodolfo Biazon, head of the strategic National Capital Region Defence Command, told me in 1988. 'Some of us thought that the soldier has the discretion to determine the legitimacy and performance of a government and, if in his judgement the government is not legitimate and its performance is below what he expects, then he has the right to come in and interfere.'

All discussion of military politics immediately prior to the fall of Marcos and during the Aquino era must start with RAM. RAM emerged publicly in early 1985; at the time it hid its subversive nature. In their Statement of Common Aspirations, its leaders wrote:

> Our efforts shall be geared towards the attainment of the AFP's new thrusts of uplifting the morale and welfare of every man and woman in uniform; enhancing the operational effectiveness of the military establishment; and restoring our people's faith in their armed forces so that in the long run we shall be able to contribute our share of building a just, peaceful and progressive society where all Filipinos live in harmony and with dignity.

In various early documents RAM had expressed admiration for Marcos's ideology, if not approval of his final years of rule. In referring to his 1973 tailor-made constitution, one document had spoken of how, 'We cling to the democratic ideals enshrined in our Constitution.' Another stressed adherence to Marcos's 'revolution,' saying the AFP must move to the centre of the political stage to 'perform its proper role as arbiter and active participant in the Democratic Revolution.' That same document noted: 'The book *The Filipino Ideology* serves as the ideological foundation for the movement.' This book, published under Marcos's name, was a pseudo-nationalist tract meant to justify martial law and offer an alternative to Marxism, liberalism and social democracy.

In part, RAM praised the constitution and ideology as a cover for its anti-Marcos activities. Yet this does not eliminate the possibility of a genuine adherence to Marcos's ideology despite its having broken with the Marcos government in its final years. Juan Ponce Enrile, RAM's mentor, served as Marcos's martial law administrator and was one of the architects of his so-called democratic revolution. After the fall of Marcos, Enrile opposed Aquino's decision to abolish Marcos institutions like the *Batasang Pambansa* and the martial law constitution.

RAM's campaign to reform the army focused on corruption, favouritism and increasing combat efficiency. For RAM leaders schooled by American instructors in theories of the national security state an important reason for doing this was to enhance the AFP's counter-insurgency effectiveness. Shortly after Mrs Aquino came to power, navy captain Rex Robles, a RAM leader who had headed Enrile's national defence study group, told me that RAM had considered Marcos a 'counter-insurgency failure. We expected the NPA to win eventually if Marcos stayed in office,' he said.

RAM's first power play coincided with the ascendancy of the civilian anti-Marcos movement. Only when Marcos's agents uncovered RAM's plot in February and forced it onto the defensive did the conspirators consider a coalition with Aquino. The advent of Aquino did not end RAM's plotting and she faced an early challenge to her authority from Enrile and RAM in the God Save the Queen episode (see Chapter 10). On that occasion Aquino relied on her chief of staff, Gen. Ramos, to suppress the coup and, in the process, he increased his stature in pro-democracy circles. But despite democratic pretensions Ramos remained a power broker and soon showed his ability to turn loyalty to his advantage by manoeuvring Aquino into dismissing Enrile as defence minister. The showdown between Enrile and Ramos — the first of several to come — firmly established the two main factions in the AFP. One centred on Ramos and included the official chain of command. The other focused on the RAM Core Group, which, though dispersed from Ministry headquarters, went on organizing. The military made matters more difficult for itself by failing to punish the RAM coup makers seriously. Some of the conspirators were removed from their posts, but none faced court martial or was dismissed from the service. That two top RAM bosses, Gregorio 'Gringo' Honasan and Eduardo 'Red' Kapunan, were assigned important training posts would come back to haunt the leadership later.

Two months after the God Save the Queen debacle, I met Brig.-Gen. Jesus de la Cruz at his headquarters near Baguio. De la Cruz, an ally of Ramos's, served as regional AFP commander in a fervently pro-Marcos region in the north-western Philippines. He said that private armies of various Ilocano war-lords continued to roam the coastal plains, many carrying firearms authorized by Col Honasan. I asked him what authority Honasan had to issue such orders. He replied: 'None.'

RAM continued to recruit military support after its first coup attempt. It exploited the economic discontent and low morale of poorly-paid soldiers. It also condemned the government for being soft on communism and for demonstrating an alleged bias against the military. This bias, RAM said, manifested itself in the Human Rights Commission's investigation of abuses by military men. Further, RAM attacked the political and military leadership for lacking a counter-insurgency strategy and for poor leadership. In the process, it exploited long-simmering conflicts between Ramos's PC (Philippine Constabulary) and the other major branches of the service.

The year 1987 was one of struggle within the AFP. RAM continued to organize. The Marcos loyalists attempted another coup. The struggle reached a climax with the August coup attempt described at the beginning of this chapter. RAM forces, led by Gringo Honasan, attacked Malacanang and seized the general headquarters at Camp Aguinaldo, portions of Villamor airbase, the government television studios and a nearby hotel; 53 individuals, mostly civilians, died in the attacks and in the sporadic fighting which lasted throughout the day. In the end RAM was defeated and the general headquarters gutted by fire. Honasan and other leaders slipped into the darkness.

The failure of the coup forced RAM underground. The arrest of Gringo Honasan in late 1987 seemed to have brought his and RAM's role to an end, but Honasan escaped and renewed his campaign to overthrow the Aquino government underground. Many suspected the underground RAM of involvement in right-wing death squad activity; in any case it continued to sow intrigue within the AFP.

Meanwhile Ramos moved to consolidate his control over the AFP and his influence within the government. He had already used the threat of instability after earlier coup attempts to push successfully for the removal of leftists from the government and for the further emasculation of the human rights committee.

The government responded to the 28 August coup attempt by increasing the AFP's budget. In addition, Aquino now made Ramos secretary of national defence and dismissed her executive secretary, Joker Arroyo, a former human rights lawyer who was much hated by the AFP. Congress rejected pleas for an internal security act, but moved towards the enactment of tougher anti-subversion laws.

New cabinet members, many drawn from business or conservative politics, were notably more comfortable working with the AFP than with the anti-Marcos activists who had preceded them. One example of this occurred in the Department of Local Government. Aquilino Pimentel, Aquino's first choice for the position, had an uneasy relationship with the military leadership. His replacement, Jaime Ferrer, won acclaim from them (and corresponding notoriety from human rights advocates) for having joined the military in supporting anti-communist vigilantes.

RAM continued to criticize the AFP leadership for lacking a strategy and for incompetence. The Marcos era had never suffered from a shortage of counter-insurgency operation plans. But in the 1980s the inability of the regime to cope with growing insurgency became clear. Marcos's military acted as a praetorian guard. Gen. Ver ordered an inordinate number of troops to be stationed in and around Metro Manila when most of the regime's armed opponents were concentrating their efforts in the countryside. Also, Marcos and Ver gave field commanders little flexibility. They reorganized the AFP so that 'regional unified commanders,' reporting directly to Ver, had overall control over military affairs in the country's 13 regions. Ver used this structure to consolidate his control over the entire AFP. Regional commanders, most of whom owed their position to loyalty to Marcos and Ver, felt limited in their ability to act without the specific go-ahead from general headquarters.

Neither Ver nor his subordinates were very creative military thinkers. Under Ver, life in the AFP was centred on the garrison, with field operations being merely short-term forays. They were also poor diplomats and poor disciplinarians, and intra-service rivalries periodically exploded into violent confrontations. But the AFP's most significant handicap was the Marcos regime's utter inability to win the hearts and minds of the population. Human rights abuses, the gross flaunting of wealth, economic injustice and the absence of any meaningful ways of participating in political life fuelled opposition sentiment. In the countryside the NPA provided an attractive alternative to the corrupt government.

The US government recognized this in its 1984 Philippines NSSD (National Security Study Directive): 'The US government does not want to remove Marcos from power to destabilize the GOP [Government of the Philippines],' wrote the study's authors. 'Rather, we are urging revitalization of democratic institutions, dismantling 'crony' monopoly capitalism and allowing the economy to respond to free market forces, and restoring professional, apolitical leadership to the Philippine military to deal with the growing communist insurgency.' Washington's call for reform came too late to save Marcos but not the AFP. After the February revolution, many Filipinos gave the AFP a second chance. Instead of fighting for a discredited regime, the AFP leadership could now portray itself as the defender of a popular leader and democratic order.

The new government had two alternatives in responding to the communist-led revolutionary movement. It could genuinely seek a political settlement, a path which would demand negotiations, radical reform and further development of people power. Or it could continue with counter-insurgency, which would require new strategies, a stronger AFP and reform of the military's worst abuses.

At first advocates of the two conflicting positions clashed within the government; however, counter-insurgency advocates always outnumbered and outgunned supporters of a political settlement. Even as peace talks proceeded, the AFP built up its fighting capabilities. Within months of Cory coming to power, the military launched a full-scale offensive against rebel positions in the Cagayan Valley of the northern Philippines.

Around the same time, US Secretary of State George Shultz visited Manila and expressed confidence in Aquino's approach to the insurgency. He assured reporters that the Philippine government was doing the same things to fight the insurgents as 'we are in El Salvador.'

The peace lobby continued its efforts but with only limited success. The government's refusal to appear to be making concessions to the rebels doomed negotiations to failure weeks before the ceasefire ended. The time had come, in President Aquino's tough new rhetoric, to 'unsheathe the sword of war.'

Counter-insurgency involves military, political and civic action aimed at defeating an insurgent movement. Ileto and Ramos, both US Military Academy graduates, accepted the same general framework but clashed over priorities. Gen. Ileto, who had led the Scout Rangers in combating the *Huk* rebellion and whom Aquino had appointed defence minister after Enrile's dismissal, gave greater prominence to the military dimension. He sought to send special forces into the jungles for weeks at a time in pursuit of the highly mobile guerrillas. Ramos took a more holistic approach, an approach shared by most policy makers in the US as well as the current commanders of the AFP. In early 1985 Ramos had told a gathering of executives in Manila that:

> We are dealing more with a political problem than a military threat. Our purpose then must be to destroy the political appeal of the CPP. As long as that party is intact, we have achieved nothing, even if we destroy the NPA. On the other hand, if we destroy the political appeal of the CPP, the NPA will wither away.

Ramos also emphasized a fast-track approach to counter-insurgency, which 'pursues the concept of fighting the CTs [communist terrorists] in a war of quick decision and not a war of attrition, the latter being synonymous to the CPP/NPA's protracted war.' Both Ramos and Aquino have repeatedly expressed the desire to defeat the NPA by the end of her presidential term, a goal that even some military men call unattainable.

The main components of Ramos's approach included the concentration of forces in provinces in which the guerrillas were most active, the use of special military teams based in the community to counter the underground's political infrastructure, civic action and the destruction of legal left groups, as well as traditional military operations. Aquino's victory gave Ramos the opportunity to test his theories in more favourable conditions than had existed during Marcos's time. Even as he was waging battles for control of the AFP against Enrile, the RAM boys and Ileto (who had been replaced by Ramos as secretary of national defence after the 1987 coup attempt), he and his colleagues were working hard to develop tactics to fit the actual conditions and framework they favoured.

'As an initial step,' Brig.-Gen. Mariano Adalem, commanding general of the AFP, told the *Manila Chronicle* in 1988:

> you must isolate the rebels from the people's support and having isolated them it will be easier for you to go after them in military operations. We found that out of practical necessity, no matter how much you like to engage the enemy and kill them in close combat, if they hide among the sympathetic population or the population who gives them protection because they are afraid, what can you do?[1]

In a 1988 paper, an official from the National Defence Department listed some of the components being used in the military's political war:

1   Heightened psychological pressure against the insurgents in the centres of population, applied primarily to the political will of the people, expressed through the local governments and *Bantay Bayan* (civilian volunteer organizations).

2   Intensified police action, undertaken by the territorial forces (the PC, the INP, and Cafgu's active auxiliaries).

3   Countryside military offensive, staged by the AFP regular forces acting as mobile forces against dissidents pushed out of the population centres (by both of the above) as well as against those in established guerrilla bases in the hinterlands.

The outline excluded what became the most prominent weapon in the AFP's counter-insurgency arsenal: the SOT (Special Operations Team). Brig.-Gen. Adalem started using them in Mindanao in 1984 to dismantle the rebels' grassroots political structures. He told the *Manila Chronicle* interviewer:

> The SOT is in itself complete. It has military operations. It advocates rehabilitation and economic development that will have to be done largely by our civilian counterparts. It relies on a very strong intelligence network to be able to identify the people's needs. Then, psychological operations which include an information drive to inform the people that no matter how deficient other people see our democracy it is still better than the alternative that the NPAs are proposing.[2]

Brig.-Gen. Biazon, who had used SOTs during his tenure as AFP commander in Metro Manila, described the SOTs when we talked in 1988:

The Special Operations Teams are soldiers too, but soldiers who are not for combat, but rather to focus on the teaching of the evils of communism, evils of the CPP-NPA's activities. They also try to dismantle the political infra-structure of the CPP-NPA in the *barangays*. If they are trying to organize the people there for say mass movements or teaching the idea of communism, then the SOT is countering that by organizing the community for simple projects such as cleanliness, vigilance against simple crimes and teaching the people, especially people around factories, that the infiltration of the KMU in the labour movement is designed towards forcing the collapse of the national economy.

Shortly before speaking with Biazon I had visited Valenzuela, a working-class town north of Manila, and found an SOT encamped in the community centre of a poor *barrio* bordering a new city dump. The soldiers had come to Manila from Mindanao where they had spent years fighting the MNLF (Moro National Liberation Front). Prior to their assignment, they had undergone training in urban counter-insurgency.

Members of the KMU painted a disturbing picture of the SOT's poli-tical operations. Soldiers showed *The Killing Fields* in factories and at community gatherings and identified the NPA with the Khmer Rouge. They accused the KMU's local organizers of belonging to the CPP or the NPA's Manila-based Armed City Partisans. Army officers delivered anti-communist lectures to captive audiences in local factories, in which they described the KMU as a communist front organization working to close factories rather than to win better pay and working conditions. After numerous unsolved killings of activists pinpointed by the military as members of the CPP, several organizers curtailed their public activities. Biazon justified the political and psychological war waged against the KMU by telling me 'this is an organization that is deliberately and inten-tionally organized and infiltrated by the CPP/NPA to force, as I said, the collapse of the economy.'

The military, however, does not limit its attacks to groups identified with the national democratic movement. Maris Diokno's description of an encounter with the AFP's chief of civil military relations, Brig.-Gen. Honesto Isleta, illustrates the wide brush with which the military paints popular movements red. 'We were in a forum together at a high school here at UP,' Diokno told me. 'And it was a forum on vigilantes, so I was against and of course he was for':

In the open forum, he goes on and explains there are two forms of subversion in this country. The first is armed struggle. Fine. I accept that. The second is mass action. Of course my eyebrows go 'hey.' I say 'Mass action?'

He goes: 'Yeah it's all these SMAs...'

So I whisper to him: 'Explain.'

He goes: 'Subversive mass activists.'

That's the one thing I like about dealing with the military. Each time I meet with them my vocabulary is enriched. I come home with a new term.

He says: 'These SMAs, these are the guys who go to Mendiola and rally there, and go to the US Embassy and rally against the bases, blah, blah, blah blah.'

And he's talking to young people, high school students.

So I said: 'You know General, I just want to ask a question, because I'm undergoing an identity crisis.' I said, 'Just last week I was with the farmers at their commemoration of the Mendiola massacre.' I said, 'Well, I don't belong to the farmers group, but I am for land reform, does that make me an SMA?'

And I have to put it in those terms because those are very young people, now he goes around school after school talking like this.

And he says: 'No, if you were SMA, you wouldn't be around.'

I figured, 'What is mass action?' Armed struggle, I know, that is in the hills, but SMA? I mean mass action is here and now.

He adds onto that: 'You know, actually, many of these like those who go to the US Embassy and fight the bases, these people are really misled and misguided.' So I said: 'Excuse me General. I'm opposed to the US bases and I'll never stop opposing those US bases and the US Embassy is my favourite rallying place. You are telling me I am misguided!'

He goes: 'Oh no, Miss Diokno here is opposed to the US bases out of principle.'

So I said: 'Thank you.'

But when I related this story to some friends, they said: 'Well you can get away with that because you're a Diokno.'

Perhaps the most telling line in that exchange was Gen. Isleta's comment: 'If you were an SMA you wouldn't be around.' The statement reminds us that behind the rhetoric of politics and civic action is an armed force and a shooting war. The deaths and disappearances of activists demonstrate the danger of being tagged a subversive by the military.

A series of reports by human rights groups and the Philippine Senate brought this home. In December 1988, Amnesty International declared: 'Several consistent and apparently reliable reports of torture show that extensive legal safeguards against incommunicado detention, ill treatment and torture are being ignored. Military intelligence agents are reported to have subjected detainees to severe beatings, electric shocks, stabbings, near suffocation with plastic bags or water, and sexual abuse.' The report added, 'Similar abuses in police stations have been reported.'[3]

That report followed an earlier Amnesty International document revealing a pattern of liquidations committed by the AFP. 'Since mid-1987 political killings carried out by government and government-backed forces in violation of the law have become the most serious human rights problem in the Philippines,' wrote Amnesty International in January 1988. 'Most of the victims have been suspected supporters of the communist insurgency, many of them members of legal left-wing organizations.'[4] Task Force Detainees claimed that the police and military had arrested nearly 12,000 people for political reasons between the start of Aquino's term and 21 November 1988. It called most of the arrests illegal and attributed them to raids on slums by troops searching for rebels. It claimed the government held 659 political prisoners as of 21 November.[5] The *Far Eastern Economic Review* reported in its 15 December 1988 issue:

> In the two years and nine months that Aquino has been in office, for instance, there have been some 220 reported disappearances. This is lower than the 114 cases reported annually in the last three years of the Marcos administration, but the numbers have been increasing since 1986. So far this year there have been close to 100, with a high proportion representing individuals who are members rather than officers of leftist organizations in the student and labour sectors.[6]

This tactic of targeting lower level people emerged after several highly visible legal left activists either died during or survived ambush attacks. The deaths of Rolando Olalia and Lean Alejandro, the bloody attacks on Bernabe Buscayno and Nemensio Prudente, fit a pattern of violence against the legal left. The attacks on Prudente, an independent leftist and university president, followed a demonstration in which police officers, angered by NPA attacks on their comrades, called for 'death to Prudente.'

Despite the brutal side of its campaign, the military emphasizes the need for civilian support for and involvement in the counter-insurgency programme. 'You see, our mayors now must work double time,' noted

Gen. de Villa in an interview with the *Manila Chronicle*. 'Once we remove the threat in any given area then the civil side of government, principally the mayor and the other support services, must work double time so that the loyalty of these people will not change again.'[7]

In addition to the national Peace & Order Council, the government established local counterparts to help deliver services and mobilize the public in the counter-insurgency campaign. 'We are actually in effect organizing a nationwide vigilante system for a total war against communism,' Secretary of Local Government Luis Santos told me. Despite this and the president's restoration of a law banning membership in either the CPP or PKP, the military continued to push for new laws that would make their fight easier. Military officers backed the restoration of the death penalty and floated the idea of a National Security Act which would implement a national identity-card programme, restrict the freedom to organize, to strike and to protest, and reduce the legal protections for suspected subversives. This proposal, however, encountered resistance from the progressive block in the Senate, civil libertarians and, even more, conservative democrats.

While the military shows no hesitation in intervening in the political system to push counter-insurgency, it does not push for the one thing that could bring a just and lasting peace to the Philippines, namely changing from an unjust social order to one that is fairer.

In order to implement its plans the military leadership has had to address the organizational and morale problems left by the Marcos dictatorship. It has also found itself confined by the new constitution banning the CHDF (Civilian Home Defence Forces) and other para-military groups. Similarly, the government faced a constitutional mandate to separate the INP (Integrated National Police) from the AFP. The INP and the CHDF had added about 90,000 men and women to the 160,000 regular AFP personnel. They played an important role in counter-insurgency operations on a local level, but the CHDF's abysmal human rights record compelled changes.

The defence leadership replaced the 13 regional unified commands with six area commands. It delineated the responsibilities of the area unified commanders, letting them know clearly what they could and could not do without the express permission of general headquarters. This was in response to a complaint from the field that under Ver everything had been controlled from headquarters. The reorganization gave area commanders operational control over all troops in their region.

Improving the ratio of combat to non-combat forces posed a more difficult challenge. Ileto confirmed that the AFP had only 70,000 effective combatants in mid-1987.[8] Traditionally it suffered from a top-heavy administration and a concentration of troops in Metro Manila. But the danger posed by coup attempts and Armed City Partisan actions pinned down significant numbers of troops in the Manila area, away from the main military fronts.

What to do with the CHDF raised more complex political issues. Distaste for the CHDF was strong enough to have all para-military units proscribed by the constitution. However, the military places a great deal of importance on direct citizen involvement in the counter-insurgency drive to supplement the regular armed forces.

The vigilante groups, which proliferated after Aquino came to power, were an extension of this campaign. First supported by local military officers and anti-communist mayors, governors and war-lords, as they spread, they got official national support. Widespread suspicion also developed that foreign anti-communist groups (and perhaps the CIA) supported their development.

The Senate Committee on Human Rights issued a scathing denouncement of the vigilantes signed by 11 senators:

> Many vigilante groups have become notorious for harassing, torturing and executing civilians. The existence and operations of many vigilante groups subject the local population to a grip of paralysing, debilitating fear that greatly hampers their ability to work for their livelihood and the welfare of their families and communities. Such fear also prevents them from exercising their constitutional right to organize and collectively solve their community problems.

Vigilante groups provided temporary relief while the military and government sought an alternative structure for civilian counter-insurgency efforts. The alternative they settled on involved the division of the civilian anti-communist forces into two components — the unarmed *Bantay Bayan*, which would perform intelligence and neighbourhood watch functions, and the armed Cafgu (Civilian Armed Forces Geographic Units). 'People really see [Cafgu] as a CHDF with another collar,' said Brig.-Gen. Adalem.

> Well, maybe so, except for training. The CHDF were just taken over by the war-lords, but here now you will have to be a member of the reservists. Second, this is going to be officer led. It wasn't before. And then better selection because if we can throw in that the community participates, they will probably select somebody who is responsible and known not to be abusive.[9]

Some of the qualifications look better on paper than in fact. For example, virtually every adult who attended at least high school is considered a reservist as military training has been a mandatory part of the curriculum.

Second, local political bosses who might select Cafgu members are often more responsive to the demands of the ruling structure than their community. And finally, there are no guarantees that officers assigned as Cafgu commanders will respect the wishes of the public.

That actual violations of human rights still continue raises doubts about the AFP's commitment to eliminating the gravest abuses. But the need to improve the military's public persona has led its top officers and their American advisers to raise the human rights issue. As Walden Bello writes:

> [A] major reform demanded by the Pentagon was a curb on the abuse of civilians by the military — a common practice that was seen in Washington as one of the main causes of the NPA's popularity. According to the NSSD, this was to be achieved both by tightening up on military discipline and by providing better pay to recruits so as to diminish the incentive to steal food and property from villagers.[10]

Discipline, equipment, morale and pay clearly remain problems within the AFP. Soldiers received a 60 per cent pay rise as part of the post-28 August 1987 concessions to the military; however, pay for enlisted men remains very low. Shortages of boots and uniforms still require some combat troops to wear rubber sandals and tattered uniforms. Such factors do not make for high morale.

A centrepiece in the drive for public support has been the value formation programme, which seeks to inculcate Christian values in the military and to change its image. Francisco Nemenzo offered a harsh critique of the value formation programme soon after the military introduced it:

> So much hope is pinned by the pious Cory Aquino government on the so-called value formation programme of Ramos and Ileto. This is an exercise in futility. No amount of seminars will teach the old rascals new manners and right conduct. The doctrine of civilian supremacy can be written on every page of the constitution and preached in every military parade. Every soldier can be required to swear fidelity to democracy. But all this will come to naught when the chance to grab power arises.
>
> Now that our soldiers have been politicized, we might as well politicize them properly. They should be made aware of the disastrous consequences of military rule in other countries; and how military intervention, far from solving any problem, compounds and makes it worse. In a language they understand, they must be made to grasp the rationale for civilian supremacy. And above all, they must be helped out of the simplistic Cold War ideology which perceives politics in black and white.... Anti-communism as a means

of motivating the soldiers can be detrimental to democracy; it is the ideological root of contemporary fascism.[11]

Nemenzo suggested that the government introduce his ideas to the Philippine Military Academy, but needless to say neither the AFP nor the state adopted his proposals. Instead, training continues to follow its traditional anti-communist ideological format.

Soldiers are taught that the danger stems from the ideology of communism, not from the existence of an unjust social order. Instructors do not teach the officers and troops to distinguish between the armed left and its unarmed counterpart. They are not even taught to distinguish between varieties of left-wing ideologies. The AFP brass, government officials and US advisers all contribute to this orientation. AFP leaders deny being strongly influenced by the United States, but the US plays an important role in the ideological formation of the modern Philippine army. Virtually every high-ranking officer in the AFP has undergone advanced training in the United States. US lecturers regularly visit the National Defence College.

US input comes from several sources, but an important one is JUSMAG (the Joint US Military Advisory Group). JUSMAG coordinates visits to US facilities by AFP officers wishing to learn to operate US-supplied weapons and equipment or to study intelligence, military command, psychological warfare and other military sciences. JUSMAG also organizes joint exercises involving US and Philippine troops. It works with the AFP to improve its intelligence capabilities and may send advisers into the field.

I spent a morning inside JUSMAG headquarters with three US officers, a marine colonel and two army majors, discussing training programmes. The three noted that all training programmes, especially IMET (International Military Education & Training Program), which brings foreign personnel to US military schools for instruction in civil-military operations, psychological warfare, counter-insurgency and logistics, provide a way in which the US can influence Filipino thinking and win lasting friendships within the AFP. A Marcos-era report by the Philippine Command & General Staff College summed it up this way: 'It is apparent that other than providing security assistance, IMET/P[hilippines] aims at gaining allies for the host country [i.e. the US] in the guise of education and training packages.'[12]

In 1986 the US spent $2.2 million on IMET programmes for the Philippines. About 460 Philippine soldiers and officers participated. The US-Philippine military relationship does not stop with training and education. The AFP depends on the US for virtually all its heavy equipment, sophisticated weaponry and transport supplies. 'At present, the Navy, maybe the Air Force are almost completely dependent on the US,' Col Oscar Florendo told me:

> I am talking of ships, big ones. Although we have small ones which we build ourselves, but you cannot call them a real navy because we do not have the capability. For the more than 75 troopships, I think it is almost 100 per cent coming from the States. And our aircraft, I think 85 per cent we have to depend on the United States, although right now I think we are buying some from Italy.

This relationship between the US and Philippine military has led many critics to look at the AFP campaign against the NPA within the context of the low-intensity conflict strategy being promoted by the US internationally. The Philippine military leadership rejects this idea. From its perspective it is simply continuing in its own tradition of counter-insurgency — a tradition that involves close cooperation with the US. From an outside perspective, however, what is being done in the Philippines does resemble US strategy elsewhere. With US support, but without troop intervention, the AFP is fighting a politico-military war against not only an armed insurgency, but also virtually all radical movements.

Since Aquino has come to power, the AFP has scored some important, though not decisive, victories in that war. It has arrested important leaders of the underground movement, captured revealing documents, reclaimed some hinterland areas from rebel influence and damaged numerous open left organizations. Despite this, the AFP leadership has been unable to solve its own internal problems. The extent of involvement in the December 1989 coup demonstrated the depth of division within its ranks, the appeal of an ideology that places the military at the forefront of political action, and the inability of the civilian and military leadership to control restive elements in the army.

Ironically, these attempted coups have occurred as the government has adopted more and more elements of an agenda shared by RAM and Ramos — anti-communism, limited democracy and restrictions on the freedoms of a civil society. Indeed it is important to remember that neither faction of the army promises to withdraw from politics and defend an open democratic system. In this they have a great deal in common with other conservative forces, including the US and its allies.

19

Foreign Powers

As Francisco and I walked over the rolling hills of his native Bicol region, our conversation drifted from guerrilla war to basketball and unrequited love. His black Converse All Stars gripped the dusty path, his US-made M-16 bounced against his bulky body. When he was growing up he had worshipped Bill Russell and Wilt Chamberlain, the American basketball giants of the 1960s. Francisco had played basketball well enough to join a regional all-star team in a tournament in the Visayas. He laughed at his team's ill-fated attempt to win the tournament. 'We were the shortest team involved,' he said. 'All we won were the spectator's hearts. We became the crowd favourites.' At college Francisco's interests had drifted away from the sporting world, but he had been unable to escape the US influence. Francisco had studied agriculture and his academic adviser had prodded him to write his thesis on wheat and soy bean intercropping. 'Imagine,' he said to me, 'wheat and soy bean intercropping. We're a tropical country. Where do we grow wheat and soy beans?'

As we approached his *nipa* hut we stepped up our pace. Francisco wanted to listen to the VOA (Voice of America) news. Whenever he could Francisco, a committed member of the CPP, listened to the VOA news on a small transistor radio in the distant hills of his native land. He had reached a personal accommodation with the US and things American. He opposed US dominance of his nation and culture, he rejected those aspects of US influence considered foolish, but he accepted the borrowed Americanisms he liked: basketball, Converse All Stars, an M-16 and even the VOA. Francisco's struggle with things American reflects the struggle the entire Philippine nation is undergoing. His personal compromise presents a possible outcome. He did what Raul Manglapus had recommended: He 'cut the American father figure down to brotherly size, or perhaps cousinly size.'

America looms large to Filipinos. I have often stood on the triangle of grass formed by the convergence of the main streets of Makati and, surrounded by the stunted skyscrapers of the business district, listened to their political speakers. The buildings themselves represent US involvement in the Philippines. The big ones house the RCA, the Bank of America, Citibank and other US corporations. Around the corner is a popular cinema. On any given day, two, three, even four Hollywood films flash across its screens. Nowhere, however, can the impact of US cultural and economic influence be more graphically observed than at the US Embassy on Manila Bay. Each morning, hundreds of Filipinos line up on the pavement in front of the embassy to await their turn to be interviewed for a visa.

Links in the popular mind reflect a shared history. Formal ties between the US and the Philippines, which are rooted in decades of struggle and collaboration, suffered a difficult period in the mid-1980s. Debates in Washington over the future of the Marcos regime were acrimonious. American liberals and pragmatic conservatives greeted the advent of Cory Aquino's presidency with genuine glee. They believed a new era in US-Philippine friendship and cooperation was being born. When Cory visited Washington in September 1986, members of the capital's establishment greeted her with fawning admiration. They fêted her at an official State Department dinner and applauded wildly as she spoke to a joint session of Congress. But the exuberant reception was not universal. Vice-President George Bush and President Aquino had an awkward meeting. Neither could forget Bush's sorry performance as Reagan's errand boy five years earlier, when Bush had lavished praise on Marcos for his commitment to democracy.

If Bush had acted uncomfortably in Aquino's company, President Reagan behaved deplorably. He waited until April, two months after her accession to the presidency, before telephoning to congratulate her on her victory. Later he erred by speaking to Marcos on the telephone when they had both been in Hawaii. Reagan had refused to grant Aquino's visit the status of a 'state visit,' an honour ordinarily accorded visiting heads of state. But when the two did meet, Reagan turned on the charm and promised to continue delivering economic aid. Thus, despite Reagan's discomfort, the US government went about patching up its relationship with the Philippines and with Cory Aquino's government. Realists in Washington wanted a strong relationship to strengthen US interests. In Marcos, they had had an increasingly hated ally; in Cory an extremely popular potential friend.

Money quickly became the weapon of choice in the US diplomatic arsenal. Aside from turning on a bilateral aid pipeline, the US renewed its efforts on behalf of the Philippines at the IMF, the World Bank and the ADB (Asian Development Bank). It also launched a showy effort to unite the world capitalist powers in a special Philippine Aid Programme, also known as the Mini-Marshall Plan, or MAI (Multilateral Aid Initiative). For its policy to work, the US needed assistance from the other major foreign power in the Philippines, Japan. In the aftermath of the Second World War Japan had become a junior partner to the US in South-East Asia. The expansion of Japanese prosperity, especially in the 1970s and 1980s, had accelerated Japanese involvement. Japan had increased its penetration of the Philippine market and, while Filipino dancers and construction workers lined up to find jobs in Japan, Japanese investors and tourists flocked to the country. Philippine resources, notably timber and tuna, found their way to Japan and Japanese aid poured in, both directly and through the Manila-based ADB. By the mid-1980s, an ascendant Japan had come of age as a full partner with the US in the exploitation of the Philippine economy.

But the US remains the obvious target for nationalist criticism. For, aside from its economic involvement, it plays an important military role, is a leading cultural influence and has never stopped short of direct political intervention in the affairs of the nation. The US military presence tops the list of concerns shared by the two countries. Filipinos worry about the US military bases, about the social costs of having them there and their effect on Philippine sovereignty.

Olongapo is located on Subic Bay, a two-hour drive north of Manila on the South China Sea coast. The US navy controls the magnificent natural harbour of Subic Bay and, without it, Olongapo would have no reason to exist. Magsaysay Street ends at the front gate of the naval base. It is a gaudy strip lined with girly bars, pizza joints, leather shops and T-shirt vendors selling products emblazoned with slogans befitting the young, often red-necked warriors of the US navy. Rock-and-roll and country-and-western music blare from the nightclubs along the boulevard. Local bands play note-for-note renditions of American and British hits. Singers contort their voices in perfect mimicry of imported records. On Magsaysay Street sex is sold. Clubs entice sailors with promises of beautiful dancing girls, mud and oil wrestling and female boxing. Off the main street and outside town near the Subic Bay beaches, the shows become increasingly vulgar and daring. Naked women performing the most unusual acts with their private parts, bananas, beer bottlecaps and their patrons' coins and bills.

Young girls flock from around the country to work in Olongapo. Many seek work as maids in American homes or as waitresses in fine restaurants. Often they drift into the bars and prostitution. The girls keep track of the schedules of the ships of the Seventh Fleet, anxiously awaiting the arrival of aircraft carriers and their escorts, knowing the ships bring hundreds of sailors and lots of loose change. The sailors also bring unwanted visitors: disease, children, heartache. The women, often anxious to find a way out of the Philippines, go on working despite AIDS, VD, unwanted pregnancies and rejection by their families. Marriages do occur between bar girls and sailors, but the US navy discourages them. 'Most of these marriages fail,' a navy officer inside the base told me. 'We can't stop the marriages, but we can warn both parties about the difficulties they may face.'

But even those bar girls who enter marriages for the wrong reasons can be luckier than the others. Marriage gives the woman rights, a child born out of wedlock becomes the woman's burden when the father's ship sails away. Amerasian children abound in Olongapo's population of street children. Even Olongapo's mayor bears an American name. Fast-talking Richard Gordon holds court in Olongapo's city hall just as his father and mother did before him. The Gordons had ruled Olongapo as Americans when the US had held authority over the town and as Filipinos when the Philippines gained control.

Gordon defends the bases in the same rapid cadence in which he attacks President Aquino's government. He reels off facts quicker than I can write them down. More than 200,000 people in the Olongapo area depend on the US military for some or all of their income; 70,000 Filipinos work on Subic or Clark Air Base in the neighbouring province of Pampanga. The bases generate more than US$1,000 million a year in revenues in the country aside from 'rent' paid by the US.

Gordon's sentiments reflect the thinking of much of his constituency. Few residents of Olongapo or of Angeles City near Clark Air Base want the bases closed. In 1986 my colleague Terri Taylor and I spent part of a day strolling through Olongapo asking people for their opinions on the bases. None wanted them closed. Polls have also shown that a majority of Filipinos support their continued presence and, though opinion polls in the Philippines are notoriously inaccurate, this does partially reflect the allure of the US to the Filipino. Most Filipinos outside the vicinity of the bases rarely think about them at all, but when they do the immediate economic ramifications can easily overwhelm whatever nationalist sentiments they might hold.

Nationalists see the bases as the embodiment of all evil. Not only do they attract the sort of social degeneracy described above, but, they argue, they could act as a magnet for attack should the US become embroiled in a war with the Soviet Union or another Pacific power. They can also be used as a springboard for US intervention in the Philippines or other Asian nations and, besides, they violate Philippine sovereignty. Philippine nationalists have been arguing against the bases on the grounds that they violate Philippine sovereignty from as long ago as

1947. A decade later Claro M. Recto warned against total annihilation within 30 minutes of the outbreak of a third world war, for 'missiles stockpiled here will be the prime targets of enemy attack.'[1]

The nationalist argument that the bases exist to serve US, not Philippine, interests gained ground in recent years. American officials have long denied it. They say the bases, which they refer to as 'US facilities on Philippine bases,' exist to defend the interests of the US, the Philippines and their regional allies against the Soviet threat.

Many analysts reject the US contention about Clark and Subic providing a counterweight to the Soviet base at Cam Rahn Bay across the sea on the Vietnamese coast. They argue that Cam Rahn Bay, itself a former US base, is a much less significant outpost than either Clark or Subic. The US confirmed this by belittling initial queries emanating from Moscow offering to exchange Soviet withdrawal from Cam Rahn Bay for US withdrawal from the Philippines. In addition, arguments regarding the Soviet threat may be rendered moot should the Cold War continue its decline.

The US claims that, apart from their strategic role the bases strengthen Philippine defences. This is a matter of much dispute. Nationalists argue that the presence of the bases on Philippine soil increases rather than reduces the chance of attack by a hostile foreign power. Secondly, agreements between the US and the Philippines do not require US military support for the Philippines in the event of a conflict. As UP Professor Roland Simbulan noted:

> While it is called Mutual Defence Pact, this treaty, however, does not really require one party to expect aid from the other in case of an attack. It merely, and weakly, promises that the US will only retaliate in the event of an external attack on the Philippines, 'in accordance with its constitutional processes.'... This is really just one way of saying that if one was attacked, the other will think about it.[2]

When Japan attacked the Philippines during the Second World War, the US, then the colonial power in Manila, beat a hasty retreat. Filipinos, especially self-conscious nationalists, remember their abandonment at the time of greatest need. 'What would happen if such a need arose again?' they ask.

The US permanently stations 15,000 troops in the Philippines. Some serve at the headquarters of JUSMAG (Joint US Military Advisory Group) in Quezon City, and at small installations scattered throughout the country, but the vast majority call Clark or Subic home. Clark hosts the US Thirteenth Air Force and Subic Bay the US Seventh Fleet.

Filipino fears about the US using their territory for its foreign adventures are anything but theoretical. The US has used Clark and

Subic as staging grounds for intervention in China, the Soviet Union, Korea, Indonesia, Indo-China, and, some would argue, Iran. In 1900, US troops dispatched from the Philippines helped to suppress the Boxer Rebellion and to defend US trade with China. From 1918 to 1920 troops sent from the bases joined tsarist and other anti-Soviet forces fighting in Siberia. The US dispatched planes from Clark Air Base to Korea soon after war broke out in 1950. In 1958 CIA-piloted planes left Clark to bomb Sumatra and to drop supplies to right-wing military rebels fighting against President Sukarno. When Iranian students seized American hostages at the US Embassy in Tehran in 1979, the US used Subic Bay as a staging post for the warships of the Seventh Fleet sent to the Persian Gulf. Use of the bases, however, peaked during the Vietnam war. As Simbulan noted:

> Clark and Subic were the busiest bases in South-East Asia. They were the hub of an air war that dropped 25 million tons of bombs on Indo-China, more bombs than were exploded on Europe, Africa and Asia throughout the Second World War and the Korean War combined.... Clark served as the Vietnam War's main logistical staging area, with close to 50 huge transports per day flying personnel and cargo to Vietnam. Meanwhile, Subic Naval Bases became a focal point for support for the Seventh Fleet whose operations ranged through the entire Indo-Chinese coastline.... In one 30 day period, the Subic base command shipped to South Vietnam 164,000 tons of ammunition.[3]

Much of the Subic Bay installation looks like anything but a source of controversy. Residential areas resemble middle-class American neighbourhoods. Commercial establishments and offices border nicely maintained roads. Ballparks, clubhouses, cinemas and woodlands promise wholesome entertainment. Sprawling workshops offer jobs to Filipinos and Americans. But an ugliness pervades. I listened as a Filipina doctor complained about the disrespect she was shown by American nurses and doctors. I witnessed the discomfort of an African-American naval officer and heard her complain about the open racism of many lower-ranking white sailors. I listened to the leader of the Filipino employees' union as he complained about the low wages Filipino workers receive in comparison with employees doing comparable work on US bases in Japan and Korea.

When originally signed in 1947, the Military Bases Agreement granted the US even wider rights than it enjoys today. Extra-territorial rights denied the Philippine courts jurisdiction over criminal offences committed by US servicemen. Later modifications of the treaty, spurred by Philippine complaints, cut its effective length from 99 to 44 years with a new expiry date in September 1991. In the 1950s the US agreed to recognize Philippine judicial authority for violations of Philippine laws by US military personnel on the bases. All too often, however, the US ships home soldiers and sailors charged with crimes against Philippine law. And these are not always petty crimes. The US government has even helped accused murderers escape the clutches of the Philippine courts.

The US retained the right for ships and planes armed with nuclear weapons to call at Clark and Subic on a regular basis even after Filipinos had approved a constitution with an anti-nuclear provision. A more thorny question is: Does the US store nuclear weapons on Philippine soil? A 1977 study by the State Department's Bureau of Politico-Military Affairs pointed to the presence of such weapons in describing the fate of the nuclear weapons stored at Clark and Subic as a severe problem should the bases be closed or relocated. A later study by the Institute for Policy Studies, however, stated that nuclear weapons previously based in the Philippines had been removed. The current status of nuclear weapons at Clark and Subic is unclear.

Less dramatic, but troubling all the same, is the use by the US of Philippine land, air and sea space for conventional military exercises using live ammunition. Jet fighters swoop out of the sky over Philippine villages in attempts to approximate combat experiences. Fighters unleash barrages of rocket and gunfire on the sprawling Crow Valley at Clark. More than a few Filipinos have been killed after straying into the target area.

The bases are also central to a wide range of US military and economic programmes in the Philippines. One week after signing the Military Bases Agreement, the two countries reached a Military Assistance Agreement aimed at developing the AFP (Armed Forces of the Philippines). The agreement covered supplies, armaments, training and advice. The Philippines considers the financial package to be rent. The US calls it aid. The wording reflects the American contention that the bases serve both countries.

Negotiations over the future of the bases have often seen both sides manoeuvre to get the best deal. During the Marcos era, for example, negotiations stalled when the dictator wanted to assuage nationalist dissent at home. In 1976 Marcos rejected a five-year US $1,000 million aid package only to accept a virtually identical proposal in 1979. Marcos's dependency on the US for military and economic aid forced the dictator to agree to terms favourable to the US. At the same time, the Carter administration's desire to keep the bases reduced its resolve to confront the Marcos regime over its human rights record.

Because of the bases, the Philippines was one of the top ten recipients of US foreign aid during the Marcos period. The interim agreement reached by the Reagan and Marcos governments in 1983 even further increased the amount of aid to be delivered by the US. But during Marcos's final years in office the US government used aid as a weapon to pressure Manila into reforming the AFP and, despite the Reagan administration's requests, reduced the amount of aid delivered. It subsequently made up the difference between promised and delivered aid during the first years of the Aquino era.

In the fiscal years 1987 through 1989, the Reagan administration asked for $320 million in Military Assistance Program grants and $343 million in ESF (Economic Support Fund) grants and loans. Congress in fact agreed to the $350 million in military aid and upped the ESF monies to $548 million. For 1990, with a new enlarged bases assistance pact in place, George Bush, the new US president, asked for a 60 per cent increase in military assistance. He also sought $160 million in ESF monies and an unrelated $200 million for an initial contribution to the MAI (Multilateral Aid Initiative).

'We want to help rebuild the democratic institutions destroyed during the Marcos years,' noted Bryant George, a USAID official responsible for dealing with US and Philippine voluntary organizations in Manila during a 1989 meeting at the State Department. George emphasized the concept of institutional pluralism. However, the organizations USAID supports represent only a narrow swathe of Philippine politics and are actively involved in attempts to eliminate the Philippine left. For example, one of the largest recipients of US government support was the Asian-American Free Labor Institute, an organization dominated by the right wing of the US labour movement, which works with the TUCP (Trade Union Congress of the Philippines). Via the TUCP and the military, the US hopes to destroy the radical KMU (May First Movement).

US support accounts for about 83 per cent of the AFP's procurement, operational and maintenance budget. The US had used its bases as staging grounds for covert operations against Philippine insurgents in the 1950s and 1970s. Today the US government denies any direct involvement in the Philippines' civil conflict, though allegations that US jets fly reconnaissance missions for the AFP and that the US is directly involved in intelligence operations may well be true. That the US dramatically increased its CIA strength in the Philippines following the fall of Marcos lends credence to this view. Certainly communist-led rebels believe that the US Air Force flies such missions for its Philippine allies. When in 1988 an NPA (New People's Army) hit squad attacked US personnel in

Angeles City, its primary target was the pilot its members held responsible for such flights.

An anti-communist obsession guides US military policy in the Philippines. JUSMAG's central mission is to help the Philippines combat its internal enemies: today most notably the CPP and NPA. JUSMAG's role in training Philippine troops became apparent when I visited an AFP encampment in an urban slum just outside Manila. An officer noted that his troops had undergone training with US forces in the Philippines before taking up their new posts. I asked Brig. Gen. Rodolfo Biazon, commander of the National Capital Region Defence Command, about this, but he played down the US training. I then asked the JUSMAG officers. They said the Philippines specifically requested training in an urban setting. 'It was a three-week course covering basic topics but with an emphasis on urban warfare. Our Special Forces gave insights on this that were not specific, more on the lines of how we would do it — checkpoints, patrols, etc.'

According to the US officers, American forces teach skills essential to regular warfare and to combating the larger units being fielded by the NPA. They teach communications, map reading, marksmanship and weapon maintenance, skills 'basic to being a good soldier.' 'We want to enhance the capability of the unit that is going to win the war, the squad,' said a US navy colonel. 'We train the young NCO, get the squad out into the bush, never give them the chance to get bad habits.'

One aspect of the training programmes emphasized by the US is the relationship developed between the two country's soldiers on a personal level. One JUSMAG officer described it as brotherhood. 'We can't place a price tag on these relationships,' he said. 'We're building relationships, making friends, that will last a lifetime. And these are the people who will be running the AFP for many years to come.'

Via JUSMAG, which incorporates US military attachés who maintain relationships with AFP leaders and American lecturers who visit the National Defence College, the US has a strong influence on Philippine military policy. Some critics accuse the US of actually establishing policy for the Philippine military. This, I find, unfair to the leaders of the AFP who have at least as much experience and intelligence as their American counterparts. The relationship is more complex.

After so many years of cooperation with US military officials, Philippine officers have taken on many Western ideas as their own. The US so succeeded in shaping the ideology and methods of the AFP that it no longer needs to exercise complete control, as it did during the colonial era. The US can now rely on more subtle ways of influencing policy. 'They're wary of our specific advice,' noted one JUSMAG officer. 'But we do have an immeasurable influence on policy. This Special Operations Team concept is not a product of the Philippines only, not only the US, but the British as well. They read, they study.'

This is not to say that Pentagon strategists do not think about Philippine strategy and advice, or influence their Philippine counterparts. Whether the advice is worth following is unclear. Walden Bello made this critical observation of US strategic thinking on the Philippines:

> On the advisory level, US strategists are seeking to forge a coherent response to the NPA's growing military prowess and archipelago-wide reach. One hint of emerging US-AFP strategy is found in a recent intelligence assessment suggesting that 'the nationwide spread of the CPP/NPA is vulnerable to a region-by-region (anti-guerrilla) campaign since it has thinly overextended itself and is not capable of reinforcing or putting up a stand on that basis.' According to one report, the Pentagon has advised that military firepower be concentrated on a single island in a 'decisive show of force against the insurgents.' Reportedly, the island under consideration for such a drive is Negros, where the NPA has experienced a rapid rate of growth in recent years.
>
> This approach may have some appeal to strategists in Washington, but reveals the Pentagon's continuing inability to understand a fundamental characteristic of the insurgency: that it has been carried out by an organizationally decentralized force whose units are expected to be entirely self-reliant. Hence, isolating Negros will not hamper NPA operations in the rest of the archipelago. But the NPA's most likely response — stepped up attacks in other parts of the Philippines — will prevent the AFP from concentrating its resources on Negros for any length of time.[4]

Many Filipinos consider the ideological impact of US military thinkers dangerous. Following the 1987 coup attempt, rabid nationalists accused the US of plotting the entire adventure. Coup leader Gringo Honasan's close relationship with a US assistant army attaché and that attaché's attempts to stave off an attack on the rebel forces had sparked off the speculation.

Senator Raul Manglapus, who later became secretary of foreign affairs, suggested that the coup plotters' thinking had been influenced by right-wing Americans brought in to lecture at the National Defence College. Manglapus's reference to right-wing Americans raises another aspect of US involvement in Philippine military affairs. A plethora of civilian international anti-communist groups, some with suspicious connections to covert US agencies, appeared in the Philippines following the fall of Marcos. Causa International, the anti-communist front of Revd Sun Yung Moon's Unification Church, staged a major conference at the Manila Hotel before settling down to work. It was attended by Vice-

President Salvador Laurel and his wife, Celia Laurel, who have remained active supporters. Causa has provided Philippine anti-communist groups with educational materials, films and lecturers.

When Marcos fell the WACL (World Anti-Communist League) and its local affiliate stepped up their activities. The appearance of WACL leader John Singlaub, who visited the country in 1986 and 1987, raised speculation, for Singlaub, a retired US army general and leading backer of the Nicaraguan *Contras*, claimed to be laying the ground for a search for treasure allegedly left in the Philippines by retreating Japanese soldiers at the end of the Second World War. Singlaub attracted attention by meeting leaders of the defence establishment and by visiting parts of the country troubled by the insurgency. The WACL, Causa, the Christian Anti-Communist Crusade and other similar groups certainly developed close ties with the anti-Aquino right in the Philippines.

Given the anti-communist obsession of US policy makers, some people were surprised that the first example of overt US military intervention in Philippine affairs during the Aquino era saw US forces pitted against right- rather than left-wing rebels. But that is what happened when the US sent its jets into the air to provide support to pro-Aquino forces during their showdown with mutinous soldiers in December 1989. US forces did not engage in actual combat, but their presence did raise the spectre of future US military involvement in the Philippines.

A final aspect of US involvement is in the area of covert operations. In 1987, *Newsweek* and the *San Francisco Examiner* reported that President Reagan had authorized stepped-up CIA operations against the radical left, while approving a $10 million secret allocation to the AFP for enhanced intelligence gathering operations. The CIA also bolstered its Philippine operations by adding 12 agents to its roster of 115 operatives.[5]

The US provides the Philippines with significant aid for several reasons. Clearly the most important of these is the need to meet its promises *vis-à-vis* the bases. Secondly, the US foreign policy establishment, obsessed as it is with fighting communism, wants to help the Philippine government fight the NPA. Finally, the US government has to be concerned about private US investment and trade.

From the US perspective, total investment and trade with the Philippines does not amount to much. In 1985 the Philippines accounted for less than 0.6 per cent of US exports and 0.7 per cent of imports. Neighbouring Taiwan, by comparison, accounted for 2.1 per cent of US exports and 5.0 per cent of imports. Despite this, US-Philippine traders and investors have long influenced government thinking, and more so since many of the US's largest corporations and banks became active in the Philippines.

From the Philippine perspective, US economic involvement is overwhelming. A US document released in 1985 notes that 'The United States is the Philippines' largest trading partner for both imports and exports. Five years ago, the US and Japan were competing on an almost equal footing, but the US share has gradually increased.'[6] A paper released by the US government in 1987 notes that the US took about 35.5 per cent of Philippine exports while providing 24.9 per cent of its imports. Total trade between the two countries amounted to nearly $3,000 million in 1986.

A study released in 1988 by IBON Databank further revealed the extent of US economic penetration. In 1986 US investments amounted to $2,700 million or 56.8 per cent of the foreign equity invested in the Philippines. In 1987 the American Chamber of Commerce in the Philippines noted that US corporations earned 1,115 million pesos (or $52 million at the 1989 exchange rate) over the previous five years. Of these earnings, the companies repatriated 84 per cent.[7] The IBON study described links between 193 Philippine companies and US firms and another 31 corporations with 'mixed Filipino and American stockholders.' As many as 92 Philippine companies had links with Japanese corporations and 48 with British firms.

While the US remained the leading foreign investor, Japan's role steadily increased. According to IBON, US investment grew at an annual rate of 25 per cent while Japanese investment increased by 36 per cent per annum. Japan's increased involvement in the Philippine economy reflected its ascendancy as an economic power and its march towards greater involvement in the overall economy of South-East Asia. By 1988 Japan had emerged as ASEAN's (Association of South-East Asian Nations) largest trading partner. That year, Prime Minister Noburo Takeshita appeared at an ASEAN summit in Manila to offer a three-year $2,000 million aid package, wider access to the Japanese domestic market and increased Japanese investments in the region.

Japan's subsequent private and public involvement in the Philippine economy have demonstrated its commitment to the plan laid out by Prime Minister Takeshita. In 1989 a consortium of Japanese investors signed an agreement aimed at infusing $1,000 million in fresh investments into the Philippine economy. The total amount of aid from Japan has actually surpassed that of the US. For the fiscal year 1990, Japan has promised to deliver close on $1,000 million in aid, which is $400 million more than the US. While this reflects Japan's emergence as an economic superpower, it does not signify a substantial shift away from the US on the part of the Philippines. Despite the infusion of Japanese money Filipinos continued to distrust Japanese motives. The collective memory of the Second World War had lingered, while that of the Philippine-American War had all but vanished. *Hapon*, the Filipino word for Japanese, is still synonymous with that of 'enemy' in much of the country.

While the US exercises tremendous cultural influence and fairly openly participates in the political life of the nation, Japan takes a back seat. American officials offer solicited and unsolicited advice to Philippine politicians and use aid for political ends. Japanese officials, however, use aid for economic ends while quietly supporting most of the political and military goals of the US. The Philippines depends on the US and Japan for the bulk of its foreign aid, investment, exchange and trade. But aid and investment from (and trade with) the EC, Canada, Australia, ASEAN and other Asian countries also contribute to the Philippines' dependency on foreign support. During the first four months of 1988, for example, Taiwan surpassed both the US and Japan as the leading source of new investment.

Not all Philippine ties with other countries are bilateral. With economic globalization, the US has been increasingly adopting a collaborative approach to aid. The principal conduits for such collaboration have been the IMF and the World Bank. In Asia, the Manila-based ADB performs a similar function. These bodies have assumed a progressively more important role. In return for loans and favourable credit ratings, these international financial institutions require borrowers to meet various conditions. This gives the IMF and World Bank tremendous influence over economic policy throughout the Third World. Economic policy in places like the Philippines often represents a compromise between competing domestic forces and foreign creditors and their allies.

In 1988, the Philippines' foreign debt amounted to $29,000 million. Aside from the multilateral institutions, the Philippines owed money to more than 400 private banks and various foreign government agencies. The debt trap has severely limited the Philippine government's ability to confront its many problems. Servicing the debt places tremendous demands on its budget and foreign exchange earnings. To keep afloat, the government is constantly hunting for new funds, which has led it to make countless concessions to its creditors.

The drift towards multilateralism took on new meaning when members of the US Congress proposed a Mini-Marshall Plan soon after Marcos fell from power. The plan, loosely modelled after the US' postwar assistance programme for Europe, later became known as the MAI.

Its framers sought to inject significant amounts of fresh aid for a period of five years to be used to build a healthy economy led by a strong private sector. When the MAI started to take shape it offered much less than originally suggested. In 1989 the leading donors pledged what advocates of the plan called $3,500 million for the first year of the programme. But critics, including Solita Monsod, who resigned as head of the National Economic & Development Authority in disgust, claimed that the programme had only offered $250 million in new aid — most of that from the US.

Despite its obvious shortcomings, the Philippine government put tremendous energy into pursuing the MAI. It developed a half-baked plan aimed at convincing the donors of their worthiness, reshuffled the cabinet and cut off the debate over debt restructuring, just to curry favour with the MAI's funders.

The shift towards greater dependency was especially frustrating for nationalists who had originally believed that Marcos's fall would present an opportunity to change direction. When President Aquino came to power she faced pressure to alter her nation's relationship with the world, especially with the US. Cory's bitterness towards Reagan and US officials who had backed Marcos weighed against the fact that she had spent a good part of her life in the US. She harboured warm feelings towards those Americans who had helped her during her exile. And, like other members of the Philippine élite, her family prospered through business dealings with US concerns.

Aquino's circle of advisers revealed similar schizophrenia towards America. Some came from the tradition of nationalist struggles. Former senators, Lorenzo Tanada and José Diokno, the most prominent nationalist advocates, were widely admired senior statesmen in Aquino's entourage. Aquino, however, drew the majority of her advisers and cabinet members from the élite. These men and women, many of them educated in American schools, had prospered in partnership with US business. They feared a future cut off from the West.

Soon enough it became apparent that the committed nationalists, who argued for such things as the immediate closure of the military bases and the repudiation of part of the foreign debt, would have little influence in official Manila during the Aquino era. Aquino excluded nationalists from positions in the financial and economic ministries. The foreign policy debate that emerged involved moderate nationalists who favoured some change and traditional thinkers who favoured the Western-oriented status quo.

Raul Manglapus returned from his exile in the US as a moderate advocate of an independent foreign policy. Many Filipinos found this surprising, for Manglapus had first emerged as a public figure as one of the bright boys of Ramon Magsaysay's CIA-engineered presidency. Before going into exile, Filipinos knew Manglapus as an 'America boy,' but his US experience had irked him. He had felt that the US government had mistreated him and his fellow exiles at the request of Marcos. In addition, during his exile, Manglapus, an intellectual, had come into contact with militant nationalist thinkers. Two of his closest associates, Bonifacio Gillego and Gaston Ortigas, had moved firmly into the nationalist camp.

Manglapus had come to view the US as an errant friend. He did not want to break with it, as those who chanted anti-imperialist slogans on the streets of Manila did, but foreign policy, he believed, should reflect Philippine needs rather than US positions. Left to his own devices, Manglapus might have made the effort to lay the foundations for a more independent foreign policy, but his small steps towards independence paled in the face of the power of traditional views on foreign policy. The gap between rhetoric and reality remained large as the Philippines continued to pursue a dependent course of development. This reality reduced even Manglapus to mendicancy as he shuffled between diplomatic meetings in pursuit of loans and dole outs.

Aquino's government made numerous concessions — including import liberalization, investment code reform and adoption of austerity measures — to the international financial community as it pursued new loans. It tied itself ever more closely to its foreign creditors in 1989 by signing a new LOI (Letter of Intent) to the IMF. The LOI met the conditions set by the IMF in return for about $900 million in new credit and $400 million in contingency funds. 'Unlike most common standby arrangements with the IMF, which commit the country to deliver a set of economic targets within a year, what we have entered into this time is the so-called extended fund facility (EFF),' noted the editors of *IBON Facts and Figures*. 'The EFF allows the IMF to step in not just for one year but for three years.'[8]

In the LOI the government outlined a programme designed to increase revenue collection and cut government spending, while avoiding the imposition of new taxes. It also promised to cut subsidies to service-oriented public corporations like the National Power Corporation and the National Food Authority. Such measures instantly resulted in higher food and power prices. In addition, the government vowed to accelerate its thrust towards privatisation. It set a 50 per cent target for December 1990 while providing no protection for employees made redundant.

Supporters of the LOI argue that it will clear the way for the rescheduling of existing debts, open the doors to new loans and facilitate the delivery of monies under the MAI. Rep. José de Venecia, for example, claimed that the LOI would facilitate the entry of $15,000 million over three years. Nationalists and leftists disagreed. 'Glossed over is the fact that our foreign debt will likewise increase by about 50 per cent, perpetuating the debt dependence mentality,' claimed IBON's editors.[9]

The government's dependence on foreign aid, investment and support for its military could play an important role in determining the future of the US military bases beyond 1991. On 17 October 1988, the US and the Philippines reached an agreement covering the final two years of the existing military bases agreement. The US agreed to try to deliver $481 million in aid during each of those years. Advocates of the bases argue that this money, coupled with the more than $370 million that enters the Philippine economy as wages for base employees, purchases by US military personnel and base contractors' fees, provides ample reason for extending the existing base treaty.

While refusing to comment directly on her plans for the future of the bases, Aquino is viewed as favouring a short-term extension of the agreement. She alone will not, however, determine the fate of the bases. The Senate must approve treaties and it has been influenced by nationalist ideas. Negotiations over their future were set to start in December 1989, but the coup intervened and complicated matters, for Aquino had to ask for support from the Clark-based US Air Force during the coup. Opposition to the bases is central to the agenda of Filipino nationalists, along with freedom from debt and nationalist industrialization. 'I do not see how you can be a Philippine nationalist and still support the bases,' Sen. Wigberto Tanada once told me. The mere presence of the bases violates Philippine sovereignty. But short of challenging the entire economic system, anti-bases activists have not presented a viable economic alternative.

A short-term extension of the agreement, perhaps with a general US commitment to withdraw within the next decade or so, seems to be the most likely outcome of the talks. While this would not satisfy the nationalists, it would fit in with the Aquino government's economic and security considerations. Other possibilities include a joint operating agreement, or withdrawal from Clark and some of the less significant facilities, coupled with a new lease for Subic and key communications facilities. Straightforward eviction would demand a reassessment of Philippine foreign policy, something the Aquino government has not shown an interest in doing — so that is unlikely.

Whatever the government opts to do will provide a gauge with which to measure the impact of nationalism on Philippine politics and the way

Filipinos view themselves and their nation. Nationalism remains a minority sentiment in the Philippines. Nationalists continue to complain about the culture of colonialism and colonial mentality of their countrymen. Many Filipinos have an idealized view of America and Americans. It is a view that comes from their educational experience, from the TV programmes and films they watch, and from the stories relatives in the US tell them. Attraction to foreign-made consumer items strengthens the bond many Filipinos feel towards America. Education in English introduces many Filipinos to American ideas and values.

The impact of US culture on the Philippines may, however, appear much greater than it actually is. Despite the love of basketball, apples and American movies, Philippine culture differs greatly from that of America. Where Americans emphasize the individual and the nation, Filipinos think of the family and extended family. Where religion plays a secondary role in the lives of many Americans, it is the centrepiece of Philippine life. Where Americans get straight to the point, Filipinos often beat around the bush trying to avoid hurting people's feelings or losing face.

Still, no matter how thin the veneer of Americanism actually is, many Filipinos believe in an American ideal, an American dream. From time to time I have heard Filipinos actually talking about becoming a US state, as if that would solve the country's problems. This idea may not be very prevalent, but its persistence indicates a crisis of identity for the Philippine nation, which finds itself in a love—hate relationship with both the US and itself. In fact before the nationalists can play an important role in setting out a political and economic agenda for the nation, they must change the way the majority of Filipinos look at themselves and at the world around them.

The Philippines continues to struggle with its own place in the world. How will its relationship with the US develop? How will it confront the problems of debt and dependency? How will it relate to the Third World? How will it emerge from that shadow of its former foreign master? Will it emerge from the shadow? The progress of the bases talks will provide a way of measuring its advancement over the last half century. But many other issues must be resolved before the Philippines finds its place in the world.

The Filipino people must find a solution to their identity crisis, just as Francisco (the guerilla we met in chapter 12) did for his own. Francisco accepted the American things he liked and felt were a part of himself, but rejected the alien impositions. He emerged from his struggle strong, self-confident and Filipino. His nation now needs to do the same.

20

Religion and Philippine Society

At noon, members of a religious congregation looked to the sky and saw a spinning, dancing sun. In that sun they saw an apparition. The Virgin Mary was bringing a message to the faithful. Newspapers reported the appearance, TV crews flocked to the congregation's outdoor chapel, the country's religious leaders had to respond. 'Maybe they were just hungry,' joked Manila's Jaime Cardinal Sin. 'This happened at noon, maybe they were seeing things because they put off eating too long.'

Filipinos take religion seriously. Religious holidays and festivals attract fanatical participation. Once a year thousands gather in Manila's Quiapo district for the procession of the Black Nazarene. Men, mostly the urban poor, whip themselves into a frenzy trying to get close enough to touch the statue of the baby Jesus, with the expectation of salvation. On Holy Week, a handful of Christians have themselves nailed to crosses as a symbol of devotion and a plea for divine favours. Other men practise self flagellation expecting forgiveness for their sins. On All Souls Day Catholics flock to the cemeteries to commune with the dead. With this sort of conviction, politics and religion make a powerful combination. Time and time again, organized religion has demonstrated its ability to influence political and social life. The Spaniards used the Roman Church to create a colonial culture. Early Filipino nationalists struggled for control of the Church as they launched their crusade for Philippine independence. Americans recolonized the Catholic Church and introduced Protestant strains. In more recent times, Ferdinand Marcos lifted martial law to present a visiting pope with a more benevolent face. The Protestant and Catholic Churches played essential roles in hastening the fall of the Marcos dictatorship.

Over 90 per cent of all Filipinos consider themselves Christian, 80 per cent Catholic (5 per cent are Muslims, see chapter 21). Within the Christian community, there are not only Catholics, but Protestants, members of significant national churches — the *Iglesia ni Kristo* and the Aglipayan (or Philippine) Independent Church — sects and charismatic groups as well. Modern Philippine Christianity has tangled roots. The

Spanish colonials built a Church on a foundation of native religions that worshipped a plethora of gods, goddesses and demigods, most of whom explained one sort of natural phenomenon or another. The Spaniards did not obliterate these earlier religions, but brought in a more powerful God who eventually laid claim to the affections of most Filipinos.

Throughout the colonial period, generally minor nativist schisms occurred in the Church. Other schisms had a deeper impact. Gregorio Aglipay's Philippine Independent Church emerged early in the century and continues to have a significant following. Another schism that prospered, the *Iglesia ni Kristo*, remains under the control of its royal family, the Manalos.

The final layer of Philippine Christianity entered with the American colonials. Missionaries from various Protestant Churches flooded the country seeking out followers among dissident Catholics and mountain people left unconverted by the Spanish colonials. The descendants of some of their converts, men like Jovito Salonga and Fidel Ramos, would become prominent national leaders.

Missionaries still come to the Philippines. Many belong to the 'born again' Churches that grew in the West in the 1970s and 1980s. Messianic leaders continue to break with the existing Churches and lead their followers into the wilderness. Through it all, however, the Roman Catholic Church remains the most significant religious body in the Philippines and one of its most important political battlegrounds.

Factionalism prevents the Catholic Church from presenting a monolithic façade. During the Marcos period, the Church found itself torn between dictatorship and godless communism. Church leaders had close social relations with the rich and powerful. On the other hand, as segments of the Church began to adapt to the reality of class conflict, demands emerged for a 'preferential option for the poor.' Grassroots struggles between the religious left and right split the Church and put extreme pressure on its leaders and theologians.

The Christian left is itself diverse: national democrats, social democrats, independent activists and Jesuit-influenced reformers. Many clergy, nuns and lay people of all denominations working at a local level joined the struggle for justice and national liberation during the Marcos era. Church-based social action centres, human rights groups and BCCs (Basic Christian Communities) developed what Bishop Francisco Claver describes as a 'liberational thrust.' But the religious right did not ignore grassroots work either.

In 1984 I walked through a sprawling Davao City slum with a local community organizer. Though a stronghold of the left, each of the slum's parishes contained a small Catholic Church and a fundamentalist

Protestant mission. My guide, a member of the NDF, noted with displeasure the fundamentalists' ability to attract the disenchanted with promises of a better life after death. A few days later, on a ferry in western Mindanao, I met an American missionary, a Baptist, full of energy and commitment to saving souls endangered by the communist influence.

The presence of an American missionary in rural Mindanao suggested international support for the grassroots efforts of the religious right. Big money and the celebrities of the US religious right supported the efforts of the missionaries in the field. Television evangelists played on the national networks, Jesus rallies toured the country and periodically Pat Robertson's 700 Club arrived to provide minor charity and bibles.

Twice towards the end of Marcos's reign, Jerry Falwell came to Manila to rally fundamentalists behind the ailing dictator. I attended one rally (a national prayer breakfast) at the Manila Hilton. Affluent businessmen filled the room with their families. They cheered as rosy-cheeked singers belted out gospel tunes in sweet southern US voices. They cheered and shouted Amen! as Falwell filled the room with bombastic rhetoric. 'The Philippines and the United States: We have something very important in common! We were born free!' the preacher shouted to the applause of his audience. 'The future of the United States and the Philippine Islands is personally intertwined. The march of communism and Marxism-Leninism cannot be stopped unless countries like yours and ours stick together!'

The danger of right-wing religion becomes painfully clear in depressed rural areas. Local war-lords and political bosses exploit animist and folk Christian traditions to form fanatical armed groups among the very poor. Such groups have been responsible for the slaughter of Muslims, community activists, religious leaders and suspected communists. Charismatic sect leaders lure members by promising a future free of sickness, hunger and death. Many use amulets or oils that leaders claim render the user invincible.

The Revd Brendon Lovett of St Mary's Seminary in Ozamis City partly attributes the success of these groups to the failings of mainstream Christianity. As Fr Lovett put it one storm-swept afternoon: 'The fanatics can be seen as an index of our failure. What has been given to them as Christianity does not help them to cope with their world. The only answer is community.'

Christians genuinely interested in social change and justice emphasize the communal aspects of their religion, which often takes the form of involvement in the BCC (Basic Christian Community) movement. BCCs emerged in the Philippines during the late 1960s and early 1970s. Political scientist Robert Youngblood writes that:

> The programs linked Latin American ideas of consciousness-raising, pioneered by Paolo Freire among the poor in Brazil, and the notion of a small Christian community, with American community-organizing concepts already in use in the Philippines. The establishment of Christian communities provided the context not only for discussing Church and community problems in terms of the Gospel, but also for engaging in collective action in the search for solutions. The BCC-CO [Community Organization] was aimed at breaking the dependency syndrome of the marginalized and dispossessed by helping them become agents of their own liberation.[1]

This liberationist thrust of the BCCs makes conservatives in the Church and elsewhere see a communist endeavour. In Bacolod City, for example, planters consistently opposed Bishop Antonio Fortich's support for the more than 1,500 BCCs in his diocese for what Fortich sees as one simple reason: 'The BCCs are espousing land reform.' Fortich's enemies call him *Kumander Tony*, a nickname that carries connotations of an NPA commander. They threatened his life and burned his home and office. Members of the local élite make no secret of their distaste for the man and the type of Church he has built in Negros Occidental. Ramon Lacson told me of their disillusionment with the Church. He suggested the Church should respect landowners' rights, adding that he rarely if ever attends Church services any more.

Fortich's priests and lay workers suffered even more than their bishop. In 1984 the military arrested three priests and six lay workers for allegedly murdering a local government official and involvement in the left-wing underground. They became known as the Negros Nine. Their real crime was active involvement in BCCs. Under intense international pressure, the courts dropped the charges, but the government deported the two foreign priests involved: Brian Gore and Niall O'Brien.

That the military considered BCCs criminal organizations was really no secret. In an influential paper written for the Ministry of National Defence in 1978, Col Galileo Kintanar described 'a dangerous form of threat from the religious radicals.' He thought that their potential as 'an infrastructure of political power' was most threatening.[2] Contact between BCCs and the revolutionary movement does exist and some priests and nuns working with BCCs also work with the national democratic movement. I in fact met members of the underground who had become involved with BCCs before leaving to take on clandestine work.

In conducting research for his book on the NPA, William Chapman found a particularly strong connection between the BCCs and the national democratic underground in Negros. A European priest in Negros told him: 'We in the BCC-COs believe quite simply that capitalists are the devils and that there can be no compromise with them, and so we must help design the new socialist system. There is no alternative to a socialist society.' After a pause, the priest added, 'But the New People's Army and the Communist Party have a definite programme and there is no alternative but to go with it and try to help them.' Chapman cited the same priest as saying, 'In my experience, there is no one at the grassroots level of the BCC-CO who is opposed to violence.'[3]

But such a generalization is inaccurate. O'Brien, Gore and other priests in battle-scarred Negros had resisted the allure of revolutionary violence in building their BCCs. During one of my visits to Negros in 1987, members of a BCC actually held a march in protest against NPA violence. During the same visit, Bishop Fortich told me that all of his more than 100 priests are actively involved in BCCs at the grassroots level. Not even the military accuses them all of being members of the underground. It would be unfair to identify the country's diverse BCCs with any single political tendency. It is more accurate to say, as Bishop Francisco Claver, head of NASSA (National Secretariat for Social Action), does, that the BCCs allow members to make political choices as a community. As he put it:

> The more conservative bishops would think they are a front for the under-ground, precisely because the underground has tried to use them, but the fact is the vast majority of Basic Christian Communities are not under the thumb of the left, they are just going on by themselves, you know, very slowly. As far as I can see, the Basic Christian Community is more of a structure where-by you can make choices, like joining the NDF or joining the government, but doing so in a critical, effective way.

Why do conservative bishops view BCCs as a front for the under-ground? In part this can be traced to redbaiting by the military and provincial conservatives, and in part to the actual influence of left-wing Christians in some communities. But, as Fr Ed de la Torre noted, it is also rooted in the fear of change, change in the Church and in society.[4]

The debate over BCCs raises questions about the general overall direction of Christian Churches in the Philippines. The radical religious left see Christianity as an inspiration for far-reaching change. They seek the Kingdom of God on earth, and so priests, pastors, nuns and laity form BCCs, human rights groups, mass organizations, political parties and, in some cases, guerrilla armies. Liberal and conservative Church people accept a more traditional theology. The mainstream Catholic and Protes-tant Churches accept the concept of Christian social action only so long as it remains charitable and developmental.

Practice rather than theology has determined the shape of the Christian left. Liberation theology, especially the Latin American version, has had an inspirational impact. But the need to find a practical outline for change-oriented social action has led the Christian left to confront and explore Marxism. This has generated several responses: wholesale acceptance of ideological Marxism-Leninism; use of Marxism and structural analysis as a tool; critical collaboration with the Marxist left; and the development of such alternative (and to varying degrees anticommunist) ideologies as Philippine social-democracy and Christian democracy.

Fr Frank Navarro accepted Marxism and became a guerrilla leader in northern Mindanao. He sees no conflict between dialectical materialism and his belief in God. As he argues: 'Science has not proven that there is a God. But neither has it proven that there is no God. Some key goals of Marxism and Christianity are similar. Both aspire to total liberation. The only difference is that Marxism is more scientific, this-worldly, while Christianity is other-worldly and idealistic.[5] The Marxist-Christian dialogue has led Christian left intellectuals to pursue a theology more in tune with the needs of Philippine society, a theology that would incorporate the Christian inspiration of liberation theology with more practical considerations. A priest explained: 'Perhaps the most important task of liberation theology now is to liberate us from goal-oriented thinking and action; lead us into a "how to" form of thinking and action; lead us into what is now being called the "Theology of Struggle".'[6]

The CNL (Christians for National Liberation) represents the far left in Philippine Christianity. De la Torre and 71 other young Church radicals set it up as a legal national-democratic group for the religious in 1972, a few months before Marcos imposed his dictatorship. Martial law forced the CNL underground where it joined the CPP (Communist Party of the Philippines) in organizing the NDF. Originally a vehicle for involving institutional Church people in the national-democratic movement, by 1985 the CNL had expanded its mission to 'conduct political work among the Christian faithful who wish[ed] to develop political involvement in the context of their Christian faith.' The CNL also adopted the 'national-democratic transformation of the Churches' as its responsibility, saying that 'the battle over the moral influence of the Church has become crucial.'[7]

De la Torre and his colleagues played a rather modest role in the revolutionary process during the movement's early days. 'We are bourgeois, no matter how petty,' they wrote in 1972. 'Hence the renunciation of a leading role (a very Christian temptation). Workers and peasants are the main bearers of humanization and liberation.'[8] Time and the growth of the movement, however, have thrust many religious people into leading roles, not just in the CNL, but in other of the clandestine national-democratic movement's organizations. De la Torre, for example, played an important part in organizing the NDF, Fr Eduardo Balicao became a leader of the CPDF (Cordillera People's Democratic Front) among tribesmen of the northern mountains, and Fr Frank Navarro plays an important part in the NPA in northern Mindanao. A former priest, Luis Jalandoni, represents the NDF abroad. The military says Jalandoni belongs to the CPP's central committee. In Davao and Manila, nuns do a lot of work in the legal national-democratic movement. Some privately admit to being members of clandestine organizations.

How do members of the Church justify their involvement in an armed struggle? Some have quite simply replaced the dogmas of their Church with the most dogmatic aspects of Maoist-derived communism. Some reason that the armed struggle is a necessary ingredient in the creation of a godly society, others that revolutionary violence is a response to state violence. The most common answer I have heard, however, is that participation in the armed struggle is the highest form of service to God's people. As Fr Navarro explained:

> I was never really contented with my parish work. The people were poor, but I was not involved in truly solving the causes of their poverty. Armed struggle is the highest form of service. One offers not only his time, money or effort. He offers his life. If lay people can offer their lives, how much more a priest who has been trained to give his total being to service?[9]

Though Navarro describes himself as a Marxist, he also considers himself a faithful priest and, albeit rarely, still celebrates mass in the *barrios* of the guerrilla zone. Fr Eddie Balicao, who went on indefinite leave from the Church before going underground in 1985, also performs religious functions when asked to do so by the *barrio* residents of his guerrilla zone. 'There is no contradiction between faith and revolution,' he told me. 'I believe in a liberating Lord, in Jesus the liberator.' Like others, Balicao joined the CNL before going underground. He worked in a number of human rights groups but grew frustrated with 'looking at things in terms of human rights alone without tackling basic problems.'

The meeting of Christianity and Marxism in the Philippines has not only affected religious people. Though founded by materialists and atheists, the Communist Party attracts support from diverse faiths. I have encountered Christians — from Catholics to a Jehovah's Witness — in leadership positions at all levels. The most visible groups within the Christian left are the Church-backed organizations involved in human rights advocacy, grassroots development, student organizing, and labour and peasant support. Many of these fall within the national-democratic orbit. Other groups however, operate independently and sometimes in opposition to the NDF and its legal counterparts.

Sr Christine Tan, who exemplifies the independent Christian left, has long lived and worked with the urban poor in Manila. She served on the Con Com (Constitutional Commission) where she joined the progressive, nationalist block in advocating radical reforms. When the Aquino government began its drift to the right, Tan quickly spoke out, despite her lifelong friendship with the president. 'The Church has never been so powerful,' she told me, 'as it is today. The sad part is, the Church is not using that power for the interest of the people.' Yet, unlike her counterparts in the CNL, she does not see changing the Church as a primary part of her mission. 'I have been a religious for more than 30 years, and I have learned you just do it [social or political action] yourself. I did not become a nun to change the Church.'

On the summer day Sr Christine and I had sat drinking Coca-Cola in her ramshackle convent in a Manila slum, she had expressed confidence that Filipino Christians could work for social change outside the confines of the national-democratic movement, which she considers arrogant. In the community, Sr Christine and her colleagues had helped residents gain confidence to protest and establish cooperatives and other economic ventures. In the Church, she had been the provincial superior in the Association of Major Religious Superiors when it had established task forces on human rights and social justice. In the broader political movement, she had worked in organizations and alliances devoted to nationalism and peace. Though Sr Christine had said that she could not accept the communist ideology, she was not at the forefront of efforts to develop a progressive theological alternative to dialectical materialism. This task was taken on by a group of Jesuit intellectuals at Ateneo de Manila University, whose work has now resulted in the authentic humanism of the social-democratic movement.

In describing authentic humanism, Fr Romeo Intengan wrote: 'The responsibility of human beings transcends in many ways their earthly and individual lives. Each human person is responsible to God, or at least to his or her fellow human beings of the present as well as of the future generations, whose lives he or she will in some way affect by his or her action or inaction.'[10] Some Christian activists were critical of Intengan and his colleagues, particularly Christian national democrats, who joined in condemning the alleged clerico-fascism of the social democrats. Even the more thoughtful ones condemned the movement. 'We were especially amused by those who tried to foist social democracy on us as the Christian alternative,' wrote Ed de la Torre in the early 1970s. In the same paper, he said, 'Opposed to the revolution and to anything Marxist, they sought to come up with a comprehensive Christian alternative that eventually got baptized as social democracy. Although clearly reformist, they had to assert that they were radical because of the temper of the times.'[11] The social democrats nevertheless gained significant support amongst students at Ateneo and in other élite Jesuit schools. They also came to influence religious, especially Jesuit, activists by providing a theology of social action and analysis that was opposed to dialectical materialism and to unity with the Marxist-Leninists of the CPP and NDF.

Sectarianism has blighted development on the religious left as well as in the wider society. The national democrats in Church-backed human-rights groups foolishly ignored the plight of social-democrat and other politically incorrect prisoners during the Marcos period. Later, social democrats and Jesuits joined conservative Church leaders in what amounted to a purge of national democrats from the leadership of the bishops' NASSA.

More than 100 bishops belong to the CBCP (Catholic Bishops' Conference of the Philippines). While it has backed some (mostly agrarian and environmental) reform, the CBCP is rather conservative. The bishops have failed to take stands on such pressing social issues as nuclear weapons or the US military bases; and they have not questioned the morality of the existing social and economic system, choosing instead to focus on the corruption within that system. The vast majority of the bishops are staunch anti-communists. Some even support anti-communist vigilantes. 'Our bishop has always encouraged people to join *Nakasaka* in his sermons because it is peace loving and God fearing,' the Uzi-toting governor of Davao del Sur told me, referring to the vigilante group he and the local military commander had organized.

Jaime Cardinal Sin represents the conservative mainstream of the Philippine Church hierarchy. During the Marcos era he gained a reputation as an outspoken foe of the dictatorship, but that image was only partially correct. While, to their credit, Sin and the majority of his colleagues rarely put obstacles in the way of activist anti-Marcos groups within the Church, they also seldom took the lead in criticizing the regime. Today Sin is as quick to defend the Aquino government and the military, as he is to attack leftists in the Church and society. This kind of political conservatism, which is matched by a theological traditionalism on such concerns as the role of women in the Church, divorce and population control, goes part of the way towards explaining the lack of serious concern about social justice. But there are other reasons. One is the need to protect the Church's position. Just as the bishops must respond to pressure from the grassroots, they must also respond to pressure from the right.

In most parts of the Philippines, the bishops are an integral part of the local élite. Many come from affluent backgrounds. They socialize with political, economic and military leaders. They bless their homes, marry their children and bury their dead. Donations from the wealthy allow the Church to prosper and the bishops to live comfortably. A few bishops, like Claver and Fortich, may call on the rich to share their wealth with the poor or get out of the Church, but the majority look the other way. A second important source of pressure on the bishops to remain conservative comes from the military, which make it difficult to be a Christian radical. Priests, nuns and lay workers disappear, or are killed or gaoled. Christian activists in the open movement are labelled communists, and thus criminals. In at least one case, an entire religious order was identified as subversive by the local military command. In Cebu, the military refers to Redemptorist priests as Redempterrorists.

Aside from these outside pressures, conservative groups within the Church also affect the bishops' thinking. Opus Dei is the most prominent of such groups in the Philippines. Backed by the Pope, this affluent lay order operates an influential economic research centre and graduate school in a Manila suburb, the Centre for Research & Communication, which engages in liberation theology bashing. Institutionally, however, the most conservative force working on the Catholic hierarchy is the Vatican. As elsewhere, it looks askance at any form of Christian-Marxist cooperation. It urges the Church leadership to concentrate on evangelization and such traditional moral causes as resistance to divorce, birth control and abortion.

The real influence of the Catholic Church, however, lies in its dioceses, parishes, schools, priests, nuns and lay workers. Its institutions exist in all the country's urban communities. Each diocese and many parishes maintain social-action centres. Traditionally, these centres provided charitable relief to impoverished parishioners and victims of natural calamities. In the 1960s Church social action incorporated a developmental thrust. Church workers began to address the causes of poverty through small-scale economic development. But progressives found this insufficient. 'The problem is, when you go into development work you find out that often times people are poor because they are denied access to resources,' said Bishop Claver. 'The whole problem of social injustice comes in. Now, when you work for social justice, you work for the liberation of people.'

The liberationist thrust in social-action work developed alongside a radicalization of many Christian social-action workers. By the late 1970s and early 1980s, Christian leftists had become the most active social-action workers. Many sympathized with open and clandestine national-democratic organizations. These radicalized Christians came to control the national and regional secretariats for social action. With the support of some sympathetic bishops, the Christian left gained a foothold in the institutional Church and used its influence in NASSA to support BCCs, human rights campaigns, critical publications and mass organizations of peasants, workers and the urban poor.

Critics have complained about NASSA also funding the armed underground and this remains a controversial issue. The bishops have failed to produce any substantial evidence, but it is fair to say that, because of the priorities of some field workers, some of the money earmarked for projects or legal organizations working in the countryside may well have made its way to the armed left. Concern about links between the national-democratic movement and the Church's social-action network first led Mindanao's bishops to withdraw support from the Mindanao-Sulo Pastoral Conference Secretariat in 1982. That forced MISSSA (the Mindanao-Sulo Secretariat of Social Action), which had merged with it, to separate. In 1985, the Mindanao Bishops dissolved MISSSA. 'The move to [reorganize] seems to be a manifestation of the authoritarian attitude of the bishops in the conservative mainstream within the Church,' wrote Fr Justiniano Cabazares, a former MISSSA executive secretary in 1985.[12]

MISSSA's big brother, NASSA, was safe so long as Marcos remained in power. But as soon as he fled, conservatives within the Church, including Cardinal Sin, began a steady attack on it. Lengthy newspaper reports claimed to prove communist infiltration. The bishops launched an investigation. Concrete questions about NASSA focused on a single department, the projects department, which reviews the proposals of local organizations for international Catholic funding agencies. Few serious questions were raised about NASSA's other departments. But in the frenzy of battle the NASSA controversy came to symbolize the fight between right and left in the Church.

Members of the moderate Christian left entered the fray. They sought to save NASSA's liberationist thrust while rescuing it from radical or national-democratic control. In the end the reformers won. The bishops voted to reorganize NASSA under the supervision of Bishop Claver. Claver asserted that NASSA would continue to pursue charitable, developmental and liberational work, but in a different manner and with a different thrust. As Claver told me:

> Our problem is not that we should not go into liberational work, it is how. Does this mean that therefore we have to tie up with political groups like the

NPA and the NDF? Or should we tie up with the government? Our position on this is: 'Well, you can tie up with anyone, but you must maintain your identity as a Church, and therefore if the means they use are against what we ordinarily accept as Christian, then we have to say no.'

The defeat suffered in the tussle over NASSA has not eliminated the involvement of radicals in the institutional Church. Leftists remain involved in social-action work on the local level, they continue to work in staff positions at NASSA, and still run an extensive network of human rights organizations, such as Task Force Detainees, the Ecumenical Movement for Justice & Peace, and the Philippine Alliance of Human Rights Advocates. These organizations make use of parish priests, diocesan social-action directors and religious educators and nuns scattered throughout the country to monitor human rights abuses, to campaign for the release of political prisoners, to put pressure on local political and military officials, and to organize seminars and teach-ins on issues of concern to the left.

A similar network exists within the Protestant Churches. Human rights desks, organizations of Protestant students, lawyers and clergy, a Commission on Tribal Filipinos and other such groups make up the Protestant left. These organizations utilize the Protestant network throughout the country and are generally supported by the liberal NCCP (National Council of Churches of the Philippines).

Church politics attracts the attention of outsiders, but does not take up all the time of religious workers. The vast majority of the bishops and most parish priests are not revolutionaries out to change the world, but Christians seeking the salvation of souls. Bishop Claver and Fr John Carroll found the bishops' top three priorities in 1988 to be 'ministry of the word,' 'worship and sacramental ministry,' and 'pastoral programmes for communities and tribes.' Community organization, i.e. promoting pressure groups among farmers, fishermen and the urban poor, ranked 13th out of 14 priorities.[13] Indeed, while the political impact of the Church is important, the moral or traditionally religious reach is even greater. Many Filipinos may rarely see a priest, but most celebrate the Christian holidays and rituals with fervour. I was in the outback of Bicol just before Holy Week in 1987. In one village we visited on a mountain top deep in the interior, the residents said a priest visited once a year. But this did not stop them from celebrating their religious rites. As we entered the village we heard the men gathered to sing a religious *pasyon*. And this in a CPP-controlled *barrio*.

Religious fervour is especially strong during moments of crisis when many — President Aquino included — seek the solace of prayer. Shortly after one of several coup attempts, Cory and a handful of her cabinet members appeared on national television praying with their rosaries to seek God's help in saving the nation. Escapist? Yes, also the source of organized Christianity's tremendous influence in the Philippines. Faith in Christ and in the Church gives religious leaders tremendous scope to mobilize and influence people. At times this faith manifests itself in extremes: in members of the *Iglesia ni Kristo* voting as their spiritual leader tells them to, in fanatics going into battle armed only with *bolos*, but protected by magic amulets and oils. At other times it is more difficult to quantify. The February revolution was in large part a religious festival. Participants carried religious icons into battle. Praying nuns knelt in front of oncoming tanks. Cardinal Sin gave people confidence that God was on their side. Similarly, but in a different vein, the presence of priests and nuns on the left allows believers to view movements for change as moral and godly choices.

Philippine Christianity is not a uniform force. Within it are the various forces present in society as a whole. Yet the Churches do not simply mirror society. Religious and active lay people tend to be more involved in social issues than the average Filipino. They can command institutions of broad political and moral impact. Hence the continued efforts of the Christian left to gain a foothold in the institutional Church. And hence the importance of winning Church people to the side of change.

21

Mountain Tribes and Cultural Minorities

Pedro considered himself educated in the ways of the modern world. When his wife gave birth to their son he refused to abide by the tribal tradition of bathing the newborn in the cold rushing waters of the Chico River. Pedro explained how the cold water could shock the fragile child. His neighbours listened politely. They believed the cold waters washed away evil. But they knew Pedro to be an intelligent young man and thought he might know something they did not. 'My son unfortunately fell ill,' Pedro told me as we waited for our host to finish preparing the rice and sweet potato we would eat for dinner. 'It was a minor sickness, the kind young children often get, but it was enough to convince the people I had done wrong, I had broken tradition, I had displeased the spirits.'

It is difficult to break with tradition in tribal villages, for in these mountain villages traditions define a unique culture, community and people. To break with centuries of practice requires a very good reason. Unlike the Aetas or Negritos, whose minority status stems from racial distinction, the majority of tribal Filipinos (whether national or cultural minorities) earned their separate identities during the Spanish period. While most of the Filipinos forced to submit to the conquerors had added a layer of Hispanic culture (usually Catholicism) to their folk traditions, the Islamic Moros, the animistic Igorots (who were descended from an early wave of migrants from the Asian mainland) and the scattered tribes of other mountain ranges had defended and preserved their cultural heritages.

US and Philippine conquest and encroachment in the south and in the mountain regions during the 20th century had a far greater impact on minority communities and cultures. But the new *conquistadores* failed either to integrate fully or to eliminate minority cultures. Partial integration then led to more sophisticated forms of resistance, as tribal leaders and young intellectuals became increasingly aware of their uniqueness and oppression by outsiders. Cooperation across tribal lines in the northern Cordillera mountains and across ethnic lines in the Islamic south emerged in the 1960s and since.

In 1983 the NCCP (National Council of Churches in the Philippines) identified 5,951,344 Filipinos as belonging to native minority groups. It counted 2,527,302 Muslims in 13 ethnic groups; 716,702 members of the seven major Igorot tribes of northern Luzon's Cordillera mountains; numerous tribals in the Cagayan Valley, Mindoro, Palawan and Mindanao and the scattered Negrito groups.[1] Other sources have placed the Muslim population at between 4 and 7 per cent of the national population of over 60 million and between 17 and 33 per cent of the southern population. At the beginning of the American period, Muslims made up more than 90 per cent of Mindanao's population, a ratio that dwindled with Filipino migration from Luzon and the Visayas.

Filipinos and Americans alike have treated tribal Filipinos as curiosities. In 1904, for example, the St Louis Exhibition in the US featured a display of natives of the Cordillera. Exhibition organizers brought Igorot tribesmen to Missouri so that American audiences could view their primitive life-style. Such cultural exploitation still continues. It often involves natives in traditional dress preforming dances for tourists, or posing for photos for a few pesos. As recently as 1968 the Philippine diplomat, Carlos Romulo, proclaimed that 'the Igorots [were] not Filipinos.' In 1983 the NCCP sponsored a fascinating dialogue between Christian and Muslim Filipinos, which revealed numerous misconceptions on both sides: 'Christians are submissive, easily bowing down to the influence of Western culture.' 'Muslims are backward.' 'Christians are a bunch of land grabbers.' 'Muslims are slave traders.' 'Christians are exploiters.' 'Muslims are bloodthirsty.' 'Christians are abusive. They are killers. Their soldiers are stained with Muslim blood.' 'Muslims are traitors.'[2]

Such attitudes have grown out of a history of conflict, conquest, encroachment on tribal lands and colonial education. Increased contact has brought both new hostilities and a tendency, among more progressive Filipinos, to recognize common historical experiences and to respect cultural differences. Contact between outsiders and tribal or Muslim Filipinos has historically been regarded by the latter as a disaster. Government policy has encouraged Tagalogs and Visayans to settle in Islamic and tribal areas. The outsiders' familiarity with modern laws embodying the concept of private property in land has led to the usurpation of traditional lands.

The rush to development without consultation — which started early in the American era and peaked during the Marcos years — accelerated the process of alienation and conflict. Transnational corporations and big

Filipino capitalists saw the mineral and forest resources of tribal areas as a wealthy last frontier waiting to be exploited for 'national development'. A corrupt state urged the tribals to make a sacrifice for the common good. But exploiting the natural resources and damming the rivers merely benefited the export-oriented industries, while bringing ecological destruction to many a mountain area. But this exploitation of natural resources in the tribal and Muslim areas also integrated the minorities into the Philippine economy. Had that economy been healthy and the government kept the minorities' welfare in mind, economic integration might have benefited them. But since integration grew out of the destruction of traditional economies through ecological destruction and land grabbing, integration merely exacerbated their impoverishment.

Despite the failure of the government's programmes, the Marcos era did, however, unintentionally bring with it the seeds of a healthy social integration of minorities into the Filipino nation, an integration based on unity in diversity rather than on cultural assimilation. This happened when Marcos's opponents came to respect the minorities, especially the Moros and Igorots, for their resistance to the dictatorship. This respect led the national-democratic movement to become involved with the Igorots in the Cordillera. Social democrats (or, in other places, the NDF) began to cooperate with the MNLF (Moro National Liberation Front) and, after the fall of Marcos, they managed to gain limited autonomy under the Philippine constitution.

While minority groups share certain experiences with the majority, they share more with one another. For example, they retain much of their pre-colonial culture; they share a history of economic marginalization; and their forced integration has introduced them to a decadent culture. Nomadic groups have lost their mobility, stationary ones their land. Outsiders have introduced an array of diseases and vices. The introduction of consumer goods and, with it, the destruction of local alternatives have increased poverty and unhealthy assimilation.

Moros and Igorots proved to be potent foes of conquest and assimilation during the Marcos years. They found in their history and culture the roots of cooperation across tribal or communal lines. They also found a cause around which they could unite their diverse communities against the dictatorship's encroachment. Their different approaches to national development and identification coincided with a political and cultural awakening that shook not just the minority community, but the entire nation.

Although Islam had dominated the deep south during the Spanish era, an Islamic nation had never in fact materialized. Islamic people, called Moros by the Spaniards, had always regarded themselves as members of

different communities, sharing a common religion and similar folk traditions, but divided by language, leadership and economic pursuits. In the
1980s the largest of the 13 major Muslim groups, the Maranaw,
Maguindanao and Tausug, each with over half a million members, occupied distinct territories in Lanao, Cotabato and Sulu.[3] *Datus* (meaning
rulers and descendants of rulers) led small communities. More powerful
datus led combinations of communities. By the 1800s separate Sulu,
Maguindanao and Lanao sultanates existed, but the real power still rested
with the *datus*.[4]

When, towards the end of their rule, the Spaniards started to assert
their authority in the south, the Muslims responded in much the same
way as people in other parts of the country. Some offered fierce resistance, others collaborated. Collaboration and conquest then changed the
whole nature of Muslim leadership. The *datus* adapted by assuming
government office, by joining political parties, and by taking advantage
of land laws to claim their own holdings while extending control over
their followers. In areas where the Muslims lost their previous majority
status to new settlers, there was a disintegration of the traditional leadership; where they remained a major group, cooptation took place. In either
case, the traditional leadership failed to serve the interests of the population and Muslim communities remained amongst the poorest in the
Philippines. Official statistics released as recently as 1986 show the two
Mindanao regions, which have large Muslim populations, to be the
poorest on that island. T.J.S. George painted an even bleaker picture at
the beginning of martial law. 'The wretchedness of the people contrasted
violently with the luxury in which traditional leaders lived,' George
wrote in his study of the Muslim uprising of the 1970s. 'Not only were
the leaders unconcerned about the lot of the poor; they routinely monop-
olized all government patronage meant for the indigent, including educational scholarships.'[5]

But even as class stratification accelerated within the already frag-
mented Moro community, a flood of settlers to Mindanao during much of
the 20th century robbed Muslims of their majority in all but a few
provinces. In the 1960s vicious campaigns by Christian landowners to
seize political power in the region — marked by the emergence of
fanatical groups, such as the *Ilaga* (Rats) — and savage massacres contributed to the growing animosity on the part of the Muslim communities. Violence and miserable conditions — poverty, the failure of
the traditional leadership, alienation from the surrounding nation, discrimination and ethnic oppression — formed the backdrop to the Moro
revolt. But changes had to occur within the community before the
uprising became possible. Most important, the Moro communities

needed an alternative leadership and ideology to confront their modern enemies.

Nur Misuari and Hashim Salamat played leading roles in the Moro drama of the 1970s and 1980s. The son of an impoverished Samal-Tausug family from Sulu, Misuari had attended UP (University of the Philippines) in the early 1960s on a scholarship. At UP he had joined such Marxist-influenced groups as New Asia and KM (*Kabataang Makabayan*), but never rejected his Islamic heritage. George notes that while Misuari retained many Marxist lessons well into his career as a political leader, he had held onto 'such deeply rooted Islamic dogma' as the idea that 'sovereignty was immutably vested in Allah.' George goes on to say that 'by 1966 Misuari [had] made his decision: he would devote his life and talents to the cause of Muslims rather than to the downtrodden as a class.'[6] Retaining his Islamic faith had played an important role in Misuari's early entry into Moro politics. While at UP he had attracted followers with his charisma, compassion and intellectual power. His associates included the sons of traditionally powerful families. Hashim Salamat, a member of the influential Pendatun-Matalam clan in Cotabato's Maguindanao-dominated Moro community, was among them. Salamat, who was to emerge as an important rival to Misuari in the 1980s, says he first became involved in the Moro struggle in 1962, as a student in Cairo. Salamat told Philippine journalist José Lacaba that the MNLF (Moro National Liberation Front), his first group, had not sought to 'take up arms against the Philippine government but to launch a sort of reform movement, to reform Muslim society in Mindanao.'

The MNLF grew out of the cooperation of Muslim students and young intellectuals. Their education in Manila and the Middle East had exposed them to Marxism and Islamic radicalism. Misuari started an organization for the four largest Muslim ethnic groups (the Maranaw, Maguindanao, Tausug and Samal) while studying and teaching at UP. During the same period he had also linked up with members of the still dominant, though corrupt, 'royal' families. George writes that:

> For the traditional leaders, Muslim autonomy meant the recognition and reinforcement of their power. Misuari's vision of Muslim destiny included the elimination of the old leaders and his own installation at the helm. He might have renounced Marxism, but his notions of justice for Muslims rested firmly on Marxist principles of egalitarianism, a restructuring of power relations within the Muslim community, the liquidation of the privileged class he loathed. The contradiction between his and his patrons' positions was more than a generational gap; it was an ideological divide.[7]

Misuari used this troubled partnership to generate support. But he presented a conception of identity far removed from the feudal identity fostered by the traditional leaders. Instead, he presented the masses with a Bangsa Moro national identity, one which cut across ethnic lines, while also rejecting the sobriquet Muslim Filipino.

Misuari and his colleagues captured the common heritage, alienation and aspirations of a Muslim population catalysed by a series of tragedies that included the 1968 Jabidah massacre, the murders perpetrated by the *Ilaga*, and the declaration of martial law. Through passionate advocacy of the rights of the Moro community and the Islamic poor, Misuari provided the Muslim community with an alternative leadership and identity. The vehicle for that leadership would be the MNLF, a group born, says Hashim Salamat, in 1968, four years before it came out into the open.

Misuari believed in the Maoist theories of a protracted people's war. He inspired his associates with his advocacy of armed struggle and even persuaded some of the *datus* with connections in the Muslim world to send him and other young Moros abroad for military training. The *datus* expected to control Misuari, as George points out:

> Soon the *datus* regretted their move, for the guerrilla training programme gave Misuari the independence he needed. While they were still abroad, he put the finishing touches to his ambitious underground organization, the Moro National Liberation Front; his fellow trainees elected him chairman. The MNLF had a separate sword arm, the Bangsa Moro Army, which began to be put together as groups of trainees returned to their hideouts in Mindanao.

> The MNLF began to dissociate itself from the *datus* whose assistance was essential for its initial sustenance. The fervent young liberationists shared Misuari's view that the hereditary leadership was feudal in character. One 'field commander' in the Cotabato area told an interviewer once that Muslims had only contempt for *datus* who 'wheeled and dealed' in politics. He added: 'Although these people call themselves Muslims, they are a party to the oppression being waged against the Bangsa Moro People. They are our enemies.'[8]

The falling out with the traditional leadership had a price, especially in Lanao and Cotabato where the warrior tradition was weaker than in Misuari's native Sulu. The MNLF lost much of its original strength in Lanao and some in Cotabato, but it still maintained its multi-ethnic leadership and character. In fact, the MNLF emerged as the first important Muslim political organization to cut across ethnic and geographic boundaries. As researcher Lela Noble notes, its founders were 'self-consciously Muslim rather than Maranao, Maguindanao or Tausug.'[9]

War exploded in the south soon after the imposition of martial law. Early battles involved forces other than the MNLF, but by the end of 1972, it had become the most potent military force. In late 1972 raging battles erupted in Zamboanga, Cotabato and elsewhere in Mindanao. Well trained, well equipped rebel forces overran government positions on an almost daily basis, several Cotabato towns fell into rebel hands and thousands died.

An eerie calm fell over Mindanao during the second half of 1973. It was not to last. In February 1974 fighting erupted anew on the island of Jolo in Sulu. Fighting broke out spontaneously when 20 marines set out to collect weapons in compliance with Marcos's ban on private firearms. Angry Muslims slaughtered them. The local military commander then called on his troops to avenge their deaths. But rebel forces entered Julo town *en masse*. The subsequent battle raged for several days with naval ships bombarding the town, Air Force jets straffing and shelling, and tanks rumbling through the streets. The MNLF pulled out its main force, but left behind snipers to harass the enemy. Estimates put the death toll at 400 to 1,000 civilians, 150 to 200 rebels and an undetermined number of army troops.

For the remainder of 1974 and 1975 Sulu and parts of Mindanao were battered by war. At its peak the MNLF had between 20,000 and 30,000 armed members. Noble reports that 'as it consolidated organizationally, it also extended its control through significant areas of Mindanao and the Sulu Archipelago. It broadened its external base of support from people like Qaddafi and Tun Mustapha [Sabah's chief minister, a descendant of a Sulu family] to all states connected with the Islamic Conference.'[10] But not everything went well for the MNLF. In Sulu some Moros blamed it for bringing war and destruction to Julo town; Amnesty programmes lured away some rebels; and disputes between leaders and ethnic groups within the MNLF troubled the organization and led to some defections.

In 1975 Tun Mustapha fell from power in Sabah. His territory had provided the MNLF with a secure base and his government had acted as a conduit for foreign aid. Noble made clear the impact: 'Aid from Sabah was drastically curtailed by late 1975. MNLF units henceforth had to depend mostly on weapons and ammunition captured in encounters with the Marcos military or bought from the corrupt troopers. Consequently, resistance groups which had joined the MNLF primarily to secure their weapons supply had little incentive to remain loyal.'[11]

By 1975 conditions were ripe for negotiating. The MNLF and the Moro community had shown themselves capable of waging a costly struggle against a state also confronting a slowly growing insurgency elsewhere. A negotiated settlement that would recognize the MNLF and deliver some autonomy to the Moro people appeared possible. The Muslim nations took the lead and the Islamic Conference recommended bringing the MNLF, the Philippine government and a ministerial commission involving Libya, Saudi Arabia, Senegal and Somalia into the negotiations.

From the government perspective, too, the time seemed ripe. Not only was the Moro war costing a tremendous amount, but it was also tarnishing the image Marcos had been trying to project of himself as a benevolent and popular Third World leader. Perhaps most significantly it was costing him much needed contacts in the oil rich Arab world — and at the very time of the first great oil crisis. The first talks took place in Jedda, Saudi Arabia in 1975. The parties reached an agreement in Libya on 23 December 1976. That pact, known as the Tripoli Agreement, called for the immediate cessation of hostilities, the implementation of autonomy in 13 provinces (eight with Christian majorities) and further talks to iron out details of the accord. For both sides the agreement represented a compromise. The MNLF gave up its claims to independence in all 21 provinces while, in the words of Lela Noble, 'the principles agreed to follow closely the MNLF demands. Within areas of the "Autonomy for Muslims in the southern Philippines," Muslims were to have the right to establish their own courts, schools, and administrative system. The Autonomy was to have a legislative assembly, executive council, special regional security forces, and economic and financial system.'12

But the Tripoli Agreement contained dangers for the MNLF. First, the MNLF was not specifically mentioned in relation to the formation of either a provisional government, which Marcos had the power to appoint, or subsequent legislative or executive councils. Second, the Agreement stated that, 'the Government of the Philippines shall take all necessary constitutional processes for the implementation of the entire Agreement.' This set the stage for Marcos to exercise his black magic in the form of a plebiscite on autonomy.

The MNLF believed the agreement gave it a right to power in the south. Libyan leader Muammar Al Qaddafi had advanced this position during a meeting with Imelda Marcos in early 1977. According to Qaddafi, he and Imelda had reached an agreement on implementation that included the following step: 'A provisional government for the autonomy to be formed by a decision of the President of the Republic in which the concerned parties from Moro National Liberation Front and the inhabitants of the areas of the autonomy take part.'13

Despite the agreement with Qaddafi Marcos staged a referendum. Qaddafi, the MNLF and Islamic Conference representatives protested, but to no avail. As Noble reports: 'The results of the referendum were similar to those of all votes held under the martial law regime. Marcos got what he wanted: opposition to the inclusion of certain provinces, opposition to the degree of autonomy presumably wanted by the MNLF, and support for two autonomous regions under central control.' The new autonomous regions included only ten of the 13 provinces mentioned in the Tripoli Agreement.[14]

Marcos did not completely fool the MNLF leadership. Misuari had always considered betrayal a possibility. He saw the ceasefire period as a time to regroup for further combat, but the MNLF failed to overcome its organizational problems during the lull. Festering differences within the leadership (differences rooted in ethnic and ideological diversity) exploded into open factionalism. Problems also arose because the Tripoli Agreement had neutralized the MNLF's foreign supporters. When the MNLF resumed its pursuit of independence, it did so without significant material support from the Islamic world. Marcos had further weakened the MNLF by shrewdly using the new autonomous regions to shore up the traditional Muslim leadership.

Various theories have been put forward to explain the split within the MNLF and the defection of numerous leaders during the post-Tripoli period. Dimas Pundato, a former MNLF official turned faction leader, attributes the split to tribal rivalry and to Misuari's imposition of Tausug domination on the MNLF's central committee. Others cite Misuari's resumption of a war of independence. Observers and participants alike credit Marcos with contributing to the MNLF's troubles. Whatever the reasons, the divisions in the MNLF put a stop to its grand project of building a Moro nation. It had grown weak just as the need for creative, democratic leadership was greatest and traditional leaders and Marcos's new partners took advantage of the situation to exploit the Muslim masses for their own benefit.

Ultimately, the autonomous governments resulted not in the empowerment of the Moro people but in the strengthening of repressive structures. These structures revitalized elements of the traditional leadership and brought into the local élite former rebels willing to cooperate with the Marcos dictatorship. These forces gained the upper hand in the struggle for power in Moro land. Though badly bruised and factionalized, the MNLF did not, however, disappear. Misuari and his comrades — now mostly Tausug and Samal — remained active in the Middle East with troops still in the field on the Zamboanga Peninsula and Sulu.

Having broken with Misuari, Hashim Salamat found support in the Muslim areas of the Cotabato provinces and parts of Lanao and set up his own organization. In 1984 it became known as the MILF (Moro Islamic Liberation Front) and, though often incorrectly labelled fundamentalist, it attracted the Moro poor through its opposition to oppression by foreigners, Filipinos and the Moro élite alike. Like Misuari's MNLF, the MILF continued sporadic military and political activity in the region.

Other groups popped up as well. Dimas Pundato established his own MNLF-Reformist wing in the early 1980s. Traditional leaders cum anti-Marcos politicians Rashid Lucman and Salipada Pendatun formed a Bangsa Moro Liberation Organization and moved in and out of alliances with Misuari and Salamat prior to the elderly politicians' deaths in the 1980s.

Despite their difficulties, the rebel groups, especially the MNLF and the MILF, maintained a considerable following in parts of Mindanao during the waning years of Marcos's rule. The MNLF's position changed again with the rise of opposition to the Marcos regime in the 1980s and the rapid advance of the popular movement that culminated with Cory Aquino's victory. The situation catalysed the MNLF and its factions to grab the political initiative and reassert their importance in the Moro community.

At first Aquino was favourably disposed towards the MNLF, for she and her supporters shared its anti-Marcos stance. A political link had already been made between Misuari's MNLF and a portion of the Aquino movement. Ninoy Aquino had met Misuari and other Moro leaders during their exile and expressed sympathy. Also, the social democrats had worked closely with the MNLF in the 1970s. In fact, they had shared camps in Mindanao and Sabah prior to the MNLF's banishment from Malaysia. Butz Aquino had met Misuari shortly before his sister-in-law became president and regarded him as essential to any peace plan for Mindanao. The new government sought negotiations with a unified Moro front. The Moros, however, could not present a united front and Cory decided to meet Misuari herself. They met in Jolo in September 1986.

The meeting resulted in a cessation of hostilities and, in January 1987, the two sides signed an accord in Jedda, Saudi Arabia, setting the stage for future negotiations. They agreed to 'continue discussion of the proposal for the grant of full autonomy to Mindanao, Basilan, Sulu, Tawi-Tawi and Palawan subject to democratic processes.' In addition, the government panel, headed by Aquilino Pimentel, agreed to present President Aquino with a proposal to suspend 'pertinent provisions of the draft constitution on the grant of autonomy to Muslim Mindanao in the scheduled plebiscite on 2 February 1987, to allow the MNLF to undertake democratic consultations with the people of Mindanao and its islands.'

Aquino, however, insisted on presenting the entire constitution to the electorate. This triggered an MNLF campaign against ratification, but an overwhelming majority of the voters in Muslim Mindanao approved the constitution. The government's position hardened, and the talks proceeded along a very rocky road. The two parties held formal talks in the Philippines between February and May 1987. They failed to produce an agreement. The MNLF refused a final offer from the government which would have resulted in an executive order creating a ten-province Regional Executive Council with significant MNLF representation and greater powers than the existing Marcos-created autonomous governments. Rejection ended the government's courtship with the MNLF. The MNLF turned its attention to diplomatic efforts in the Muslim world and posturing in the Philippine media. The ceasefire continued with reports of violations coming from both sides.

The pursuit of talks with the MNLF had divided the Aquino cabinet. Some government officials and members of the first family actively courted various Moro factions, while others strongly opposed any talks or concessions. Meanwhile, all the attention given to the MNLF and the hot rhetoric from all sides fanned the flames of fear amongst Christian Filipinos. The talks had also generated animosity among more moderate Moro guerrilla and political forces. Exclusion angered them. The focus on the MNLF had highlighted the disagreements between the various ethnic and political groups within the Moro community.

By the time the government had staged a plebiscite on its proposed autonomous region in November 1989, it had succeeded in alienating the most progressive segments of the community and in restoring power to the more backward elements. Besides, it had not secured support from either the Muslim or Christian residents of Mindanao for its plans. Voters rejected the government's proposal of a limited autonomy: Muslims because it offered too little, Christians because it gave away too much. This did not augur well for those concerned with relations between Muslim and non-Muslim Filipinos. The Moro community emerged from the talks factionalized and with no clear unified leadership. Guerrillas continued to operate outside the political system, while traditional leaders and rebel returnees enjoyed powers granted by the state. Local war-lords and bandits, siding with whoever they could gain the most from, complicated the picture.

Despite their failure to capitalize on the fall of Marcos, the guerrillas continue to hold the key to peace in the south. With all their weaknesses, the Moro rebel groups still symbolize the cause of Muslim unity and empowerment in the Philippines. The MILF and the MNLF-Reformists seem committed to using this appeal to further the cause of autonomy. The MNLF represents a more problematic picture. Its recognition by the government has strengthened its appeal, but its diplomatic posturing and failure to achieve a settlement have cost it its credibility. Also, the MNLF has not made clear who its allies and foes will be, especially in provinces with significant Christian populations.

The left underground in the shape of the NDF (National Democratic Front) cannot be ruled out as a force in Muslim Mindanao. It has been very cautious in its relations with the various Moro factions, opting not to favour one over the other, while also avoiding the appearance of interfering in Moro politics. The NDF bases its practice on a vow to support the Muslim people's right to self-determination. More recently, however, there have been signs of NDF influence within the Moro community. A number of legal Moro organizations have sprung up over the last few years which use language similar to that of the national-democratic organizations. Also, in 1985, the NDF Mindanao council announced the formation of an NDF organization for Moros. The NDF's entry into Moro land suggests a strategy similar to the one it pursued in the Cordillera, where the majority of rebels sought to preserve their separate identity within an archipelago-wide revolutionary movement.

Like the Moros, the people of the rugged Cordillera belong to various ethnic groups. Outsiders imagined a united group of Igorots or mountain people long before they thought of a cohesive front of their own. Even the use of the term 'tribe' to describe the seven major ethno-linguistic groups drew more on convenience than on reality. In fact, the village traditionally formed the highest level of organization known to the people of the Cordillera. Different groups did use treaties, like the *bodongs* (peace pacts) of the Kalinga and Bontoc peoples, to give some order to relations between often warring villages.

Periods of resistance marked the Spanish era in the Cordillera. William Henry Scott notes how difficult it was for the Spaniards to subjugate the Cordillera and to stop the flow of untaxed tobacco from the mountains in the 19th century. According to him, the occupation of parts of Ifugao required an average of one soldier for every 26 inhabitants as late as the 1890s, when 'the occupation of the Cordillera was still a military occupation, dependent on lowland sources for its foods, funds and guns, and its points of occupation were lonely outposts in the midst of unsubmissive tribes.' Even tribes in areas occupied by the Spaniards rejected the trappings of Hispanicization whenever possible. When the Spanish troops pulled out, supposedly subjugated Igorots rejected their new-found Christianity for traditional ways.[15]

Colonialism and resistance created an Igorot identity. Igorot anthropologist and activist, Joanna Carino, points out that:

> Under the onslaughts of the sword and the cross, the lowland *barangays* were slowly assimilated into the centralized colonial order. While their lowland brethren were undergoing the colonization process, the Igorots, except for those in some areas in Benguet and Abra, generally did not experience Spanish colonial rule. The price that the Igorots had to pay for independence from colonial rule was that they became different from their colonized brethren.[16]

The terrain made Igorot resistance possible. As the NPA would discover in the 1970s, the Cordillera — with its soaring peaks, deep canyons and rushing rivers — is uniquely conducive to guerrilla war and popular resistance. It is a rugged, beautiful land understood best by its traditional residents. The people of the Cordillera carved lovely and productive agricultural terraces from the steep slopes of the innermost mountains. A common love of the land grew up among the various tribes and villages which would serve as a point of unity when the Cordillera people finally joined to fight their common enemies during the Marcos era.

American mining corporations started operating in the 20th century where tribal peoples had previously tapped the earth for its metals and gems. Paths turned to roads to bring produce from the high plains of the Cordillera region to lowland markets. Baguio rapidly grew into a rest and recreation centre for US colonial officials and later for foreign tourists seeking an escape from the sweltering heat of the plains. New laws opened the Cordillera plateaux to lowland migrants and stripped the tribes of their ancestral rights to the unterraced slopes. Timber companies began to fell the Cordillera's pine forests for profit. Native culture became a sideshow for foreign tourists seeking authenticity amidst the dominant colonial culture of the accessible lowlands of the archipelago. The coming of outsiders did not mean the integration of the Igorots into mainstream Filipino culture. Exposure led some to convert to Catholicism or the Protestant faith brought by American missionaries; many learned English and Western ways from these Protestants in the 20th century, but many remained true to their old beliefs.

These trends accelerated during the Marcos era. New dams wiped out tribal villages; loggers slashed away at the forests; and miners stripped hillsides in pursuit of gold and other riches. Dictatorship and massive corruption speeded up the exploitation in the Cordillera as did the exhaustion of resources in other parts of the country. Now marginalization and underdevelopment characterize most of the Cordillera villages, practically all of which do without electricity, running water and sanitary facilities. Many can only be reached by trekking an hour to a day from the nearest road. Villages in which the indigenous economy has survived primarily practise subsistence farming, with a bit of cash income from native crafts. Other Igorots, pushed off the land, are reduced to penury. During the Christmas season, beggars from the mountains flood Baguio, Manila and other cities.

Against this backdrop the Marcos regime launched two major schemes in the Cordillera, which sparked off massive resistance and made way for the successful entry of the NPA. Marcos granted Herminio Disini's CRC (Cellophil Resources Corporation) a huge timber concession in Abra and announced plans to build a series of dams across the Chico River in Kalinga-Apayao and in the mountain province.

The NPA first entered the Cordillera in early 1971, when the CPP assigned Abriano Aydinan to his native Ifugao, but it had little success for nearly a decade. In 1974 the organizers of the mountain branch of the NPA assessed their efforts in Ifugao and, frustrated by the slow growth, decided that the Ifugaos did not feel themselves to be part of the Philippine nation. They also noted an absence of feudalism and recommended the formation of an army separate from the NPA, the ILA (Igorot Liberation Army), and an independent political organization, the FITL (Federation of Igorot Tribes for Liberation).

The local group abandoned the project in 1975 when the CPP rejected its recommendations. According to a 1986 NDF document:

> A much too narrow political line was the FITL-ILA's weakness. Being localist, it tended to gloss over national concerns. It stressed the ethnic component of the Cordillera struggle, sacrificing this struggle's class character. Since it failed to identify the class enemies of the Cordillera masses, it was unclear on whether non-minorities or lowlanders should be considered targets of the 'Igorot war of liberation.' It was, therefore, a political line divisive in nature.

But the effort signified the beginnings of both an attempt to develop an analysis of the Cordillera within the national-democratic movement and of tension between some in the Cordillera and others in the CPP leadership. Tension haunted the revolutionary movement in the Cordillera until a split in 1986.

Efforts in the Cordillera began to pay off when spontaneous protests erupted against the Chico River dam project and the CRC concession. In 1977 an NPA team moved in and offered assistance in the fight against the dam. Significantly, the movement cultivated links with village elders and adapted itself to progressive aspects of the local culture, while gently prodding the community to drop its more backward practices. In 1979 the NPA also began to operate in Abra, where Tingiuian people were resisting the CRC project. Again recruits from the militant local movement flooded the NPA. Among them were four priests, two of whom — Fr Conrado Balweg and Fr Bruno Ortega — would become NPA leaders in the Cordillera and key figures in the split that occurred after Aquino's rise to power.

Meanwhile, the national leadership of the CPP developed a more sophisticated analysis of the Cordillera and minority peoples. This occurred as leaders of the movement, like Tony Zumel, spent time in the Cordillera, and natives of the Cordillera, like Ignacio Capigsan, rose in the ranks of the CPP. 'The national minorities have the right to liberate themselves from oppression and determine their own destiny,' proclaimed the 1977 version of the NDF programme. 'The right to self determination includes the right to secede from a state of national oppression or to choose autonomy within a state that guarantees the equality of nationalities.' In the early 1980s the CPP sanctioned the development of the CPDF (Cordillera People's Democratic Front), which would become the vehicle for the underground national-democratic movement in the Cordillera and the voice of the Cordillera within the NDF. With the development of the CPDF came a still more sophisticated analysis of the Cordillera. It laid the groundwork for deeper involvement of the NDF in the region but also helped catalyse the ultimate split within the movement in the Cordillera.

As the majority of Cordillera revolutionaries moved towards the CPDF, a Cordillera nationalist faction began to emerge, which rejected the proposition that semi-feudalism described the source of oppression in the Cordillera. It instead promoted an indigenous system in which the *bodong* formed the core of the governing structure and collective traditions the heart of the economic system. But the nationalist ideology and practice were riddled with contradictions. Cordillera nationalists rejected the influence of lowlanders in their revolutionary movement and proclaimed themselves separatists. Yet when Cory became president this group actively pursued a far less radical settlement with her government than that demanded by the national democrats.

This can partially be explained by the personalities involved, notably priest-turned-guerrilla Conrado Balweg. After recruiting Balweg, the underground assigned him to its unit in the Bugnay area of Kalinga-Apayao. Bugnay was a hotbed of resistance to the Chico River dams and Balweg emerged quickly as a spokesman for the NPA and a folk hero. But he also became a Cordillera nationalist and, according to the CPDF, eventually a disciplinary problem. He and his supporters retaliated by accusing the national democrats of plotting his murder.

The developing tension exploded into a nasty split soon after Aquino became president. Balweg left the movement in April 1986, along with

Fr Bruno Ortega, members of an important NPA squadron and a faction of the Cordillera Bodong Association, to establish the CPLA (Cordillera Peoples Liberation Army). 'Rather than continue participation in a national revolution propelled — in the classic Marxist formulation — by exacerbations in class contradictions within society, intensified by imperialist intervention,' wrote UP instructor Ed Maranan, 'the CPLA of Balweg has chosen to cut off the Cordillera as a separate area for liberation, where the mountain people shall have full autonomy — independence even from the present government.'[17] The CPLA rejected the notion that class conflict exists in the Cordillera. Instead it developed an all encompassing minority-majority based analysis. In part, this was a reaction to the left's insistence on labelling the Cordillera's problems semi-feudal. But by 1986 the national democrats' analysis had become much more sophisticated and logical.

The national democrats recognized that classic feudalism was limited in the traditional Cordillera. The movement noted that modern economic integration in the Cordillera followed capitalist lines in vegetable and cash-crop production for the national market, craft production, and mining and electronics assembly for the overseas market. Still, the CPP insisted that the Cordillera was under the domination of a semi-feudal national economic and political order and thus suffered from feudal domination. In a later document, released by the CPDF in 1987, it recognizes that while 'the Cordillera is well known for its natural wealth, ... its people are poor, exploited, oppressed. This is due to three major problems. They include: imperialist and comprador-bourgeois encroachments on the people's lands; fascist terrorism; and national oppression.' In theory, the CPDF had sought to create an autonomous Cordillera government within the confines of a national-democratic state. Its organizers saw the CPDF, a coalition of mass organizations within the Cordillera, village and tribal councils and individuals, as the framework for that government.

Balweg, by contrast, sought to use the traditional *bodong* as the framework for a Cordillera government:

The Cordillera Bodong Administration/CPLA structure started in the mass movement itself. This structure was an expression of the political decision of the different tribes to confederate as one and bring out a new form of society while retaining their identities and political structures as tribes. This is what we call an indigenous system wherein structure is in the context of the alignment of political forces in relation to the means of production which is the land. This is also what we call now the Cordillera Bodong, fruit of the mass movement in the Cordillera, at the same time an offshoot of the traditional *bodong* from which they have come out with something new, in their attempt to defend their rights as a people. The traditional *bodong* is the recognition given by a tribe to another tribe. The Cordillera Bodong is a confederation of the different communities of the Cordillera who in the past were separated and lived independently. But now they could no longer be that independent any more because of the need for unity in order to survive the oppression of a system from the outside which has colonized them for so many years. It is necessary that for their political will to be one, it must have its own expression in the context of translating this into their economic and cultural life.[18]

Balweg's CPLA entered talks with the Aquino government. The CPDF had adhered to the NDF's policy of national negotiations only. After the initial setback caused by the rift, the CPDF had recovered; some CPLA members had returned to it and the organization had picked up steam elsewhere. The CPLA thus negotiated from a position of weakness, in which its military forces had come to consider the revolutionary movement as the enemy. In response, the CPDF accused it of becoming little more than a paramilitary arm of the AFP. That the CPDF held firm in the face of splits and intensified military operations was impressive. Doubly so since the issues that first allowed the NPA entrance into Cordillera society — the Chico River dam and the CRC concession — had long been settled in favour of the Cordillera communities.

Government efforts in the region — to create an autonomous government (so far approved by voters in only one province) and to improve the winding mountain roads — seem unlikely to alter the political landscape so long as outsiders control the modern economy and the indigenous economy lies in ruins. The goals of empowerment, autonomy, and social and economic transformation remain as viable today as they were when the NPA made its first bumbling overtures to the people of the region. So too does the goal of developing a new identity. In the south, the MNLF has tried to develop a Moro identity outside the confines of a Philippine nation. This has led to conflicts with Christians who might otherwise support a radical movement. In the Cordillera, revolutionaries have worked to build a pan-Igorot identity within the framework of Philippine nationalism. This project has laid the foundation for a new nation, but its future depends on the development of a strong movement in the rest of the country. Both the Cordillera and Moro people have contributed to this broader movement by showing the possibilities of building a national identity free of much of the damaging inheritances of a longstanding colonial culture.

22

Culture and Society

James Fallows lambasted a 'damaged culture' in an influential and controversial article in the *Atlantic Monthly*. My wife, a Filipina lawyer, complained of a 'culture of corruption and complacency.' The *Manila Chronicle* editorialized about a cultural lack of discipline. Progressive nationalists regularly denounce the many traces of colonialism in Philippine culture. Some attribute all the nation's cultural shortcomings to the country's colonial heritage.

Cynics believe that Philippine culture condemns the nation to eternal damnation and permanent poverty. More thoughtful critics, however, admit something is wrong and call for cultural change. They see a culture that has never been given the chance to flower; a culture burdened by a history of colonial, élite and dictatorial imposition; a culture, in fact a nation, that has never fully evolved as a healthy independent entity. The best of these critics include artists and intellectuals, activists and government officials, revolutionaries and reformers seeking to revamp schools, the entertainment industry and the media with institutions promoting a strong national culture.

A 1988 study on the Philippine character by Senator Leticia Shahani reveals many of the weaknesses of modern Philippine culture. It starts by listing seven strengths including family orientation; joy and humour; flexibility, adaptability and creativity; hard work and industry; faith and religiosity; ability to survive: and *pakikipagkapwa-tao* (helpfulness, generosity and sensitivity). Shahani also discussed negative characteristics:

1 Extreme personalism — Filipinos view the world in terms of personal relationships. One of the manifestations is the necessity for the establishment of personal relationships before any business or work relationship can be successful.

2 Extreme family centredness — While concern for the family is one of the Filipinos' greatest strengths, in the extreme it becomes a serious flaw. Excessive concern for the family creates an in-group to which

257

the Filipino is fiercely loyal to the detriment of concern for the larger community or common good.

3 Lack of discipline — This trait often results in inefficient and wasteful work systems, violation of rules leading to more serious transgressions and a casual work ethic leading to carelessness and lack of follow-through.

4 Passivity and lack of initiative — In many ways, it can be said that the Filipino is too patient and long-suffering. Too easily resigned to his fate, he is thus easily oppressed and exploited.

5 Colonial mentality — This is made up of two dimensions: a lack of patriotism and actual preference for things foreign. This trait results in a cultural vagueness or weakness that makes the Filipino extraordinarily susceptible to the acceptance of modern mass culture which is often Western.

6 Kanya-Kanya ('to each his own') syndrome — This is evident in the tendency to bring others down and in the drive for power and status that is completely insensitive to the common good.

7 Lack of self-analysis and self-reflection — There is no felt need to validate hypotheses or explanations of things. There is also the tendency to be satisfied with rhetoric and to substitute this for reality.

Contradictions abound in Shahani's report. But, of course, as in all cultures, contradictions abound in Philippine culture. Philippine society is not the only one to have such contradictions. Unfortunately, the political and economic system and much of the cultural machinery tends to accentuate the negative.

Let us look at some of Shahani's points. First, the colonial mentality. Though this affects Filipinos of various classes it is most prevalent among the educated. Aside from cultivating tastes in things foreign, from travel to consumer items, the élite has traditionally looked for partners and investments abroad. It holds the opinion that: 'If things get really bad, I can always go to the States.' This has contributed to the failure of Philippine capitalism to keep pace with development elsewhere in the region.

Learning from Shahani's criticism of passivity and lack of initiative would help the nation move forward on a democratic path. Complacent individuals allow others to make decisions of importance to the nation. Individuals and entire communities depend far too much on leaders.

Utang na loob further enhances the power of leaders. Translators often use the English 'debt of gratitude' to define it, but this fails to convey the significance of *utang na loob*, through which a debtor may owe a lifelong commitment. *Utang na loob* becomes dangerous when a peasant or farm worker feels he owes a landowner for some act of paternal benevolence, such as payment for medicine for a sick child, for burial of a parent or for food during lean months. The debtor may decide he owes his master a lifetime of service on the hacienda and loyalty at election time. Benjamin Pimentel Jr of *National Midweek* encountered the political impact of *utang na loob* during a visit to the Bicol region. 'We always vote for the master's rooster,' Pedro Ordoves told him. 'We couldn't refuse him after all he's done for us. So when he says we should be for this candidate, we follow.'[1]

Though Shahani's report provides a good start for analysing Philippine culture, it ignores other manifestations like escapism, attitudes to women and corruption. Escapism manifests itself in flights of fantasy and the lure of emigration. Fantasy, seeking solutions to a problem that are clearly out of reach, finds its roots in the Philippines' Christian tradition. The belief in a better world after death contributes to the fatalism of many Filipinos. But the passage of time has added new layers to the Filipino fantasy life — the dream of striking it rich through simple good fortune, marriage, gambling, searching for hidden treasure, scheming or moving abroad.

Emigration, as a fantasy and reality, has numerous detrimental affects on the nation and the individual. For every overseas job opening scores of often skilled workers apply. Con artists promise non-existent jobs in return for exorbitant fees. More important, the dream of success abroad interferes with the individual's dedication to succeeding in the Philippines, with the export labour market draining the domestic workforce of its best workers and many of its brightest college graduates.

Women in the Philippines find themselves in an odd position. Many doors are open to them and they can enter virtually every profession and responsible position in the public and private sectors. Yet society expects them to manage a house, maintain their virtue and provide their men with sexual gratification. Among Catholic Philippines, who are not allowed to divorce, there is a flourishing macho tradition in which the men pursue their sexual fantasies, have extra-marital relations, and often keep two families.

Economic pressures can push poor unskilled Filipinas into prostitution. With a ready market of foreign tourists, US servicemen and Filipino beerhouse patrons, prostitution flourishes and with it the woman's alienation from her community, separation from her family,

bouts of severe depression and loss of self-respect. Combine the lure of
foreign shores with sexuality and you find another source of alienation
and exploitation, the mail-order bride business, which unites struggling
Filipinas with lonely foreigners, often in rural areas of Japan, Australia,
New Zealand, Western Europe and North America. In her own society, a
Filipina linked with a foreigner is a target for snide comments and disrespect from strangers. She becomes a prostitute in the eyes of those who
know no better. A woman in the Philippines might also find herself the
victim of sexual violence. Rape, though not always acknowledged, is not
an uncommon crime. And some men approve of beating wives when
they get out of hand. As one Filipina noted, some do this to 'prove they
are the head of the family.'

Corruption, however, may well be the most serious problem in
Philippine culture. It is so widespread in the Philippines today that it
must be considered a cultural phenomenon. Bribes are taken as travellers
pass through customs, 'grease money' provides services, government
officials seal deals in exchange for a cut of the profits, businessmen
avoid paying taxes by bribing the collector, and politicians pay off
journalists. The most visible corruption, however, is in the police force.
In 1988, a woman stopped for a violation could get off with a 10-peso
bribe, for a man it was 20 pesos.

Corruption coupled with gullibility has brought a proliferation of
frauds and charlatans. Many Filipinos accept faith healers — who claim
to operate, repair damaged organs and remove unwanted growths without
knives, scalpels or other tools — as a normal part of the health-care system. Inventors and pseudo-scientists have wasted the energies of legitimate scientists with their fantastic claims. While I was in the Philippines I watched the media going gaga over a man who claimed to have
invented a car engine that used water as fuel. Legitimate scientists had to
examine the car to debunk the inventor's obviously fraudulent claims.
They discovered a petrol tank neatly hidden away.

Many of the cultural problems confronting Filipinos flourish in the
socio-economic system. Systematic poverty and structural inequality
give the Filipino masses little to strive for at work and little reason to
apply themselves to their jobs. Domination by foreigners and domestic
élites creates a culture of complacency and leadership orientation. Violence by the masters of society legitimizes it as a response for society as
a whole.

Religion, especially Roman Catholicism, has had a mixed impact on
the country's culture. It has contributed to the construction of a Filipino
identity, but it has also encouraged such harmful traits as fatalism, escapism and, until recently, acceptance of the status quo.

Education has also had a tremendous impact on Philippine culture. During the Spanish period educational institutions helped create an enormous gap between the mass of Filipino people and the educated élite. American rule resulted in a popular educational system, the institution of English as the language of instruction and the teaching of American values. The first two decades of independence saw the further development of an American-style school system run by Filipinos. Marcos introduced a bastardized nationalism into the schools. Bilingual (Filipino and English) education became the order of the day and, with it, an increased emphasis on Philippine history and culture. But the leadership confused education with indoctrination and schools became centres for propagating the myths of Marcos and his New Society.

Today, however, aspects of all these periods survive in the Philippines' jumbled education system. State schools suffer from underfunding, overcrowding and a serious shortage of teachers. (Teachers earn far less than other college graduates.) Provincial schools, in particular, are badly understaffed and are often forced to close their doors. The results can be devastating. Once the Philippines had one of the highest literacy rates in the region. A 1983 study, however, identified 5.8 million Filipinos over the age of ten as illiterate and found the rate to be climbing as more and more students failed to finish elementary school. The study found a 60 per cent drop-out rate by fourth grade.[2] Even those who finish high school are worse off in comparison with earlier generations. A 1987 study by the Philippine Normal College found that many third-year college students 'could not apply simple mathematical concepts to day-to-day problems involving two or more steps, and they would rather memorize than analyse.' They answered an average of only 50 per cent of the questions correctly on an English test intended for high-school graduates.

Philippine education also fails to inculcate a sense of pride in the nation and its history. Once I asked two graduates of highly regarded Manila universities to share some Filipino folk tales. They could not come up with any. At the same time Philippine history takes a rather benign view of the nation's colonizers. 'The majority of history books present the Americans as the saviour,' Dr Wilfredo Villacorta, a professor at de la Salle College and a member of Aquino's Con Com (Constitutional Commission), told me. 'There's much to credit the US for. However, there were also evils that came with the Americans.'

Critics often attribute this to the role foreign money plays in curriculum development. As columnist Hernando Abaya wrote in the *Manila Chronicle*:

The way Philippine history is being taught in the elementary and secondary levels of our public and private schools perverts the truth because the mass-produced World Bank textbooks merely reinforce the colonial outlook among the young. Such perversion not only distorts the students' sense of history but undermines as well their sense of identity, the sense of belonging to a particular race or nation. In a word, at this early stage, their sense of patriotism and pride as Filipinos is already impaired.[3]

It is not just in the humanities that the education system's orientation is questionable. Science and technology teaching is geared to an advanced industrial society. The medical school trains doctors in Western-style, high-tech medicine, and the agricultural school even prepares some students for farming in a temperate climate.

Perhaps the most controversial legacy of American rule has been the use of English in education. With the spread of American education, English developed some of the characteristics of a national language. Most Filipinos learned a bit of the language, but with the tremendously high drop-out rate, true English literacy became the possession of an educated élite. English intensified the cultural differences between the educated élite and the masses of under-educated farmers. It opened doors for that élite (government posts, jobs with transnational companies, travel, and the world of literature and films) while slamming the door on the great mass of vernacular speakers. Opportunity became synonymous with English literacy.

The imposition of English has also caused a rather subtle problem. Whereas Filipino languages evolved in a Philippine setting — with words to express the intricacies of the Philippine experience and character, English will always be foreign. Countless Filipino phrases cannot be properly translated into English. While appropriate as a global language and a window on the world, it fails to capture uniquely Filipino experiences. How can an emerging national intelligentsia express itself in an alien language? And how can it reach the vernacular-speaking public?

Marcos's government started to develop an indigenous national language based almost entirely on Tagalog, which it called Filipino, but it took some time to catch on. The Cebuanos and Visayans resisted the new language, which they saw as an artificial imposition, and the older generation felt far more comfortable with their local dialects. With Filipino came a bilingual education system. Teachers used English for some classes and Filipino for others. The idea had merit, but, given the poor state of Philippine education, bilingual education created a generation inadequate in both languages.

Popular culture has brought a basic comprehension of the new 'native' tongue. As Joseph Estrada, star of countless action pictures, pointed out, 'the movie industry was the first place where we used our national language. Most people in Mindanao learned our language through the movies.' But if popular culture (for example, locally-produced films, *komik* books, the tabloid press and television) has made a positive contribution towards developing a national culture, there are negative aspects as well. In general, mass popular culture seeks to entertain without informing, to attract audiences with colourful fantasies and, in some cases, to translate the worst aspects of colonial culture into the language of the Filipino masses. 'Manila's movies are still exploiting the escapist tendencies of the mass public,' director and actor Behn Cervantes told me in an early 1989 letter.

While major film companies like Regal Films churn out snappy melodramas, irrelevant comedies and bloody action pictures for fun and profit, less reputable studios mass-produce soft-core pornography (called bold pictures) for exhibition in public cinemas and hard-core sex flicks called 'pene' (for penetration) for underground circulation. The porn film industry is part of a flourishing sex-trade culture, which includes night clubs with everything from go-go girls girating in skimpy bikinis, to nude models and live sex shows. A counterpart gay male industry exists as well.

Film is among the most popular media in the country. The reach of television is also spreading rapidly, especially near the cities. Different programmes and networks appeal to different classes. Filipino programming is generally aimed at lower-middle class and mass audiences. Philippine television hit a low point in the 1980s with a spate of demeaning contests. Grandmother Madonna featured elderly women dancing and lip-synching to Madonna records, Grandfather Jackson featured older men prancing to Michael Jackson tunes. Among the worst programmes are variety shows featuring attractive, but talentless children of affluent families. Skilled promoters turn their young stars into teen-idols and producers pinpoint them for the movies.

Neither Philippine television nor Philippine music can be written off as all bad or all foreign. Much of it in fact owes a lot to the fiesta tradition, where communities gather for colourful celebrations and feasts. These events emphasize community and fun. Local folk let their hair down and demonstrate their artistic prowess in talent shows, parades and beauty contests. But television and the music industry have taken this part of Philippine culture, commercialized it, sapped it of its communal content, and thrown in a strong dose of Western influence.

The spread of English as the language of the educated Filipino has done serious harm to the spread of vernacular literature. Only a handful of serious writers work in Filipino languages. Rather, it is *komik* books, religious tracts, film magazines and tabloid newspapers that are written in Filipino, Tagalog and the widely-used combination of Tagalog and English, Taglish. Apart from updated folk tales and religious tracts, most mass-produced Filipino literature has no redeeming social value. *Komiks* and the local film industry are much the same. Melodrama and action dominate with a strong dose of fantasy thrown in for good measure. Movie magazines focus on the romantic lives of the stars and advance publicity for the latest films. The tabloid press combines sensationalized accounts of violence, political and criminal, with gossip, cheesecake and sports.

The Philippines is a sports-crazed nation. Asia's only professional basketball league plays virtually year round, its teams strengthened by imported American players. A running craze has swept Manila with scores of fun runs, marathons and other distance races. Every March, scores of cyclists set out on the punishing Tour of Luzon. Boxing, cock fighting, motorcar rallying and horse racing are popular. But in sport, as in other aspects of Philippine culture, there is a gap between rich and poor. The rich may enjoy poor people's sports (like boxing, cock fighting, running and basketball) but the poor cannot participate in the rich men's games like motorcar and horse racing. The same can be said of literature, films and other art forms.

Western élite culture does not suit Philippine society. There is an inevitable clash between it and the needs of an impoverished Asian state with an underdeveloped sense of nationhood. It has been obvious since at least the 1960s that national development requires a strong national culture. Even Marcos attempted to develop some form of counter-culture to support his New Society and used Philippine folk tales and traditions in an attempt to increase his popularity. He filled Malacanang and public places with paintings of himself and Imelda as *Malakas* and *Maganda* (literally 'strong' and 'beautiful'), the mythical first Filipinos. Imelda appointed herself cultural tsar and urged local artists to present a positive national image of the 'true, the good and the beautiful.'

In response to lobbying by the arts community, President Aquino created the PCCA (Presidential Commission on Culture & the Arts). But despite this, critics still questioned the government's commitment to art and culture in general and to nationalist culture in particular. Debates continue over how the state should perform its role as patron of the arts. There has been a huge controversy over censorship. Mrs Aquino appointed Manoling Morato chief film and video censor, but he imposed his own strict sense of morality on the film industry. While few publicly mourned the demise of 'bold' pictures, many criticized his attacks on more artistic — and socially relevant — films. On several occasions

Morato's board has demonstrated an inclination to censor more than sex. The board forced a well-regarded television documentary team to delay showing a programme on the urban poor, which the censors declared one-sided, before an outburst of protest forced its airing.

Other attempts to clamp down on the media involve other branches of government. These have included the temporary closure of opposition radio stations, the cancellation of controversial programmes on public TV and radio, and bans on interviews with members of both the right-wing underground and the NDF. The government imposed harsher censorship during the state of emergency that followed the 1989 coup attempt.

Political forces contending for power in the Philippines have their own cultural programmes. Both the social and national democrats advocate creating a culture based on nationalism and science. The social democrats add humanism. They organize mass-based cultural troops, run extensive education campaigns, and promote pride in native culture and Filipino identity. But intellectuals, artists and educators play an important role as well.

> Historically, the Philippine intelligentsia failed to set a positive tone for the nation-building process. As writer and bookseller F. Sionil José pointed out: The Filipino intelligentsia imbibed much of the élitism of its colonial master while it paid noisy homage to the grand ideals of justice, freedom and nationhood. Introverted, self-satisfied and smug, it identified its interest basically with that of the power élite from whence most of its members came. It was more concerned with the form rather than the substance of democracy for even with its American orientation, it paid scant attention to the ancient exploitation of the peasant and the land hunger of the masses of people. It had ignored what an American reformer, Wendell Phillips, had so aptly put: 'If you hold land and land is in the hands of a few you do not have a democracy, you have an oligarchy.'[4]

There was a historic failure of the Filipino intelligentsia to serve the masses of impoverished citizens. José pointed out that the idol of Philippine nationalism, Claro M. Recto, opposed agrarian reform rather than side with President Magsaysay.

Truly there were exceptions. Lawyer and government official, Pedro Abad Santos, cast his lot in with the peasantry as founder and leader of the Socialist Party. The Lava brothers did the same as leaders of the PKP (*Partido Komunista ng Pilipinas*). But these men were always a minority among intellectuals. That seemed to be changing in the 1960s when intellectual turmoil spread from college campuses and bohemian beer houses to the streets. Martial law created new difficulties. Tight control of the media, which gave artists and intellectuals access to the public, excluded independent thinkers. Imelda's cultural institutions co-opted the less committed intellectuals and artists.

Cultural guerrillas emerged from a process started in the 1960s which led to the convergence of a new nationalism, a bohemian counter-culture, radical politics and the discovery of the Philippines' Third World identity. But it was not until the 1980s that an alternative culture flourished in the era of activism that followed the assassination of Ninoy Aquino. Demonstrators carried banners painted by radicalized visual artists. New theatre troupes presented socially relevant plays on the street. Musicians sang traditional protest songs and new compositions at demonstrations. Even film makers managed to produce controversial political pictures. The alternative press published nationalist and dissident writers.

The advent of the Aquino government confronted intellectuals and artists with a dilemma. Should they enter the government, work with government cultural institutions, or maintain their independence? Aquino's initial cultural action pointed to a modestly reformist approach to Philippine culture. The new president appointed Lourdes Quisumbing to head the Ministry of Education, Culture & Sports. Quisumbing moved from the presidency of a Catholic girls school, Maryknoll College, to head the largest government department. During her three-and-a-half years in office, she pushed for competence in education and decency in culture. Though laudable, it was not enough to build a healthy national culture. That task remains in the hands of artists, writers, performers, intellectuals and common Filipinos.

Some Filipinos sought to pursue their cultural work while serving the government. A play by Foreign Secretary Raul Manglapus opened in Manila soon after his appointment. Sen. Estrada made an anti-bases film. Meanwhile, independent artists and intellectuals laboured to create a healthy national culture. Following the departure of the Marcoses, the new government opened the doors of Imelda's CCP (Cultural Centre of the Philippines), a huge compound of theatres, museums, a film production centre and convention halls to artists of various leanings. Along with the traditional fare of ballet and classical and pop music, the Centre hosted festivals of new drama, exhibitions of experimental and political art, craft shows and the like in a self-conscious effort to develop a national culture. CCP President Maria Theresa Escoda-Roxas told an interviewer in 1986:

> Art can be used in many ways. It can serve to rebuild the values we have lost. We can use it to make us realize that wherever one comes from, north or south, all of us are Filipinos. And there are elements in our arts and culture

that we share in common. We have a very rich tapestry with many threads that bind us together.[5]

The numerous theatre groups are an example of the breadth of activity in the alternative arts sphere. Alternative theatre companies range from UP Repertory to the KMU's *Masa*, and from the internationally known PETA (Philippine Experimental Theatre Assembly) to UP *Peryante*, an organization of students and ex-students. Doreen Fernandez, an English professor at Ateneo de Manila, described the work of PETA during the martial law era: 'PETA... is oriented towards theatre relevant to Philippines reality: contemporary plays by Filipinos, updated folk-theatre forms, adaptions of foreign plays by Filipinos, experimental forms using music and dance — all with some direct and significant relation to current issues of Philippine life.'[6]

The post-Marcos era has opened doors for PETA, allowing it to produce such overtly political, overtly anti-fascist plays as *Macli-ing,* a look at the life and death of Kalinga leader Macli-ing Dulag. While avant-garde writers and artists push their craft forward, the poster-and-slogan style remains a strong influence in community and movement-based arts groups. I sat through several such productions during rallies and conventions in Manila and must admit that while the drama was often stirring and encouraging to the already committed, it certainly did not open doors to the apolitical or less active.

The music world too has individuals and groups swimming against the tide of dominant commercial tastes and a close-minded industry. The alternative music space includes scores of folk singers who admittedly borrow from Western stylists, but who nevertheless convey a strong Filipino presence in their message and singing style. More daring artists incorporate native rhythms and instruments into their performances.

Aside from those traditionally called artists, scores of independent intellectuals and activists contribute to the process of cultural development. Small magazines like *National Midweek*, *The Diliman Review*, *Solidarity* and *The New Progressive Review*, as well as the underground press, provide writers with an outlet for their essays, fiction and reportage. A handful of bigger publications publish a surprising number of dissident essayists and columnists. Small publishing houses make available the works of Filipino writers in Filipino and English, and many of these writers are quite radical.

Feminists and liberation theologists readily challenge the traditional way of thinking in the Philippines. A feminist critique has influenced much of the alternative culture though it has barely dented the sex-ploitative mass culture. A handful of films featuring strong female characters and the impressive work of a number of female journalists have laid the groundwork for assaults on the domination of mass culture by sexually oppressive or demeaning images.

Minority activists and movements have made a tremendous contribution to the process of cultural change in the Philippines. The increased presence of proudly self-conscious tribal Filipinos in society has launched a rediscovery of indigenous Philippine culture. The construction of a national culture — rooted in indigenous values, informed by science and exposure to the world — is a central element of the nation-building process. Economic and political development and national and human liberation cannot occur in a country culturally oriented to its former colonial master and mired in a morass of corruption and complacency. For a new culture to prosper, it must, F. Sionil José suggests, appeal to the broadest swath of Philippine society — the farmers to which we turn in the next chapter.

23

Agrarian Politics

Manila is misleading in that its urban sprawl is uncharacteristic of the Philippines. Most Filipinos live and work in the countryside, tilling their own smallholdings or farming the land of others. More than any other issue, agrarian reform divides the country into haves and have-nots, conservatives and progressives. The inequitable distribution of land (and of the fruits of the land) has generated protest, rebellion and even revolution.

President Aquino rose to power on the hopes of the rural population. She promised agrarian reform and economic justice. The people believed her. But for the rural poor, the promises of the February revolution were broken. At first, both the Ministry of Agrarian Reform and the Ministry of Agriculture made a point of consulting farmers' organizations, including the radical KMP (*Kilusang Magbubukid ng Pilipinas*). But the ministers concerned, Heherson Alvarez and Ramon Mitra, resigned within a year to run in congressional elections in early 1987. Technocrats replaced them, but pledged to continue to serve the agrarian population.

In mid-1987 I met an under-secretary of agriculture, who was critical of previous notions of focusing simply on increasing output. Instead of depending on the expensive technologies of the green revolution, which had driven many small farmers out of business, the government would emphasize services such as marketing, technical advice and infrastructural development, with the aim of 'making farming profitable.' Productivity, he said, would increase along with the profits. But the Department of Agriculture's scheme relied on market economics in a country with a dangerously weak domestic consumer base. It also begged the question of 'profitability for whom?' The small farmers, peasants and landless workers could only profit if an agrarian-reform programme succeeded in giving them control of the land and in creating a large enough domestic market to accept their produce.

Government awareness of the problems of inequitable distribution of land did not vanish when Aquino came to power. In mid-1988, Philip Juico, then secretary of agrarian reform, told me: 'It is generally assumed that 20 per cent of the population owns 80 per cent of the land.' Statistics support Juico's contention, though not the idea that oligarchs have complete control of the country's farms. Old landed families do dominate such commercial crops as sugar, coconut and (in conjunction with foreign capital) bananas and pineapples, but the countryside has seen significant changes in patterns of land ownership.

Some agrarian capitalists own or lease enormous tracts of land. Through leases and management contracts transnational corporations control huge farms in Mindanao — Dole has 50,000 hectares in South Cotabato, Del Monte 24,000 in Bukidnon, and Guthrie at least 8,000 in Agusan. But the biggest change has been the growth of a new class of small and medium-sized absentee landowners. Middle-class professionals — teachers, soldiers, small businessmen, doctors and lawyers — have been buying relatively small farms to supplement their earnings. Rarely do these town dwellers move to the farms. Instead they enter share-cropping agreements with peasant families or hired wage labourers. These new landowners have accelerated the trend towards absentee ownership, which began when the more astute old plantation families diversified into manufacturing and finance.

Most of those who work the land do not own it or own too little to make ends meet. Many work other people's land as wage labourers or tenants. The World Bank noted these and other characteristics of rural poverty in 1988:

> About 70 per cent of all poor families live in rural areas, the majority of these are small farmers. Fifty-eight per cent of all rural families now live below the poverty line, compared to 48 per cent a decade ago. The majority are involved in corn, rice or coconut production with corn farmers being the poorest. Wages are the second most important source of income among the poorest, followed by family sustenance activities. Low-income agricultural families are characterized by high levels of underemployment, small farm size, large family size, limited use of modern technology, and low levels of education. The majority do not own the land they till; or cultivate other farms as tenants or lessees in addition to their own. Most poor farmers do not use fertilizers or pesticides, do not have access to irrigation, nor have access to credit. More than one-third of the rural poor have not completed elementary school while another tenth had never attended schools. [1]

Farmers' organizations add details to the description. One says most tenancy agreements require the tenant to give the landowner 60 per cent of the harvest while bearing two-thirds of the production costs. Leasehold arrangements mandate the payment of 25 per cent of the total harvest with the farmer shouldering all production costs.

My travels confirmed the hardships faced by the rural population. From the northern Cagayan Valley to Mindanao's southernmost provinces, I visited rural families in tiny one-roomed houses of wood, bamboo and *nipa* or *acogon* grass. Diets normally consist of white rice supplemented by small amounts of fish and vegetables. Only on special occasions do farm families taste chicken or pork. The poorest of the poor, having given up the struggle on the plains, head to the mountains where they slash and burn, plant for a year or two, sap the soil of its nutrients, and move on. I visited a slash-and-burn farming community in Kalinga-Apayao. A handful of families lived in a cluster of shacks at the foot of several hills, on which scattered struggling banana plants, sugar cane, yams and small amounts of rice grew. We sat together chewing sugar cane. Men, women and children wore tattered dirty clothing. Of course they had no running water or electricity. The children had no chance of health care or education.

For close to a year Cory Aquino hemmed and hawed on the issue of agrarian reform. She refused to meet militant peasant representatives, she failed to issue an executive order on agrarian reform, and her Constitutional Commission side-stepped the issue by accepting agrarian reform in principle, but leaving details to the government. The government only appeared to wake up to the urgency of the issue when 13 pro-agrarian reform marchers were massacred outside Malacanang Palace in January 1987.

Mrs Aquino then quickly appointed a Cabinet Action Committee and progressive members of the government went into the field to meet peasant organizations. Finally, after rejecting a series of drafts, Mrs Aquino signed an executive order on agrarian reform a few days before Congress convened in July. The executive order disappointed all involved. Landowners vowed to fight any attempts to take their land. Peasants objected to sections mandating payment for land. But most of all, peasant organizations expressed outrage at Aquino's decision to leave to a rural élite-dominated Congress such key aspects as timetables for land transfers, and the amount of land landlords and absentee landowners could keep.

Congress did not disappoint its landed benefactors. Despite the good fight put up by Rep. Bonifacio Gillego, Sen. Agapito 'Butz' Aquino and a few others, it passed an emasculated law in June 1988. 'The recently-signed Comprehensive Agrarian Reform Act of 1988 is said to have merged the demands of landlords and peasants,' declared the broad-based CPAR (Congress for a People's Agrarian Reform) shortly after the enactment of the new law.

A closer examination of the act belies these claims. The said law is not a compromise. While it invokes social justice and the welfare of farmers and farm workers, it contains loopholes by which landlords can evade a genuine agrarian reform and retain their land-based wealth and power. The seemingly pro-farmer provisions are effectively cancelled out or rendered meaningless by other pro-landlord provisions. The act is a deception.

CPAR spelled out its objections in more detail. Broadly these were:

1 The retention limit of five hectares for the landowner automatically exempts 51 per cent of the total private agricultural land area. In addition, qualified heirs of landowners retain three hectares each, whether actual tillers or not. Assuming an average of two legal heirs per family, at least 75 per cent of all private agricultural lands will not be covered. Moreover, the scope of CPAR is reduced even further by the 10-year reprieve given to commercial farms or lands devoted to commercial livestock, poultry and swine-raising, aqua-culture and orchards, among others.

2 Landlord corporations that merely distribute part of their stocks to tillers are not obliged to redistribute their lands to tillers/farm workers. Under this scheme, farm workers will be getting only a minimal share in the corporation and will have no significant participation in its decision making.

3 Final determination of compensation rests solely with the landowners and the Department of Agrarian Reform and the Land Bank of the Philippines. The farmers have no say.

4 All public agricultural land used by multinational corporations (MNCs) shall be distributed to the workers within three years, beginning the year the law shall take effect. Succeeding provisions, however, allow MNCs to continue leasing the land with the approval of the government or the beneficiaries to whom the lands may be transferred. Furthermore, Section 72 allows the lease, management, grower or service contracts in private lands to continue even if these lands have already been transferred to their beneficiaries. These are the loopholes through which foreign and domestic corporate interests can retain control over vast land holdings.

Not long after the agrarian-reform act became law, I visited Secretary of Agrarian Reform Philip Juico in his Quezon City office. As a technocrat, he found it difficult to hide his own disappointment with the new law, but vowed to do his best to make agrarian-reform work. To some, the government's failure to develop a workable agrarian-reform programme was inevitable. After all, landlords and agrarian-based capitalists had played a leading role in the anti-Marcos revolt, and were well represented in the post-Marcos Congress and in Aquino's inner circle. Once in office, President Aquino did not find agrarian reform a compelling issue.

Opposition to agrarian reform was anchored in the rural élite, with strong backing from middle-class absentee landowners (and bankers who had extended loans to agribusiness). Many farm owners refused to register their lands as required by law. Planters backed up their arguments with threats of violence, and they did control private armies and vigilante groups. Rabid foes of agrarian reform often made it seem as if the government favoured a more meaningful brand of change than it actually did. 'It would seem today that this government would look at the landowner as if we were criminals,' Ramon Lacson, a sugar planter in Bacolod City, told me. Like other landowners, Lacson attributed unrest among farm workers to outside agitation, rather than to the poverty of those who worked the land owned by others.

> You see, with agitators coming in, it has estranged some of the landowners from their farm workers, so there is a hardening of positions on both sides, This is very unhealthy. When it was before, the landowner could go to his farm any time, stay with his people, talk with his people and the labourers could go to the landowner any time for their problems.

The agrarian reform law reflects the distribution of power in Philippine politics. If numbers had mattered, a meaningful land-reform law would have sailed through Congress. Virtually all public-opinion polls show overwhelming support for land redistribution as a source of social justice. Even middle-class urban Filipinos support reform, though do not seem to understand its urgency. In addition, some powerful institutions have lined up behind it. The CBCP (Catholic Bishops Conference of the Philippines) has urged the government to enact a sweeping programme and even the World Bank has added its voice. This has not, however, been enough to overcome opposition from the landed.

Central to the fight for agrarian reform is a conflict between a militant peasant movement and the landed élite. Peasant and farm-worker organizations have overcome cultural taboos to mobilize a sophisticated movement. The active core remains relatively small, but it has demonstrated an ability to influence a much larger mass. The movement is a significant social force, and one that seems to be growing. The KMP, for example, claimed to have 700,000 members in the late 1980s. KMP members seized control of fallow land and land formerly controlled by Marcos cronies and started planting, despite opposition from the government and the military. In other locations, KMP affiliates have negotiated better deals with landowners. On a national level, the KMP plays a leading role in organizing demonstrations and campaigns.

But the peasant movement does not consist solely of the KMP. Remnants of the Federation of Free Farmers, a moderate, Church-backed organization, exert some influence in isolated areas. But its leadership lost much of its legitimacy through silence during the Marcos years and an alliance with Juan Ponce Enrile in the early Aquino years. The National Farmers Organization, a TUCP (Trade Union Congress of the Philippines) affiliate, has a small following. It is led by former *Huk* commander Luis Taruc. The mainstream of the peasant and pro-agrarian-reform forces, however, joined to form the CPAR (Congress for a People's Agrarian Reform) in May 1987. The alliance was made up of 14 groups. The KMP brought the largest contingent into it, but other organizations led by social democrats, socialists and local personalities share in its leadership. Acrimonious debates have periodically marked the CPAR's stormy history, but the alliance has been flexible enough to allow constituent groups to pursue independent activities outside its umbrella.

Underground groups also participate in the struggle for agrarian reform. The CPP and NDF provide a revolutionary alternative to legal strategies and campaigns. The armed struggle has attracted the bulk of its support from angry and frustrated rural people. In the process, it has generated hope and created heightened expectations in the countryside. Some of this has fuelled the broader movement for radical agrarian change.

All three of the major national alliances advocating genuine agrarian reform — the KMP, the CPAR and the CPP/NDF — believe the primary goals should be social justice and equity. They also believe that peasants and farm workers should receive the land free — on the grounds that they had earned the right to own it through years, even generations, of labouring under exploitative conditions.

The programmes of the three groupings have certain features in common. They believe agrarian reform should affect all types of farms. All favour cooperative development and the free distribution of land. All believe peasant organizations should play a leading role in determining the nature of agrarian reform and policy. Yet all three recognize the difficulty of implementing a sweeping programme all at once. They call for interim steps — rent reduction, the elimination of usury, and the transfer of the burden for paying for supplies to the landowner. They share a belief that agrarian reform should be empowering. This manifests itself in the CPAR advocating that PARCs (People's Agrarian Reform

Councils) take on the task of implementing agrarian reform, in the KMP contending that agrarian reform should be a joint undertaking of the government and popular organizations, and in the CPP constructing underground peasant organizations wherever it operates in rural areas. 'The PARC[s] will be composed exclusively of representatives of farmers, farm workers, fishermen and other direct beneficiaries,' proclaims the CPAR. Such democratic councils would be anathema to the landowners as they would provide an entry point for radical organizers into positions of power and challenge the élite's monopoly.

Cooperatives also appeal to rural activists. Farm workers view them as a possible alternative to capitalist agribusiness. The NFSW (National Federation of Sugar Workers), a Negros-based union affiliated with the KMU and the CPAR, has experimented with production cooperatives, as have BCCs. A final shared component of the CPAR, KMP and CPP agrarian-reform programmes is strong opposition to foreign agribusiness controlling large tracts of farm lands to produce for export. All three groups want agriculture 'Filipinized,' with the CPAR endorsing 'ownership and management transferred collectively to direct producers.'

Aside from advocating agrarian reform as a state policy, many peasant and farm-worker organizations try to implement their own version in those areas where they are strong. The CPP does this as a principal form of organizing as we witnessed in Bicol (see chapters 1 and 12). Several CPAR affiliates have small agrarian-reform projects underway — either with the consent of a landowner or through unsanctioned occupation of the land. The KMP practises land occupation more frequently than other groups. It has initiated actions in Bicol, Laguna, Central Luzon and elsewhere. In some cases experiments have resulted in land being divided between participant farmers. In other places the KMP has promoted cooperative ventures.

Hacienda Tison presents a good example of the promise agrarian reform holds for the poorest of the country's rural population. The plantation stretches from the seaside town of Victoria to the foothills of the inland mountains dividing Negros. It covers some 700 hectares of plains and rolling hills. At the peak of the sugar crisis in the mid-1980s the landowner stopped planting on the hilly extremity of the plantation and this put 32 families out of work.

Tossed out on their own, the former farm workers no longer felt bound to the *haciendero*. Their survival would now depend on their own hard work and the strength of their organization, a local chapter of the Small Farmers Association of North Negros. The farm workers decided to farm the land they had long occupied. To avoid unwanted trouble, they entered negotiations with the landowner over control and use of the land.

The negotiations were continuing when I visited, but the landowner had not tried to stop the farmers' endeavour. The new cooperative had sought the assistance of the PRRM (Philippine Rural Reconstruction Movement), a non-governmental body working with people's organizations in Negros and other parts of the country. The farmers, in conjunction with PRRM's agriculturalists, collectively planted food crops on the former sugar fields overlooking the valley and the sea. They launched duck- and hog-raising projects.

A young woman serving on the cooperative board spoke of the continuing difficulties confronting her community. Though field and animal projects provide the villagers with most of their food needs, they sorely lack money. 'We still have to go into the hills to cut wood for sale as firewood, lumber or charcoal,' she said. 'It is the only source of income we have.' Still, she and others feel optimistic about the future — especially if they can negotiate a deal for the title to the land — for they are hoping to extend their livestock projects into small-scale commercial ventures. Unlike peasant communities I have visited in Bicol, Cagayan and elsewhere, where cooperatives face opposition from a tradition of individual work patterns, the residents of *Hacienda Tison* show little resistance to the idea of cooperative farming.

Some critics of agrarian reform claim that there is a contradiction between land reform and increased productivity, that breaking up the country's farms would reduce productivity and lose economies of scale. Advocates of agrarian-reform do not ignore questions of productivity, but argue that land reform is merely an essential part of a more comprehensive policy of agrarian reform, which includes rural development and supports industrial development. I asked Boy Morales, the director of PRRM, for his comments:

> In overall terms, the issue is democratization, not just political democracy, but socio-economic democracy and in those terms, land reform is essential. But as far as simple productivity is concerned, I think that all you need to do is look at how productive our farms are now in relation to Taiwan or Japan, for example. There, on one hectare you can really earn. On one hectare, how much do we earn? You'll see the big disparity there.

Advocates see agrarian reform as part of an overall economic development programme aimed at redistributing wealth and generating greater equity, increasing rural productivity and encouraging national industrialization. In its programme, the CPAR described agrarian reform as aiming:

> to free and develop the productive powers of agrarian workers, farmers and fishermen from the forces that deprive them of resources and initiative. It is

designed to promote nationalist industrialization by widening the national market, rechanelling the agricultural surplus into industrial investments and labour for industrial development, and the establishment of self-sufficient local industries controlled by the rural masses.

The KMP proposes that the state support the establishment of basic industries by providing farm inputs, fertilizers, pesticides and other essential goods for increasing productivity. Currently, the country's agricultural economy depends heavily on foreign implements and technology.

In essence, the debate is not between those who favour development and productivity versus those who favour land reform, but between partisans of at least three very different approaches to development and economic justice. On the one side are those tied to the existing structures. These individuals, mostly members of landed families and the political and economic élite, claim an inherent right to own the land and, faced with the prospect of rural unrest, promise to pursue a course of national development to benefit all Filipinos. So far this class has failed the nation. Its practices have created a vast pool of impoverished labourers and peasants. Profits from the land have not been converted into a sound and productive industrial sector.

The second group, the partisans of agribusiness, generally members of the modernizing élite, propose an alternative based on a modern, but heavily concentrated, private agricultural sector. But the success of agribusiness has long depended on low wages, mechanization, large landholdings and marketing monopolies. Large-scale agriculture has created unfair competition for small farmers, depressed prices for some agricultural products, and destroyed large tracts of land. Large ventures have also been responsible for land grabbing from poor communities, and the transfer of economic power to foreign corporations.

The situation in the countryside has driven organized peasants, farm workers and their allies to seek radical solutions. This third group advocates agrarian reform as part of a much-needed programme of radical, social and economic change to bring about a just and equitable society. They have long viewed economic democracy as a prerequisite to development. In recent years, as we shall see, their drive for rural change has been supplemented by a growing awareness of the damage being done by current ecological practices.

24

Environmental Politics

When the residents of *Hacienda Tison*'s village lost their jobs in 1985, they immediately faced the problem of survival and turned to the obvious solution — harvesting the natural resources near their village. Few resources remained on the plains. The ancestors of the current planters had seen to that by stripping the lowlands of the lush tropical forests and planting a green sea of sugar cane. So the villagers took to the neighbouring mountains with hand saws, axes and matches. They cut trees for charcoal, firewood and lumber. They cut trees for their own use and for sale in the nearby towns. They cut trees without thinking of the impact on the land and the nearby seas. They cut trees thinking only of survival, not thinking of ecology or the environment.

Together poverty and greed have stripped the once bountiful archipelago of its resources. Today the Philippines faces an environmental disaster. Wealthy loggers, agribusiness and impoverished slash-and-burn farmers threaten total destruction of the now scattered rain forests. About 105,000 hectares of forest cover disappear each year, giving the Philippines one of the fastest rates of deforestation in the world. Siltation from eroded mountain slopes, mine tailings, residential waste and blast fishing endanger the rivers, rice paddies, mangrove swamps, coral reefs, lakes and seas. The survival of the Philippine eagle, the *tamaraw*, the mouse deer, the Palawan peacock and other endangered species is in doubt because of man's thoughtless encroachment.

About the only bright spot for the Philippine environment is a growth of ecological consciousness among a vocal and active portion of the population. Though environmentalists would like to see more environmental consciousness within government, the DENR (Department of Environment & Natural Resources), until 1987 the notoriously corrupt Ministry of Natural Resources, has fallen into the hands of men and women whom most of the country's environmental activists find acceptable. The powerful Catholic bishops issued a ground-breaking pastoral letter on the environment in early 1988. And, most significantly, citizens' groups focusing on environmental concerns have sprung up in Manila and other parts of the country.

The emerging movement is, however, not yet strong enough to reverse decades of destructive habits. Manila's parks remain littered with trash. Small industries continue to dump unfiltered waste directly into rivers and estuaries. And, despite the rhetoric of sustainable development, the government has yet to find a balance between economic concerns and environmental protection. Development is still largely based on the exploitation of dwindling natural resources — the development plan presented by the government in 1989 ignores environmental concerns. 'It is not a pretty picture,' said Amado Tolentino, who had grown up on the island of Mindoro and now heads the government's Environmental Management Bureau. Mindoro is home of some of the archipelago's tallest mountains, an internationally known beach resort with lovely white sandy beaches and coral reefs, and the endangered *tamaraw*. Growing up on Mindoro meant growing up with nature. Tolentino fondly recalls swimming in a river running through his home town. Sadly, the waters are now polluted. Children today must seek their pleasure elsewhere. 'Lately,' he said, 'I have been looking at the rivers whenever I go out, and I cannot encounter one which is with clean waters the way I remember them when I was young.' Environmentalists consider water pollution the country's second most serious environmental problem. Deforestation is the most daunting. Deforestation in a mountainous country like the Philippines results in an array of problems. Soil erosion on denuded hillsides leads directly to siltation of rivers and rice paddies and damage to the coastal environment and nearby reefs. Deforestation is also the prime threat to the country's wildlife.

A 1988 report by the ADB (Asian Development Bank) notes that 60 per cent of the Philippines' forest lands are either cleared or denuded. The DENR believes that only 25 per cent of the total land area has adequate forest cover. Many believe the Philippines' forests could disappear by the early 21st century if current land use practices continue. To address the problem, the government has sought help from the ADB for an intense reforestation programme. It is also searching for ways of arresting the ongoing deforestation and of protecting existing forests. But the ADB says it could take 100 years to revegetate the already denuded forests. As Dr Celso Roque, a physicist and under-secretary for the environment, said in 1988:

> I tend to believe it is going to be quite difficult to reforest these areas. Unlike the temperate forest, it is quite difficult in the tropical area because most of the organic material in the tropical rain forest is in the trees. There is very little organic matter in the soils and these soils are very thin. Definitely, I do

not think you can recover the original forests with the variety that is associated with the tropical rain forest — having thousands of species per hectare — I do not think you will ever recover that.

The Philippines' ecological problems are the result of bad policy decisions, and of economic practices that favour short-term gain over long-term ecological and economic health. Ever since Spain opened the Philippines to the emerging global economy in the late 18th century, export-oriented production of crops has defined the archipelago's economic role and contributed to the destruction of the forests and the environment. To clear fields for large-scale agriculture, the new *hacienderos* stripped the plains of their forests, while mining and logging concerns raided the mountain areas.

Sugar, coconuts, bananas, timber, gold and other minerals became the largest earners of hard currency for the Philippine élite. The emergence of a manufacturing sector in the 1950s did not radically alter the situation. Gareth Porter and Delfin Ganapin note how: 'The dynamics of the Philippines' external economic relations since the mid-1960s added to the pressures on the natural resource base by forcing economic policy to emphasize short-term and medium-term export earnings. The Philippines' growing debt and dependence on renewed borrowing increased the Marcos regime's emphasis on export crops in the country's development strategy.'[1] The expansion of export agriculture in the 1970s contributed to deforestation in at least three ways. First, it created new plantations, with firms practising clear felling and other destructive activities. Second, dependence on fickle foreign markets left planters and farm workers at the mercy of overseas consumption. When markets dried up, unemployed workers had little choice but to turn to the forests for survival. And third, it used a tremendous amount of land, but provided few jobs for displaced peasants. This forced farmers who had previously worked on relatively stable, small lowland farms to seek earnings elsewhere — either in over-crowded cities or on the fragile mountain slopes.

'The number one cause of deforestation today is fire,' Domingo Abadilla, an environmental activist, told me. Between 14 and 17 million Filipinos, about a quarter of the country's population, live in the upland areas set aside by law as forest lands. Most of these upland dwellers practise shifting cultivation and slash-and-burn farming; most have moved to the uplands in recent decades; and most are impoverished. Their practices put tremendous pressure on an environment once protected by traditional upland dwellers — today's tribal Filipinos. As Under-Secretary Roque said:

In ancient times, this [slash-and-burn agriculture] was a perfectly ecological practice. You know, each family could probably cultivate about a hectare or two and this does not result in permanent damage. But now, people have been moving into the uplands, which is quite difficult to control, in fact we cannot control it. There are so many of them that the forest cannot recover.

Many concerned Filipinos see irresponsible logging and slash-and-burn farming as part of a single cycle destroying the forests. I asked Maximo Kalaw Jr, who was president of a large environmental group, the Haribon Foundation, about the debate over the causes of deforestation. He responded, 'That is baloney. That is so because the whole system is responsible.'

On the simplest level, the logger opens the forest up to the slash-and-burn farmer. He cuts the roads that the lowlander follows into the hills. If he is irresponsible, he leaves the concession area unguarded after cutting the virgin growth. He may also abandon his employees once he has completed the operation, leaving them to initiate slash-and-burn cultivation. 'The approach of most logging companies was to cut and get out,' noted Porter and Ganapin. 'Enormous profits could be earned in the first cut, but most companies had no incentive to use sustained yield methods of logging, since they would have to wait at least 25 years for the next cut.'[2]

Other factors are involved. Traditionally, the government has been lax about enforcing its own logging regulations. The timber industry has broken laws requiring selective logging and reforestation with impunity. The government has had too few forest guards to enforce its laws. Endemic corruption in the agencies responsible for licensing and monitoring the industry has allowed further destruction, for short-sighted loggers find it more profitable to bribe government officers and practise illegal methods. 'Basic to this,' said Kalaw, 'is it mirrors the structure of most Third World developing countries, where they give access to natural resources of the country to a chosen few. In effect, you've got this small group profiting from the resources of the entire nation.'

The problem is as complex as it is devastating. Activists, scientists and government officials offer an array of solutions. The most popular seems to be to impose a ban on logging and timber exports, but this too is controversial. According to the industry's statistics, logging companies, sawmills and plywood producers employ 212,000 workers with an estimated 1,060,000 dependants. In addition, the industry's spokesmen say that they are not responsible for the damage. Antonio Olison, vice-president of the Philippine Wood Products Association, points his finger at the slash-and-burn farmers, the small-scale loggers and the illegal operators. Some environmentalists do not dispute this. But officials believe only a handful of the big loggers practise responsible logging. Kalaw says close to half the Philippines' licensed timber operators have overcut on their concessions. Very few loggers practise reforestation. In the long run, Roque and others would like to see the existing logging industry — save those few firms operating within the confines of the law — replaced by small-scale, community-based logging using non-mechanical methods. This, they believe, would not only halt destructive forestry, but would also attack poverty and replace destructive slash-and-burn farming with an environmentally sound activity.

The government is a long way from saving the existing forests and revegetating the denuded ones. Fortunately it is not alone. Non-governmental organizations are also contributing their efforts. Both the Haribon Foundation and World Ecologists have their own small reforestation projects, and Haribon is leading a controversial campaign to save the forests in Palawan province. LTK (*Lingkod Tao Kalikasan*, or In the Service of Man & Nature), a group chaired by Domingo Abadilla, utilizes its strong church connections to conduct ecological seminars for church workers, government employees, military men, and elected officials. In addition, some development and social justice organizations, like the PRRM (Philippine Rural Reconstruction Movement) and some BCCs have added environmental components to their work.

Bishop Francisco Claver, a supporter of the Roman Catholic Church's new environmental activism, sees these efforts as important. He told me that 'if we have small projects in every diocese in the country, we will start to have an effect.' The importance of these projects owes something to the limits of government action. Despite the resources available and the efforts of DENR environmentalists, conflicts between development and ecology and between loggers and conservationists, and simple bureaucratic red tape stand in the way of a concerted effort. This can be clearly seen from attempts to attack air and water pollution, but the best example may be found in the storm following Haribon's announcement of a plan to protect Palawan.

Filipinos call Palawan their last frontier. It is a gorgeous land of mountains rising sharply from the sea, white sandy beaches and thick forests. The national highway running along the coast is little more than a dirt track through lush growth. On the north coast there is an eight-mile-long underground river. Divers love the province's offshore coral reefs and the diversity of underwater life. By Philippine standards, Palawan has remained relatively untouched. Forests still cover about 54 per cent of the land area. A small population makes Palawan one of the less crowded Philippine provinces. But pressure is building. Silica mines near the town of Roxas have stripped several hills of trees and soil. Mine tailings pollute the nearby bay. In Honda Bay blast fishing and coral gathering have begun to take their toll of the reefs. Developers clear mangrove swamps to build small resorts. The island's two logging concessionaires stand accused of illegal and destructive practices while slash-and-burn farmers — mostly migrants from other islands — are beginning to eat away at the forests. Palawan loses 19,000 hectares of tree cover every year.

Haribon campaigned for 'a ban on commercial logging, collection and trading of wildlife and the declaration of Palawan as an integrated protected area.' Local officials, businesses and the local bishop responded quickly and negatively, accusing Haribon of intruding in a purely local situation. Among those lined up against Haribon was House speaker Ramon Mitra. Maximo Kalaw explained:

> In Palawan it is more like a model of the old system. There is only one big man and one political patron. In Palawan, it is sad to say, the people have not yet gotten out of that dominance and woken up to the fact that they have to protect their resources. Nobody has told them that instead of one man, the community should get the benefits from these resources.

Haribon's campaign has drawn fresh attention to environmental issues, but with opposition from the Palawan establishment and its congressman, total success seems unlikely. What a local élite can accomplish faced with mounting pressure from environmentalists and even residents became clear recently on the island of Marinduque.

In 1988, after years of legal battles, the DENR ordered Marcopper to stop dumping waste from its copper-smelting plant into a bay. Local fishermen, with the help of the LTK, had complained that the plant was destroying the bay and Sr Aida Velasquez, a chemist with LTK, had provided scientific evidence of the damage the plant was causing. But Marcopper appealed to the Office of the President, which intervened and overruled the DENR's decision. According to Sr Aida, all the local officials on Marinduque sided with the company because of business connections. In addition, a national government agency controlled a large portion of the company's stocks.

Ironically, the Philippines has rather strict laws regulating pollution, but they are, however, often ignored. Officials have launched countless campaigns against vehicle and industrial pollutants, but denizens of Manila continue to choke on thick black clouds of diesel exhaust while most of the country's rivers are either dead or dying. 'Would you believe,' said Tolentino, director of the Environmental Management Bureau, 'that the two environmental agencies before, our predecessors — the Environmental Council and the Pollution Commission — were the lowest

budgeted of the government system in the past years.' Funding is but one
of the problems confronting the DENR and environmentalists. Sr Aida
Velasquez says:

> There is a need for an independent environment authority. The difficulty with
> the set-up of the Department of Environment & Natural Resources is that the
> exploitation aspect and the protection aspect are all under the same man. It is
> really very difficult for him to take up both jobs. The protection always
> suffers, that is what has been going on for years.

The secretary, Factoran, does give protection a higher priority than did
his predecessors. With his encouragement President Aquino has declared
the ten years from the middle of 1989 Philippine Environmental Decade.
And, apart from his attempts to arrest deforestation, he is spearheading
an effort to clean Manila's rivers and South-East Asia's largest lake.

The DENR promotes the idea of sustainable development, i.e that to
attack both poverty and ecological destruction, this generation should use
only what it needs and should replace whatever possible. But the idea has
not sunk in. Indeed the powerful CCAP (Coordinating Council on the
Philippine Aid Programme) outraged environmentalists by ignoring their
concerns in a development plan presented to the country's foreign creditors in 1989. The government's main priority is economic growth and development. Its thrust has been towards deregulation. Environmental
regulation does not mix well with a deregulated economy. A handful of
lawmakers have responded to the environmental crisis. But Senator Orly
Mercado has complained that environmental issues are not perceived as
urgent or as vote getters. This points to the political challenge facing the
environmental movement. The movement has come a long way since its
birth in the early 1970s. The successful campaign against the Bataan
nuclear power plant generated a degree of environmental consciousness.
But much remains to be done to make ecological concerns national concerns.

At the root of most environmental problems in the Philippines are
those evil twins we have seen time and time again: greed — or the
exploitation of man and nature for profit — and poverty. To break the
cycle of environmental destruction the Philippines needs a policy that
will attack exploitation and poverty at their roots. Piecemeal proposals
like reforestation — which consider the environment separate from the
overall development framework — will not solve the problem. The war
on environmental abuse cannot be won without waging war on poverty,
exploitation, and the ill-conceived policies behind them. Fortunately
much of the most creative thinking in Philippine politics combines
ecological and social awareness.

25

Reformist Possibilities... Revolutionary Alternatives

I left the Philippines in October 1988 with mixed feelings. Events in recent months had taken the lustre off the country which had shone so brightly two years earlier. I could not help but be depressed by the continuing violence, the endless poverty, and the seemingly unbridgeable gap between rich and powerful and poor and powerless. Could things ever really change? More and more people asked that question as the days passed. Many gave up. The queues outside the US and Japanese embassies and the overseas employment agencies seemed to grow longer. Many Filipinos seemed ready to give up not on themselves, but on their nation. My wife revisited the Philippines six months after we had departed. Prices had gone up. Manila seemed dirtier than ever. The poverty seemed to have become more visible.

It came as no surprise several months later when the RAM boys, Marcos remnants and their spin-offs, tried to shoot their way to power in the 1989 coup. Popular support for the Aquino administration had been waning and the militarists had always believed that they had the answers. That few people agreed with them did not really matter to the rebellious men in uniform.

Real hope lies, not in the mutinous soldiers, but in the thousands of Filipinos who continue to struggle for a better life and a brighter day. Some outstanding individuals in government and the private sector stand out from their humdrum colleagues and continue to strive to meet the expectations they had developed during the anti-Marcos struggle. Thousands of workers and peasants continue to risk life and limb in mass movements for justice and peace. Church people, students and professionals have given up the comforts of a middle-class life to live and work as activists amongst the impoverished majority. Artists and intellectuals push on in their efforts to forge a strong national culture. Thousands continue to wage an armed struggle to free the country from centuries of foreign and élite domination.

Cory Aquino has failed to carry forward the torch of justice and peace. Her government has fallen into the old trap of counter-insurgency. It has paid lip-service to the causes behind the insurgency — poverty, inequality and injustice — but has failed to pursue the programme of economic development and redistributive justice it had promised. Conservative élite forces once again dominate the government. Elements of the old rural oligarchy share power with the emergent urban élite, the military and the survivors among Marcos's political and financial cronies. After a false start, the US has regained its footing and, with its allies, most notably Japan, plays an influential role.

Many analysts writing about the Aquino government focus on the conflicts within this dominant group. Certainly such conflicts have affected the Aquino government's performance. However, by focusing on issues within the ruling block, critics have ignored the fundamental conflicts in Philippine society. The main one, which pits the haves against the have-nots and the nationalists against an alliance of élite and foreign interests, raises questions about the whole future course of the nation's development. It does not simply ask how the nation will produce wealth, but who will benefit from it. The wealthy alliance of the domestic élite and foreign interests steers an essentially conservative course, defending private interests, favouring unrestricted market economics and generally ignoring the question of social justice. These conservative forces have stood in the way of substantive change, resisting the modest proposals of the reformers in Aquino's first cabinet, blocking any meaningful agrarian reform and killing the idea of a political settlement between the NDF (National Democratic Front) and the Aquino government. On the other side of the equation are the forces fighting for change — the mass organizations of peasants and workers, the political parties and movements that support them, and the radical intellectuals who work in the media and in the schools.

From an uncertain position in the early days of the Aquino government, the balance of power has shifted in favour of the most conservative elements of society. Very quickly it became apparent that change would not come easily. The picture need not, however, be painted solely in sombre colours. The conservative élite may well dominate society for some time to come, but the possibilities of reform, of an eventual political settlement with the communist rebels, or of victory by the revolutionary movement cannot be ruled out. Continued élite domination depends not only on the maintenance of the existing balance of power in the political arena, but on keeping religious power in the hands of the most conservative bishops, on maintaining some degree of control over the military, and on alliances with the US.

For all its shortcomings the February 1986 revolution did create a democratic opening, which has given some life to reform-oriented forces in Philippine society. That space narrowed during the first four years of Aquino's rule, effectively shutting out the radical left and reducing the space available to the more moderate groups of the extra-parliamentary left. It also narrowed the options available to parliamentary reformers.

To succeed, a reform movement in the Philippines would need an organized and constantly mobilized mass base, one which could be called upon to stand up against the right-wing backlash and even fight the armed forces of the right (both private armies and the AFP). The mass organizations led by the social democrats and independent left are at present too small to fill such a role. The leaders of these groups hope to build their organizations but face a long and difficult task. Short of radical reform — either through the advent of a left-leaning government or a political settlement with the guerrillas — the Philippines faces a violent future. During the ceasefire, NDF negotiator Tony Zumel told me something that has stuck in my mind ever since. 'In our country,' he said, 'every serious movement for change must eventually confront the armed might of the state.' According to him, the AFP would always stand in the way of radical change.

In the Philippines today guerrilla armies are a reality. Moro armies, for all their weaknesses, keep turning up in the south. The NPA (New People's Army) fights on in most of the country. Even the social democrats have not broken up their small guerrilla groups. Finding a solution to the nation's problems will necessarily involve the guerrilla groups and the political organizations behind them. The government hopes it can destroy them. Cory Aquino has said she hopes to defeat the insurgency by the time her term expires in 1992. Even some military men find this highly unlikely.

The CPP and NPA had some difficulty responding to the emergence of the Aquino government, its obvious popularity and the opening of a democratic space. Aquino's early popularity slowed down the NPA's growth and even led to some defections, but the NPA has essentially remained as potent as when Aquino came to power. Though still limited to about 10,000 full-time fighters, it influences 20 to 25 per cent of the population and wages war in most of the country's provinces. But the revolutionary movement is far larger than the NPA. An extensive underground network stretches from southern Mindanao to northern Luzon. And, for the first time in Philippine history, radical mass movements of peasants, workers and slum dwellers actually exist in most provinces and cities in the country. Though often restricting their activities to open political acts, these movements share a common ideology and common goal with the revolutionary underground.

The Aquino government's failure to deliver on its promise to bring justice to the poor has left the guerrillas with fertile ground to sow. With Aquino's popularity waning and her term coming to an end, the rebels may well find themselves in an improved, though still difficult, situation. Notwithstanding their somewhat inadequate reaction to the changeover from Marcos to Aquino, the revolutionaries have shown themselves to be capable organizers and leaders. Masses of peasants and workers have come to respect their courage and their concern. But the decisive battles (military and political) between the state and the guerrillas are yet to be fought. Each side has scored some important victories since Marcos fell. The government has slowed down the growth of the insurgency and captured several key leaders. It has broken the rebels' hold over more than a few communities by exploiting their mistakes, promising better services and clean government, and by using a terror of its own. But the revolutionary organizations have survived the government's peak of popularity and their own confusion. They presented a rather agreeable public face during the ceasefire and peace talks, and appear capable of recovering from the arrests that occurred in 1986 and 1988.

The government has adopted a classic strategy of counter-insurgency to contend with the rebels, whereby it attempts to combine sometimes brutal military operations with political, economic and civic action aimed at destroying the rebels' political infrastructure. It has tried to coordinate the efforts of all branches of government towards the single goal of eliminating the guerrillas. But even assuming the government overcame its own problems — corruption and a divided military — and defeated the CPP and NPA, it would still not bring the country the lasting peace its people so desire. In its focus on counter-insurgency, the government has denied the insurgent movement its legitimacy. As it stands, the NDF represents the overt aspirations of perhaps one-fifth of the Philippine population. Tens of thousands of otherwise ordinary Filipinos have already decided to risk their lives in a war for what they believe will be a better Philippines.

The NDF programme attempts to articulate the concerns of a far larger portion of the nation's people. Every day, NDF members bring their revolutionary message to the people. Though often fearful at first, their poverty and the realization that the government has done little to improve their lot leaves them susceptible to rebel arguments. In addition, the continuation of human rights abuses by landowners and members of the AFP gives further cause for anger among the poor. A military victory over the NPA and the political neutralization of the NDF without addressing the injustice built into the Philippine political and economic system would only postpone the inevitable conflict between a government of the rich and an impoverished population.

Peasant uprisings have dotted the landscape of Philippine history, with the current insurgency being but the most recent and widespread of them. In the 1890s, in the 1950s and again in the 1980s, a domestic élite successfully captured control of a popular movement just as the struggle against a hated enemy was at its height. Emilio Aguinaldo, Ramon Magsaysay and Cory Aquino represent a common tendency in Philippine history. Aguinaldo seized control of the first independence movement from Andrés Bonifacio in a bloody coup, while Ramon Magsaysay appropriated the slogan of land for the landless and led the masses of Central Luzon away from the *Huk* rebellion. Aguinaldo surrendered first to the Spanish and later to the Americans, but the war for independence continued with poorer Filipinos flocking to the cause of the rebels. Magsaysay neutralized the agrarian rebellion by promising justice and hope in the future. Magsaysay died, the system remained the same, the hope faded, a new and eventually bigger insurgent movement sprang from the ashes of the old.

Cory Aquino came to head a popular movement against a hated dictator. She offered the dream of peace and freedom and justice. The dream lives on. But the promise has been broken. The country's future lies in the fulfilment of that promise.

Notes

Note: To cut down on the number of footnotes appearing in the text I have limited their use to selected sources. I have not footnoted interviews, press conferences, speeches or forums, primary documents or reports identified in the text, or historical information (including quotes) derived from several sources.

1. The Unfinished Revolution

1. Benedict J. Kerkvliet, *The Huk Rebellion: A Study of Peasant Revolt in the Philippines*, (Berkeley, Los Angeles and London, 1977), pp. 6-9.
2. Communist Party, *Revolutionary Guide on Land Reform*, (CPP Central Committee, 1977).
3. Malou Mangahas, 'Inside Malacanang: Cory's Silence on Human Rights Abuses is Deafening,' *Manila Chronicle*, 15 November 1987, p. 9.
4. Task Force Detainees, *Human Rights Update*, November 1989.
5. John T. Marlin, Immanuel Ness and Stephen T. Collins, *Book of World City Ratings*, (New York, 1986), pp. 528, 554-8.
6. 'Editorial: No Excuse for the Chaos in the Streets,' *Manila Chronicle*, 19 December 1987, p. 4.
7. 'Man Killed in Dispute over Nativity,' *Malaya*, 24 December 1987, p. 7.

2. Colonialism and an Emerging Nation

1. Renato Constantino, *A History of the Philippines*, (New York and London, 1975), pp. 28, 37.
2. *Ibid.*, p. 37.
3. *Ibid.*, p. 26.
4. Alfred W. McCoy, 'The Social History of an Archipelago,' in Alfred W. McCoy and Ed C. de Jesus (eds), *Philippine Social History: Global Trade and Local Transformations*, (Quezon City, 1982), p. 6.
5. Dennis M. Roth, 'Church Lands in the Agrarian History of the Tagalog Region,' in McCoy and de Jesus, p. 134.
6. Mariel N. Francisco and Fe Maria C. Arriola, *The History of the Burgis*, (Quezon City, 1987), p. 40.
7. McCoy, 'Social History', p. 8.
8. Constantino, *A History*, p. 158.

3. From Rebellion to Revolution

1. Constantino, *A History*, p. 141.
2. *Ibid.*, pp. 155-6.
3. *Ibid.*, p. 156.

4. *Ibid.*, p. 216.

4. The Road to Independence

1. Constantino, *A History*, p. 319.
2. James Allen, *The Radical Left on the Eve of War: A Political Memoir*, (Quezon City, 1985), p. 15.
3. *Ibid.*, p. 29.

5. From Liberation to a New Colonialism

1. Kerkvliet, p. 151.
2. *Ibid.*, p. 152.
3. Francisco and Arriola, p. 140.
4. Kerkvliet, p. 237.
5. Francisco and Arriola, p. 141.
6. Petronilo Bn. Daroy, 'On the Eve of Dictatorship and Martial Law,' in Auroroa Javate-de Dios, Petronilo Bn. Daroy and Lorna Kalaw-Tirol (eds), *Dictatorship and Revolution: Roots of People Power*, (Metro Manila, 1988), pp. 10-11.
7. Stephen Rosskamm Shalom, *The United States and the Philippines: A Study of Neocolonialism*, (Quezon City, 1986), pp. 142-3.

6. The Marcos Era

1. Carmen Navarro Pedrosa, *The Rise and Fall of Imelda Marcos*, (Manila, 1987), p. 75.
2. *Ibid.*, p. 91.
3. Francisco Nemenzo, 'Rectification Process in the Philippine Communist Movement,' in Lim Joo-Jock and S. Vani (eds), *Armed Communist Movements in Southeast Asia*, (Hampshire, 1984), p. 74.
4. Nemenzo, 'Rectification,' pp. 75-6.
5. José F. Lacaba, *Days of Disquiet, Nights of Rage: The First Quarter Storm and Related Events*, (Quezon City, 1982), p. 69.
6. *Ibid.*, p. 84.
7. Philip Shabecoff, 'Protest Movement in the Philippines Widening Rapidly,' *New York Times*, 12 March 1970, p. 10.
8. Nemenzo, 'Rectification,' pp. 83-4.

7. Dictatorship

1. T.J.S. George, 'Mr. Marcos and a Reverse Revolution,' *Far Eastern Economic Review*, 30 September 1972, p.11.
2. Ninotchka Rosca, *Endgame: The Fall of Marcos*, (New York and Toronto, 1987), p. 23.

3. T.J.S. George, 'Ferdinand Marcos on a Fateful Move,' *Far Eastern Economic Review*, 30 September 1972, p. 12.
4. Roberto D. Tiglao, 'The Consolidation of the Dictatorship,' in *Dictatorship and Revolution*, p. 45.

8. The Fall

1. 'President's News Conference on Foreign and Domestic Issues,' *New York Times*, 12 February 1986, p. A12. See also Sandra Burton, *Impossible Dream: The Marcoses, The Aquinos, and the Unfinished Revolution*, (New York, 1989), pp. 360-1.
2. Bernard Weinraub, 'Reagan Praises 2-Party System of the Philippines: He Reserves Judgement on Charges of Fraud,' *New York Times*, 11 February 1986, pp. 1, A8.
3. *Ibid.*
4. Raymond Bonner, *Waltzing with a Dictator: The Marcoses and the Making of American Policy*, (New York, 1987), pp. 435-40.

9. Why Change?

1. Amnesty International, *Amnesty International Report 1984*, (London, 1984), p. 250.
2. World Bank, *The Philippines Poor, What is to be Done?* (Washington, 1988), pp. 1-2.
3. Amado Guerrero (José Maria Sison), *Philippine Society and Revolution*, (Oakland, 1979), p. 64.
4. *Ibid.*, pp. 64-5.
5. *Ibid.*, p. 65.
6. World Bank, p. 2.

11. Forces for Changes: Cory Aquino's Left Wing

1. James Clad, 'Tainted Watchdogs: Aquino's Commission on Good Government Accused of Malpractice,' *Far Eastern Economic Review*, 17 September 1987, p. 23.

12. Forces for Change: The Underground

1. Liz Beltran (pseudonym), 'A Fitting Crown,' *Liberation*, November 1986, pp. 11-12. See also Beltran, 'Sowing Hope in San Fernan,' *Liberation*, 15 December 1986, pp. 9-12.
2. NPA General Command, Political Department, 'New People's Army Reaps Tremendous Gains in Face of Intense Enemy Campaigns,' *Ang Bayan*, December 1987, p. 8.
3. NPA General Command, 'Heed New Cries for Battle and Victory,' *Liberation*, 7 April 1989, pp. 4-5.

4. Celso García (pseudonym), 'Sabotage as a Revolutionary Weapon,' *Ang Bayan*, September 1987, pp. 12-15.
5. *Ibid.*

13. Forces for Change: The Mass Movement

1. *Ang Bayan*, Special Release, 12 January 1988.
2. Rene E. Ofreneo and Amelita M. King, 'Labor Relations in the Marcos Era: Implications for the Aquino Government,' in *Labor's Vision of the Economic Recovery*, (Quezon City, 1986), p.4.
3. 'May the Hearts and Minds Follow,' *The Economist*, 9 September 1989, p. 40.

14. Forces for Change: The Debate

1. CPP Central Committee, 'Party Conducts Assessment, Says Boycott Policy was Wrong,' *Ang Bayan*, May 1986, pp. 1-3.
2. Guerrero, 'Specific Characteristics of our People's War,' in *Philippine Society and Revolution*, pp. 181-2.
3. 'Bourgeois Elections and Parliament: Props for Counter-Revolution,' *Ang Bayan*, March 1987, pp. 4-8. Pilar Victoria (pseudonym), 'A View of the Current Situation and Revolutionary Tasks,' *Ang Bayan*, April 1987, pp. 8-15.
4. CPP Central Committee 'Carry Forward the People's Democratic Revolution 'til Victory,' *Ang Bayan*, December 1987, pp. 1-5.
5. Guerrero, *Philippine Society*, pp. 138-9.
6. Carol Victoria (pseudonym), 'A Reply to the Resolution,' *Praktika*, August 1986, p. 64.
7. *Ibid.*, pp. 66-73.
8. Edicio de la Torre, 'The Politics of Popular Democracy,' in *Two Essays on Popular Democracy*, (Quezon City, 1986), pp. 5, 9.
9. 'US-Aquino Regime's Peace: A Mask for Fascist Violence,' *Ang Bayan*, February 1987, pp. 1-3.
10. Celso García, p. 13.
11. 'Mass Support Shall be Decisive,' *Liberation*, March-April 1988, p. 6.
12. José Maria Sison, *Monthly Review*, December 1988, p.8.
13. Flor Eugenio (pseudonym), 'Joema's Crisis,' *National Midweek*, 16 March 1988, p. 44.

16. Popular Democracy

1. 'When a Zigzag Turn is Shorter than a Straight Route,' *Praktika*, 14 May 1986, pp. 21-2.
2. For examples see Amado Guerrero, 'Our Urgent Tasks,' in *Philippine Society*, pp. 255-9, 160-2.
3. De la Torre, 'Popular Democracy,' p. 5.

4. Edicio de la Torre interviewed by Lester Ruiz, 'On the Post-Marcos Transition and Popular Democracy,' *World Policy Journal*, Spring 1987, reprinted by Social Pastoral Institute, 1987, pp. 12-13.
5. De la Torre, 'Popular Democracy,' p. 5.
6. 'Our Most Pressing Tasks,' *Liberation*, April-May 1984, p. 2

17. Obstacles to Change

1. Walden Bello, 'Asia's Miracle Economies: The First and Last of a Dying Breed,' *Dollars & Sense*, January-February 1989, p. 12.
2. John McBeth, 'The Boss System,' *Far Eastern Economic Review*, 14 September 1989, pp. 36-9.

18. A People's Army?

1. Gemma Nemenzo Almendral, 'The People Have to Support Us,' *Manila Chronicle*, 15 May 1988, p. 18.
2. *Ibid.*
3. Amnesty International, *Philippines: Incommunicado Detention, Ill-Treatment and Torture during 1988*, (New York 1988), pp. 1-21.
4. Amnesty International, *The Philippines, Unlawful Killings by Military and Paramilitary Forces*, (London, 1988), p. 1.
5. Task Force Detainees, *Human Rights Update*, December 1988.
6. José Galang, 'Dubious Disappearances,' *Far Eastern Economic Review*, 15 December 1988, p. 42.
7. Malou Mangahas, 'Dismantle the NPA's Political Network,' *The Manila Chronicle on Sunday*, 12 June 1988, p. 18.
8. Ninotchka Rosca, 'Two Views on Guerrilla War,' *National Midweek*, 1 July 1987, p. 5.
9. Almendral, p. 18.
10. Walden Bello, 'Counterinsurgency's Proving Ground: Low Intensity Warfare in the Philippines,' in Michael T. Klare and Peter Kornbluh (eds), *Low Intensity Warfare: Counterinsurgency, Proinsurgency, and Antiterrorism in the Eighties*, (Quezon City, 1988), p. 166.
11. Francisco Nemenzo, 'A Season of Coups,' *Diliman Review*, 5 & 6, 1986, p. 25.
12. Bello, 'Proving Ground,' p. 167.

19. Foreign Powers

1. Renato Constantino (ed.), *Vintage Recto: Memorable Speeches and Writings*, (Quezon City, 1986), pp. 206-7.
2. Roland G. Simbulan, *The Bases of Our Insecurity: A Study of the US Military Bases in the Philippines*, (Quezon City, 1983), p. 84.
3. *Ibid.*, pp. 195-6.
4. Bello, 'Proving Ground,' p. 176.

5. *Newsweek*, 23 March 1987, cited in Bello, 'Proving Ground,' p. 177.
6. Ibon Databank Philippines, *Directory of TNCs in the Philippines*, (Manila, 1988), pp. 20-30.
7. *Ibid.*
8. 'The Letter of Intent to the IMF,' *Ibon Facts and Figures*, 15 April 1989, p. 1.
9. 'LOI: A Bitter Deal?' *Ibid.*, p. 2.

20. Religion and Philippine Society

1. Robert Youngblood, 'Basic Christian Communities and the Church-State Conflict,' *Diliman Review*, November-December 1985, p. 43.
2. *Ibid.*, pp. 45-6.
3. William Chapman, *Inside the Philippine Revolution: The New People's Army and its Struggle for Power*, (New York and London, 1987), pp. 205-6.
4. Edicio de la Torre, *Touching Ground, Taking Root: Theological and Political Reflections on the Philippine Struggle*, (Quezon City, 1986), p. 202.
5. Pen Guerrero (pseudonym), 'Ministry in the Mountains,' *Liberation*, April-May 1987, pp. 8-10.
6. Brian Allan, '"Liberation Theology:" What is it?' *Breakthrough*, October-December 1984, p. 8.
7. De la Torre, *Touching Ground*, p. 207. Abdul Ulap, 'A Revolutionary Faith That Moves Mountains,' *Liberation*, January-February 1985, p. 9.
8. De la Torre, *Touching Ground*, p. 119.
9. Guerrero, 'Ministry,' p. 9.
10. *Political Line*, pp. 5-6.
11. De la Torre, *Touching Ground*, p. 57.
12. Justiniano Cabazares, 'Social Action on Trial,' *Communications*, December 1985, pp. 43-4.
13. John J. Carroll and Francisco F. Claver, 'The Pastoral Priorities of the Philippine Bishops: A Report on a Survey,' *Philippine Studies*, 1st Quarter 1984, p. 25.

21. Mountain Tribes and Cultural Minorities

1. 'Minority Map of the Philippines,' *Sandugo*, 2nd Quarter 1983, pp. 18-19.
2. 'Muslim and Christian Students Dialogue,' *Sandugo*, p. 5.
3. 'Minority Map.'
4. Jeremy Beckett, 'The Defiant and the Compliant: The Datus of Maguindanao under Colonial Rule,' in *Philippine Social History*, p. 392.
5. T.J.S. George, *Revolt in Mindanao: The Rise of Islam in Philippine Politics*, (Kuala Lumpar and Oxford, 1980), p. 209.
6. *Ibid.*, p. 198.
7. *Ibid.*, pp. 199-200.
8. *Ibid.*, pp. 200-2.

9. Lela Noble, 'The Muslim Insurgency,' in Daniel B. Schirmer and Stephen Rosskamm Shalom (eds), *The Philippine Reader: A History of Colonialism, Neocolonialism, Dictatorship, and Resistance*, (Boston, 1987), p 195.
10. *Ibid.*
11. *Ibid.*
12. *Ibid.*, p. 196.
13. Col Muammar Al Ghaddafi, 'The Marcos Ghaddafi Letters,' in *Aide Mémoire on the Mindanao Peace Talks: Position of the Philippine Government Panel*, (Manila, 1987), p. 34.
14. Noble, p. 196.
15. William H. Scott, 'The Spanish Occupation of the Cordillera in the 19th Century,' in *Philippine Social History*, p. 54.
16. Joanna K. Carino, 'From the Mountain Fastnesses: A Cry for Justice,' *Diliman Review*, March-April 1985, p. 7.
17. Ed Maranan, 'Development and Minoritization,' *Diliman Review*, 5 & 6, 1987, p. 10.
18. 'Forum,' *Diliman Review*, 5 & 6, 1987, p. 42.

22. Culture and Society

1. Benjamin Pimentel, 'Feudal Fetters,' *National Midweek*, 30 September 1987, p. 15.
2. Information provided by former Secretary of Education Lourdes Quisumbing.
3. Abaya, *Manila Chronicle*, cited in author's notes.
4. F. Sionil José, 'The Filipino Intelligentsia: Trapped in a Bog of its own Making,' *Solidarity*, May-June 1988, p. 6.
5. Benjamin Pimentel, 'New Directions for the CCP, Interview: Bing Roxas,' *National Midweek*, 15 October 1986, p. 5.
6. Doreen Fernandez, 'Artists, Writers and Intellectuals and the Culture of Crisis,' *The New Progressive Review*, 3 (1), p.38.

23. Agrarian Politics

1. *The Philippines Poor*, p. 2.

24. Environmental Politics

1. Gareth Porter and Delfin Ganapin, *Resources, Population, and the Philippines*, (Washington, 1988), cited in James Goodno, 'Clear Cutting the Future: Greed, Poverty Threaten Philippine Forests,' *Dollars and Sense*, December 1989, pp. 6-8.
2. *Ibid.*

Bibliography

Newspapers, periodicals, news agency releases

Alternative
AMPO
Anawim
Ang Bayan
Ang Partisano
Ang Pilipino
Asian Wall Street Journal
Atlantic, The
Balai Asian Journal
Balita ng Malayang Pilipinas
Boston Globe
Breakthrough
Communications
Cordillera Quarterly
Diliman Review
Diwang Pilipino
Dollars & Sense
Economic & Political Monthly
Economist, The
Far Eastern Economic Review
Farm
Granta
Ibon Facts & Figures
Inside Asia
In These Times
Kalayaan
Kasarinlan
KMP News Dispatch
KMU International Bulletin
Liberation
Lusong

Makati Business Club Papers
Malaya
Manila Bulletin (and Bulletin
Today)
Manila Chronicle
Manila Times
Maryknoll
Mindanao Focus
Monthly Review
Mr. & Ms.
Nation, The
National Catholic Reporter
National Midweek
Navy Journal
New Asia Visions
New Progressive Review (and
New Philippine Review)
New York Times
Office of Media Affairs
Backgrounder
Philippine Agenda
Philippine Daily Inquirer
Philippine Development
Philippine Human Rights
Update
Philippine Labor Monitor
Philippine News & Features
Philippine Studies
Philippine Trade & Industry
Journal
Philippine Trade Union Report

Philippines Today   South
Pintig ng Bayan   Taliba ng Bayan
Praktika   Tao-Kalikasan
Pulang Bandila   Trend Monitor
Religious News Service   Trend Register
Rural Reconstruction Forum   Tugon
Salam   US Views
Sandugo   Veritas
Silyab   Washington Post
Simbayan   World Marxist Review
Solidarity

Books, pamphlets and selected documents

Abadilla, Domingo C. (ed.) *Forest Conservation in the Philippines, Importance of Ecological Balance: What Needs to be Done.* Manila: Columbian Publishing Corporation, 1986.

Aguirre, Brig. Gen Alexander P. and Col Ismael Z. Villareal. *Readings on Counterinsurgency.* Quezon City: Pan Service Masters Consultant, 1987.

Allen, James S. *The Radical Left on the Eve of War: A Political Memoir.* Quezon City: Foundation for Nationalist Studies, 1985.

Alliance for New Politics. 'Platform of the Alliance for New Politics,' 1987.

Alternate Resource Center. *Socio-Economic Factbook of Mindanao.* Davao City: Alternate Resource Center, 1985.

Amante, Sofronio V. (ed.) *Labor's Vision of the Economic Recovery.* Quezon City: UP Institute of Industrial Relations, 1986.

Amnesty International. *Amnesty International Report: 1984.* London: Amnesty International, 1984.

———— *Amnesty International Report: 1985.* London: Amnesty International, 1985.

———— *Philippines: Unlawful Killings by Military and Paramilitary Forces.* London: Amnesty International, 1988.

Anon. *Political Developments Leading to the Rise of Authoritarianism.* n.d.

Aquino, Belinda A. *Politics of Plunder: The Philippines Under Marcos.* Quezon City: Great Books Trading, 1987.

Aquino, Corazon C. *Republic of the Philippines Policy Statements: Speeches of Corazon C. Aquino, 22 March-5 August 1986.* Manila: Republic of the Philippines, 1986.

Armed Forces of the Philippines. *Philippine Insurgency Problem: Scramble for Mass Support.* Quezon City: AFP, n.d.

———— *A Report, March 25, 1987: A Documented Report on Davao City Violence.* Davao City, 1987.

———— *Thrusts.* Davao City: Regional Unified Command XI, AFP, April 1985.

———— *Summary of Files in Diskette 03-FM.* Quezon City: AFP, 1988.

———— *Update of CT-Related Violent Activities: As of 30 June 1988.* Quezon City: AFP, 1988.

Asedillo, Rebecca C. and B. David Williams (eds) *Rice in the Storm: Faith and Struggle in the Philippines.* New York: Friendship Press, 1989.

Asian Development Bank. *Report on the Philippine Forestry Sector Program.* Manila: ADB, 1988.

Bacani, Bishop Teodoro. *Mary and the Filipino.* Makati: St Paul Publications, 1985.

Bagong Alyansang Makabayan. *General Program of Action.* Quezon City: Bagong Alyansang Makabayan, 1985.

Bain, David Howard. *Sitting in Darkness: Americans in the Philippines.* Boston: Houghton Mifflin Company, 1984.

Bautista, J.V. *Toward a Democratic Coalition Government.* Quezon City: Nationalist Alliance for Justice, Freedom & Democracy, 1984.

Bello, Walden. *US-Sponsored Low-Intensity Conflict in the Philippines.* San Francisco: Institute for Food & Development Studies, 1987.

Bello, Walden, David Kinley and Elain Elinson. *Development Debacle: The World Bank in the Philippines.* San Francisco: Institute for Food & Development Policy and the Philippine Solidarity Network, 1982.

Bello, Walden, Peter Hayes and Lyuba Zarsky. *American Lake: Nuclear Peril in the Pacific.* Ringwood: Penguin Books Australia, 1986.

Biazon, Brig. Gen. Rodolfo. 'The Philippine Insurgency Problem: Scramble for Mass Support', *CM6,* Anniversary Issue, 1987, pp. 37-42.

Bonner, Raymond. *Waltzing with a Dictator: The Marcoses and the Making of American Policy.* New York: Times Books, 1987.

Bresnan, John (ed.) *Crisis in the Philippines: The Marcos era and Beyond.* Princeton: Princeton University Press, 1986.

Brillantes Jr, Alex Bello. *Dictatorship and Martial Law: Philippine Authoritarianism in 1972.* Quezon City: Great Books Publishers, 1987.

Broad, Robin. *Unequal Alliance, 1979-1986: The World Bank, the International Monetary Fund, and the Philippines.* Quezon City: Ateneo de Manila University Press, 1988.

Bulosan, Carlos. *America is in the Heart*. New York: Harcourt Brace & Company, 1946.

Burton, Sandra. *Impossible Dream: The Marcoses, the Aquinos, and the Unfinished Revolution*. New York: Warner Books, 1989.

Caldwell, Wallace E. and Edward H. Merrill. *The New Popular History of the World: The Story of Mankind from the Earliest Times to the Present Day*. Greystone Press, 1964.

Canoy, Reuben R. *The Counterfeit Revolution: The Philippines from Martial Law to the Aquino Assassination*. Manila: Philippine Editions, 1981.

Catholic Bishops' Conference of the Philippines. *Living Lightly Over the Earth*. Manila: CBCP, 1988.

Chapman, William. *Inside the Philippine Revolution: The New People's Army and Its Struggle for Power*. New York: W.W. Norton & Company, 1987.

Collins, Joseph. *The Philippines: Fire on the Rim*. San Francisco: Institute for Food & Development Studies, 1989.

Columbian Publishing Corporation. *The Key to Philippine Forest Conservation: The Defense of the Dipterocarps*. Manila: Columbian Publishing Corporation, 1984.

Commission on Trade Union & Human Rights. *Report of the Fact Finding Mission on Labor Repression and Militarization, Davao City-Davao del Sur, February 21-23, 1985*. Manila: Commission on Trade Union & Human Rights, 1985.

Committee of the Revolutionary Internationalist Movement. 'Open Letter to the Communist Party of the Philippines,' in *A World to Win*, 1987/8.

Communist Party of the Philippines. *Revolutionary Guide on Land Reform*. Central Committee, CPP, revised, 1977.

———— *Overthrow the US-Marcos Fascist Dictatorship, Establish a Revolutionary Coalition Government: An Urgent Message to the Filipino People*. Central Committee, CPP, 7 October 1983.

———— *Memorandum to Party Units on the Snap Election*, Executive Committee, Central Committee, 23 December 1985.

———— *Memorandum on the Congressional Elections*, Executive Committee, Central Committee, March, 1987.

———— *Program for Mass Struggles, August to December, 1987*, Executive Committee, Central Committee, 1987.

Constantino, Renato (ed.) *MAN's Goal: The Democratic Filipino Society*. Manila: Malaya Books, 1969.

———— *A History of the Philippines: From Spanish Colonization to the Second World War*. New York: Monthly Review Press, 1975.

————— *Neocolonial Identity and Counter Consciousness: Essays on Cultural Decolonisation.* London: Merlin Press, 1978.

————— (ed.) *Vintage Recto: Memorable Speeches and Writings.* Quezon City: Foundation for Nationalist Studies, 1986.

Cordillera People's Alliance for the Defense of the Ancestral Domain. *Papers and Documents from the First Cordillera People's Congress, June 1-3, 1984, Bontoc, Mt Province.* Baguio City: Cordillera People's Alliance, 1984.

Cordillera People's Democratic Front. *General Program of the Cordillera People's Democratic Front (revised draft).* CPDF Provisional Secretariat, 1986.

Corpus, Lt-Col Victor. 'Dear Pete Letter', 1986.

Cory Aquino for President Movement. *Cory: Sigaw ng Bayan si Cory ang Kailangan.* Makati: Cory Aquino for President Movement, 1986.

Diokno, José. *Anti-Americanism: Twenty-Four Questions about Filipino Nationalism.* Manila: Kaakbay Primer Series, 1984.

Ecumenical Center for Development. *Philippine Regional Profiles.* Quezon City: Ecumenical Center for Development, n.d.

Far Eastern Economic Review. *Asia 1988 Yearbook.* Hong Kong: Far Eastern Economic Review, 1988.

Feder, Ernest. *Perverse Development.* Quezon City: Foundation for Nationalist Studies, 1983.

Francisco, Luzviminda Bartolome and Jonathan Shepard Fast. *Conspiracy for Empire: Big Business, Corruption and the Politics of Imperialism in America, 1876-1907.* Quezon City: Foundation for Nationalist Studies, 1985.

Francisco, Mariel N. and Fe Maria C. Arriola. *The History of the Burgis.* Quezon City: GCF Books, 1987.

Freedom from Debt Coalition. *Questions and Answers on the Philippine Debt Crisis.* Quezon City: Freedom from Debt Coalition, 1989.

García, Ed. *The Filipino Quest: A Just and Lasting Peace.* Quezon City: Claretian Publications, 1988.

George, T.J.S. *Revolt in Mindanao: The Rise of Islam in Philippine Politics.* Oxford: Oxford University Press, 1980.

Government of the Republic of the Philippines and the National Democratic Front. *Memorandum of Agreement on a Preliminary Ceasefire.* Metro Manila: GRP, NDF, November 1986.

————— *Memorandum of Agreement on Safety and Immunity Guarantees and Physical Centers and Facilities.* Metro Manila: GRP, NDF, November 1986.

Guerrero, Amado (José Maria Sison). 'Specific Characteristics of Our People's War,' 1 December 1974. Reprinted in *Philippine Society and Revolution*.

———— 'Our Urgent Tasks,' 1 July 1976. Reprinted in *Philippine Society and Revolution*.

———— *Philippine Society and Revolution*. Oakland: International Association of Filipino Patriots, 1979.

Ibon Databank. *What Crisis? Highlights of the Philippine Economy, 1983*. Manila: Ibon Databank Philippines, 1984.

———— *Directory of TNCs in the Philippines*. Manila: Ibon Databank Philippines, 1988.

International Labour Office. *Sharing in Development: A Programme of Employment, Equity and Growth for the Philippines*. Geneva: ILO, 1974.

Javate-de Dios, Aurora, Petronilo Bn. Daroy and Lorna Kalaw-Tirol (eds) *Dictatorship and Revolution: Roots of People's Power*. Metro Manila: Conspectus Foundation, 1988.

Jenkins, Shirley. *American Economic Policy Towards the Philippines*. Palo Alto: Stanford University Press, 1954.

Jocano, F. Landa. *Outline of Philippine Mythology*. Manila: Centro Escolar University Research & Development Center, 1969.

Jones, Gregg. *Red Revolution: Inside the Philippine Guerrilla Movement*. Boulder: Westview Press, 1989.

José, F. Sionil. *Mass*. Manila: Solidaridad Publishing House, 1979.

Kaimito Media Group. *Star Trooper 2*. Makati: Star Trooper Media, 1987.

Karnow, Stanley. *In Our Image: America's Empire in the Philippines*. New York: Random House, 1989.

Kerkvliet, Benedict J. *The Huk Rebellion*. Berkeley: University of California Press, 1977.

Kilusang Mayo Uno. *Repression of Filipino Workers: A Dossier*. Manila: KMU External Affairs Committee, n.d.

———— *International Solidarity Affair Documents*. Manila: KMU, 1985.

Klare, Michael T. and Peter Kornbluh (eds) *Low Intensity Warfare: Counterinsurgency, Proinsurgency and Antiterrorism in the Eighties*. Quezon City: Ken, 1988.

Komisar, Lucy. *Corazon Aquino: The Story of a Revolution*. New York: George Brazziller, 1987.

Lacaba, Emmanuel. *Salvaged Poems*. Manila: Salinlahi Publishing House, 1986.

Lacaba, José F. *Days of Disquiet, Nights of Rage: The First Quarter Storm and Related Events.* Manila: Asphodal, 1986.

Lachica, Eduardo. *Huk: Philippine Agrarian Society in Revolt.* Manila: Solidaridad Publishing House, 1971.

Lichauco, Alejandro. *The Lichauco Paper: Imperialism and the National Situation.* New York: Monthly Review Press, 1973.

————— *Towards a New Economic Order and the Conquest of Mass Poverty.* Quezon City: Alejandro Lichauco, 1986.

Lopez-Gonzaga, Violeta. *The Sugarcane Workers in Transition: The Nature and Context of Labor Circulation in Negros Occidental.* Bacolod City: La Salle Social Research Center, 1985.

————— *Crisis in Sugarlandia: The Planters' Differential Perceptions and Responses and their Impact on Sugarcane Workers' Households.* Bacolod City: La Salle Social Research Center, 1986.

————— *Voluntary Land Sharing and Transfer Scheme in Negros: An Exploratory Study.* Bacolod City: La Salle Social Research Center, 1986.

Mahal Kong Pilipinas Foundation. *Philippine Company Profiles.* Metro Manila: Mahal Kong Pilipinas Foundation, 1987.

McCoy, Alfred W. and Ed C. de Jesus (eds) *Philippine Social History: Global Trade and Local Transformations.* Quezon City: Ateneo de Manila University Press, 1982.

Miller, Stuart Creighton. *Benevolent Assimilation: The American Conquest of the Philippines, 1899-1903.* New Haven: Yale University Press, 1982.

Morales, Horacio 'Boy'. *Forum on the Coalition Government.* Quezon City: Nationalist Alliance for Justice, Freedom & Democracy, 1984.

Morante, P.C. *Remembering Carlos Bulosan.* Quezon City: New Day Publishers, 1984.

Munro, Ross H. 'The New Khmer Rouge'. Manila: USIS, 1986 (from *Commentary* 80 (December 1985), pp. 19-38.)

National Democratic Front. *Our Agenda for a Just and Enduring Peace: Proposal of the National Democratic Front for a Negotiated Political Settlement.* NDF, 1987.

————— *NDF Draft Program.* NDF, 1988.

————— *Towards a Just and Enduring Peace.* NDF, 1989.

National Ecumenical Forum for Church Response. *Beyond the Ceasefire Talks: A Study Guide on Genuine and Lasting Peace.* Makati: National Ecumenical Forum for Church Response, 1987.

National Press Club. *Report of the National Press Club Seminar Committee on the State of the Philippine Press.* Quezon City: Foundation for Nationalist Studies, 1983.

National Press Club Committee to Protect Writers. *The Philippine Press: Under Siege, Vol. 1.* Manila: National Press Club, 1984.

————— *The Philippine Press: Under Siege, Vol 2.* Manila: National Press Club, 1985.

Nationalist Alliance for Justice, Freedom & Democracy. *Basic Documents and Resolutions of the First National Assembly.* Quezon City: Nationalist Alliance for Justice, Freedom & Democracy, 1984.

Nemenzo, Francisco. 'Rectification Movement in the Philippine Communist Movement,' in Lim Joo-Jock and S. Vani (eds) *Armed Communist Movements in Southeast Asia.* Hampshire: Grower, 1984.

Ofreneo, René E. and Esther P. Habana. *The Employment Crisis and the World Bank's Adjustment Program.* Quezon City: UP Institute of Industrial Relations, 1987.

Partido Demokratiko-Sosyalista ng Pilipinas. *Philippine Democratic Socialism: Maximum Programme.* Quezon City: PDSP, 1987.

————— *Philippine Social Democracy (The People's Alternative): Minimum Programme.* Quezon City: PDSP, 1987.

————— *Political Line.* Quezon City: PDSP, 1987.

————— *Programme of Action from 1987 to 1991.* Quezon City: PDSP, 1987.

Partido ng Bayan. *Constitution of the Partido ng Bayan.* Metro Manila: PNB, 1986.

————— *Programme of Action.* Metro Manila: PNB, 1986.

Pedrosa, Carmen Navarro. *The Untold Story of Imelda Marcos.* Manila: Pedrosa, 1969.

————— *The Rise and Fall of Imelda Marcos.* Manila: Bookmark, 1987.

Philippine Institute for Development Studies. *Economic Recovery and Long-Run Growth: Agenda for Reforms.* Quezon City: Philippine Institute for Development Studies, 1986.

Philippine Military Academy. *Bulletin of Information.* Baguio City: Philippine Military Academy, 1986.

Pil, Teresita Veloso. *Philippine Folk Fiction and Tales.* Quezon City: New Day Publishers, 1977.

Pineda-Ofreneo, Rosalinda. *The Manipulated Press: A History of Philippine Journalism since 1945.* Mandaluyong: Cacho Hermanos, 1984.

————— (ed.) *Foreign Capital and the Philippine Crisis.* Quezon City: UP International Studies Institute of the Philippines, 1985.

Pomeroy, William. *The Forest.* New York: International Publishers, 1963.

————— (ed.) *Guerrilla Warfare and Marxism.* New York: International Publishers, 1968.

———— *American Neo-Colonialism: Its Emergence in the Philippines and Asia*. New York: International Publishers, 1970.

Project 28 Days. *Bayan Ko! Images of the Philippine Revolt*. Quezon City: Veritas Publications and Communications Foundation, 1986.

Quijano de Manila. *Joseph Estrada and Other Sketches*. Manila: National Book Store, 1977.

Ramos, Elias T. *Philippine Labor Movement in Transition*. Quezon City: New Day Publishers, 1976.

Reform the AFP Movement. *Crossroads to Reform*. Metro Manila: Reform the AFP Movement, n.d.

Republic of the Philippines. *The Tripoli Agreement of December 23, 1976*. Manila: Peace and Development Panel for Mindanao and the Cordilleras, n.d.

———— Constitutional Commission of 1986. *The Constitution of the Republic of the Philippines*. Quezon City: HEAR Enterprise, n.d.

———— Office of Media Affairs. *The Philippines Today: Stability amid Change*. Manila: Office of Media Affairs, 1984.

———— Ministry of National Defense, Office of Media Affairs and the President's Center for Special Studies. *The Communist Insurgency in the Philippines*. Manila: Office of Media Affairs, 1985.

———— Office of the President. *The Situation in the Philippines: 7 December 1985*. Manila: Office of the President, 1985.

———— Sandiganbayan. *People of the Philippines versus Brig. Gen. Luther Custodio, et al, Decision*. Manila: Sandiganbayan, 1985.

———— *1986 Philippine Statistical Yearbook*. Manila: National Economic and Development Authority, 1986.

———— National Economic and Development Authority. *Medium-Term Philippine Development Plan, 1987-1992*. Manila: National Economic and Development Authority, 1986.

———— National Environmental Protection Council. *Philippine Environment Report: 1984-85*. Quezon City: National Environmental Protection Council, 1986.

———— Ministry of Agrarian Reform. *Agricultural Tenancy Act and Code of Agrarian Reforms*. Quezon City: Public Information Division, Ministry of Agrarian Reform, 1986.

———— *The Government's Commitment to Mindanao: Policy of the Aquino Government, 20 August 1986*. Manila: Peace and Development Panel for Mindanao and the Cordilleras, 1986.

———— *Aide Mémoire on the Mindanao Peace Talks: Position of the Philippine Government Panel*. Manila: Philippine Information Agency, 1987.

———— Board of Investments. *The Omnibus Investments Code of 1987.* Makati: Department of Trade & Industry, 1987.

———— Department of Agriculture. *Policies, Priorities, and Medium-Term Program of Action.* Quezon City: Department of Agriculture, 1987.

———— Peace and Development Panel for Mindanao and the Cordilleras. *Primer on Mindanao Peace Talks.* Manila: Peace and Development Panel for Mindanao and the Cordilleras, 1987.

———— *Point-by-Point: Government's Response to MNLF Demands.* Manila: Peace and Development Panel for Mindanao and the Cordilleras, 1987.

———— *1988 Investment Priorities Plan.* Makati: Department of Trade & Industry, 1988.

———— *Investment Opportunities in the Philippines.* Department of Trade & Industries, 1988.

———— *Primer: Foreign Investment Policies in the Philippines.* Makati: Department of Trade & Industry, 1988.

———— Senate. *The Senate Speaks: A Collection of Speeches by the Senators of the Republic.* Manila: Senate of the Congress of the Philippines, 1988.

———— Senate Committee on Justice and Human Rights. *Report on Vigilante Groups.* Manila: Senate of the Congress of the Philippines, 1988.

Richards, Pablo. *Our Struggle is Against the Idols.* Ozamis City: Center for the Study of Religion & Culture, 1984.

Salgado, Pedro V. *The Philippine Economy: History and Analysis.* Quezon City: Salgado, 1985.

Salvosa, Benjamin. *Reform or Revolution.* Baguio City: Baguio Colleges Foundation Press, 1972.

Sanchez, Cesar. 'The Dear Pete Letter: A Backgrounder,' in *Rank and File,* 12-25 December 1986.

Sandoval, Romulo A. (ed.) *Prospects for Agrarian Reform under the New Order.* Quezon City: NCCP-URM and REAPs, 1986.

San, Juan Jr. *E. Buluson: An Introduction with Selections.* Manila: National Book Store, 1983.

———— *Crisis in the Philippines: The Making of a Revolution.* South Hadley: Bergin & Garvey Publishers, 1986.

Schirmer, Daniel B. and Stephen Rosskamm Shalom. *The Philippines Reader: A History of Colonialism, Neocolonialism, Dictatorship, and Resistance.* Boston: South End Press, 1987.

Shalom, Stephen Rosskamm. *The United States and the Philippines: A Study of Neocolonialism.* Quezon City: New Day Publishers, 1986.

Shultz, George P. *Philippine Reforms and the US Interests: The US Role in Consolidating Democracy*. Manila: US Information Service, 1986.

Simbulan, Roland G. *The Bases of our Insecurity: A Study of the US Military Bases in the Philippines*. Metro Manila: Balai Fellowship, 1983.

Sison, José Maria. *On National Democracy*. Quezon City: Aklatang Gising Na, n.d.

———— *Onward with the Struggle for National Democracy: Unite to Dismantle the US-Marcos Dictatorship and Establish the Democratic Coalition Government*. Quezon City: Nationalist Alliance for Justice, Freedom & Democracy, 1984.

———— *Post Election Views*. Mimeograph, 1984.

———— *Prison and Beyond, Selected Poems, 1958—1983*. Metro Manila: Free José Maria Sison Committee, 1984.

Sison, José Maria and Rainer Werning. *José Maria Sison and the Philippine Revolution: An Interface with Dr Rainer Werning*. Draft version, 1988.

Tadem, Eduardo C. *Mindanao Report: A Preliminary Study of the Economic Origins of Social Unrest*. Davao City: Afirm Resource Center, 1980.

Task Force Detainees. *Trends: A TFDP Report on Political Detention, Salvaging and Disappearances, January-June, 1984*. Quezon City: Task Force Detainees, 1984.

Third World Studies Center. *Marxism in the Philippines*. Quezon City: Third World Studies Center, UP, 1986.

———— *Marxism in the Philippines: Second Series*. Quezon City: Third World Studies Center, UP, 1988.

Torre, Edicio de la. *The Philippines: Christians and the Politics of Liberation*. Quezon City: Socio-Pastoral Institute, n.d.

———— *Touching Ground, Taking Root: Theological and Political Reflections on the Philippine Struggle*. Quezon City: Socio-Pastoral Institute, 1986.

———— *On the Post-Marcos Transition and Popular Democracy*. Quezon City: Socio-Pastoral Institute, 1987.

Torre, Edicio de la and Horacio R. Morales Jr. *Two Essays on Popular Democracy*. Quezon City: Institute for Popular Democracy, 1986.

United Nationalist Democratic Organization. *Toward a Just Society*. Makati: Unido, 1985.

United States Government. *Your Guide to Clark AB, Republic of the Philippines*. Air Force, 3rd Tactical Fighter Wing, Clark Air Base: USAF, n.d.

———— *Foreign Economic Trends and their Implications for the United States, Philippines.* Washington: Department of Commerce, various editions.

———— *Philippine Economic Trends Report.* Manila: US Embassy, various dates.

———— *Survey of Current Business.* Washington: Department of Commerce, 1985.

———— *Background Notes: Philippines.* Washington: Department of State, 1986.

———— *Grant Agreement Between the United States of America and the Republic of the Philippines for the Budget Support Program.* Manila: US Embassy, 1986.

———— *Background on the Bases: American Facilities in the Philippines.* Manila: US Information Service, 1986.

———— *Windows of opportunity: PVO Co-financing Projects.* Manila: USAID, 1988.

Villa-Real, Brig.-Gen. Luis A. *Threats to Philippine National Security In the Year 2000: Insurgency and Economic Crisis.* Manila: National Intelligence Coordinating Agency, n.d.

Villegas, Edberto M. *Studies in Philippine Political Economy.* Manila: Silangan Publishers, revised, 1984.

Woddis, Jack. *Armies and Politics.* New York: International Publishers, 1977.

Index